MARC BLOCH: A LIFE IN HISTORY

MARC BLOCH:
A LIFE IN HISTORY

CAROLE FINK

Department of History
University of North Carolina, Wilmington

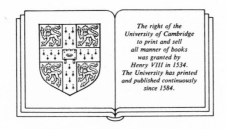

The right of the
University of Cambridge
to print and sell
all manner of books
was granted by
Henry VIII in 1534.
The University has printed
and published continuously
since 1584.

CAMBRIDGE UNIVERSITY PRESS

Cambridge

New York   Port Chester   Melbourne   Sydney

Published by the Press Syndicate of the University of Cambridge
The Pitt Building, Trumpington Street, Cambridge CB2 1RP
32 East 57th Street, New York, NY 10022, USA
10 Stanford Road, Oakleigh, Melbourne 3166, Australia

First published 1989

Printed in the United States of America

Library of Congress Cataloging-in-Publication Data
Fink, Carole.
Marc Bloch : a life in history / Carole Fink.
p.   cm.
Includes index.
ISBN 0−521−37300−X
1. Bloch, Marc Léopold Benjamin, 1886−1944.   2. Historians−
France−Biography.   I. Title.
D15.B596F56   1989
994'.0072024−dc19
[B]   88-32216

British Library Cataloguing in Publication applied for.

ISBN 0−521−37300−X hard covers

TO STEFAN HAROLD FINK
AND JOLIE FINK

Contents

vii

Illustrations

Preface

A biography should begin with two explanations, for the choice of the subject and for its treatment. Marc Bloch was one of this century's most brilliant historians. He was also a patriot and a Jew, a soldier and a leader of the Resistance. As the co-founder of an influential scholarly journal and a prolific author and teacher he would no doubt still be remembered. But his character and fate also placed him in history itself, in the struggle to liberate France, for which he paid with his life.

Here is an ideal subject for a historian of contemporary Europe, a figure who lived in important and tumultuous times, from the Dreyfus Affair to the Holocaust, through two world wars and the Nazi occupation. Bloch's life had a poignant symmetry: He spent his first and last year in Lyon, began and ended his teaching in Montpellier, and spent seventeen years in his ancestral homeland, Alsace, before returning to a Paris much changed since his youth. The unifying thread was France, the *patrie* that had emancipated and educated his forebears and given him the opportunity to serve, the proud republic of 1906 and 1918 that he watched falter and collapse in 1940, the main subject of his broad research and the object of his last efforts. Marc Bloch's strong sense of national identity was not uncommon in his generation in France and in the Western world. What makes him extraordinary were the added qualities of humanism, liberalism, and cosmopolitanism and the intelligence, wit, and imagination that enabled him to transcend the narrow barriers of time and place and become one of those individuals we rightly call heroes.

This first biography of Marc Bloch, based largely on unpublished materials, is an intellectual and political study that seeks a coherent picture of the man, his ideas, and the world he inhabited. No doubt my effort to achieve a human balance has occasionally resulted in overemphasis on certain elements and neglect of others. This study draws on insights from several disciplines, but there is no grand theory behind it. In faithfulness to my subject, I have sought to separate the real Marc Bloch from the legends, to render his reality in its proper texture and contours, to revive his voice and his milieux, and to relate the life of a complex, courageous intellectual who though killed four and a half decades ago is remembered and esteemed even outside the halls of academe.

It is a pleasure to acknowledge my gratitude to those who have aided and sustained the writing of this book. In 1986–87 I was honored by a fellowship at the Woodrow Wilson International Center for Scholars in Washington, a splendid workplace and stimulating scholarly environment, wonderfully near the National Archives and the Library of Congress. As the first occupant of the Cardin Chair in the Humanities at Loyola College in Maryland in 1987–88, I had the privilege of gaining time to write, together with the opportunity to teach two courses as a guest member of the History Department. I thank the University of North Carolina at Wilmington for granting me a two-year leave. I have also been the grateful recipient of research awards from the American Association of University Women, the American Philosophical Society, the Inter-University Centre for European Studies in Montreal, and the University of North Carolina at Wilmington, and travel-to-research-collection awards from the National Endowment for the Humanities and the Southern Regional Educational Board.

My work has been enriched by the opportunity to read papers before the following organizations: the Association of Historians of Eastern North Carolina, the Southern Historical Association, the American Historical Association, and the international colloquium held in Paris in 1986 to commemorate the centenary of Marc Bloch's birth; and to present lectures on Marc Bloch at Brown University, Brandeis University, Harvard University Center for European Studies, New York University, Vassar College, the Graduate Center of the City University of New York, the University of Göttingen, the Catholic University of America, Georgetown University, the University of Maryland, and the Woodrow Wilson Center.

Finally I should like to express my thanks to a number of individuals who have made special contributions to this daunting but deeply satisfying study. First to Etienne and Gloria Bloch, with profound appreciation for their warmth and generosity. To my former teachers Hsi-Huey Liang and the late Hans W. Gatzke for their inspiration. To my friends and colleagues Denise Artaud, Rebecca Boehling, John Day, Hilda Godwin, Ruth Gratch, Waltraud Heindl, Peter Kilby, Roberta Knapp, Melton McLaurin, David Marwell, and Evelyn Schnetz, for many kinds of support and comradeship. To Peter Loewenberg and Rudolf Binion for sharing their insights on biography. To Diane de Bellescize for her helpful suggestions and kind hospitality in Paris. To Professor Dr. Karl Ferdinand Werner for his enthusiastic endorsement. To Maurice Aymard for making important materials available to me. To William Harris for his excellent maps. To Snežana Cockburn and Tim Nix for their able assistance at the Wilson Center. To my former students Richard Rayburn, Juanita Slaughter, and Andrea Tyndall, my most avid questioners and supporters. To the reference department of Wilson Library at UNC–Chapel Hill for their patience with my abundant requests, and to the library staffs of UNC–Wilmington, the Wilson Center, and Loyola College for their efficiency and helpfulness. To Terry Benjey and John Dysland for helping me overcome the complications, and experience the benefits, of using a computer. To Frank Smith, who has been a most congenial and perceptive editor and Jane Van Tassel, a very skillful and tactful copy editor. To Seymour Fink for his loyal attachment to this work. And to the two to whom this is dedicated, my love and high hopes.

Wilmington, North Carolina   C.F.

Acknowledgments

Figs. 1, 12, and 23 were executed by William Harris; Fig. 28, a British Crown Copyright/MOD map, is reproduced by permission of the Controller of Her Britannic Majesty's Stationery Office.

Figs. 2, 6, 9, 13, 17, 20, 24, and 27 were obtained from Roger-Viollet, Paris.

Fig. 22 is from the collection of the Musée d'Histoire Contemporaine–BDIC (Universités de Paris).

Fig. 30 is reproduced courtesy of the editorial board of *Annales: Economies, Sociétés, Civilisations.*

Fig. 29 was given by Mme. Robert Boutruche.

Fig. 5 was given by Daniel Bloch.

Fig. 19 is from the author's personal collection.

Figs. 3, 4, 7, 8, 10, 11, 14, 15, 16, 18, 21, 25, and 26 were generously provided by Etienne Bloch.

Abbreviations

For fuller descriptions, see the Note on Sources.

ADBR	Archives Départementales du Bas-Rhin, Strasbourg
ADH	Archives Départementales de l'Hérault, Montpellier
AESC	*Annales: Economies, Sociétés, Civilisations* (1946–)
AH	Marc Bloch, *Apologie pour l'histoire*, 7th ed. (Paris: Armand Colin, 1974)
AHES	*Annales d'Histoire Économique et Sociale* (1929–38)
AHR	*American Historical Review*
AHS	*Annales d'Histoire Sociale* (1939–41, 1945)
AN	Archives Nationales, Paris
BN	Bibliothèque Nationale, Paris
BNUS	Bibliothèque Nationale et Universitaire, Strasbourg
Carnet	Marc Bloch, Carnets de guerre, 1914–18, Etienne Bloch Collection (EBC)
CdF	Archive of the Collège de France
CDJC	Centre de Documentation Juive Contemporaine, Paris
CP	*Les Cahiers Politiques* (1943–45)
EBC	Etienne Bloch Collection, La Haye, France
ED	Marc Bloch, *L'étrange défaite: Témoignage écrit en 1940*, 2d ed. (Paris: Armand Colin, 1957)

xvii

Historique	"Historique du 72e régiment d'infanterie," in Bloch's file "Souvenirs de guerre" ("SG"), EBC
HP	Letters of Marc Bloch and Lucien Febvre to Henri Pirenne, Courtesy of Professor Bryce Lyon, Brown University, Providence, R.I., and Count Jacques-Henri Pirenne, Hierges, France
HRF	Marc Bloch, *Les caractères originaux de l'histoire rurale française*, new ed. (Paris: Colin, 1952)
IF	Archive of the Institut de France, Paris
JM	Journal de marche, 272e régiment (1914–15), 72e régiment (1915–18), Service Historique de l'Armée de Terre, Château de Vincennes (SHV)
MH	Marc Bloch, *Mélanges historiques*, 2 vols. (Paris: S.E.V.P.E.N., 1963)
MHS	*Mélanges d'Histoire Sociale* (1942–44)
NARS	National Archives and Records Service, Washington, D.C. Germany AA T-120: Captured records of the German Foreign Ministry, Series T-120 OSS: U.S. Office of Strategic Services USDS: U.S. Department of State
RACEP	Records of the American Council for Emigrés in the Professions, Library of the State University of New York at Albany
RB	Letters of Marc Bloch to Robert Boutruche, courtesy of Mme. Boutruche, Montpellier
RFA	Rockefeller Foundation Archives, Tarrytown, N.Y.
RH	*Revue Historique*

RS	Marc Bloch, *Rois et serfs: Un chapitre d'histoire capétienne* (Paris: Champion, 1920)
RSH	*Revue de Synthèse Historique* (1900–30) (superseded by *Revue de Synthèse* (1931–))
RT	Marc Bloch, *Les rois thaumaturges: Etude sur le caractère surnaturel attribué à la puissance royale particulièrement en France et en Angleterre*, new ed. (Paris: Gallimard, 1983)
SF	Marc Bloch, *La société féodale*, 2 vols. (Paris: Albin Michel, 1939–40)
SG	Marc Bloch, *Souvenirs de guerre, 1914–1915* (Paris: Armand Colin, 1969)
"SG"	Marc Bloch file, "Souvenirs de guerre, 1914–1918," EBC
SHV	Service Historique de l'Armée de Terre, Château de Vincennes

1. Forebears

My great-grandfather was a serving soldier in 1793;...my father was one of the defenders of Strasbourg in 1870;...I was brought up in the traditions of patriotism which found no more fervent champions than the Jews of the Alsatian exodus.[1]

Marc Bloch was descended from Jews of eastern France. One of the oldest surviving family documents, a letter by his great-grandfather Gabriel (Getschel) Bloch, was written from the battlefield at Mainz in 1793 (5 Tamouz 5554) in Alsatian Hebrew, using Hebrew characters. The twenty-three-year-old volunteer tersely related the costly defense against the attacking Prussians, assured his father of his faith in God and the protection of his forebears, and expressed his hope for peace and a prompt return to the family home in Wintzenheim in Alsace.[2] Son of the merchant Benjamin Marc (Wolf) Bloch, Gabriel Bloch was the first of his family to enjoy the fruits and pay the price of the emancipation legislation of 1790 and 1791, to which Alsatian Jews – long consigned to poverty and ghetto conditions – responded. As an enlisted man, the peddler Gabriel Bloch was both the scion of an orthodox past and the creator of a new tradition, which enabled his great-grandchild to assert his citizenship a century and a half later.[3]

Gabriel Bloch's son Marc (1816–1880) started another tradition

1 ED, pp. 23–24.
2 Original copy in the possession of Etienne Bloch. Useful background in Zosa Szajkowski, "French Jews in the Armed Forces during the Revolution of 1789," in Jews and the French Revolutions of 1789, 1830, and 1848 (New York: Ktav, 1970), pp. 544–75.
3 ED, p. 23. I thank Dr. Henry Bloch-Michel for a copy of the official translation of this letter, dated 13 Oct. 1941, which likely figured in Marc Bloch's efforts to counter Vichy's legislation on racial exclusion, giving proof of five generations of French citizenship and his family's extraordinary services to the nation.

I

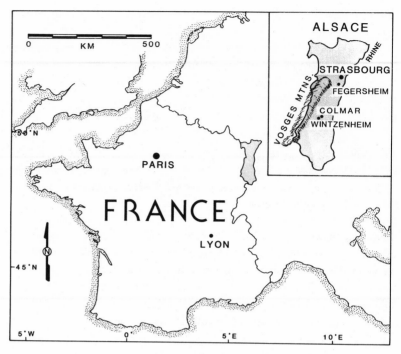

1. Map of France and Alsace

as a teacher. Orphaned at age eleven, he was tutored by an uncle and developed a passion for learning. A disciple of Rousseau, he was the first Jewish student at the Ecole Normale d'Instituteurs of Colmar. After studying for a year at the Ecole Normale in Nancy to perfect his French, he held a modest post for the next twelve years as a schoolmaster (*instituteur*) in the village of Fegersheim outside Strasbourg. There, on 23 August 1847, he married Rose Aron, the daughter of the learned Talmudist Rabbi Alexandre Aron of Fegersheim and grand-daughter of the grand rabbis of Karlsruhe and Metz. On 21 July 1848 a son was born to Marc and Rose Bloch, whom they named Gustave. Two years later the family moved to Strasbourg when, ranking first in a regional competition, Marc Bloch was named director of the newly opened Ecole Israélite de Strasbourg. He now left the village world of Fegersheim for the

2

Alsatian capital, profiting from its flourishing cultural life under the Second Empire.[4]

Though of relatively modest circumstances, Marc Bloch's family lived comfortably at 6, rue des Francs-Bourgeois, where he taught four courses in Jewish subjects. The school attracted students from the leading Jewish families, and in 1864 its director was named the official Hebrew translator before Strasbourg's civil tribunal. The Blochs had two more sons, Oscar, born in 1861, and Louis, born in 1864. They spent the Jewish holidays and summer vacations in nearby Fegersheim with Rabbi Aron, who made an indelible impression on his grandsons, not only with his learned orthodoxy but also with his fascinating tales and anecdotes and the warmth of his personality. Aron's death in 1874 cut the family's tie with its traditionalist and village roots.[5] Marc Bloch's own world was shattered in 1870, first by a stroke at age fifty-four, then by the siege and bombardment of Strasbourg by the Prussians. Forced to submit to German control of his school and to teach in German, Marc Bloch failed to regain his full capacities. At age sixty-two he was obliged to retire, and after an extended period of decline he died two years later, on 9 November 1880.[6]

Gustave Bloch, who was thirteen years older than one brother and sixteen years older than the other, had been considered a prodigy since his earliest youth. Trained first in his father's school, he studied at the lycée in Strasbourg, where he won all the first prizes and came under the influence of the ancient historian Emile Belot, his colleague later at Lyon. Even more important was the influence of Alexandre Aron. During their walks on the Alsatian plains, he confided in Aron. The diminutive, eloquent rabbi conversed with his gifted grandson and imparted many enduring lessons. Gustave Bloch saved all his grandfather's letters, cherished his memory, and,

4 Information on Marc Bloch's professional career in ADBR, Série T, Fonds du Rectorat. The marriage contract of 1847, documents pertaining to Marc Bloch's education and career, and a detailed family history by his youngest son, Louis (1864–1944), EBC.

5 Alexandre Aron's obituary in *Journal d'Alsace*, 9 Aug. 1874.

6 Condolence letter to Marc Bloch's widow, undated, from the members of the Consistoire Israélite de la Basse-Alsace, EBC.

when his own end came, asked for a religious funeral out of respect for his pious ancestor.[7]

In 1864, at age sixteen, Gustave Bloch left Alsace for Paris to prepare for the entrance examinations of the prestigious Ecole Normale Supérieure on the rue d'Ulm. He arrived in the capital an admitted provincial romantic.[8] Living at the Springer Institution, a Jewish residence, where he would be followed seven years later by Henri Bergson, Bloch attended the Lycée Bonaparte, studied philosophy, and placed second in his class.[9]

Four years later, in 1868, he placed first in the *promotion* for the Ecole Normale Supérieure. Founded in 1795 "to educate teachers [to] carry out the ideas of the Enlightenment" and shaped largely under the First Empire, the Ecole Normale continued to produce graduates who formed an elite corps of lycée and university professors under the regime of Napoleon III.[10] According to his later recollections, the bright, exuberant Alsatian was disappointed by the Ecole's intellectually sterile atmosphere and its traditionalist curriculum based primarily on rhetoric and philosophy, which was ill-suited to professional training. He was unsympathetic to Bonapartism, which he blamed for depriving French university life of the fruits of contemporary German scholarship and for perpetuating the stultifying and pedantic academic environment that ultimately weakened the nation.[11]

---

7 Résumé of Gustave Bloch's life in the obituary written by his student, Jérôme Carcopino ("Gustave Bloch," in Ecole Normale Supérieure, Association Amicale de Secours des Anciens Elèves, *Annuaire* [Paris, 1925], pp. 86–109).

8 AH, pp. 150–51, which Marc Bloch later used to illustrate "lag" (*décalage*) in a particular generation.

9 AN, F17 4201, 9042. Cf. Louis M. Greenberg, "Bergson and Durkheim as Sons and Assimilators: The Early Years," *French Historical Studies* 9, no. 4 (Fall 1976): 622.

10 Robert Smith, *The Ecole Normale Supérieure and the Third Republic* (Albany: State University of New York Press, 1982), pp. 5–18.

11 His predecessors Alfred Rambaud (*promotion* of 1864) and Gabriel Monod and Ernest Lavisse (1865) were similarly dissatisfied with the superficiality of their historical instruction at the Ecole Normale: William R. Keylor, *Academy and Community: The Foundation of the French Historical Profession* (Cambridge: Harvard University Press, 1975), pp. 23–24, 36–39; Carcopino, "Gustave Bloch," p. 88.

Nevertheless, entry into one of the *grandes écoles* was a considerable step upward for Gustave Bloch. The Ecole Normale, which prided itself on a democratic tradition and a selection of candidates from all regions, religions, and classes of France, gave him the opportunity to imbibe the political, cultural, and intellectual atmosphere of France's capital. Here he established a fine scholarly record and acquired what a later colleague termed the *culture générale* of those who came of age in the 1870s – a taste for art and literature, concern for social causes, a boundless curiosity, and dedication to the scientific spirit.[12] Here a third-generation emancipated Jew became an assimilated and cosmopolitan Frenchman.[13]

Gustave Bloch arrived in Strasbourg for the summer holidays of 1870 in time to experience the seven-week German siege. He was one of the first to enlist in the civilian militia organized by General Ulrich to extinguish fires and rescue victims. The bombardment of Strasbourg caused heavy casualties and material destruction, including damage to its famous cathedral, before Ulrich finally surrendered on 27 September. The municipal library, with its valuable manuscript collection, had been destroyed. Bloch was unable to continue his studies.

In the preliminaries of peace at Versailles on 26 February 1871, France ceded Alsace and a large part of Lorraine to the new Second Reich. This was formalized in the Treaty of Frankfurt of 10 May 1871, in which article 2 stipulated the terms for those who wished to opt for French nationality. After several unsuccessful efforts to obtain a teaching post in a French lycée, Gustave Bloch decided to return to the Ecole Normale. At this time, more than 159,000 Alsatians (about 15 percent of the total population and 21 percent of the heavily Catholic Haut-Rhin, but only 10 percent of Bloch's native département of Bas-Rhin) left for the interior, where they would contribute significantly to the politicial, economic, and cultural life of the Third Republic. The exodus also deprived the pro-

12 Gustave Lanson, "Discours," 5 Dec. 1923. EBC. Gustave Bloch's scholastic records in AN, 61 AJ 182, 183.
13 Wladimir Rabi, *Anatomie du judaïsme français* (Paris: Editions de Minuit, 1962), pp. 65–66.

vince of their skills and independence during a critical period of almost five decades of German rule.[14]

Back in Paris, Bloch found changes in the Ecole Normale; the defeat by Prussia reinforced the pressure by French academics for reforms and led eventually to government support for major personnel and curricular changes.[15] Gustave Bloch appears to have fallen under the influence of Fustel de Coulanges, whose lectures on ancient France introduced a new vibrance and scholarly rigor into the rue d'Ulm. In 1872 he passed the *agrégation* with a first in letters.[16]

Gustave Bloch left Paris at age twenty-four for his first teaching post as a classics professor at the lycée of Besançon with an awakened enthusiasm for history.[17] A year later he won an appointment to study archaeology at the Ecole Française d'Athènes, but was assigned to the branch institute in Rome, which was headed by the *normalien* Albert Dumont. Originally a joint venture with Prussia, the Institut Archéologique de Rome had its German support cut off in 1871 at the behest of the Second Reich. Dumont argued against maintaining the Rome institute as a practicum for the older better-endowed Athens school. He urged the establishment of an independent French institution in Rome to provide first-class archaeological training and "exceed the work of the Germans," who with their facilities, research, major chairs, and journals dominated the field. Gustave Bloch was therefore present during the founding years of the new Ecole Française de Rome, which began in 1873 with five hearty students.[18]

14 Letters to Ministère de l'Instruction Publique, 29 May, 8 June, 6 Sept. 1871, AN, F17 22468; Gustave Bloch, Option pour la nationalité française, 28 June 1872, AN, BB 31 47. Also Alfred Wahl, *L'option et l'émigration des Alsaciens-Lorrains (1871–1872)* (Paris: Ophrys, 1972), and François-Georges Dreyfus, *Histoire de l'Alsace* (Paris: Hachette, 1979), pp. 248–55.

15 Claude Digeon, *La crise allemande de la pensée française (1870–1914)* (Paris: Presses Universitaires de France, 1959), chaps. 5–7.

16 See report by M. Jaquinet on the *agrégation*, AN, F17 22468. More accomplished in the written than the oral presentation, Bloch was described as an "esprit réfléchi, sagace et ferme, dont la distinction se cache d'abord sous des façons et une tenue assez rudes et incultes."

17 AN, F17 22468; Carcopino, "Gustave Bloch," pp. 88–89.

18 *Le Temps*, 19 July 1874; records in AN, F17 4129/4130.

Under Dumont's direction, the Ecole Francaise de Rome flourished. Officially chartered in 1875, the school moved from the charming Villa Médicis, which it had shared with the French art academy, to the sumptuous Villa Mérode. There was a warm spirit of camaraderie between the students and the youthful Dumont, who taught courses in archaeology and prudently managed the school's external relations. He pleaded with Paris for more ample resources and compensated for his sparse library holdings by arranging loans from the Germans. Historical research at the Ecole was modeled on the critical tradition of Barthold Georg Niebuhr and Theodor Mommsen.

Gustave Bloch, who studied Roman administrative history and specialized in epigraphy, received excellent reports. He had two stays in Athens, in the fall of 1874 and the spring of 1876; but he preferred Rome where, still under the influence of Fustel de Coulanges, he sought to investigate the civilization that had left so important an imprint on France. For three years, between the ages of twenty-five and twenty-eight, Bloch patiently examined texts as well as the sites and monuments of antiquity and developed his intuition and his concrete sense of the past, which would supplement his philological and historical research. Bloch's Roman years, rich and happy, were highlighted by his friendships with Dumont and with French artists, sculptors, archaeologists, and diplomats.[19]

Gustave Bloch returned to France in 1876. On Dumont's recommendation he was appointed to the Faculty of Letters of the University of Lyon to teach a new course in Greek and Latin antiquities. His inaugural lecture announced his adherence to a new doctrine of classical history. According to Bloch, the "reconstitution of the reality of the past (*la réalité disparue*)" should explore all types of testimony; it demanded an energetic examination of texts and monuments and a persistent comparison of both. This diligent labor required diverse and rare qualities: "an exact and complete knowledge of the facts, the first condition of all certitude; a largeness of vision which, in addition to facts, seeks reasons; a sensibility able to

---

19 AN, F17 13600; Dumont to Ministère de l'Instruction Publique, AN, F17 22468; Carcopino, "Gustave Bloch," pp. 90–92.

distinguish styles and epochs; an imagination which reproduces the sentiments of another age; and the finesse to grasp the most subtle nuances." Gustave Bloch represented a determined and "reflective eclecticism," which he practiced and passed on to his students.[20]

The new returnee from Rome doubtless raised some hackles among the senior faculty of Lyon with his ambition and novel ideas. Protected by his former lycée professor, Belot, and supported by his *normalien* and Roman colleagues Charles Bayet and Léon Clédat, Bloch found his place at Lyon as a historian. He was a popular, well-respected lecturer, received the highest ratings for his teaching, and in 1882 was recommended to direct a new course at Lyon in archaeology and epigraphy. The specialist in ancient Rome was capable of both filling the amphitheater and providing expert historical training.[21]

On 26 March 1878 Gustave Bloch married Sarah Ebstein two months short of her twentieth birthday. Ebstein had been born in Lyon to an Alsatian family. Within a year of the marriage, their first son, Louis Constant Alexandre, was born. Seven years later, when Gustave Bloch was thirty-eight, there was a second son, whom they named Marc Léopold Benjamin. Upon his father's death in 1880, Bloch had brought his mother to Lyon, and she remained with him until her death fifteen years later.[22]

During this time Gustave Bloch's career accelerated. In 1884, at the Sorbonne, he successfuly defended his doctoral thesis on the origins of the Roman Senate. The official report was commendatory. It recognized the self-made historian, *agrégé* in letters at the Ecole Normale, who had been teaching at a university for several years without a doctorate, and pronounced him the strongest, most mature candidate in a long time. The judges wrote, "This small, stout, swarthy, and bearded man...has a remarkably sure and vigorous

20 Carcopino, "Gustave Bloch," pp. 92–93.
21 AN, F17 22468; notes by Sarah Bloch, undated, EBC.
22 Gustave Bloch also brought his two brothers, who formally opted for French citizenship, to Lyon, where they began business careers. *ED*, p. 23.

    On the occasion of her return to France, Rose Bloch carried hidden in her baggage the aged national flag which had flown over her husband's school during the siege of Strasbourg and which Gustave and Sarah Bloch subsequently displayed on all national holidays. Louis Bloch, Family history, EBC.

spirit, enhanced by firm and correct speech."[23] For ten years Gustave Bloch had investigated the obscure period of Rome's first centuries, concentrating on the patrician Senate as a key and enduring institution. Well informed by his Roman experiences and combining Fustel's view that history was a series of questions, not all of which could ever be resolved, with what he understood of the Germans' discipline and erudition, Gustave Bloch was eclectic and comparative in his presentation. He delighted in puncturing errors bequeathed by ancient sources, and reflected what would be his abiding interest in the people.[24]

Paris now beckoned. Failing in his candidacy for the Collège de France, Gustave Bloch was nominated for the professorship of ancient history at his alma mater, the Ecole Normale Supérieure, and began officially on 1 January 1888. Eleven years later, he was named an officer of the Legion of Honor on the basis of his services at the Ecole Normale. In 1904, when the Ministry of Education reunited the Ecole with the University of Paris and abolished its separate teaching faculty, Bloch was given a chair in ancient history at the Sorbonne, where he remained until his retirement in 1919.[25]

Nicknamed le Méga, Gustave Bloch was a formidable figure at the rue d'Ulm.[26] He appears to have inherited Fustel's role among the normaliens as a scrupulous scholar and demanding teacher, exuberant

---

23 Report on the thesis defense, 23 Feb. 1884. AN, F17 22468. There is an interesting parallel with Alphonse Aulard, who left the Ecole Normale in 1871 as a specialist in modern literature, later trained himself with great passion and patriotism in the political study of the French Revolution, and became mentor to dozens of eminent historians. Keylor, Academy, pp. 68–70.

24 Gustave Bloch, Les origines du Sénat romain (Paris: E. Thorin, 1883); review by Willems in RH 2 (1885): 164–75.

25 Carcopino, "Gustave Bloch," p. 97; AN, F17 22468.

26 Raoul Blanchard, Ma jeunesse sous l'âile de Péguy (Paris: Fayard, 1961), pp. 224–25; Paul Dimoff, La rue d'Ulm à la Belle Epoque, 1899–1903: Mémoires d'un normalien supérieur (Nancy: G. Thomas, 1970), pp. 33–34; Edouard Herriot, Jadis: Avant la première guerre mondiale (Paris: Flammarion, 1948), pp. 70–71; Hubert Bourgin, De Jaurès à Léon Blum: L'Ecole Normale et la politique (Paris: Fayard, 1938), pp. 30–31; Lucien Febvre, "Marc Bloch et Strasbourg: Souvenirs d'une grande histoire," in Mémorial des années 1939–1945, Publication de la Faculté des Lettres de l'Université de Strasbourg (Paris, 1947), pp. 171–72; and esp. Carcopino, "Gustave Bloch," pp. 97–100.

but unsentimental, with a powerful, picturesque vocabulary. Small, portly, bearded, and bald, he compensated for a lack of physical grace with his "imperturbable probity." Straightforward, undogmatic, precise, and frank, his lectures gave students the opportunity to witness the process of his thought; several listeners responded by choosing ancient history as their vocation. His legendary brutality with careless student presentations was balanced by his warmth and affection for his protégés. He shared his experiences and the fruits of his research with them and exhibited exceptional fairness, kindness, and concern over their lives and careers.

Active as a scholar, Bloch produced several articles, reviews, and short monographs, maintaining his old interest in the plebians of ancient Rome.[27] In 1900 he contributed a volume to Lavisse's series on the history of France. Inspired by Fustel and nourished by his investigations in Lyon, his book, *La Gaule indépendante et la Gaule romaine* was an ambitious popular study from the Stone Age to the fifth century. As a patriot, Bloch aspired to supplant the Germans' dominance of this field; but this foray into unfamiliar terrain involved a risk for a nonspecialist who instinctively emphasized Roman influences over the traditions of ancient Gaul. Most foreign reviews were favorable, but French experts pointed out their colleague's deficiencies. His last two works, *La république romaine* (1913) and *L'empire romain* (1921), brief general studies of the formation and decline of Rome's political and social system, were well received.[28]

Gustave Bloch was one of the group of assimilated Jewish savants who, encouraged by the liberal, reformist atmosphere and institutions of the Third Republic, entered disciplines once alien to their people. His lifelong friends from the Pension Derenbourg, Arsène and James Darmesteter (born in 1846 and 1849), descendants of generations of biblical scholars, became authorities in medieval French and Oriental philology; Bloch's future colleague Emile Durkheim (born in 1853), son of an Alsatian rabbi, became France's leading sociologist; Henri Bergson (born in 1859), son of a Polish

27 Gustave Bloch, "La plèbe romaine: Essai sur quelques théories récentes," *RH* 106 (1911): 70–77.
28 Review by Salomon Reinach in *Revue Archéologique* 19 (1924): 389; Carcopino, "Gustave Bloch," pp. 101–3.

Jewish musician of Hassidic ancestry, was his generation's most influential philosopher; and Gustave Bloch himself brought to ancient history his background of learning and culture, national and republican pride.[29] A devoted citizen, Bloch was committed to educational reform and justice. He worked for improvements in pedagogy at the Ecole Normale, calling for the addition of *culture scientifique* to its *culture générale*. He later became a Dreyfusard and member of the Ligue des Droits de l'Homme.[30]

When world war erupted in 1914, Gustave Bloch insisted on remaining in Paris close to the front, where his two sons were in combat. Still teaching, and working on *L'empire romain*, he followed the fighting with horror at the carnage, anguish at the loss of friends and students,[31] fear for his sons, pride in their courage and accomplishments, and a strong belief in France's cause. He participated in the committee of the patriotic Ligue Civique presided over by his colleague Ernest Denis.[32] Victory brought him the honor of representing the Sorbonne at the ceremonies reopening the University of Strasbourg, where his son Marc had been named professor.[33] He was ecstatic at the sight of the tricolor flying over Strasbourg's cathedral and made an emotional pilgrimage with his son to Fegersheim.

Then he retired to his country home in Marlotte, which contained

29 Rabi, *Judaïsme français*, p. 67; Michael Marrus, *The Politics of Assimilation: The French Jewish Community at the Time of the Dreyfus Affair* (Oxford: Oxford University Press, 1980), pp. 100–10.

30 Gabriel Monod, "La pédagogie historique à l'Ecole Normale Supérieure en 1888," *Revue Internationale de l'Enseignement* 54 (1907): 199–207; Martin Siegel, "Clio at the Ecole Normale: Historians and the Transformation of an Elite Institution in France, 1870–1904," *Findings* 2 (1981): 15–19; Robert Smith, "L'atmosphère politique à l'Ecole Normale Supérieure à la fin du XIXe siècle," *Revue d'Histoire Moderne et Contemporaine* 20 (1973): 248–69; Carcopino, "Gustave Bloch," p. 104.

31 Gustave Bloch (letter to Davy, 17 Nov. 1917, AN, MI 318 1) mourned the death of Emile Durkheim ("another casualty of the war"), following by two years the death in combat of Durkheim's only son; cf. *RH* 127 (Jan.–Apr. 1918): 204–5.

32 Bourgin, *Jaurès à Blum*, p. 31; Gustave Bloch to Jérôme Carcopino, 24 July 1916, 3, 10 Jan., 7 Oct., 3 Nov. 1917, 1 Apr., 1 Aug., 29 Dec. 1918, Carcopino papers, IF; to Georges Davy, 17 Nov. 1917, 27 Jan. 1918, AN, MI 318 1.

33 Gustave Bloch to Carcopino, 24 Feb. 1919, Carcopino papers, IF.

a small colony of academics. In the mornings he read ancient history and Rousseau, in the afternoons took walks with his wife in the nearby forest, and in the evenings socialized with friends. He returned to Paris twice a year to see his older son and two grandsons, who were attending his alma mater, renamed the Lycée Condorcet. He visited Strasbourg again and participated in the scintillating *réunions du samedi* organized by his son Marc and his colleagues on the Faculty of Letters. In October 1921 he traveled to Paris to receive a medallion and the homage of his colleagues and former students. He also began a new work, a social and political history of the Roman republic from 146 to 44 B.C. Illness and deaths, especially that of his older son Louis on 16 March 1922, contributed to Bloch's emotional and physical decline. He suffered from jaundice and crises of breathing, developed severe heart problems, and lost a third of his weight. Gustave Bloch died at age seventy-five, on the night of 3 December 1923, after a calm reassurance to Sarah Bloch: "Je suis bien."[34]

34 *Bulletin de la Faculté des Lettres de l'Université de Strasbourg*, 2 (1923–24): 92; Carcopino, "Gustave Bloch," pp. 105–9. Also Sarah Bloch to Simonne Bloch, Marlotte, 11, 20 Nov. 1923; to Marc Bloch, undated and 22 Nov. 1923, along with Dr. Gaillard's three letters to Marc Bloch, 8 Oct. and two undated, on Gustave Bloch's illness, and eulogy by Carcopino, 5 Dec. 1923, EBC.

2. Education

My classmates and I considered ourselves the last of the generation of the Dreyfus Affair.[1]

Born of defeat, civil war, and the delicate constitutional compromise of 1875, the Third Republic was a paradox: "an unusually stable society, with equally unstable politics."[2] During the four decades before World War I, France had more than fifty cabinets; but its successive coalition governments forged significant social and educational reforms and pursued a moderately successful foreign and colonial policy. Despite some serious recessions, the country was prosperous. Though lagging behind Germany, Great Britain, and the United States, France under the Third Republic became a modern industrial nation and remained an international leader in the arts, literature, and medicine.

Marc Bloch was born in Lyon on 6 July 1886. The family left for Paris before he was two years old. Though Bloch spent his entire youth, adolescence, and young adulthood in the capital, all his official documents would record his birthplace in France's second city, which he would get to know more than a half-century later during the last year of his life.[3]

1 *AH*, p. 151.
2 Eugen Weber, *A Modern History of Europe* (New York: Norton, 1971), p. 801. Another historian, restating the paradox, has written: "Created by the aristocracy, administered by the upper and middle bourgeoisie, governed by the lower bourgeoisie, and dominated by the peasantry." Gordon Wright, *France in Modern Times*, 3d ed. (New York: Norton, 1981), p. 284.
3 See Bloch's remarks on the significance of names and places in a review late in life (*AHS* [1940]: 62): "Un nom d'homme ou de lieu, si l'on ne met derrière lui des réalités humaines, est, tout bonnement, un vain son; qu'aux yeux de l'historien un fait existe seulement par ses liaisons. Etre 'précis,' c'est se tenir proche du concret; ce n'est pas étiquer, à tour de bras, des tiroirs vides."

13

Bloch was raised during the Third Republic's golden age in a capital still celebrated for its beauty and intellectual enterprise, and now also a center of heavy and light industry, national and international finance, mass culture and communication. Lacking direct experience of the debacle or the spirit of *revanche*, Bloch was the offspring of a generally liberal and progressive regime whose dominant republican principles also stimulated significant antidemocratic elements. By the accident of birth Bloch was in the middle – between those who created and shaped the republic and those from the extreme left and right who would challenge its political, intellectual, and philosophical premises.[4]

Little is known of Marc Bloch's childhood; he seldom spoke of it, and there are few records. For about twenty years the family lived in the southern part of Paris, at 72, rue d'Alésia, in the 14th arrondissement. Bloch's parents exerted considerable influence over him. Gustave Bloch, already in his forties, began his younger son's historical training at an early age. Sarah Bloch, intelligent, musically talented, and a meticulous organizer, was devoted to her husband's career and to her sons' education. The slight, reserved Marc Bloch idolized his extroverted older brother. Although separated by seven years, they were close and congenial. Louis Bloch went on to study medicine and specialize in pediatrics. By the time of World War I, he had married the daughter of a Sorbonne professor, had two sons, and was laboratory chief of the diphtheria section of the Hôpital des Enfants Malades.[5]

Bloch's family was typical of many Alsatian Jews, who were republicans, liberals, and patriots. Severed from their roots and kin and from all memories of the ghetto, they claimed the capital as their home, the Revolution as their liberator, and the Third Republic as their benefactor. France represented a noble and rational ideal of morality, liberty, and civilization to which they could adhere.

4 John Eros, "The Positivist Generation of French Republicanism," *Sociological Review* 3 (Dec. 1955): 255–57.
5 Mare Bloch's tributes to his parents: "A mon père, son élève," dedication of *RS*, and "Avant propos," *RT*, pp. vi-vii; manuscript of 10 May 1941 instructing that the flyleaf of *AH* read: "In memoriam matris amicae." Personal memorabilia in "Souvenirs sur les disparus" (Papa, Louis), EBC. Information on Louis Bloch-Michel's medical career in AN, AJ 16 6500, 6525.

2. Paris: rue d'Alésia, ca. 1890

3. Marc Bloch with his parents and grandmother

15

4. Louis Bloch (1879–1922)   5. Marc Bloch

Neither chauvinists nor xenophobes, French Jews struck a balance between fierce Jacobin patriotism and the antinationalism of the left.[6]

Bloch's early schooling no doubt reinforced his devotion to the motherland. The Third Republic was a dynamic laboratory of pedagogic reform. Spurred by the challenge of the Second Reich, school reformers saw public education as "a thaumaturgic answer to France's political and social ills after Sedan."[7] The Ferry Laws between 1879 and 1886 created a centralized, standardized national system of education substituting "civic education" in the public schools for the now outlawed religious instruction. History, a means of healing the wounds of invasion and defeat by reviving past glories, became the showpiece of the curriculum. Spurred by the work of Ernest Lavisse, French textbooks were rewritten to foster national pride in young minds; and the first generation of republican

6 ED, pp. 23–24. Cf. Julien Benda, La jeunesse d'un clerc (Paris: Gallimard, 1936), pp. 27–28; Michael Marrus, The Politics of Assimilation: The French Jewish Community at the Time of the Dreyfus Affair (Oxford: Oxford University Press, 1980), pp. 97–99 and passim.
7 Barnett Singer, "From Patriots to Pacifists: The French Primary School Teachers, 1880–1940," Journal of Contemporary History 12 (1977): 414.

schoolmasters were renowned for their militant patriotism.[8] Sports and physical fitness were also emphasized during Bloch's youth as skills necessary for individual and national regeneration.[9]

Marc Bloch is unlikely to have received a Jewish education or witnessed any religious observance at home. Like most assimilated French Jews, Gustave and Sarah Bloch regarded traditional Judaism as a relic of the past, a sign of separation and obscurantism that had been overcome by a century of citizenship and progress since the Revolution.[10] "Education" thus meant training and preparation to enter the mainstream of French life. Through its schools and competitive examinations, the republic had given all segments of the population access to its elite institutions and to hitherto limited-entry positions in government, the army, the arts, the press, law, medicine, and academic life, where French Jews made contributions disproportionate to their general numbers.[11]

A reaction was predictable. In the year of Marc Bloch's birth, 1886, Edouard Drumont's popular two-volume work *La France juive* appeared. It assembled a motley group of charges against the Jews and the Third Republic and was an instant success; over 100,000 copies were sold within a year of publication. *La France juive* signaled the birth of modern French anti-Semitism. Economic,

8 Pierre Nora, "Ernest Lavisse: Son rôle dans la formation du sentiment national," *RH* 222 (1962): 73–106. See also F. Wartelle, "Bara, Viala: Le thème de l'enfance héroïque dans les manuels scolaires (IIIe République)," *Annales d'Histoire de la Révolution Française* 52, no. 3 (1980): 365–89. Singer, "From Patriots to Pacifists," pp. 413–34, discusses the change in this group after World War I.

9 Jean-Pierre Rioux, "L'ardeur sportive à la Belle Epoque," *Histoire* 14 (1978): 76–78; Dominique Lejeune, "Histoire sociale et alpinisme en France à la fin du XIXe et au début du XXe siècle," *Revue d'Histoire Moderne et Contemporaine* 25 (1978): 111–28. Bloch enjoyed mountain climbing. According to his military records, he was a passable horseman but was unable to swim.

10 Marrus, *Politics of Assimilation*, pp. 9–50; Benda, *Jeunesse*, pp. 30–31. Bloch did have a prayer book, in French translation, dated 1848, EBC.

11 Robert Byrnes, *Antisemitism in Modern France* (New Brunswick, N.J.: Rutgers University Press, 1950), p. 97. The *Archives Israélites*, which each year recorded Jewish appointments, promotions, and other successes, toward the end of the nineteenth century rejoiced that there "were enough Jews in the Institut to form a minyan" (Wladimir Rabi, *Anatomie du judaïsme français* [Paris: Editions de Minuit, 1962], p. 67); however, almost all of these eminences were non-practicing Jews.

political, racial, and ideological accusations, together with the techniques of mass communications and modern politics, were added to the old religious accusations and legal discrimination against the Jews. Borrowing a pseudo-scientific label from the Germans, French anti-Semites insisted that despite their emancipation and assimilation, the Jews maintained a corporate identity that threatened the nation. As individuals they could never merge with the French people, since they lacked the racial, historical, and religious essentials of "Frenchness." In this vein, Pierre Drieu La Rochelle, who was born in 1893, had one of his literary characters voice outrage that his cherished "old complex [French] culture" had been tarnished by the Jews' leap from the synagogue to the Sorbonne.[12]

Before the eruption of the Dreyfus Affair, French Jews tended to minimize anti-Semitism, deeming it an imported (German) phenomenon and responding cautiously or with the silence of disdain.[13] Once Dreyfus was arrested, the issue could not be ignored. Whether real or not, his iniquity was touted by the Jews' enemies as a blemish on the entire community: "Les Israélites français" again became "des Juifs," an unassimilable, separate nation.[14]

Faced with so potent a threat to their identity and security, French Jews reacted prudently. Gustave Bloch initially believed that Dreyfus was guilty, for he found it difficult to conceive that the army, venerated as the nation's shield, had erred or that a French officer had been persecuted for his religion.[15] Contrary to opinion at

12 Drieu La Rochelle, *Gilles* (Paris: Gallimard, 1962), p. 112. Also Henri Dagan, *Enquête sur l'antisémitisme* (Paris: P. V. Stock, 1899). Useful studies include: Hannah Arendt, *The Origins of Totalitarianism* (New York: Harcourt Brace & World, 1966), pp. 79–88; J. B. Duroselle, "L'antisémitisme en France de 1886 à 1914," *Cahiers Paul Claudel* 7 (1968): 49–70; Jacob Katz, *From Prejudice to Destruction: Anti-Semitism 1700–1933* (Cambridge: Harvard University Press, 1980), pp. 292–300; Stephen Wilson, *Ideology and Experience: Anti-Semitism in France at the Time of the Dreyfus Affair* (Rutherford, N.J.: Fairleigh Dickinson University Press, 1982); Zeev Sternhell, "The Roots of Popular Anti-Semitism in the Third Republic," in Frances Malino and Bernard Wasserstein, eds., *The Jews in Modern France* (Hanover, N.H.: University Press of New England, 1985), pp. 103–34.
13 Marrus, *Politics of Assimilation*, pp. 99, 122–43.
14 Simon Schwarzfuchs, *Les Juifs de France* (Paris: Albin Michel, 1975), pp. 271–77.
15 Interview with his grandson, Jean Bloch-Michel.

the time, and now, the Alsatian captain was not the first Jew to serve on the General Staff, nor were Jews unusual in the ranks of French army officers.[16] Indeed some liberal Frenchmen, including Jaurès, considered the sentence extremely lenient in view of the magnitude of the charge of aiding the hated Reich. The struggle for revision was initiated by the tireless and devoted Dreyfus family, the courageous Jewish nationalist Bernard Lazare, and the liberal politician Joseph Reinach. But Dreyfus was saved also by the crucial support of non-Jews – Picquart, Zola, Scheurer-Kestner, and Jaurès – who transformed the case into a national rather than a parochial issue and mitigated the Jews' sense of isolation. The widespread rumors of a "syndicate," which portrayed the efforts for revision as a well-financed conspiracy to rule and ruin France, no doubt reinforced the prudence of Dreyfus's co-religionists and their determination to demonstrate their loyalty as French citizens to the principle of equal justice under the law.[17]

At the Ecole Normale Supérieure, the Dreyfusard cause was originally led by the socialist librarian, Lucien Herr, and by Gabriel Monod, founder and editor of the *Revue Historique*. It was later joined by the dean of students, Paul Dupuy, the Germanist Charles Andler, the literary historian Gustave Lanson, the mathematician and vice-director of the Science Division Jules Tannery, and Gustave Bloch. Reportedly a model of republican and Dreyfusard sentiment, the Ecole was actually divided into two camps. Indeed, the Affair split the entire French academic establishment and swept academicians "into the unfamiliar world of mass meetings, political rallies, and journalistic polemics."[18]

The Dreyfus Affair was the pivotal event of Marc Bloch's youth.

16 Rabi, *Judaïsme français*, p. 67; Doris Bensimon-Donath, *Socio-démographie des Juifs de France et d'Algérie: 1867–1907* (Paris: Publications Orientalistes de France, 1976), pp. 167ff.
17 Wilson, *Ideology and Experience*, pp. 411–13. Cf. Nancy L. Green, "The Dreyfus Affair and Ruling Class Cohesion," *Science and Society* 43, no. 1 (1979): 29–50; also the excellent Nelly Wilson, *Bernard Lazare: Anti-Semitism and the Problem of Jewish Identity in Late Modern France* (Cambridge: Cambridge University Press, 1978).
18 Robert Smith, *The Ecole Normale Supérieure and the Third Republic* (Albany: State University of New York Press, 1982), pp. 87–94 and passim; William Keylor, *Academy and Community* (Cambridge: Harvard University Press, 1975), pp. 144–45, 251 n. 6; Wilson, *Ideology and Experience*, pp. 405–6.

He was eight when Dreyfus was arrested on charges of treason. Despite the army's efforts at secrecy, after the story was trumpeted by Drumont's *Libre Parole* on 29 October, the General Staff expedited the court-martial, with its falsified documents, and Dreyfus was hastily convicted, sentenced, and deported to his solitary confinement on Devil's Island.[19] Marc Bloch was nine when Colonel Piquart, named chief of the army's Statistical Section in July 1895, began his investigation, and he was ten when Lazare's pamphlet *Une erreur judiciaire: La vérité sur l'Affaire Dreyfus*, published in Brussels, appeared in Paris and sparked the Dreyfusard cause. He was twelve the year the storm broke in 1898, with Zola's "J'accuse," Esterhazy's flight, Henry's suicide, and the judicial decision to reopen the Dreyfus case. Zola's charges stimulated anti-Semitic riots in the Latin Quarter as throughout France and Algeria, with lootings, beatings, and cries of "Death to the Jews!"[20]

Just after Bloch's thirteenth birthday, between 7 August and 9 September 1899 the army was forced to retry Alfred Dreyfus before another court-martial at Rennes. Not unexpectedly, he was pronounced guilty with "extenuating circumstances." The president of France, Emile Loubet, immediately granted clemency, which Dreyfus accepted on condition that it would not prejudice the continuing efforts to establish his innocence. The Dreyfusards were now ascendant. In July 1906, when Marc Bloch turned twenty, the Rennes judgment was overturned by the Court of Appeals. Dreyfus was made a *chevalier* of the Legion of Honor and, by an act of parliament, reinstated in the army.[21]

The Dreyfus Affair had a profound impact on Marc Bloch.

19 David B. Ralson, *The Army of the Republic* (Cambridge: Harvard University Press, 1967), pp. 212–15; cf. Jean-Denis Bredin, *L'Affaire* (Paris: Julliard, 1983).

20 Wilson, *Ideology and Experience*, pp. 106–24; George Weisz, *The Emergence of Modern Universities in France* (Princeton, N.J.: Princeton University Press, 1983), p. 353; Marrus, *Politics of Assimilation*, pp. 222–23; Arendt, *Totalitarianism*, pp. 106–17.

21 Dreyfus was promoted to major although on the basis of his ability and training and in the ordinary course he might well have become a lieutenant-colonel; Piquart, on the other hand, who had been dismissed for his role in the affair, was given the maximum promotion, from lieutenant-colonel to brigadier general. Ralson, *Army of the Republic*, p. 296.

6. "The Traitor: Degradation of Alfred Dreyfus" in the court of the Ecole Militaire, 5 January 1895. Engraving by H. Meyer in *Le Petit Journal*, 13 January 1895

According to his own brief testimony, he adhered to the older generation and felt separated from those just behind him. When he entered the Ecole Normale Supérieure in 1904, it was the end of an illustrious era. Typical *normaliens* between 1890 and 1904 had been devoted republicans: antidoctrinaire and antihierarchical, Jauresian socialists, patriots without chauvinism, and generally free-thinkers without strong religious affiliation or prejudice. Many students joined the faculty in signing petitions to revise the Dreyfus

21

judgment.[22] The "young men of 1905" were different: "Frank irrationalists or even antirationalists," angered or alienated by the Dreyfusards' revenge against the church and the army, they looked more to Péguy than to Jaurès for inspiration.[23] During the dark times forty years later Bloch recalled Péguy's dauntless philo-Semitism during the Affair and shared the poet-journalist's distaste for "temporality"; but he preferred Jaurès's more lucid and serene historical perspective.

Bloch shared none of his father's illusions about France's military leadership. The Dreyfus Affair produced in him a negative image of its snobbery, anti-Semitism, and antirepublicanism, its narrow educational system and jealous protection of its autonomy vis-à-vis the political and judicial sectors of the state. Bloch soon saw military life firsthand. In the wake of the Dreyfus Affair, the law of 1905 established universal service but reduced the term from three to two years. Bloch took advantage of the previous exemption available to those already attending university. He volunteered, and served in the 46th Infantry Regiment in Pithiviers between September 1905 and 1906. On requesting leave from the Ecole Normale, Bloch reassured the dean of students that the benefits to his physical development might compensate for a year of what he delicately characterized as "intellectual repose."[24]

Bloch also acquired a profound skepticism of the press. While

22 Jérôme Tharaud and Jean Tharaud, *Notre cher Péguy* 1 (Paris: Plon-Nourrit, 1926), p. 134; Robert Smith, "L'atmosphère politique à l'Ecole Normale Supérieure à la fin du XIXe siècle," *Revue d'Histoire Moderne et Contemporaine* 20 (1973): 267.

23 H. Stuart Hughes, *Consciousness and Society* (New York: Random House, 1958), pp. 334–58. See also Frank Field, "Jaurès, Péguy, and the Crisis of 1914," *Journal of European Studies* 16 (1986): 45–57.

24 Bloch to Dupuy, Paris, 27 Sept. 1905, AN, 61 AJ 110. Bloch entered as a "three-year volunteer" under the old law of 1889; article 23 enabled university students to apply for the *bénéfice* of resuming their studies after one year of active duty. On his return to the Ecole Normale in 1906 Bloch, placed "en disponibilité de l'Armée active," was attached to the regiment of Fontainebleau. He was promoted to corporal on 18 September 1906 and to sergeant on 18 March 1907. "Registre matricule du recrutement" 9 (1907): 4277, SHV; also République Française, "Constatation de services militaires," 9582 (9 Mar. 1950), EBC.

acknowledging the commercial and time constraints under which even the best journalists operated, many years later he was still insisting that their "stereotyped psychology" and "rage for the picturesque" placed them at the forefront in the gallery of "fomenters of lies (*fauteurs de mensonges*)."[25]

Perhaps Bloch's fascination with courtroom procedure was related to the Dreyfus Affair. He insisted that the historian be a thorough, if imperfect, interrogator of "witnesses" (the documents). Certainly his lifelong preoccupation with fraud and error had been stimulated in his youth. Six years after Dreyfus's triumph, on the eve of World War I, Bloch at the awards ceremony at the lycée of Amiens presented a catalogue of recent scholarly forgeries. In his discourse on fabricated documents and plagiarist historians, he singled out the case of the brilliant Vrain-Lucas, who, like the inventive Colonel Henry, had answered his challengers by continuing to manufacture letters of Pascal and Galileo.[26]

Bloch also became sensitized to the collective manifestations of distorted reality, the *fausses nouvelles* (rumors and misinformation) that could be stimulated by human misperception, miscalculation, and the frailty of memory as well as by extraordinary circumstances. All the stock items of modern anti-Semitism had surfaced in the furor over the Dreyfus case; but their content and dissemination were not at all "spontaneous." Although Bloch's thinking was rooted in late-nineteenth-century rationalism and positivism, he acknowledged the inevitability of rumor and falsehood. He strongly advised his students in 1914 to adopt "the critical spirit," the response of intelligent beings to the challenges of the present as well as the past:

The alert individual who is aware of the rarity of exact testimony is less prompt than the uninformed to accuse an erring friend of lying. And when one day you take your place in the public arena in some great debate, whether to scrutinize a cause too quickly judged or to vote for a man or an

25 *AH*, pp. 88–89.
26 Address delivered 13 July 1914: *Critique historique et critique du témoignage* (Amiens, 1914), p. 5 (autographed copy in Duke University Library, Durham, N.C.). In 1942 Bloch inserted the forgeries of the Dreyfus Affair in his list illustrating that "la fraude, par nature, enfante la fraude" (*AH*, p. 88).

23

idea, you must never forget the critical method. It is one of the routes that lead toward the truth.[27]

Finally, the outcome of the Dreyfus Affair reinforced the conviction of assimilated French Jews that their legal emancipation a century earlier could not be reversed by the counterrevolution: by the church, the royalists, and their supporters in the army, the towns, or the countryside. According to the principles of 1789, they were not a Jewish nation residing in France but were "French citizens of Jewish origin" whose rights had been affirmed by the law and by the political process. In return they were willing to pledge their complete loyalty to the nation in which they had eagerly merged themseleves. Marc Bloch during his crucial adolescent years had witnessed the trial and vindication of these ideas and emerged exceptionally confident of their endurance.

Bloch had in the meantime also made excellent progress as a student. After three years of study at the elite lycée Louis-le-Grand, he passed the *baccalauréat* on 6 July 1903 in Classical Instruction (Letters and Philosophy) with the distinction "très bien." Each year he had been ranked at the top of his class and had won first prizes in history, French, English, Latin, and natural history. A year later, still short of his eighteenth birthday and after barely a year in the *cagne* (the preparatory course for the Ecole Normale Supérieure), he passed the rigorous entrance examination with high marks in history and was awarded a scholarship. In his letter of recommendation, Bloch's lycée headmaster described him as an "excellent student, with originality and finesse," a professor's son with "considerable prospects for success."[28] That summer Marc Bloch made his first trip to England. It was the year of the Entente Cordiale, but he was less impressed by the splendor of Chamberlain's London than by the

27 *Critique historique*, p. 7.
28 AN, 61, AJ 233. Information on the lycée supplied to the author by the librarian of Louis-le-Grand; see also AN, MI 318 I. The commemorative volume *Louis-le-Grand, 1563–1963* (Paris, 1963) surprisingly omits Bloch from its graduates admitted to the Ecole Normale Supérieure (p. 189); it includes memoirs by Bloch's slightly older and younger contemporaries Raoul Blanchard and Maurice Baumont that stress the rigors of the *cagne* (pp. 233–39, 241–44).

7. The *promotion* of 1904 at the Ecole Normale Supérieure. Marc Bloch is seated on the right.

masses of the homeless unemployed crowding the benches of the Embankment.[29]

Marc Bloch arrived at the rue d'Ulm on 1 November 1904, the year that the Ecole Normale Supérieure was united with the University of Paris. A spate of reforms took place designed to merge the Ecole's resources with the Sorbonne. The rigid boarding-school routine (the *internat*) was abolished; faculty were given appointments at the university; and, except for one required course in the history of French secondary education (taught by Emile Durkheim), *normaliens* were supposed to take all their courses at the Sorbonne. In his inaugural address on 23 November the new director, Ernest Lavisse, urged the *normaliens* to serve the nation by dedicating themselves to becoming well-trained teachers.[30]

29 Bloch to André Siegfried, 4 May 1931, Siegfried papers, Fondation Nationale des Sciences Politiques, Paris.
30 Address reprinted in *Revue Internationale de l'Enseignement* 43, no. 2 (1904): 481–94; also Gabriel Monod, "La réforme de l'Ecole Normale," *RH* 84 (1904): 78–87, 308–13.

In fact, the 1904 reforms proved less effective than expected. Though stripped of its own faculty and curriculum, the Ecole Normale retained its distinctive intellectual climate. During Bloch's tenure many professors continued to conduct small classes and seminars at the rue d'Ulm. The *"normalien* spirit" did not, as some hoped or feared, dissolve. Admission standards remained high, and the Ecole, attracting the Third Republic's brightest youth, continued to produce journalists, politicians, jurists, and diplomats as well as teachers.[31] Its traditions of political activism and service to the republic survived. In World War I, slightly over 800 *normaliens* were mobilized, and 239 were killed.[32]

At the Ecole Normale Bloch joined an elite group, separated from others by its own expressions and ironic, occasionally sarcastic, humor and linked to each other by the universal *tutoiement* as well as lifelong personal and professional bonds. At the rue d'Ulm Bloch established his longstanding friendships with the geographer Philippe Arbos (1882–1956), the sociologist Georges Davy (1883–1950), the Sinologist Marcel Granet (1884–1940), the Hellenist and future librarian of the Ecole Paul Etard (1884–1962), the mathematician Paul Lévy (1886–1940), the philosopher Emmanuel Leroux (1883–1942), the classicist Louis Séchan (1882–1968), and the jurist Jacques Massigli (1886–1971).

Ten of the forty-one students in Bloch's *promotion* of 1904 died between 1914 and 1919, among them several of his closest friends. Three of the most brilliant – Antoine-Jules Bianconi (1882–1915), Maxime David (1885–1914), and Ernest Babut (1875–1916) – were killed in combat. Two died of illness. Casimir Julien Vaillant

---

31 Smith, *Ecole Normale Supérieure*, pp. 72–78, 84–86. The 1904 reform also added a number of externs, and a few women were finally admitted after 1927.
    The biography of another member of the *promotion* of 1904 (Lucienne Gosse, *Chronique d'une vie française: René Gosse, 1883–1943* [Paris: Plon, 1962], pp. 36–59) provides useful details about student life at the Ecole during Bloch's era.

32 After the collapse of 1940 a larger number of *normaliens* joined the Resistance and led its ranks than collaborated with the Germans or with Vichy. Gosse, *Chronique*, pp. 355–421. Jean Guéhenno, *Journal des années noires (1940–44)* (Paris: Gallimard, 1947), p. 313; Smith, *Ecole Normale Supérieure*, pp. 98, 126–29.

(1883–1918), a specialist in ancient languages and grammar, who was Bloch's colleague in 1913–14 at Amiens, died at age thirty-five a month before the war was over and just after assuming the post of assistant headmaster in Rouen. Emile Besch (1884–1919), who may have been Bloch's closest friend, was stricken with tuberculosis as a youth. Forced to give up his literary studies, he spent long periods at Berck, a small resort town on the English Channel, where through visits and correspondence he stayed in contact with his former classmates. During the war, Besch taught for three years very close to the front in the lycée of Bar-le-Duc and then was evacuated to Caen in Normandy, where he continued to write and read. Suffering from his inactivity, worry over his many friends in the trenches, and the pain of a debilitating illness, Besch succumbed at Berck on the night of 14–15 March 1919, a day after Marc Bloch was demobilized.[33]

Bloch's progress through the Ecole Normale was ostensibly smooth and successful. He was awarded the *licence* after his first year, during which he had written a treatise analyzing the use of the words *vassi* and *vassali* in the capitularies of Charlemagne. At the end of his second year, under the supervision of the medievalist Christian Pfister, Bloch earned the *diplôme d'études supérieures* (D.E.S.) with a thesis on the social and economic history of the region south of Paris. Following his last year, he placed second in the *agrégation* in history and geography.[34]

Bloch acquired his professional training at a time when French historians were undergoing an important period of self-evaluation. Four decades earlier, a pioneering generation of scholars, led by Ernest Renan, had fought to establish a new discipline of pro-

---

33 Bloch's poems "Au magnifique cacique Bianconi" and "Davidiana" and his letters and cards from Besch, 1909–18, in personal file, "Souvenirs sur les disparus," EBC; also unsigned obituary (by Marc Bloch?), "Besch (Emile) 1884–1919," in Ecole Normale Supérieure, Association Amicale de Secours des Anciens Elèves, *Annuaire* (Paris: 1920), pp. 53–57; information supplied by P. Petitmengin, Bibliothécaire de l'Ecole Normale Supérieure, 14 July 1984. In his will of 1 June 1915 (EBC) Bloch mentions his *normalien* friends.
34 Pfister to Emile Boutroux (Director, Fondation Thiers), 3 Mar. 1909, AN, MI 318 1. Bloch's Ecole Normale records in AN, 61 AJ 17, 186, 233; Sorbonne: AN, AJ 16 4966.

fessional history, based on objective, "scientific" criteria that would distinguish them from the clerics, politicians, journalists, and dilettantes who wrote about the past. Their "critical spirit" challenged the prevailing romantic literary treatment of history. The reformers' model was Germany, where well-endowed, full-time specialists assembled in institutes and universities, conducted painstaking research, and trained students in methodology.[35]

Successive governments in the 1880s and 90s, spurred by the republic's rivalry with the church and the Second Reich, were receptive to the reformers' scientific goals. Building on reforms begun under Napoleon III and responding to pressures from the business, scientific, and academic community, the Third Republic began modernizing its university system. In 1884, the philosopher and former *normalien* Louis Liard was appointed Director of Higher Education in the Ministry of Public Instruction. Working closely with his former colleagues, Liard for the next eighteen years prepared and directed major institutional changes. Under increased enrollment pressures, the University of Paris was expanded, and provincial centers were created, new faculty positions and scholarships were established, and the curriculum and examinations were revised.[36] Because of its central role in shaping national consciousness and through the crucial contributions of historian-reformers such as Renan and Lavisse, the discipline of history profited remarkably from governmental support and patronage. In Paris and in the provinces the number of history chairs on the university

35 Ernest Renan, *La réforme intellectuelle et morale* (Paris: M. Lévy Frères, 1871). Also Martin Siegel, "Science and the Historical Imagination: Patterns in French Historiographical Thought, 1866–1914" (Ph.D. diss., Columbia University, 1965), pp. 2–121; Keylor, *Academy and Community*, pp. 19–54; *AH*, p. 80.

36 George Weisz, "The Anatomy of University Reform, 1863–1914," in Donald N. Baker and Patrick J. Harrigan, eds., *The Making of Frenchmen: Current Directions in the History of Education in France, 1679–1979* (Waterloo, Ontario: Historical Reflections Press, 1980), pp. 363–79; also Antoine Prost, *Histoire de l'enseignement en France, 1800–1967* (Paris: A. Colin, 1968); Fritz Ringer, *Education and Society in Modern France* (Bloomington: Indiana University Press, 1979); George Weisz, "Le corps professoral de l'enseignement supérieur et l'idéologie de la réforme universitaire en France, 1860–1885," *Revue Française de Sociologie* 18 (1977): 201–32.

faculties increased dramatically along with official support in terms of salaries and research subventions.

With history the centerpiece of these reforms, historians were nonetheless sensitive about their secondary position behind the world-famous French sciences of mathematics, biology, physics, chemistry, and medicine. Led by Gabriel Monod, a student of Michelet who had attended the famous seminar of Georg Waitz in Göttingen, Gustave Bloch's generation had striven to emulate and exceed the Germans: to perfect their methods and techniques and to establish rigorous precepts of textual criticism, research, and writing. Even the old standard bearers of national history, like Fustel de Coulanges and Lavisse, welcomed the reinforcement of French scholarship with higher standards of erudition. Scholarly societies were created which convened local and national meetings. Two scholarly journals exemplified their historicist ideals: Founded under the Second Empire, the *Revue Critique d'Histoire et de Littérature* (1866) was devoted exclusively to learned reviews, and the *Revue Historique* (1876), founded by Monod, gathered the most eminent historians and scholarship to stimulate a more "profound understanding of the nation's history."[37]

The institutional triumph of the crusading, positivist historians led inevitably to factionalism and to challenges from outside. The political consensus of the 1870s and 80s was shattered by the test of the Dreyfus Affair. Several of the new academicians of the 1890s deprecated their elders' reverence for "German fact-grubbing" and began questioning the scientific claims of history. In 1896–97, Charles Seignobos and Charles-Victor Langlois taught the first course in historiography at the Sorbonne. A year later they published the first French manual of historical training, entitled *Introduction aux études historiques*, which intensified the debate between the specialists and their detractors. Seignobos led the struggle against both the remnants of popular, romantic history and the excesses of overly pedantic scholars. While admitting that the reconstruction of

37 Monod in *RH* 1 (1876): 38. Distancing itself from the Catholic *Revue des Questions Historiques* (1866), the *RH* pledged to avoid political and religious controversies and treat subjects "avec la rigueur de méthode et l'absence de parti pris qu'exige la science" ("Avant propos," ibid., p. 1).

the past through the examination of fragmentary documents could never duplicate the scientist's direct observation of phenomena, Seignobos insisted that history was a "process" of disciplined fact gathering and synthesis governed by the mind of the investigator.[38] Langlois and Seignobos, both Bloch's teachers, insisted on the primacy of documents and the singularity of individual events.[39] Hence, in examining nineteenth-century revolutions in his *Histoire politique de l'Europe contemporaine*, Seignobos focused primarily on individuals and political events, and stressed the importance of accidental factors over long-term causes.

Out of the Dreyfus Affair came a wave of new questions and concerns from those who sought to broaden history's scope by penetrating the political facade to uncover more profound social, economic, and cultural processes. Monod admitted in 1896 that history should concentrate not simply on great men and great events but also on the grand but slow development of institutions and on economic and social conditions.[40] With a more leftist republicanism than their teachers, a new generation, spurred by the publication of Jaurès's *Histoire socialiste de la Révolution française*, contested the predominance of mainstream political history. The historians Henri Hauser and Alphonse Aulard attempted to bring social and economic history into the curriculum; the medievalist Ferdinand Lot pressed for more interdisciplinary studies; and in 1908 a new journal dedicated to economic and social history appeared.[41]

Across the Rhine, Karl Lamprecht (1856–1915) was challenging the reigning German establishment by promoting a *total* history that subsumed all human actions, and the fierce debate he provoked

38 Seignobos, *La méthode historique appliquée aux sciences sociales* (Paris: Alcan, 1901), pp. 1, 3, 5, 116 and passim.
39 *Introduction aux études historiques* (Paris: Hachette, 1898), pp. 204, 253, 275.
40 *RH 61* (1896): 325.
41 Entitled *La Revue d'Histoire des Doctrines Economiques et Sociales*, it was renamed *La Revue d'Histoire Economique* in 1914. Ferdinand Lot, "De la situation faite à l'enseignement supérieure en France," *Cahiers de la Quinzaine*, ser. 7, 11 (1905–6): 136–38. Cf. Luciano Allegra and Angelo Torre, *La nascita della storia sociale in Francia: Dalla commune alle "Annales"* (Turin: Einaudi, 1977), pp. 158–62; Weisz, *Modern Universities*, pp. 288–89.

spilled over into French journals. Lamprecht's friend and disciple the Belgian medievalist Henri Pirenne (1862–1935), who had studied at both the traditionalist Ecole des Chartes and the reformist Ecole Pratique des Hautes Etudes, was both indebted to French positivism and skeptical of its scientific claims. In his own work on the foundations of urban civilization in the West and the history of his native Belgium, the brilliant and independent Pirenne transcended the narrow compass of his nationality and medieval training and conducted innovative studies in demography and economic history. Harking back to the goals of Jules Michelet, Pirenne advocated a history that was as subtle as the human spirit and relative as the changing nature of human reality, and that, though admittedly not an exact science, reflected the writer's awareness of the requirements and the nobility of his task. In an age of intense nationalism Pirenne also dedicated himself to promoting contacts among scholars, serving before World War I as a liaison between French and German historians.[42]

Scholars in history's sister disciplines were similarly shaking off German dominance and reevaluating their methods and goals. A new school of human geography was led by Paul Vidal de la Blache (1845–1918), co-founder in 1891 of the *Annales de Géographie* and author in 1903 of the *Tableau de la géographie de la France*, which contained his original interpretation of France's physical personality. Vidal rejected the Germans' obsession with geographical determinism – used, he believed, to justify national expansion and human and material inequality. Drawing on the older tradition of Alexander

42 Jaroslav Kudrna, "Zu einigen Fragen des Methodenstreits in der französischen Historiographie um 1900," *Storia della Storiografia* 3 (1983): 62–78; Luise Schorn-Schütte, *Karl Lamprecht* (Göttingen: Vandenhoeck and Ruprecht, 1984), pp. 287–337; Peter Griss, *Das Gedankenbild Karl Lamprechts: Historisches Verhalten im modernisierungsprozess der "Belle Epoque"* (Berne: Europäische Hochschulschriften, 1987); Bryce Lyon, "The Letters of Henri Pirenne to Karl Lamprecht (1894–1915)," *Studies of West European Medieval Institutions* (London: Variorum, 1978), pp. 161–231; also Lyon, "Henri Pirenne and the Origins of *Annales* History," *Annals of Scholarship* 1 (1980): 69–84. Bloch's ambivalence toward Lamprecht in *AH*, p. 153, and appreciation of Pirenne, *AH*, pp. 48, 81, 162.

von Humboldt, Vidal, a staunch republican as well as a skilled cartographer, insisted on the interaction and interdependence of man and the environment. He drew freely on history and other disciplines and sought a new geography, firmly tied with history, based not on national egotism or iron laws, but on painstaking study, interdisciplinary approach, and comparison.[43]

Comparison was also critical in the method of the sociolinguist Antoine Meillet (1866–1936). German scholars had long used language, along with topography and climate, to support their theories of development and dominance. According to Meillet, language, which he defined as the "spontaneous creation" of specific groups, was transmitted over space and time by various unchartable factors rooted in social reality. He therefore deemed it impossible to reconstruct the course of linguistic transmission or transformations with any precision. Notwithstanding his own innovative studies of linguistic borrowing, archaisms, and language groups at the "periphery" – all of which served as corrections and refinements in the study of toponymy – Meillet maintained his conviction that his science ultimately rested on possibilities and probabilities.[44]

A third former *normalien*, Henri Bergson (1859–1941), one of the most influential French intellectual figures before World War I, systematically attacked philosophical positivism before large audiences at the Collège de France, where he was appointed in 1904. Bergson's categories of duration and movement, memory and perception, science and intuition, gave a new dimension to historical reality. He taught Bloch's generation not to divide and dissect the past into artificial chunks of clock time and restricted space, but to develop those "variable" measurements and wide boundaries per-

43 A. Demangeon, "Paul Vidal de la Blache," *Revue Universitaire* (1918): 4–15. The *Tableau*, which formed part of the text of Lavisse's *Histoire de France*, was the fruit of ten years' labor and represented Vidal's critique of Friedrich Ratzel's *Politische Geographie* (Leipzig, 1897). Bloch (who studied with Vidal's student Lucien Gallois) offered this appreciation: 'Is not man himself the greatest variable in nature?" (*AH*, pp. 125, 159–60).

44 Meillet, "Comment les mots changent de sens," *Année Sociologique* 9 (1904–5): 1–38; also *Introduction à l'étude comparative des langages indoeuropéennes* (Paris: Hachette, 1903). Bloch's appreciation and references in *AH*, pp. 97, 101, 107–9, 130–33, 166.

taining to human time and reality that were the ultimate goal of their discipline.[45]

The most direct contribution and challenge to academic historians came from the philosopher-sociologist Emile Durkheim (1858–1917) and his followers. Having freed French social science from "Teutonic dominance," Durkheim took aim at the positivists. In the pages of the *Année Sociologique*, which he founded in 1896, and in his lectures and writing, he indicted his historian colleagues for slavishly following the Germans and for aimless fact gathering without a sound theory of human development. Expecting that sociology would become the primary discipline of scholarly synthesis, Durkheim assigned to history the merely auxiliary role of gathering the data, establishing chronology, and focusing on individuals.[46]

The debate between history and sociology, essentially between Seignobos and Durkheim, erupted in 1903 and continued almost unabated for five years, until 1908. In January 1903, before the Société d'Histoire Moderne, the Durkheimian economist François Simiand (1873–1935) issued a rebuttal of Seignobos's criticisms of social science and also launched a powerful attack on the discipline of history as practiced by Seignobos *et cie*. He singled out three of the historians' "idols": politics (the obsession with political phenomena); the individual (equating history with the actions of single notable persons); and chronology (the false preoccupation with "origins").[47]

45 *AH*, p. 153. Cf. Robert C. Rhodes, "The Revolution in French Historical Thought: Durkheim's Sociologism as a Major Factor in the Transition from Historicist Historiography to the *Annales* School: 1868–1945" (Ph.D. diss., U.C.L.A., 1974), pp. 159–77.

46 Durkheim, prefaces to *L'Année Sociologique*, in Kurt Wolff, ed., *Emile Durkheim, 1858–1917* (Columbus: Ohio University Press, 1960), pp. 341–53; Georges Davy, "Emile Durkheim," *Revue de Métaphysique et de Morale* 26 (1919): 181–98; Robert N. Bellah, "Durkheim and History," in Robert A. Nisbet, ed., *Emile Durkheim* (Englewood Cliffs, N.J.: Prentice-Hall, 1965), pp. 153–76. Bloch's appreciation of Durkheim in *AH*, pp. 63, 123.

47 Simiand, "Méthode historique et science sociale," *RSH* 6 (1903): 1–22, 129–57. Simiand, who was a strong critic of orthodox economics and *Kathedersozialismus* for their superficiality and nationalist bias, stressed the influence of history and social classes in his economic analyses. Cf. B. Damalas, *L'oeuvre scientifique de François Simiand* (Paris: Presses Universitaires de France, 1943); also Marc Bloch, "Le salaire et les fluctuations économiques à longue période," *RH* 173 (Jan.–June 1934): 1–31; *AH*, pp. 56, 103–4, 157, 159.

33

The debate heated up in May 1906 at a meeting of the Société Française de Philosophie with Simiand's laying down four "rules" for historians.[48] A year later it was Seignobos's turn to respond. In the discussion, several historians, including Gustave Bloch, took a middle position, suggesting that while there were certain "laws" in history, they generally involved relatively simple phenomena and were always liable to modification. A year later, after heated discussion between the two principals, Bloch criticized Seignobos's history-as-contingency but also denounced Durkheim's claim of objective treatment of complex human psychological facts. The sociologists maintained a more or less common front, but the historians were divided, an inevitable characteristic of an old, well-entrenched discipline that had known periodic waves of criticism and dissent.[49]

It was a nonhistorian, Henri Berr (1863–1954), who came to the rescue of history as the unifying force of human knowledge. Trained in philosophy at the Ecole Normale and a professor of rhetoric at the lycée Henri IV, in 1900 he founded still another journal, the *Revue de Synthèse Historique*. Berr was disenchanted with narrow academic specialization and hoped to draw all the human sciences together under the rubric of "synthesis." His review, often bristling with militant, polemical articles and letters, was open to practitioners of all disciplines and to scholars abroad, such as Lamprecht and Benedetto Croce. In 1904 Berr tried to solicit the views of French historians on current problems of research and teaching, but he found the majority uninterested in the debates over methodology and history's relationship to other disciplines.

Berr's enterprise was innovative, largely self-sufficient, and outside the mainstream of academic history. In 1905 he was passed over for a chair at the Collège de France in favor of the more traditional Gabriel Monod. Nevertheless, the impact of his journal on young historians was considerable. Lucien Febvre, who discovered the

---

48 "(1) Definir en termes généraux l'effet précis; (2) Entre les antécédents prendre pour cause celui qui est lié à l'effet par la relation la plus générale; (3) Expliciter l'antécédent immédiat; (4) Arriver dans la recherche des causes jusqu'à des propositions dont la réciproque soit vraie." *Bulletin de la Société Française de Philosophie* 6 (31 May 1906).

49 *Bulletin de la Société Française de Philosophie* 8 (28 May 1908).

Revue in 1902 in the library of the Ecole Normale, credited Berr with rekindling his enthusiasm for history after he had become disillusioned with the "banality" of his training.[50]

As a witness to all this ferment and debate, Marc Bloch formulated his own views of history at the ages of twenty and twenty-one.[51] Offspring of his era, he began by comparing history and science. Unlike chemistry and biology, involved with analysis and classification, history according to Bloch was essentially a process of description and narration. Like Seignobos, he concluded that all scholarly study focused on "events" and "phenomena," the former a random group of facts joined only by their temporal connection, the latter produced by analysis of related events.

Like his father, Bloch believed that scientists dealt with relatively simple phenomena, which permitted generalization and also enabled them to artificially produce phenomena; these phenomena passed through only one consciousness, that of the observer. History, on the other hand, which Bloch defined as primarily a study of "psychosocial" phenomena, passed through two – the subject and the observer – thereby offering a virtually infinite selection of interpretations.[52]

Despite the practical and human impediments to generalizations as well as history's chronological, empirical, and synthetic nature and procedures, the discipline nevertheless offered some prospect of scientific validity. Bloch took a middle point between Seignobos and Durkheim, objecting to the "false" distinction between the individual and society, which was simply a "group of individuals." Both followed certain "laws," the group's superimposed on those of the

50 Henri Berr's statement on the founding of *RSH*, trans. Deborah H. Roberts, in *The Varieties of History*, ed. Fritz Stern (New York: New American Library, 1956), pp. 250–55; Lucien Febvre, "De la *Revue de Synthèse Historique* aux *Annales, AESC* 7 (1952): 289–92; Martin Siegel, "Henri Berr's *Revue de Synthèse Historique*," *History and Theory* 9 (1970): 322–34; *AH*, pp. 115–16, 125–26, 129–30, 144.

51 Notebook, dated "1906" and "Oct 07," EBC.

52 Cf. *AH*, p. 157: "Reality offers us a nearly infinite number of lines of force, all of which converge on the same phenomenon"; and *AH*, pp. 157–58: "Historical facts are, in essence, psychological facts. They therefore find their antecedents in other psychological facts."

Je voudrais essayer de fixer par écrit
certaines idées sur la Méthodologie historique
que, ~~et que plus ou moins flottant~~
se sont développées dans mon esprit
depuis quelque temps ~~et~~, mais affectent
encore une forme ~~vague et~~ flottante et
des contours vagues —

L'histoire n'a pas d'existence
scientifique — Le progrès capital des
sciences de la vie organique a été
d'écarter cette notion d'"histoire" — Du
jour où ~~on~~ au lieu d'"hist. naturelle
on a dit "biologie", du jour où on a
cessé de décrire pour expliquer et classer

8. Bloch's meditations on history, 1906

individual. Bloch identified two areas – the study of language and the study of economic phenomena ("man's utilization of material objects") – as most suited to establishing unvarying laws, and hence the seedbed of a more scientific history. Throughout his life these areas would remain central to his repertoire as a historian.[53]

He rejected the scientific pretensions of "political economy," insisting that this German-dominated discipline was analytically unsophisticated and riddled with distortions. In 1908–9, during his study year in the Wilhelmian Reich, Bloch personally observed the reigning economic historians. At the University of Berlin he attended courses of Max Sering and Rudolf Eberstadt, and at Leipzig of Karl Bücher. Though admiring Bücher's "systematic nature," Bloch was critical of his penchant for "metaphysics" reflected in his overriding Darwinian framework of economic development and his iron laws of class – which were often contradicted by the facts.[54]

The young Bloch meditated on the historian's method and rejected absurdly complex problems or arbitrarily delimited investigations such as "the reign of Louis VII."[55] But a year later when he underwent examination for the *agrégation*, Bloch would be confronted with questions still conceived within traditional boundaries of time and geography: political life under Caius Gracchus; the role of the Fourth Crusade in the demise of the Greek Empire; church and state under Louis XIV.[56]

To alleviate the historian's isolation and technical limitations, he called for the creation of standardized questionnaires. These, drawn up and administered by groups of researchers, would yield useful proofs and correct erroneous theories. Here was the anticipation of

---

53 *AH*, pp. 108–9.
54 Marc Bloch, "Karl Bücher," *AHES* 4 (1932): 65–66. On his studies: communications to the author from Dr. Kossack, Director of the Archive of Humboldt University, Berlin, 31 Aug. 1983, 15 Feb. 1984, and from Dr. Schwendler, Archive of Karl Marx University, Leipzig, 4 Nov. 1983, 28 Feb. 1984.
55 Cf. *AH*, p. 148: "We should look to the phenomena themselves for their proper periods."
56 C. V. Langlois, "Agrégation d'histoire et de géographie: Concours de 1908," *Revue Universitaire* 17, no. 2 (1908): 277–93.

the inquiries Bloch launched thirty years later as co-editor of the *Annales*.[57]

It appears that Bloch, like his father, took a moderate position in the heated debate between traditional historians and the social scientists, between "culture" and specialization, between the popularizers and the learned scholars. He had enough distance from his father's generation to look favorably on the "prescientific" work of Voltaire and Michelet, was uncomfortable with Renan's inflated ambitions for history, and valued the work of Fustel (whose photograph was displayed in his father's study) almost as highly as that of Langlois and Seignobos.[58]

Emerging from the Ecole Normale at twenty-two, Bloch charted his course between concern for the particular and for the general, the temporal and the unchanging, the present and the past. The historian's work was to formulate useful and appropriate questions – before which Seignobos had shrunk and where the social scientists had their preconceived positions – and to find the basis for synthesis. While crediting his elders with having perfected the critical method, he likened the historian to the biologist who had an excellent microscope but was unsure what to study with it.[59]

57 Cf. *AHES* 1 (1929): 60–70, 390–98; 4 (1932): 370–71; also *AH*, p. 66.
58 Marc Bloch, "Fustel de Coulanges, historien des origines françaises," *L'Alsace Française* 19 (1930): 206–9, and "Fustel de Coulanges," *Encyclopedia of the Social Sciences* (1931), VI, p. 543; *AH*, pp. 35, 80, 81, 129, 138. Similar sentiments in Jules Isaac, *Expériences de ma vie*, I (Paris: Calman-Lévy, 1959), pp. 258–66.
59 Cf. *AH*, p. 80: "Too often the work of research still wanders aimlessly with no rational decision about where it is to be applied." Also *AH*, pp. 42, 76, 129, 146, 155.

3. The Young Historian

Is it not the nature of interesting books to provoke reflection, stimulate questions, and even raise objections and criticism?[1]

In the decade before World War I, France underwent a nationalist revival, caused in part by German saber rattling but also by the revival of monarchism, Catholicism, and militarism, as exemplified in the writings of Maurice Barrès, Charles Maurras, and Léon Daudet and in the politics of the Action Française. The "generation of 1905" were more conservative than their fathers. Among the youths who were to enter battle in 1914, there was a high regard for individualism, courage, creativity, and the prestige of bearing arms, as well as respect for authority and tradition. The Sorbonne in 1910 reverberated with "Agathon's" attacks on scholars such as Langlois, Seignobos, and Durkheim for tainting the institution with their scientism and specialization; in 1912 forty *normaliens*, a third of the student body, acknowledged that they were practicing Catholics, as compared with only three or four in 1905.[2]

1 Marc Bloch, review of Lucien Febvre, *Histoire de Franche-Comté, RSH* 28 (1914): 356.
2 "Agathon" (pseud. of Henri Massis and Alfred de Tarde), *L'esprit de la Nouvelle Sorbonne* (Paris: Mercure de France, 1911) and *Les jeunes gens d'aujourd'hui* (Paris: Plon-Nourrit, 1913). Also Phyllis H. Stock, "Students versus the University in Pre−World War Paris," *French Historical Studies* 7 (Spring 1971): 93−110; Robert Wohl, *The Generation of 1914* (Cambridge: Harvard University Press, 1979), pp. 5−18; H. Stuart Hughes, *Consciousness and Society* (New York: Random House, 1958), pp. 342−58; Eugen Weber, *The Nationalist Revival in France, 1905−1914* (Berkeley and Los Angeles: University of California Press, 1959). On the revival of anti-Semitism, André Gide, *Journals, 1889−1949*, trans., selected, and ed. Justin O'Brien (Harmondsworth: Penguin, 1967), entry 24 Jan. 1914, pp. 194−96; Romain Rolland, *Jean Christophe*, trans. Gilbert Cannan (New York: Random House, 1938), pp. 384−88.

9. Paris: rue Soufflot, ca. 1910

Marc Bloch was now entering the historical profession. Upon leaving the Ecole Normale in 1908, he left for Germany to study in Berlin and Leipzig after being turned down in the keen competition for a fellowship at the Fondation Thiers. Bloch's venture across the Rhine coincided with the eruption of the Bosnian crisis and the *Daily Telegraph* affair, both of which epitomized the diplomatic and constitutional turbulence of the Wilhelmian Reich. In the spring of 1909 Bloch returned to Paris to make a new application, which involved a medical examination, interviews with prominent members of the Institut de France, and a brief plunge into academic politics. This time successful, he went back to Leipzig for a short stay before returning to the capital in the summer.[3]

---

3 Bloch to Boutroux (Director, Fondation Thiers), 29 Mar. 1909, and to Georges Davy, n.d. (Mar. 1909?); Pfister to Boutroux, 3 Mar. 1909, Gallois recommendation, n.d. (Mar. 1909?), AN, MI 318 1, 432, 387–88, 437, 439; also Emile Besch to Marc Bloch, 9 Apr., 14 June, 23 Aug. 1909, EBC.

The Fondation Thiers had been established in 1893 by the widow of France's historian-statesman Adolphe Thiers as a residence for outstanding young scholars preparing their doctoral theses. Fellowships were awarded for a maximum period of three years, and about five students were chosen annually. *Normaliens* generally occupied a high percentage of residencies; for example, among Bloch's group three of the five had graduated from the rue d'Ulm. As a resident scholar at the Fondation, Bloch not only enjoyed the comforts of a specially constructed mansion, considerable financial support, and the opportunity for intellectual exchange with fellow scholars, but could draw upon the rich collections of the Archives Nationales, the Bibliothèque Nationale, and nearby departmental and municipal collections.[4]

Bloch's doctoral thesis was to be a study of the disappearance of serfdom in the rural regions around Paris in the twelfth and thirteenth centuries. By investigating all the available seigneurial and ecclesiastical records, he hoped to produce the first systematic analysis of the social, economic, and legal aspects of manumission in a precisely delimited area.[5]

Bloch had done the preliminary research in 1907. For his *diplôme* he had examined in the Archives Nationales the charters of the possessions of the chapter of Notre Dame in the region south of Paris. His mentor, Christian Pfister, had praised Bloch's thesis for its original conclusions. Pfister (1857–1933) was another Alsatian exile, who at the lycée Louis-le-Grand had formed a close friendship with a fellow eastern patriot, Raymond Poincaré. He had been trained at the Ecole Normale Supérieure under Fustel, Lavisse, and Monod, and after sixteen years of teaching in Besançon and Nancy was called to Paris in 1902, where he joined the more reserved medievalist Langlois. In Pfister's enthusiastic recommendation to the Fondation Thiers he stressed that Marc Bloch's proposed study of the transformation of the rural economy – a subject much encour-

4 Edme Tassy and Pierre Léris, *Les ressources du travail intellectuel en France* (Paris: Gauthier-Villars, 1921), p. 312; also *Annuaire de la Fondation Thiers* (Paris: Issoudin, 1910–13).
5 Bloch to Boutroux (his first application), 1 May 1908, AN, MI 318 1, 433–36; more on his sources in Marc Bloch, "L'Ile-de-France," *MH* II, pp. 754–64.

aged and pursued in contemporary Germany – had been neglected in France since the death of Fustel.[6]

Marc Bloch's first major historical work involved an extensive search for documentation, an innovative methodology, and a rivalry with Reich specialists. His subject was emancipation: when and where it had happened, how and at what pace it had occurred, what were the main conditions and accompanying difficulties. The points Bloch stressed in his fellowship application underscored his strong interest in the dynamic process of historical change: the social transformation of the lord–peasant relationship from a generalized control by the former over the latter's person and property to what he termed their new status of *rentier* and *petit propriétaire*; the economic transformation of the countryside through the introduction of money and credit operations, financed by the cities, to help peasants secure their freedom and the lords reap the financial benefits (this was the great "medieval economic revolution," advanced by the Leipzig professor Karl Bücher, which substituted urban markets, standards, and ideas for local ones); the demographic transformation of a once almost static rural population into a mobile workforce, as witnessed by his preliminary study of surnames based on place of origin; and the juridical transformation of the peasant's obligations to the lord – formerly variable and arbitrary – into an annual, permanent *taille*.[7]

In his study Bloch intended to use comparison, which was strongly advocated by the Durkheimians. Through the works of other scholars he would examine French regions where serfdom had disappeared earlier (Normandy) and later (Burgundy) as well as comparable regions abroad. Bloch admitted his lack of experience in the history of ideas. But since the world of thought affected all social change, which he ambiguously termed either the product or the cause of "new ideas," he announced his intention of examining contemporary religious texts, particularly sermons, for important clues.[8]

6 Pfister to Boutroux, 28 Apr. 1908, AN, MI 318, 1, 431. Report on Bloch's treatise (Apr. 1907), AN, 61 AJ 186 (the other readers were Langlois, Gallois, and Gustave Bloch). Marc Bloch, "Christian Pfister, 1857–1933: Les oeuvres," *RH* 172 (1933): 563–70.
7 Bloch to Boutroux, 1 May 1908, AN, MI 318 1, 435–36.
8 Ibid. Cf. "Vie religieuse," AN, AB XIX 3827.

The next three years were happy and fruitful ones. Bloch, from age twenty-three to twenty-six, was able to work full time as a researcher, free from financial concerns and teaching obligations and close to the documents he required, in a brilliant capital of over two and a half million inhabitants. He remained close to his parents, now in new quarters on the avenue d'Orléans, and to his brother. His life was enriched by the stimulating relationships with his *normalien* friends and fellow scholars at the Fondation Thiers: Davy, Granet, and the Hellenist Louis Gernet. These vigorous, enterprising scholars sat long hours at their worktables piled with books and notes. Bloch had adopted from his father a system of classification for all his research that would organize his wide-ranging professional work throughout his life.[9]

Bloch's work on his doctoral thesis proceeded slowly. During his first year he prepared maps of serfdom and its disappearance in the region of the Ile-de-France. He also examined serfdom itself, an institution based almost entirely on custom, which varied from place to place and over time, combining remnants of ancient slavery with medieval vassaldom.[10]

Through the vast subject of serfdom Bloch had the opportunity to explore a series of related questions that became his lifelong interests: the forms and practices of feudal justice; the end of ancient slavery; the early origins of feudalism; the development of tithes; the characteristics of the *noblesse*; the clergy's role in society and the economy; the development of commerce, currency, and credit; the history of urban society from Rome to the Middle Ages; and the social and political aspects of medieval art, literature, and architecture.[11]

9 Besch to Bloch, 29 June, 26 Oct. 1910, 6 Jan., 30 May, 13 Dec. 1911, EBC; Georges Davy, "Louis Gernet, l'homme et le sociologue," in Marcel Bataillon et al., *Hommage à Louis Gernet* (Paris: Presses Universitaires de France, 1966), p. 8. Discussion of Bloch–Gernet–Granet relationship in Jacques Le Goff's preface to *RT*, pp. iv–v. Bloch's scholarly papers (AN, AB XIX 3796–852) are arranged according to an elaborate, thematic classification system; there are samples, in reused files, of his father's similar organization.
10 Annual report of Director, Fondation Thiers, to Conseil d'Administration, 1 Oct. 1910, AN, MI 318, 1, 450–51.
11 Annual reports, 1 Oct. 1911, 1 Oct. 1912, AN, MI 318 1, 452, 453. AN, AB XIX 3796, 3798–99, 3801–2, 3804–10, 3811–15, 3820–23, 3833–34, contain Bloch's research notes of this period.

Certain elements of Marc Bloch's later history writing began to emerge. In reviving Fustel's studies of the characteristics of French rural society, Bloch began exploring the division into closed- and open-field units.[12] Carrying on the master's investigations of the origins of modern France, Bloch became a severe critic of fashionable racial theories of national identity.[13] As a convinced comparatist he pored over the basic literature of English and German legal, social, and economic history.[14] As a regional investigator he probed the countryside around Paris in great detail – the land-clearing movements of the eleventh and twelfth centuries that created the large estates; the religious developments that contributed to the formation of major ecclesiastical domains; the growth of new towns; the economic influence of Paris; the region's castles and churches as well as its terrain and climate – and he contrasted this region with other parts of France and with foreign lands.[15] Finally, toward the end of his fellowship he became interested in the policies of the last Capetians toward their peasants – the germ of the doctoral thesis, "Rois et serfs," which Bloch completed after World War I.[16]

Bloch's publications during this period reveal his critical perspective, skill with documentary sources, and ability to extract and analyze the main interrelated questions. In his first article, "Blanche de Castille et les serfs du chapitre de Paris," Bloch "corrected" the exaggerations in two fourteenth-century royalist chronicles of the significance of the queen's order in 1251–52 freeing several peasants imprisoned in the cloister of Notre Dame. Bloch traced the origins of the tax dispute between the canons of Notre Dame and the serfs of Orly that had led to the arrests, the royal intervention, the judgment against the recalcitrants, and the eventual terms of manumission. The young historian displayed expertise in the legal, political,

12 AN, AB XIX 3846, 3851, and Marc Bloch, "Note sur deux ouvrages d'histoire et d'économie rurales," *RSH* 27 (1913): 162–67.
13 AN, AB XIX 3828; review of A. Longnon, *Origine et formation de la nationalité française* (Paris, 1912), *RSH* 25 (1912): 365.
14 AN, AB XIX 3808–9, 3934; reviews in *RSH* 24 (1912): 417; 25 (1912): 105–7, 244.
15 AN, AB XIX 3813, 3816, 3833, 3848.
16 AN, AB XIX 3830. Report, Director, Fondation Thiers, 1 Oct. 1911, AN, MI 318 1, 452.

economic, and social aspects of servitude in the Paris region in the mid thirteenth century as well as the complexities of manumission: how the growing desire for emancipation among the peasantry was reinforced by the ambitious Parisian bourgeoisie and by royal officials; how clerical seigneurs, pressed by financial exigency and royal taxes, were divided over the exploitation of their peasantry; and how a relatively weak monarchy could on occasion assert its jurisdiction in its subjects' disputes.[17]

Bloch seemed to relish the task of documentary criticism, and not just for itself. It was a useful tool to rectify the findings of the growing number of enthusiastic but often inadequately equipped local savants who had sprung up in the late nineteenth century. In his article "Cerny ou Serin?" he used his skills in paleography and geography to correct one regional historian who had given the wrong name to the place where a lord had freed his serfs in 1345.[18] Moreover, Bloch used documents to illuminate interesting questions. In "Les formes de la rupture de l'hommage dans l'ancien droit féodal," based on analysis of a large number of texts, Bloch described the ceremony of the rending of the feudal bond: One party either flung or broke a piece of straw in the presence of the other. The variations in performing this nearly universal rite offered proof that feudalism was neither rigid nor uniform in its laws or practices. Bloch was also cautious with his sources. Despite evidence of a similar Frankish custom of dissolving family ties, Bloch, unlike his Reich colleagues, was careful not to assign "Germanic" antecedents to a feudal rite that developed six centuries later.[19]

Bloch's major publication of this period was a monograph on the Ile-de-France. It was the first scholarly study of this subject and the culmination of a series entitled "Les régions de la France" that had appeared in Henri Berr's *Revue de Synthèse Historique* between 1903 and 1913.[20] Berr had launched this collection as a means of com-

17 *Mémoires de la Société de l'Histoire de Paris et de l'Ile-de-France* 38 (1911): 224–72; repr. in *MH* I, pp. 462–90.
18 *Annales de la Société Historique et Archéologique du Gâtinais* 30 (1912): 157–60.
19 *Nouvelle Revue Historique de Droit Français et Etranger* 36 (1912): 141–77.
20 *RSH* 25 (1912): 209–23, 310–39; 26 (1913): 131–99, 325–50. Published as a separate monograph: *L'Ile-de-France* (Paris: Revue de Synthèse Historique, 1913).

prehending the "psychology of historical groups," which he identified within specific regions rather than in the vague concept of a *Volk*. In the spirit of *synthèse*, he had established a common format and asked his authors to evaluate the state of current scholarship and suggest work to be done.[21]

Bloch, the last contributor, raised serious questions about writing the regional history of the Ile-de-France. He outlined the region's physical aspects and acknowledged the work of local historians, though he questioned whether any of their particular insights had contributed to "general" or real history.[22] Unlike Berr's other authors, he denied the unity of his region. Franche-Comté, Lorraine, Brittany, and Normandy all had their own history and possessed a measure of geographic coherence. According to Bloch, the Ile-de-France was defined by his modest subtitle: "Les pays autour de Paris."

Though trained in geography, Bloch treated his subject primarily in historical and comparative terms: When and how did people come to settle on dry or wet plains? How do the physical features of towns and countryside record human decisions and actions? What specific characteristics constitute a region and make it distinctive from others? Bloch's first monograph denied the utility of physical studies that were not grounded in human time and change.[23]

His fellowship completed in 1912, Bloch obtained his first teaching position, a one-year appointment to the lycée in Montpellier.[24] Six miles from the Mediterranean, capital of the département of Hérault, chief city of the Languedoc, and the center of an extensive winegrowing region, Montpellier was a small university town of 66,000 inhabitants with France's oldest medical faculty. This was Bloch's first extended residence in the French provinces and in the south, his first separation from his family and friends and from the archives of Paris. With class preparation, grading, and a heavy schedule of sixteen and a half hours of teaching per week, he had almost no time to continue work on his doctoral thesis.

21 Henri Berr, "Les régions de la France," *RSH* 6 (1903): 180.
22 *RSH* 26 (1913): 151, 348.
23 *RSH* 25 (1912): 339; 26 (1913): 154, 147–48, 152.
24 Gustave Bloch to Jérôme Carcopino, 22 Sept. 1912, Carcopino papers, IF. Lycée de Montpellier, Etat du Personnel, 1 Nov. 1912, ADH.

In Montpellier Marc Bloch encountered a different world from Paris, affected less by the Dreyfus Affair than by the enduring bitterness of the religious wars.[25] In a lecture at the university in January 1913 Bloch gave his interpretation of the nation's history, stressing the diverse ethnic roots of the French people, who were descended from Ligurians, Iberians, Celts, Romans, Burgundians, Goths, Franks, Bretons, Normans, and Jews. He asserted that the modern French nation and state began to form in the tenth century from this mélange through the merging of different civilizations and the development of loyalty to the monarchy.[26]

Bloch was intent on studying royalty. In 1911 a Bonn historian named Hans Schreuer had published a dense study of French and German coronation rites beginning with their common tradition in Charlemagne and running up to the eighteenth century, with glances at English and other Continental practices. Schreuer analyzed the ceremonial rituals of anointing, crowning, blessing of the scepter and sword, enthronement, and the acts of homage as well as their political significance on both sides of the Rhine, which he related to the development of French absolutism on the one hand and to Germany's decentralized imperial power on the other.[27]

Schreuer's work got a mixed response in France. The leading sociological journal applauded its comparative research, but the historians chided Schreuer for his exaggerations, simplifications, and erroneous documentation.[28] The Schreuer debate was no doubt a reflection of a heightened preoccupation with royalty during the waning days of Europe's Old Regime. This had been stimulated by traditional Great Power rivalries and also by the recent intensification of court ceremony, especially in Berlin, the participation of crowned heads in a host of civil, national, and religious rituals, and such

---

25 Almost three decades later Bloch recalled his headmaster's warning: "There is nothing dangerous here in the nineteenth century; but be very careful when you touch on the religious wars." *AH*, p. 43.

26 "Origines de la nationalité française," AN, AB XIX 3896.

27 *Die rechtlichen Grundgedanken der französischen Königskrönung mit besonderer Rücksicht auf die deutschen Verhältnisse* (Weimar: H. Böhlau's Nachfolger, 1911).

28 *Année Sociologique* 12 (1911): 460–65; cf. Paul Fournier, "Le sacre et le couronnement des rois de France," *Journal des Savants* N.S. 11 (1913): 116–20; *RH* 108 (1911): 136; *Revue Critique d'Histoire et de Littérature* 75 (1913):50.

extraordinary occasions as the diamond jubilee of Franz Joseph's reign in 1908, the lavish funeral of Edward VII and coronation of George V in 1910, and the extravagant twenty-fifth anniversary of the reign of Wilhelm II in 1913.[29]

Marc Bloch carried the Schreuer debate with him from Paris to Montpellier. At the university library he verified Schreuer's sources and interpretations and read additional texts. He concurred with some of the writer's criticisms of Fustel — that he had perhaps exaggerated the sacred aspects of royal unction. Bloch nonetheless noted Schreuer's omissions (of Jeanne d'Arc, for example) and his inability to discriminate between prescriptive and descriptive texts.[30]

Here were the roots of Bloch's interest in sacred ceremonies as manifestations of royal power, which inspired his later book *Les rois thaumaturges* (1924). Bloch had already investigated feudal ritual. Now he turned to France's medieval kings, who had evolved their own ceremonies as manifestations of their growing political and moral authority. At the Fondation Thiers two of his colleagues, Granet and Gernet, had studied Chinese and Greek myths and ceremonies, and the brother he revered was fascinated by comparative ethnography and especially by religious psychology. Determined to "correct" Schreuer along with several other German and English studies of the French monarchy, the young Bloch conceived the idea of someday writing on the coronation ritual at Rheims, which occupied at least half the consciousness of all good French patriots.[31]

29 Arno Mayer, *The Persistence of the Old Regime: Europe to the Great War* (New York: Pantheon, 1981), pp. 136–46 and passim. In *The King's Evil* (Oxford: Clarendon Press, 1911), a work that would greatly influence Marc Bloch, author Raymond Crawfurd mentioned the happy timing of his study of the sacred power of English and French royalty.

30 Notes on sacred kingship in AN, AB XIX 3845 (with library slips from the university library at Montpellier), which include a summary and criticism of Schreuer's work.

31 Almost three decades later Bloch defined a true Frenchman as identifying with both the coronation rite at Rheims and the Festival of Federation. *ED*, p. 210. Richard A. Jackson, *Vive le Roi! A History of the French Coronation from Charles V to Charles X* (Chapel Hill: University of North Carolina Press, 1984), summarizes the scholarly debate.

The exact origins of Marc Bloch's fascination with kings and coronations will always remain obscure. Perhaps he was distant enough from the *ancien régime* and from the Bonapartist empire, which his father had detested, to view monarchy dispassionately and as a worthy topic of research. Perhaps in his youth he had absorbed the cult of Jeanne d'Arc. Perhaps also he had imbibed a small measure of Renan's mythical France – the amalgamation of monarchism and republicanism, elitism and egalitarianism – which had evolved into the present liberal state in which Jewish patriots felt proud and comfortable.[32]

In 1913 Bloch moved on to the lycée of Amiens, where two of his *normalien* friends were on the faculty. Amiens, a slightly larger city than Montpellier, had a population of 78,400 and was approximately 135 kilometers from Paris. Capital of the département of the Somme and the center of Picardy's trade, manufacturing, and transportation, Amiens was set in a marshy valley and dominated by one of France's finest thirteenth-century cathedrals.[33]

Bloch was nearing the end of his apprentice period. That year his emerging ideas were expressed on two occasions: in a review of a work by his future collaborator Lucien Febvre[34] and in a speech before the prefect and several other dignitaries at the lycée's awards ceremony in July 1914.[35]

In his critique of Febvre's history of his native Franche-Comté, the twenty-seven-year-old Bloch expressed reservations about the

32 Though remarking Renan's "exaggerations," Bloch copied verbatim the colorful passage from "La monarchie constitutionelle en France" in Renan's *Réforme intellectuelle et morale* (Paris: M. Lévy Frères, 1871) stating that what distinguished France's medieval kings from their German and English counterparts was their unique role as bestowers of justice. Their coronation derived from the kings of Israel, and as priest-kings like David they were able to "perform miracles." Research notes, AN, AB XIX 3845. On Jeanne d'Arc, whose visions Bloch considered less important than her "courage, good sense, and nobility," AN, AB XIX 3831.
33 Besch to Bloch, 13 Oct. 1913, EBC; Bloch to Davy, 30 Dec. 1913 AN, MI 318 1.
34 Review of *Histoire de Franche-Comté*, RSH 28 (1914): 354–56.
35 *Critique historique et critique du témoignage* (Amiens, 1914), repr. in AESC 5 (Jan.–Mar. 1950): 1–8.

book's flamboyant style and language[36] and about the author's grasp of medieval social and economic history. He did call the subject a "true province," worthy of study. Nevertheless, like all *pays*, this eastern county of Burgundy, which included both the Jura range and the right bank of the Saône, was primarily a product of politics and historical accident.[37]

Bloch faulted Febvre for neglecting a systematic analysis of the region's history, the growth and nature of its Burgundian patriotism, the extinction of its separatist elements, and the establishment of its French identity in the nineteenth century. Bloch was also dissatisfied with Febvre's stereotyped characterization of the "authentic Comtois." The traits he identified – prudence, level-headedness, a deliberately caustic intelligence, a high level of tenacity, and "more solidity than sparkle" – were traits common to almost all French peasants and *petits bourgeois*. Febvre's representative Comtois – Courbet, Proudhon, and President Grévy – were an arbitrary selection that ignored the distinction between ancient inhabitants and recent immigrants. Intrigued by Febvre's speculations, Bloch nonetheless insisted that the new science of collective psychology required a more "solid foundation" based on the principles of "prudence and methodical doubt."[38]

Bloch's address to the Amiens students on 13 July 1914, in which he summed up his creed as a historian, the "leading ideas" that would guide his entire career,[39] had a distinctly autobiographical tone. The poor historian, unlike his scientist colleague, was doomed to perpetual ignorance about the phenomena he investigated; and unlike his brother, the physician directly involved in the experience, the historian was forced to rely on secondhand testimonies. Like the

36 "M. Febvre appears to follow Michelet more diligently than Fustel de Coulanges. Michelet is a seductive master, but an occasionally dangerous one." *RSH* 28 (1914): 354.
37 Unified in the eleventh century by the ambitious House of Salins, Franche-Comté, which maintained a prosperous, strategically important, quasi-independent existence under the Empire, escaped absorption into the Duchy of Burgundy in 1491 when Charles VIII rejected Margaret of Austria for Anne of Brittany. Ibid. p. 355.
38 Ibid., p. 356.
39 Lucien Febvre, preface, *AESC* 5 (Jan.–Mar. 1950): 1.

examining magistrate, he attempted to reconstitute "reality" from witnesses of varying credibility. Historical criticism consisted of disentangling the true, the false, and the probable.[40]

According to Marc Bloch, humans were lazy and all too ready to accept opinion as fact. Historians had therefore developed the critical method to impose a "constant discipline" on themselves in the struggle against complacency, overwork, fatigue, and uncertainty over the results. Faced with contradictory evidence, the critical spirit must not avoid making judgments: "If your neighbor on the left says two times two equals four, and the one on the right says it is five, do not conclude that the answer is four and a half."[41]

If three witnesses presented identical testimony on a particular event, the shrewd historian must search for the plagiarist; often style of presentation and the use of active over passive words distinguished the actor from the copyist. Sheer numbers were no sure guide to accuracy; if ten or even a thousand persons insisted that the sea at the North Pole was free of ice, their testimony could be refuted by one man, Admiral Peary, who had actually been there five years earlier.[42] On the facade of the Amiens cathedral the archangel held in a balance the souls of the saved and the damned; the historian needed both as his witnesses, but he could employ neither permanently or without reservation. If no testimony was error free, no false testimony was barren of useful details. The historian's task was to dissect many whole, often beautiful and entertaining, pieces of evidence, discarding all the inaccuracies and retaining the valid bits. Roland was killed, as the chanson relates, at Roncevaux; but the historian must correct the poet, who made him die at the hands of the Saracens.[43]

Bloch stated that memory is a fragile and imperfect instrument, a mirror blemished by opaque spots that deform the image it reflects.

---

40 *Critique historique*, p. 2.

41 Ibid., p. 3.

42 However, Bloch would not have been astonished when almost eight decades later Peary's claim to have reached the pole would be challenged by an examination of evidence from his own diary. *New York Times*, 22 Aug. 1988, 5 Feb. 1989.

43 *Critique historique*, pp. 3–4.

In motion, the human intelligence, like a leaky vessel, loses the memories it has stored, and when still, faced with the facts themselves, it can perceive only a small part of the whole. The witness with the most continuous exposure to an event is usually the least reliable. Bloch quoted recent experiments proving that we observe routine things more carelessly than extraordinary ones.[44] The doctor ministering daily to a patient could be expected to give excellent testimony on the illness but a totally inadequate account of the sickroom.

It was through comparison that the historian could hope to master the labyrinth of erroneous, contradictory testimonies. He confronted each fallible witness with as many proofs as possible, and ultimately elicited the truth. True, critical historians could be accused of destroying the "poetry of the past"; it was easier to castigate scholars than submit to their rigorous standards. But the ancient poems that still moved us with their human detail were poor chronicles: beautiful stories of heroic, mysterious, turbulent times but also deformed mirrors of the real past. With no regrets that certain seductive images were being banished by the process of historical criticism, Bloch confidently asserted: "The critical spirit provides discipline for the intellect. Our first duty is to cleanse it."[45]

Fifteen days before these words were spoken, Archduke Francis Ferdinand, heir to the throne of the Habsburg Empire, had been assassinated by a Bosnian Serb at Sarajevo. The Vienna government, supported by its German ally, prepared for war against Serbia by submitting a list of unfulfillable demands. A week after Marc Bloch's Amiens address, French president Raymond Poincaré and Premier René Viviani departed for St. Petersburg to cement the 1894 alliance in the face of another war scare. Not unlike many who expected that despite some Teutonic saber rattling the crisis would soon dissolve, Marc Bloch left for a family vacation in the Swiss Oberland with his brother, sister-in-law, and two nephews. After

44 Bloch proposed that his students verify this by polling their friends over the summer holidays about the number "6" on their analog wristwatches; would they know if it was a roman or arabic number, or, as was more likely, recall that the number had been replaced by the seconds dial?
45 Ibid., pp. 6–7.

completing his work on the *baccalauréat* examinations, Gustave Bloch and his wife Sarah arrived on 29 July 1914, one day after Austria's declaration of war against Serbia. The next evening, when Russia announced general mobilization, news arrived in the village of Rosenlaui that Swiss reservists had been ordered to their posts to guard against frontier violations. This was compelling reason for the young Blochs to return at once to France before its borders were attacked or closed. On 31 July, Marc and Louis Bloch took the first Paris train from Vevey. There they had read Germany's proclamation of a "state of threatening danger of war," which was accompanied by a twelve-hour ultimatum to St. Petersburg and an inquiry to Paris about its response in the event of a Russo-German conflict. When they arrived at the Gare de Lyon on 1 August, the newspapers were reporting the assassination of Marc Bloch's idol, Jean Jaurès. Bloch's grief was somewhat mitigated when this tragedy produced no riots or civil strife. All over the city walls the mobilization decrees had appeared.[46]

The return home was also marked by the poignant sights of a silent capital and its frightened but resolute population. Paris was divided into the "nobility" – those who were leaving – and all the rest, who "seemed at that moment to recognize no obligation other than to pamper the soldiers of tomorrow." On 3 August Germany declared war on France and invaded neutral Belgium. One day later Bloch, departing for his posting at Amiens, was transported part of the way to the Gare de la Chapelle in a market gardener's wagon that had been requisitioned by a police officer. Sitting in the back, wedged between the vegetables, Bloch's emotions of exhilaration and apprehension merged with the fresh and slightly acrid smell of cabbage and carrots.[47] At twenty-eight, the young historian was off to war.

46 *SG*, p. 9; Jérôme Carcopino, "Gustave Bloch," in Ecole Normale Supérieure, Association Amicale de Secours des Anciens Elèves, *Annuaire* (Paris, 1925). pp. 104–5.
47 *SG*, pp. 9–10.

4. The Great War

The individual who is guided by reason believes, if it is necessary, in sacrificing his life to his duty and even in subordinating to it the very instinct of self-preservation.[1]

I know enough history to realize that great crises move slowly, and such poor little chaps as ourselves can only take pride in our resignation.[2]

In anticipation of a massive German attack on France, Bloch's idol, the socialist leader Jean Jaurès, had called for the creation of a national militia and a totally defensive strategy guided by "intelligence, organization, and patriotism."[3] But the French General Staff was committed to offensive warfare and an almost total reliance on a cohesive, professional army. The three-year-military-service law passed in 1913 represented the victory of the traditionalists, embattled since the Dreyfus Affair, in the struggle to democratize the French army. In this victory lay the seeds of the disasters of 1914.[4]

When the Reich, as expected, invaded neutral Belgium in August 1914, France, exactly as Schlieffen had predicted, responded with its own *offensives à outrance*. Plan 17 sent French regular troops against the German left flank in Lorraine, in the Ardennes, and at Charleroi. The ensuing series of battles, extending from Belgium

1 Jean Jaurès, *L'armée nouvelle* (1910; repr. Paris: Editions Sociales, 1977), pp. 330–31, quoted in Carnet, 1916.
2 Bloch to Davy, 16 Sept. 1917, AN, MI 318 1.
3 Jaurès, *Armée nouvelle*, pp. 80–104; Maurice Faivre, "La pensée militaire de Jaurès," *Stratégique* 25 (1985): 63–121. Strong criticisms in Douglas Porch, *The March to the Marne: The French Army 1871–1914* (Cambridge: Cambridge University Press, 1981), pp. 210–11, 246–50.
4 Jack Snyder, *The Ideology of the Offensive: Military Decision Making and the Disasters of 1914* (Ithaca, N.Y.: Cornell University Press, 1984), pp. 15–106.

to Alsace and known collectively as the Battle of the Frontiers, engaging three and a half million German, French, British, and Belgian soldiers, resulted in thousands of casualties and brought Germany its first great victory. The unexpectedly strong German right flank, consisting of a considerable number of well-trained and well-outfitted reservists, swept through Belgium, defeated the Allies at Sambre and Mons, and forced their withdrawal and redeployment all the way back to the Marne, threatening Paris itself. The architect of the debacle, General Joseph Joffre, had misallocated his forces, leaving four hundred thousand qualified reservists almost completely inactive during the opening campaigns. By late August he had modified his strategy and saved France, but had also ensured a long, bloody war on the western front.[5]

Like most Frenchmen of his generation, Marc Bloch responded to the outbreak of war not joyfully but resolutely.[6] When he left Paris on 4 August he knew that the Germans had invaded Luxembourg and penetrated French territory. In Amiens he was assigned as sergeant to the 272d (Reserve) Regiment, 18th Company, 4th Platoon. Ready for combat, he instead shared the experiences of most French reservists during the opening battles: poor leadership, inadequate equipment, chaotic arrangements, and oscillation between extremes of inactivity and frenetic activity — all well behind the scene of battle.[7]

Shortly after midnight on 9 August his regiment left Amiens for a hot, exhausting, sixteen-hour train ride to the southeast. At Sedan, site of France's humiliation almost a half-century earlier, the spirits of Bloch and his men were lightened by the news of the short-lived French capture of Mulhouse. Disembarking at Stenay, they

5 Marc Ferro, *The Great War, 1914–1918* (London: Routledge and Kegan Paul, 1973), pp. 49–55; Barbara Tuchman, *The Guns of August* (New York: Macmillan, 1962), pp. 28–43, 163–262, 341–72.
6 *SG*, pp. 9–10; cf. Henri Desagneaux, *Journal de guerre 14–18* (Paris: Editions Denöel, 1971), 1 Aug. 1914; Jean-Jacques Becker, *1914: Comment les Français sont entrés dans la guerre* (Paris: Presses de la Fondation Nationale des Sciences Politiques, 1977).
7 On the low priority of reservists in French military planning, see Richard D. Challener, *The French Theory of the Nation in Arms, 1866–1939* (New York: Columbia University Press, 1955), pp. 82–83.

made a three-hour, seven-kilometer march south to Saulmory. The next day they marched north sixteen kilometers in brutal midday heat, reaching their destination, Martincourt, close to 5 p.m. They spent the next ten days in the Meuse valley, guarding the bridges and the border region on the right bank at Baalon and Quincy, a quiet, bucolic, slightly "monotonous" time. Though enjoying the rustic pleasures of fishing, swimming, and dozing on the grass and the charm of an unknown countryside, Bloch and his idle men, watching troups of the 81st and 83rd Regiments marching east to Montmédy, were permeated with "feverish anticipation."[8]

This tranquil period ended suddenly on the night of the twentieth when Bloch's platoon was awakened and ordered to march toward the front. At Montmédy they heard cannon for the first time; the next day they saw their first shrapnel – "distant white wreaths in an azure sky." On 22 August they responded joyously to news that they would enter Belgium; a counterorder sent them on a long, hard march southeast to the town of Velosnes on the Belgian border, where they slept in a cold barn. Remaining in the area for three days, they occupied trenches in the rear of an obviously important struggle nearby. The news of the German capture of Brussels dampened Bloch's spirits. Despite the large numbers of wounded, he hoped that the French would still be victorious; but at Virton, one of the bloodiest battles of the Fourth Army's Ardennes offensive, they were beaten and driven back.[9]

Sleepless after a night of dysentery, Bloch on 25 August took part in the long, agonizing retreat that followed the Ardennes disaster. Their hurried escape was hindered by the heat, poor organization, and roads that were clogged with artillery and convoys. Passing Montmédy, they slept in a beautiful forest, only to flee precipitately hours before the enemy's arrival. The next day's forced march past Stenay was more agonizing for the famished, dispirited troops. Bloch deplored the sight of French peasants "fleeing before an enemy from whom we could not protect them. . . . Wrenched from their homes, disoriented, dazed, and bullied by the gendarmes, they were troublesome but pathetic figures." While that night the troops

8 *SG*, p. 10; Carnet, 4–20 Aug. 1914; JM, 9–21 Aug.
9 *SG*, pp. 10–11; Carnet, 20–25 Aug. 1914; JM, 20–25 Aug.

slept in a stable, the refugees remained outside in the rain. The next day Bloch saw burning villages in the direction from which they had fled.[10]

The retreat before the armies of the Duke of Württemberg and General von Hausen lasted until 7 September, with interminable marches and brief periods of rest. Bloch was bored, weary, footsore, and anxious as they moved rapidly away from the border without either fighting or knowing what was happening. Their escape route took them southwest to Grandpré, down through the Argonne forest, and across Champagne to Larzicourt on the right bank of the Marne. Then on the ninth Bloch's regiment was brusquely awakened, and he suddenly realized they were joining columns of soldiers headed for the battlefield. Seven hours later they arrived in a pouring rain near a farm named Grand Perthes, southwest of the Marne. Despite hunger and fatigue, they renewed their advance an hour later. Now at last they would fight.[11]

A half-year later, describing his first battle experience, Bloch admitted that his recollections of that crucial day, 10 September, were not "altogether precise." He retained "a discontinuous series of images, vivid in themselves but badly arranged, like a reel of motion picture film containing some large gaps and some reversals of certain scenes."[12] They marched forward under extremely violent fire from artillery and machine guns, covering just three or four kilometers in eight hours. There were heavy casualties, and Bloch himself was wounded in the arm. Nightfall brought the end of the firing, leaving the groans of the wounded and the smells of blood and death on the desolate battlefield.[13]

In the morning Bloch's colonel announced that the Germans had retreated, and the men had their first solid meal in three days. Despite the painful sights of the wounded and the vast destruction, Marc Bloch was happy on 11 September, happy to be alive.

It was not without secret pleasure that I contemplated the large gash in my canteen, the three holes in my coat made by bullets that had not injured

10 *SG*, pp. 11–12; Carnet, 25–27 Aug. 1914; JM, 25–27 Aug.
11 *SG*, pp. 12–14; Carnet, 28 Aug.–9 Sept. 1914; JM, 28 Aug.–9 Sept.
12 *SG*, p. 14.
13 *SG*, pp. 15–18; Carnet, 9 [*sic*] Sept. 1914; JM, 10 Sept.

me, and my painful arm, which, on inspection, was still intact. On days after great carnage, except for particularly painful personal grief, life appears sweet. Let those who will, condemn this self-centered pleasure. Such feelings are all the more solidly rooted in individuals who ordinarily are only half-conscious of their existence.

Bloch also rejoiced in the victory.

Perhaps if I had thought about it, I might have felt some doubts. The Germans had retreated before us, but how did I know they had not advanced elsewhere? Happily, my thoughts were vague. The lack of sleep, the exertions of the march and combat, and the strain of my emotions tired my brain; but my sensations were vivid. I had little comprehension of the battle. It was the victory of the Marne, but I would not have known what to call it. What matter, it was victory. The bad luck that had weighed us down since the beginning of the campaign had been lifted. My heart beat with joy that morning in our small, dry, devastated valley in Champagne.[14]

Now the French were in pursuit. They recrossed the battlefield and slept in a barn near Blacy which the night before had been occupied by German troops and still bore their traces. The chase resumed early the next morning. When they crossed the Marne an exhausted Bloch was exhilarated at the evidence of the Germans' hurried departure.[15]

On 16 September they reached the Argonne and stopped. They were sent to reinforce the defense of Hauzy forest. This sparsely wooded, hilly area just south of the confluence of the Aisne and the Tourbe was traversed by the Sainte-Menehould-Vouziers railway; the Hauzy was therefore a vital and exposed strategic point linking the French line in Champagne with the Argonne forest. The weather suddenly turned cold and rainy. In his first primitive shelters and trenches, Bloch watched the clay soil turn into bogs of mud. On the first dry night, while he was commanding a squad guarding the tracks, the sudden chill made Bloch feel "naked in an icy bath."[16] The men's spirits sagged as, hungry, cold, and inexperienced in this kind of warfare, they perceived that summer was over and their

14 SG, p. 18.
15 SG, pp. 19–21; JM, 11–16 Sept. 1914; Carnet, 11–16 Sept.
16 SG, p. 22.

movement had ended. In soaking rains, almost unprotected against enemy fire, Bloch's regiment doggedly constructed defense works, established liaisons, and conducted reconnaissance missions in the treacherous Hauzy forest.[17]

The next three weeks were relatively calm and uneventful. Bloch was billeted in two garrison towns, La-Neuville-au-Pont and Florent, whose comforts and rustic charm he appreciated, although by now he chafed at the absence of mail and news. Autumn brought better weather but also the distribution of woolen underwear, which presaged a long winter campaign. There were alternating periods of trench building in the fields, guard duty in the towns, a return visit to Hauzy on "the first day of classes" (1 October), and idleness, all of which ended suddenly on 11 October when they entered the dense, forbidding forest of La Gruerie.[18]

Trench warfare began in the fall of 1914 when the retreating Germans were ordered to dig in and proceeded to bombard the would-be liberators of French and Belgian soil. The western front now stabilized in a snaking line of opposing holes, ditches, and emplacements 790 kilometers long between the North Sea and Switzerland.[19] In the Gruerie forest the fortifications of the crown prince's army were manned by first-class regular and reserve troops who rarely changed their positions. Their aim was to exhaust the French defenses and eventually sweep down to the valley of the

17 *SG*, pp. 21–23; Carnet, 16–20 Sept. 1914; JM, 16–20 Sept. In the Ordre of 20 September, the 272d Regiment was commended for its five consecutive days' mission defending Hauzy against heavy enemy artillery.

18 *SG*, pp. 23–27; JM, 21 Sept.–11 Oct. 1914; Carnet, 21 Sept.–11 Oct.

19 John Ellis, *Eye-Deep in Hell: Trench Warfare in World War I* (New York: Pantheon, 1976); other useful works include: H. Warner Allen, *The Unbroken Line: Along the French Trenches from Switzerland to the North Sea* (London: Smith, Elder, 1916); Erich von Falkenhayn, *The German General Staff and Its Decisions, 1914–1916* (Freeport, N.Y.: Books for Libraries Press, 1971), pp. 43–53; C. R. M. F. Cruttwell, *A History of the Great War, 1914–1918*, 2d ed. (Oxford: Clarendon Press, 1969), pp. 106–13; J. Meyer, *La vie quotidienne des soldats pendant la Grande Guerre* (Paris: Hachette, 1966); Eric J. Leed, *No Man's Land: Combat and Identity in World War I* (Cambridge: Cambridge University Press, 1979); and Tony Ashworth, *Trench Warfare, 1914–1918: The Live and Let Live System* (New York: Holmes and Meier, 1980).

Biesme, cutting off the main road and railway line to Verdun.[20] Steadfast and resolute, consummate trench builders, and excellent marksmen, this enemy in the Gruerie was often only fifty meters away.

Marc Bloch saved two popular German poems, printed on postcards, that gave voice to this faceless, omnipresent enemy:

Argonne Forest

Know thee a destroyed forest
Where no game or birds survive,
All around roars the cannon thunder
This tiny spot of earth is called the Argonne...

Greetings from the Argonne

Here it is bleak and cold,
We sleep in caverns in the earth
Looking only toward the front, always prepared,
Ready to die for Germany's honor.
We have sworn to hold fast
Till all around us a chorus
Sounds with the longed-for notes of peace
And the destruction of our enemies,
The Frenchman, the Russian, the Brit
Along with the Belgian, Japanese, and Serb.
We need no mercenaries, barbarians, and savages,
Our nation fights for its own homeland.
For Kaiser and Reich, for wife and child
We're in the field for Germany's honor.
So here for the hundredth night
Steadfastly guarding the trenches
We send our greetings to you back there
Until the command: "Return to your homes!"[21]

20 *Histories of 251 Divisions of the German Army Which Participated in the War (1914–1918)* (Washington, D.C.: Government Printing Office, 1920), pp. 198–200, 320–23, 371–73; for example, the 27th Division (13th Army Corps, Royal Württemberg), one of the best German divisions, remained in the Argonne until the end of 1915.

21 "Argonnerwald" and "Gruss aus dem Argonnerwald," by P. Richter, 26th Division, 10th Company, found in Bloch's file "SG."

Stationary warfare assumed a special character in the Gruerie, where lanes and footpaths formed the only breaks in the hilly, frequently impenetrable thickets. There were no convenient firing positions for the infantry, no observation posts for the artillery; until winter everything was concealed by the thick foliage. Firing was continuous. By day snipers took aim from the trees, and after sunset rifle and machine-gun fire continued uninterrupted, making any movement dangerous. Each army rained showers of grenades and bombs on the other, causing heavy casualties, while the commanding officers remained far in the rear.[22]

Between 11 October 1914 and his evacuation because of illness on 5 January 1915, Marc Bloch spent several long periods in the trenches of the Gruerie; occasionally he stayed in the front lines for seven days or more. Forest warfare combined monotony and extreme danger. They would arrive and be relieved under a hail of German bullets. The first hours of settling in close to the enemy were exceedingly dangerous, as the men acclimated themselves to a new, often ill-prepared shelter. Constant bombardment and inundation wrecked the poorly constructed French trenches, which needed constant repair and necessitated dangerous forays into the open. Patrols were targets for the precise German sharpshooters. Nighttime sounds provoked dread and excessive firing until the men learned to conquer their fear of surprise attack. Bloch "learned to distinguish the sounds that comprise the great nocturnal murmur: the tap-tap of the raindrops on the foliage, so like the rhythm of distant footsteps, the somewhat metallic scraping sound of very dry leaves falling on the leaf-strewn forest floor (which our men so often mistook for the click of an automatic loader introduced into a German rifle breech)." Like James Fenimore Cooper's Mohicans and trappers he had admired as a child, Bloch learned to listen and long remembered the sounds:

Ever since the Argonne in 1914, the buzzing sound of bullets has become stamped on the gray matter of my brain as on the wax of a phonograph record, a melody instantly recalled by simply pushing a button. . . . Even

22 On the terrain, see *Verdun, Argonne, 1914–1918* (Illustrated Guide to the Battle Fields, 1914–1918) (Clermont-Ferrand: Michelin, 1931), pp. 14–16; also *SG*, pp. 28–29.

after twenty-one years, my ear still retains the ability to estimate by its sound the trajectory and probable target of a shell.[23]

There were glaring insufficiencies of matériel, reflecting shortages throughout the French army. The first month of fighting had consumed half the stockpile of ammunition. In the Gruerie the French lacked barbed wire and heavy tools for trench construction and did not have adequate telephone communication with the rear. These deficiencies were slowly rectified over the course of the year.[24] Two decades later Bloch judged his superiors harshly. By refusing to concede an inch of soil, insisting on reconquering every lost meter, and placing masses of insufficiently equipped and provisioned troops in the front lines, the French leadership made the Gruerie battles of 1914, though not of exceptional strategic importance, some of the bloodiest of the war.[25]

Quiet periods of rest in La Neuville and Florent alternated with sojourns in the heart of the Gruerie, each time in a new position. Between 17 and 20 October, Bloch's platoon survived grueling attacks of shells, grenades, and machine-gun fire, for which he earned congratulations from his adjutant and captain. He felt proud of his bearded and unkempt *poilu* appearance. On 3 November he was finally promoted to adjutant. Though regretting the loss of close contact with his men, Bloch was happy to obtain an officer's comforts: "a table, a lamp..., a quiet corner where I could read, write, or merely think or dream,...the pleasure of more polished conversation,...and more opportunity for news."[26]

Death came quite close. On 18 October for the first time he lost a close friend, a gentle miner from Pas-de-Calais, who fell literally on his shoulder. Bloch was prepared to be hit. When a bullet struck his head on 23 November he coolly reflected, "If I'm not dead in two minutes, I'll be all right." After the allotted time, he walked back to the command post, was treated at the medical station in La

23 *ED*, p. 84. Cf. *SG*, pp. 27–31; Carnet, 11–16 Oct. 1914; JM, 11–16 Oct.
24 *SG*, p. 46.
25 Marc Bloch to Etienne Bloch, 9 Apr. 1936 (EBC), details his war experiences.
26 *SG*, p. 36. Bloch assumed that a personality conflict with his captain, a man he disliked and respected little, delayed his appointment to second lieutenant: Marc Bloch to Etienne Bloch, 9 Apr. 1936, EBC.

10. Bloch in uniform, ca. 1914

Harazée, and returned to his men with a glowing, swollen eye.[27]

In December they "rested" in Vienne-le-Château, a village on both banks of the Biesme, which under constant bombardment by German artillery became an "Arras or Rheims in miniature."[28] While shells whistled, the men cleaned themselves and looted; Bloch took a candlestick, which he soon lost, and a book of poetry published in 1830, which he kept. The heavy rains created an "age of mud." The clay soil stuck to spades, clothing, and skin, spoiled food, threatened to plug the barrels of rifles and jam breeches, and added another hazard to their return to the front lines on dark winter nights. Trenches became muddy canals, needed constant bailing out, and frequently collapsed. In Vienne there was a tragic

27 *SG*, pp. 39–40.
28 *SG*, pp. 40–41; JM, 23 Nov.–1 Dec. 1914.

cave-in of a shelter that had been dug into a hill. Seven soldiers were wounded and three died, including another close friend.[29]

As the year came to a close, "home by Christmas" lay in everyone's thoughts. On 20 December an elated Bloch learned that Joffre had announced an offensive to "liberate the country," but it was a false alarm. The artillery roared, then quieted again.[30] By the end of the month they had inched their way northward to the road from Servon to Vienne-le-Château. Bloch could see an open horizon, the enemy lines, and, beyond, the belfry of Binarville: a visible if painfully unreachable goal.[31]

Bloch had more adventures. Undertaking a solo reconnaissance mission to verify the testimony of his men, he had to crawl back to the accompaniment of German rifle fire. He likened the exasperation and uneasiness of being shot at to being cornered at a social gathering by a crank. On Christmas eve there was a joyous reunion with his schoolmate and Amiens colleague Bianconi, who shortly thereafter died in battle. There was also the needless death of one of his men, a gentle Breton who spoke almost no French and expired after failing to make his illness clear to the officers and medics. There seems to have been no fraternization at Christmas between the French and Germans in the Argonne as there was in other sectors.[32]

On the night of 2 January 1915 Bloch, though ill, took up his position at the front. After a feverish, sleepless night, he asked to return to the rear. He was accompanied on foot to Vienne, driven by car to Sainte-Menehould, and then evacuated by ambulance to the hospital at Troyes, where he was treated for typhoid fever.[33]

Once the scourge of armies, typhoid became a less devastating

29 JM, 19 Dec., 1914; *SG*, pp. 41–42.
30 *SG*, pp. 42–43. Cf. Pierre Quentin-Bauchart, *Lettres août 1914–octobre 1916* (Paris: Editions de l'Art Catholique, 1918), pp. 44–45, which gives the text of the proclamation. Quentin-Bauchart was a historian and staff officer of the 272d Regiment who died at the Somme; his letters and his memoir of the retreat from Belgium and the battle of the Marne complement Bloch's *SG*.
31 *SG*, p. 43: "Lorsque nous voulions parler d'un grand procès, d'une offensive brillante, nous ne disions pas: 'Quand nous serons à Mézières' ou 'à Lille,' nous disions 'quand nous serons à Binarville.' Je crois bien qu'on n'y est pas encore."
32 *SG*, pp. 43–45; JM, 20 Dec. 1914–2 Jan. 1915. Cf. Ellis, *Eye-Deep in Hell*, pp. 172–73.
33 *SG*, p. 45; cf. JM, 3–5 Jan. 1915; Marc Bloch to Etienne Bloch, 9 Apr. 1936, EBC.

threat in World War I, thanks to the identification of its bacillus by C. J. Elberth in 1880, the introduction of Almroth Wright's vaccine in 1897, and improved knowledge of its course and treatment. Nevertheless, during the first nine months of the war the French army suffered a major typhoid epidemic that peaked in January 1915. This was due to the low rate of inoculation, especially among reservists, a less effective vaccine, inadequate sanitary arrangements, and insufficient identification of victim carriers.[34] French soldiers, physically and mentally exhausted from the long retreat, the battle of the Marne, and the prolonged periods of cold, sleepless nights (sometimes with water up to their knees) in trenches like those of the Gruerie forest, succumbed in large numbers to typhoid fever in the winter of 1914–15. Men under thirty-five, who were especially vulnerable to serious complications to the heart, lungs, and intestines as well as to pneumonia and diphtheria, recorded the highest rates of mortality. Treatment was long and arduous. The victim was immediately isolated in a special typhoid center with rigorous disinfection procedures, where he was given frequent cool or lukewarm baths to lower his temperature, stimulate breathing and secretions, and relieve tension.[35] Marc Bloch, who almost died of his illness, spent five months in treatment and recuperation, at first at Troyes and then for almost four months at the Hôpital du Collège in Royan near Bordeaux.[36]

34 H. Vincent and L. Muratet, *La fièvre typhoïde et les fièvres paratyphoïdes (Symptomatologie, étiologie, prophylaxie)* (Paris: Masson, 1917). Wilmot Herringham, *A Physician in France* (London: Arnold, 1919), pp. 103–4, estimated 50,000–60,000 French typhoid cases during the first nine months as compared with 1,365 British cases up to 10 November 1915. See also Friedrich Prinzing, *Epidemics Resulting from Wars* (Oxford: Clarendon Press, 1916), pp. 8–9 and passim, and Arthur Hurst, *Medical Diseases of War* (Baltimore: Williams and Wilkins, 1944), pp. 261–83.

35 "Contribution à l'étude des états typhoïdes," *Comptes-Rendus Hebdomadaires des Séances de l'Académie des Sciences* 160 (1915): 263–65; "Evolution générale des fièvres continues," *La Presse Médicale* (Paris) 23 (26 Aug. 1915): 317; M. Salomon, "Récentes acquisitions cliniques sur la fièvre typhoïde," in *Revue Générale de Pathologie de Guerre* (1916); and esp. Jacques Carles, "La fièvre typhoïde du combattant," *Journal de Médicine de Bordeaux* 6 (Feb. 1916): 65–68.

36 *SG*, pp. 9, 45, 53. Bloch's own military medical records are unavailable until 2036, 150 years after his birth.

Once he had recovered, he wrote the first part of his *Souvenirs de guerre* to fix his recollections of the "five astonishing months" through which he had just lived before they faded from memory.[37] Severely critical of the army leadership and of certain officers, Bloch paid tribute to his brave and generous fellow soldiers, who were mostly from modest backgrounds and primarily from rural France. He recognized that it was their contribution, their willingness to place the larger cause above narrow concerns, that had enabled France to survive.[38]

Not surprisingly, Bloch wrote his concluding comments about courage: something not easily acquired, not at all dangerous to the healthy individual, and possible for responsible leaders to reinforce.

Death ceases to appear very terrible the moment it seems close: it is this, ultimately, that explains courage. Most men dread going under fire, and especially returning to it. Once there, however, they no longer tremble. . . . Few soldiers, except the most noble and intelligent, think of their country while conducting themselves bravely; they are much more often guided by a sense of personal honor, which is very strong when it is reinforced by the group. . . . Thus I always thought it a good policy to express openly the profound disgust that the few cowards in my platoon inspired in me.[39]

Having barely escaped death, Bloch on 1 June 1915 composed his will. He expressed joy at the ultimate act of self-sacrifice for a cause he placed above his own life, confidence in France's future victory, and an affectionate farewell to his family and closest friends. He gave practically all of his military salary, bonds, and death benefit to war orphans, to the alumni association of his alma mater, the Ecole Normale Supérieure, and to organizations devoted to "preparing a more equitable and healthy society (cooperatives, the struggle against alcoholism. . .etc.)." He asked that his books and personal possessions be distributed among his friends and family. Finally he requested a "purely civilian funeral, without flowers or wreaths."[40]

On 7 June 1915, his convalescent leave over, Bloch reported to

37 *SG*, p. 9.
38 *SG*, pp. 46–50; cf. *ED*, pp. 139–41.
39 *SG*, pp. 49–50.
40 Original copy in EBC.

Morlaix, in northeastern Brittany, which was the depot of the 72d and 272d Infantry Regiments. He was dispirited to find himself among a group of soldiers and officers who clung "desperately to the dreary but safe existence characteristic of a small garrison town in the rear" and were capable of a "host of mean little maneuvers." Burning "to be useful" and impatient to face danger at the earliest possible moment, Bloch signed up as a volunteer in the 72d, a regular unit that had fought beside his own at the Marne and in the Argonne.[41]

The return to the front was uneventful. The troop train meandered slowly, the trip lasting three days and four nights. Bloch had the opportunity to observe the peaceful rear: the Loire countryside, the bustling factories at Le Creusot, and, at Is-sur-Tille, a bullying stationmaster who harassed the troops with his version of the "discipline of the front." Uncertain of his destination, Bloch ruefully discovered on 25 June that he was back in the Argonne.[42] The 72d, which during his illness had seen action in Champagne and near Verdun, had recently returned to a new sector of the eastern Argonne. On 30 June from the north the Germans launched an unsuccessful attack on the railway station of Les Islettes where Bloch had just disembarked.[43]

In mid July 1915 the crown prince led an attack by Prussian and Württemberg divisions along the entire Argonne front supported by heavy bombardment and gas, anticipating the great offensive a year later at Verdun. Although inflicting heavy losses, the Germans failed to reach their goal: the crucial road between Vienne-le Château and Le Four-de-Paris. Bloch underwent his first gas attack on 13 July; he received his first decoration for energetic leadership and defiance of danger during the French counterattack.[44]

41 *SG*, pp. 53–54; twenty-five years later, in *ED*, p. 25, Bloch recalled that he had returned to the front before he had to, as a volunteer. For the history of the 72d Regiment, see JM; also *Historique du 72e régiment d'infanterie pendant la campagne 1914–1918* (Paris: Henri Charles-Lavauzelle, 1920). Bloch's "SG" file contains a draft of this publication.
42 *SG*, pp. 54–56, the last entry, written in 1916.
43 Historique.
44 Text of his first citation in: Ordre no. 2 of the 250th Brigade, 7 Aug. 1915, Marc Bloch dossier, SHV.

Because the thick Argonne foliage had impeded accurate observation, the Germans had failed to follow up their advantage against the thinly defended French line that had held the ravine of the "Courtes-Chausses." For the time being the 72d had helped save Les Islettes. Bloch nevertheless deplored the inexplicably long French delay in constructing a more southerly truck route to Verdun while Les Islettes was daily bombarded by long-range German cannon. This was "one of the great errors of Joffre and his General Staff!"[45]

Afterward Bloch had a quiet period. The troops alternated service in the front-line trenches of the southeastern Argonne with short periods of rest in villages like La Chalade that had been totally abandoned by their inhabitants, or occasionally in shelters in the forest itself. On 23–24 September, Bloch recorded in his journal Joffre's proclamation of still another great offensive. Fifty-four French and thirteen English divisions, supported by 1,500 pieces of artillery, launched the attack in Champagne along a front of almost ninety kilometers. The army in the Argonne was assigned to divert the Germans from the thrust of the main offensive, which was halted on 13 October. Then the forest became quiet. Both sides followed a defensive policy punctuated by the struggle for saps – the mining of each other's trenches – and by brief bombing engagements.[46]

Bloch remained in the Argonne until the end of July 1916. The 72d was one of the few French regiments that did not fight at Verdun, but it nevertheless suffered heavy enemy attacks during the spring. On the night of 24 March Bloch led a detachment of grenadiers on a daring mission to distract the Germans from the main attack on their trenches and on 3 April received his second citation. He was evaluated as a superb reserve officer, intelligent, serious, devoted, and vigorous, knowledgeable in military rules and innovation, "always ready to march and give an example," and "possessing unqualified authority over his men." Finally promoted

45 Marc Bloch to Etienne Bloch, 9 Apr. 1936, EBC; Historique; also Allen, *Unbroken Line*, p. 146, and *Verdun, Argonne, 1914–1918*, pp. 16–18.
46 Carnet, 26 June–21 Oct. 1915; Historique; Cyril Falls, *The Great War, 1914–1918* (New York: Capricorn, 1961), p. 116.

to second lieutenant, he was reassigned from his section command to the post of intelligence officer and made responsible for reports on signals, aircraft, cartography, and topography.[47]

The 72d left the forest for good at the end of July to join the Joffre offensive at the Somme. After two months of training and reserve duty, it occupied the exposed front line at Bouchavesnes and withstood a series of brutal bombardments. At Bouchavesnes the chief who had chosen Bloch for intelligence work, the brilliant and brave Lieutenant-Colonel Bonnet, was killed almost beside him.[48]

During 1916, the year of the great bloody battles, Bloch had four leaves in Paris that enabled him to experience the capital under war conditions, observe the effects of bombardment, and renew contact with his parents. His brother Louis, having served the first twenty months of the war as a doctor in the front lines, had been reassigned to a bacteriology laboratory in Besançon and then in Poitiers.[49]

A new adventure began on 14 December. In the wake of the uprisings and protests against the draft in a number of Algerian cities, Bloch's regiment suddenly departed for North Africa. Dispersed in small groups in the département of Constantine, their instructions were to maintain order and, with their mobile columns patrolling the region, to assure native recruitment.[50] For Bloch it was a brusque transition, from the cold, gray Champagne battlefields to three months of the warm, sunny climate and fascinating scenery of North Africa. Once his exhaustion from the Somme subsided, Bloch used his free time to explore the cities of Philippeville, Biskra, Constantine, and Algiers and to visit Tunisia. He never-

---

47 Carnet, 1916; Marc Bloch (to Etienne Bloch, 9 Apr. 1936, EBC) minimized the incident, claiming that his most deserved but unachieved citation had been earned earlier in the Gruerie.
48 Historique; Gustave Bloch to Jérôme Carcopino, 3 Jan. 1917, Carcopino papers, IF.
49 Carnet, 13–22 Jan., 30 May–1 June, 1–21 Oct., 15–29 Nov. 1916; Gustave Bloch to Carcopino, 24 July 1916, 3 Jan. 1917, Carcopino papers, IF; Gabriel Perreux, *La vie quotidienne des civils en France pendant la Grande Guerre* (Paris: Hachette, 1966), pp. 188–201 and passim.
50 *72e régiment*, p. 9, ascribed the source of these incidents to "German espionage" made possible by the absence of metropolitan troops in North Africa.

11. Bloch (on the right) in Algeria, 1917

theless felt a bit like a "shirker" (*embusqué*) during this pleasant, relatively uneventful interlude.[51]

By late March of 1917 he was back in France, and in May the 72d was positioned west of Saint-Quentin adjacent to the English sector. The spring weather was pleasant, and activity was limited to patrols.[52] In the meantime, General Robert Nivelle, who had succeeded Joffre at the end of 1916, had launched a headlong, costly Allied attack against the Hindenburg Line that provoked widespread mutinies in the French army. Nivelle was replaced by Henri Philippe Pétain, who restored discipline and confidence and introduced the "tactics of convalescence." Awaiting a buildup in matériel and the

51 Gustave Bloch to Carcopino, 3 Jan., 7 Oct. 1917, Carcopino papers, IF; Carnet, 14 Dec. 1916–27 Mar. 1917; Historique; *SG*, p. 53.
52 Historique; Carnet, 14 May–4 June 1917.

American troops and tanks that would be essential for victory, Pétain took up the strategic defensive. He chose limited objectives and pounded them with massive artillery, tanks, and planes before the infantry moved slowly forward.[53]

In early June Bloch's regiment saw action again. Marching southeast to the region of the Chemin des Dames, it occupied a salient targeted by the Germans, who hoped to seize the crest that dominated the Noyon ravine. Between 21 June and 2 July, in the valley of Cerny-en-Laonnois, Bloch took part in the "brutal battle of the observation posts." Attacked twice by barrages of *Minenwerfer* as heavy as those thrown against the regiment at Bouchavesnes and by powerful assault troops who penetrated the front lines, its trenches and communication lines decimated by shells and its men showered with toxic shells, the 72d nevertheless held its ground.[54]

In late summer, quiet descended over the plateau of the Chemin des Dames, but there was a memorable event for Bloch.[55] The regiment was at L'Epine-de-Chevregny, north of the tiny village of Braisne. The command, seeking information on enemy strength by capturing some prisoners, ordered what Bloch termed one of its typically excessive artillery actions, which produced a lone middle-aged German sentinel.[56] On 7 September Bloch interrogated this captured reservist from Bremen, who was promptly escorted to the rear. Immediately afterwards the troops excitedly circulated a tale of extraordinary German cunning. The city of Bremen (in French

53 Guy Pedroncini, *Pétain, général en chef, 1917–1918* (Paris: Presses Universitaires de France, 1974), pp. 20–21, 40–42, 44–48, 57–62, 109, 166; also Jere Clemens King, *Generals and Politicians: Conflict between France's High Command, Parliament, and Government, 1914–1918* (Westport, Conn.: Greenwood, 1971), pp. 140–91.

54 "Rapport de M. le Lieutenant-Colonel, Commandant du 72e régiment..." (in Bloch's hand: "redigé par moi"), "SG"; Marc Bloch to Georges Davy, 16 Sept. 1917, EBC; Gustave Bloch to Carcopino, 7 Oct. 1917, Carcopino papers, IF; Cruttwell, *History of the Great War*, pp. 404–17; *72e régiment*, pp. 9–10.

55 Carnet, 7 Sept. 1917; Bloch, "Réflexions d'un historien sur les fausses nouvelles de la guerre," *RSH* 33 (1921): 53–57, also recounted in *AH*, pp. 93–94.

56 According to the regimental history, "Il y exécute, le 7 septembre, un brillante reconnaissance jusqu'à la deuxième ligne ennemie..." *72e régiment*, p. 10.

"Brème") had been confused with nearby Braisne, and the prisoner was heralded as a spy who had been planted in prewar France. From mouth to ear went the announcement: "What marvelous organizers, these Germans! They had spies everywhere. We took a prisoner at L'Epine-de-Chevregny, and what did we find? Someone who in peacetime was a merchant a few kilometers from here, in Braisne."[57]

Why, ignoring geography and reason, had they "misheard" the prisoner's origins and substituted the village on the Vesle for the ancient Hanseatic city on the Weser? To be sure, there was an error of hearing; a familiar place was substituted for a remote one. But Bloch insisted that this mistake was not at all accidental but the inevitable consequence of two widespread and profound convictions: that the Germans were capable of all sorts of ruses, and that France was menaced by traitors who had caused all its earlier setbacks and prolonged the war.[58] The auditors "confused" Braisne with Brème because they were unconsciously predisposed to distort all testimony in accordance with "commonly accepted opinion." This rumor (*fausse nouvelle*) was therefore not a spontaneous occurrence. It mirrored the fearful, suspicious collective consciousness of the moment. Originating in the rear (the cooks were a rich source of anecdotes and popular prejudices) and transported orally by gunners and fatigue parties to isolated forward positions, the "myth-making zone" was a continuous strip for the dissemination of gossip to harassed, troubled, news-hungry soldiers who were deprived of their normal and healthy capacity of "methodical doubt."[59] Already fascinated by the production of misinformation and by collective psychology, Bloch considered this war a rich laboratory to study the dissemination of *fausses nouvelles*, the alterations and variations created by different classes, groups, and nations, and the myths

57 Bloch, "Réflexions," p. 53.
58 The troops, according to Bloch, had routinely misidentified innocent lamps as enemy signals and were made apprehensive by the shadows of owls on belfry windows. Ibid., p. 54.
59 On 8 Sept. 1914, when one of Bloch's chiefs erroneously announced that the Russians had bombarded "Ber-lin" (confusing the German capital with "Lemberg," which France's ally *had* reached), he was too worn down and dispirited by the long retreat to scrutinize and reject this absurd but seductive report. Ibid., p. 54. Quentin-Bauchart, *Lettres*, p. 222, describes the same incident.

surrounding certain colorful subjects. He wondered who would write the "legendary life of the German crown prince."[60]

Now in his third year of combat, Bloch had passed repeatedly through the "eternal cycle" of violence and calm. As an intelligence officer his activities ranged between the physically and mentally demanding duties of the command trenches and the periods of rest, still in not very quiet sectors, where his tasks of "topography, observation, and information concerning the enemy" also included a host of such small, "ridiculous" functions as rendering citations into good French.[61] Writing to Davy on 16 September 1917, Bloch took time to examine the war's consequences. His health, despite wounds, illness, and privations, had proved unexpectedly resilient, but the long struggle had taxed his power of concentration.[62] Bloch found it difficult to "express clearly" the many things he sensed in a vague and confused manner. He harshly judged the professional army for its inflexibility, lack of historical perspective, and callousness toward the troops; he praised the ordinary soldiers for a courage and patience he wished to emulate. He read and admired Henri Barbusse's graphic war novel *Le feu*.[63]

The regiment returned to combat at the beginning of November in support of Pétain's offensive against the fort of Malmaison. Bloch received his third decoration, for having held his observation trench under heavy enemy shelling in order to obtain invaluable information for the command post.[64] Malmaison, a minutely planned, innovative action combining tanks, surprise, and coordination of armies, was a remarkable success. Advancing five and a half kilometers, the French demolished the fort, captured 180 guns and over eleven thousand prisoners, improved their front along the Chemin des Dames, and restored the army's morale and confidence.[65]

60 "Réflexions," p. 56.
61 Bloch to Georges Davy, 16 Sept. 1917, EBC; also Gustave Bloch to Carcopino, 3 Nov. 1917, Carcopino papers, IF.
62 Bloch's Carnet for 1917 contains a five-part work plan for his thesis; beginning in 1916, he listed books he had read or intended to read.
63 Besch to Bloch, 3 Dec. 1917, EBC.
64 Ordre de la division, 17 Nov. 1917, AN, MI 318 I.
65 Historique; John Terraine, *To Win a War* (Garden City, N.Y.: Doubleday, 1981), pp. 11–13.

The home front was also revitalized with Georges Clemenceau's appointment as head of government on 16 November, ending six troubled months of pacifist campaigns and declining civilian morale. The seventy-six-year-old "tiger" announced that his single aim was to wage "total war" (*la guerre intégrale*) at home and abroad.[66] Following Italy's defeat at Caporetto and the elimination of Russia and Romania, the Allies for the first time began to coordinate their strategy. On the vital western front there was fear that Germany would transfer vast numbers of troops from the east and launch a major attack before "the tanks and the Americans" arrived.[67]

When 1918 opened, Marc Bloch was in Champagne, expecting "another Verdun."[68] While the cold, snowy winter delayed the Germans, he returned to scholarship with a review of one of the reigning Reich medievalists, Georg von Below. Bloch criticized Below's polemical tone, careless chronology, faulty technical definitions, and the parochialism of his historical categories – typical faults of his compatriots – which he cautioned his readers to avoid "after our coming victory." Below had presented abundant and erudite proofs of the existence of a concept of the state in medieval Germany but ignored the question of popular patriotism. Bloch, for whom national consciousness preceded and formed the moral and legitimating bases of public law and power, chided Below and his countrymen for preaching that "the state is everything, the people insignificant."[69]

As expected, Ludendorff attempted the knockdown blow in the west. Between March and July 1918 the Germans launched five successive attacks, using surprise tactics, short, intense artillery

---

66 King, *Generals and Politicians*, pp. 192–218. Clemenceau's more energetic direction was noted approvingly in Gustave Bloch to Carcopino, 10 Jan. 1918, Carcopino papers, IF.

67 Ferro, *The Great War*, pp. 197–214.

68 Gustave Bloch to Carcopino, 10 Jan. 1918, Carcopino papers, IF. Marc Bloch composed a letter to his brother Louis on 27 November, to be delivered by his comrade Crassier in the event of his death (EBC).

69 Review of Below, *Der deutsche Staat des Mittelalters* I (Leipzig, 1914), in *RH* 128 (1918): 343–47; Gustave Bloch to Georges Davy, 27 Jan. 1918, AN, MI 318 1.

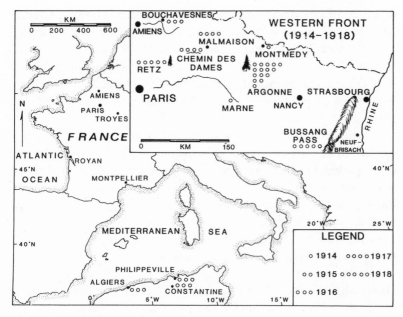

12. Map of Bloch's positions in World War I, 1914–18

preparation, storm troops, and gas. From 110 to 130 kilometers away the Germans shelled Paris with a powerful long-range gun, causing fear and confusion, high civilian casualties, and considerable destruction.[70] In April the Allies finally appointed a joint commander in chief, General Ferdinand Foch, who, radiating energy and resolve, overrode Pétain's defensive tactics.

For Marc Bloch, 1918 was a year of new challenges and reflection. His dossiers recorded the intelligence matters on which he worked, including military orders, liaisons with the British, signals, codes, topography, and propaganda. There are also his notes of his inter-

---

70 Gustave Bloch to Carcopino, 1 Apr. 1918, Carcopino papers, IF. Also Henry W. Miller, *The Paris Gun: The Bombardment of Paris by the German Long Range Guns and the Great German Offensives of 1918* (New York: Cape and Smith, 1930); Arthur Banks, *A Military Atlas of the First World War* (New York: Taplinger, 1975), pp. 184–87, which illustrates the four major bombardments and their toll.

rogations of French deserters, whom he defended before the Conseil de Guerre.[71] Bloch fully realized that this war had revolutionary consequences "not for one class alone, but for all of humanity." It would also become one of the major reference points of his life, defining heroism and human folly, technical feats and their limitations – an experience written indelibly on him and his generation.[72]

Bloch saw military action in several sectors of the re-ignited western front. Stationed east of the Argonne in early March, he was twice caught in German gas attacks. On a week's leave in Paris he witnessed the beginning of Big Bertha's damage. He spent April moving about in long, fatiguing marches during the massive German offensive that reached to within thirteen kilometers of Amiens. Sent to that city twice in May, he was able to confirm that his completed minor thesis (*thèse complémentaire*), deposited before the outbreak of the war in the Amiens library, had survived the bombardment. Though mainly engaged in instruction and training, the 72d Regiment was under fairly constant fire from long-range artillery and aircraft.[73]

When the Germans launched their massive attack against the French front on the Aisne in June 1918, Bloch was in an exposed front-line position at Villers-Cotterêts, southeast of the forest of Retz. Beginning at daybreak on 12 June and using gas to erode French resistance, the Germans pounded the French lines and inflicted heavy casualties – including killing Bloch's liaison officer – but they were eventually stopped. In its counterattack, the 72d,

71 "SG." Background in Guy Pedroncini, "Les cours martiales pendant la Grande Guerre," *RH* 252 (1974): 393–408.
72 Carnet, 1918 (quotation from Barrès); also *ED*, p. 141. Cf. Carole Fink, introduction to Marc Bloch, *Memoirs of War, 1914–15*, trans. Carole Fink, new ed. (Cambridge: Cambridge University Press, 1988), pp. 64–73; David Englander, "The French Soldier, 1914–18," *French History* 1, no. 1 (1987): 49–67; Stéphane Audouin-Rouzeau, "Les soldats français et la nation de 1914 à 1918 d'après les journaux de tranchées," *Revue d'Histoire Moderne et Contemporaine* 34 (Jan.–Mar. 1987): 66–86.
73 Historique, pp. 10–11; JM, 1–13 Mar. 1918; Gustave Bloch to Carcopino, 1 April 1918, Carcopino papers, IF; Carnet, 1 Jan.–21 May 1918; *72e régiment*, p. 11.

supported by tanks and engaging in fierce hand-to-hand combat, recaptured over a kilometer of the front, taking hundreds of prisoners as well as rifles and other matériel.[74]

On his thirty-second birthday, 6 July 1918, Bloch received his fourth decoration. He was cited as a "remarkable officer" who under the recent violent bombardments had conducted many daring reconnaissance missions, providing his chief with crucial information and setting a "beautiful example of courage and cool resolution in the accomplishment of his missions."[75] It was said that the heroic defense in the forest near Villers-Cotterêts had helped to save Paris.[76]

On 16 July Bloch's regiment, depleted by its recent losses, beat a "terrible" retreat to Arsy, on the right bank of the Oise. Bloch soon perceived, however, that this was the preliminary to a French counteroffensive two days later. The Germans had failed to batter their way to Paris. Now the Allies, bolstered by American troops, effectively applied *offensive à outrance*. Bloch took part in the costly attack on Villemontoire, which was heavily defended by German machine guns and took five days to capture. On 2 August the enemy began the retreat that step by step forced him back to the Rhine.[77]

Promoted to captain on 18 August, Bloch took only a minor part in the final stages of the war. First, the 72d was transported by rail and truck almost three hundred kilometers to the Vosges, where for a short time it linked up with an American regiment. It then moved to the northwest along the Meurthe valley to a series of relatively calm sectors. When it reached Nancy, Bloch had a two-week leave. In mid October in the forest of Parroy there were some reconnaissance missions, producing a number of prisoners and weapons as well as useful intelligence.[78]

---

74 Carnet, 12 June–11 July 1918; Projet de causerie pour les officiers des compagnies, (July) 1918, "SG"; JM, 1 June–9 July; *72e régiment*, pp. 11–12.
75 Ordre de la 87e division d'infanterie no. 115, 29 June 1918, Marc Bloch dossier, SHV.
76 *72e régiment*, p. 12.
77 Carnet, 16 July–2 Aug. 1918 ("Départ des boches, nous poursuivons"); Gustave Bloch to Carcopino, 10 Aug. 1918, Carcopino papers, IF; *72e régiment*, p. 13.
78 Carnet, 7 Aug.–20 Oct. 1918; *72e régiment*, p. 14.

In late October the 72d was carried by truck back to Champagne, where it was held in reserve outside Vouziers during a joint French-American attack on the forest of Boult.[79] On 5 November the regiment was retired from action and ordered on a forced march back to Châlons for still another embarkation to the east. In piercing wet and cold, under occasional shelling and with inadequate lodgings, Bloch and his men marched south over the roads he had traversed in 1914 – now littered with German and English trucks and tanks – through a scarred, desolate landscape. He had reached L'Epine, nine kilometers from the Marne, when the armistice was signed on 11 November.[80] Bloch signed the telegram for the regimental commander, Lieutenant-Colonel Mignon, announcing the end of hostilities.[81]

The final act came quickly. Within three days Bloch left the Marne by rail and returned to Lorraine. Following the Moselle up to its source in the Vosges, the 72d headed toward Alsace. On 24 November when it crossed the frontier at the Bussang pass, Bloch for the first time entered the land of his ancestors.[82] Following a triumphal march through the towns and villages of Upper Alsace – Bollviller, Feldkirch, Rouffach, Pfaffenheim, and Niederhergheim – accompanied by warm, colorful receptions by the inhabitants, the regiment established its headquarters on the Rhine, near Neuf-Brisach. Before settling down to the duties of a peacetime military bureaucrat in liberated Alsace, Marc Bloch obtained a twenty-day leave and returned to Paris for a joyful reunion with his family.[83]

79 Carnet, 21 Oct.–5 Nov. 1918; 72e régiment, pp. 14–15.
80 Carnet, 5–11 Nov. 1918.
81 "SG."
82 Carnet, 14–24 Nov. 1918.
83 Carnet, 25–30 Nov. 1918; 72e régiment, p. 15; Gustave Bloch to Carcopino, 29 Dec. 1918, Carcopino papers, IF.

5. Strasbourg

In Strasbourg France must do better than Germany.[1]

We were good workmen. . . . [Were we] good citizens?[2]

A historic crossroads of Western Europe, Strasbourg lay on an often bloody religious, political, and linguistic frontier. Before its capture by Louis XIV in 1681, the free imperial city had been the site of some of the major struggles of the Reformation, leaving it with Catholic, Lutheran, and Calvinist congregations along with an ancient Jewish community. After a century of French rule it became the borderland of the Revolution. The "Marseillaise" was written here, and Alsatians like Bloch's great-grandfather had trekked loyally through on their way to the battlefield. The University of Strasbourg was established by the Protestants in 1621. Tolerated by the Bourbons and abolished in 1793, it was reconstituted by Napoleon in 1808 and incorporated into France's centralized state system of higher education. Despite some significant political and economic changes, throughout most of the nineteenth century the inhabitants of the Lower Rhine capital had clung to their native language, customs, and religions, creating a culture separate from "the interior" and from the greater part of Alsace.[3]

German rule altered the face of Strasbourg, introducing a host of Reich soldiers, administrators, businessmen, and teachers and a

1 Christian Pfister, "L'Université de Strasbourg," *Revue Politique et Littéraire* 59, no. 24 (17 Dec. 1921): 760.
2 *ED*, p. 218.
3 Pfister, "L'Université de Strasbourg," *Revue Politique et Littéraire* 59, no. 23 (2 Dec. 1921): 721–28; no. 24 (17 Dec. 1921): 753–56. Also Franklin L. Ford, *Strasbourg in Transition, 1648–1789* (Cambridge: Harvard University Press, 1958); Georges Livet and Francis Rapp, *Histoire de Strasbourg des origines à nos jours* III (Strasbourg: Editions des Dernières Nouvelles d'Alsace, 1982).

spate of new laws, industries, and cultural institutions. There was also a building boom that demolished the old city ramparts and erected expanded new walls, broad green suburban living spaces, and a handsome modern university and medical school. The Germans rebuilt a combined municipal and university library with over a half-million volumes which, until World War I when it was surpassed by Harvard, was the largest in the world.[4] Following the failure of their efforts to convince the Strasbourgeois of Germany's physical and spiritual superiority, the Reich's representatives belatedly tried to win the inhabitants' loyalty by showing sensitivity to their local culture. But Strasbourg never became a German city. In 1919 it retained its identity as a medium-sized Rhenish town of 167,000 people with its traditional insularity and unique mélange of tongues, faiths, and politics.[5]

The entry of the French army into Strasbourg on 22 November 1918 marked a new era: After more than four decades, the Reichsland was about to return to French sovereignty. Its premier scholarly institution, the Kaiser-Wilhelms-Universität Strassburg, would revert to French control.[6] Early in the war the French government had prepared for the reunification of Alsace-Lorraine's institutions with the political, economic, legal, and educational institutions of

---

4 Johannes Ficker, *Die Kaiser-Wilhelms-Universität Strassburg und ihre Tätigkeit* (Halle: Buchhandlung des Walsenhauses, 1922), p. 43. Friedrich Meinecke, in *Strassburg/Freiburg/Berlin 1901–1919: Erinnerungen* (Stuttgart: Koehler, 1949), pp. 7–58, evokes five eventful Strasbourg years between 1901 and 1906.

5 German Strasbourg had grown from 85,000 in 1871 to 178,000 in 1910. The postwar drop was due to the exodus of Reich soldiers, businessmen, and civil servants. Urban transformation in Pierre Feder and Astrid Gidoni, *Strasbourg naguère, 1855–1945* (Paris: Payot, 1979); Office Municipal de Statistique de Strasbourg, *Comptes-rendus statistiques de la ville de Strasbourg* (Strasbourg: Imprimerie Alsacienne, 1934), pp. 58–69; German failure in Dan Silverman, *Reluctant Union: Alsace–Lorraine and Imperial Germany, 1871–1918* (University Park: Pennsylvania State University Press, 1982); Lucien Aaron (pseud. Georges Delahache), "Strasbourg 1918–1920," *Revue de Paris* 27 (1 Aug. 1920): 487–513.

6 On the history of the German university, see John E. Craig, *Scholarship and Nation Building: The Universities of Strasbourg and Alsatian Society, 1870–1939* (Chicago: University of Chicago Press, 1984), pp. 29–202; also Silverman, *Reluctant Union*, pp. 82–83.

13. Foch entering Strasbourg

the *patrie*. In 1915 study groups appointed by the Ministry of Foreign Affairs and the Ministry of War formulated proposals for a new French university in Strasbourg to facilitate the reabsorption of Alsace and promote France's intellectual and cultural prestige in Europe. In late 1917 the Service d'Alsace-Lorraine, attached to the

Ministry of War, set up a subcommittee of seven Paris professors to plan higher education in the two provinces. The historian Christian Pfister, Marc Bloch's principal teacher, compiled the results of their deliberations in a ninety-one-page report that was approved by both ministries during the last days of the war.[7]

The Pfister report urged that the new University of Strasbourg be endowed with staff and facilities to supplant its German predecessor and compete with universities across the Rhine. It would fulfill the "special mission" of reintegration by maintaining some Alsatian professors and retaining a faculty of theology. Significantly, this wartime committee of patriots (four of the seven planners were of Alsatian origin) stressed that Strasbourg would become a French university, with standards and curriculum identical to the interior. There was no inclination to experiment with an international university or to implement radical reforms on the newly liberated soil. Pfister, in his plan for the Faculty of Letters, set the staff at the same size as the German university but asked for a shift in emphasis to modern languages and literature, the continuation of a chair in psychology, and the establishment of France's first chair in sociology.[8]

On 7 December 1918 the Kaiser-Wilhelms-Universität, closed down by order of the French occupation authorities, ended its illustrious forty-six-year history. Except for the Alsatians, the faculty were summarily dismissed and within the next month were

7 France, Ministère des Affairs Etrangères, *Procès verbaux de la Conférence d'Alsace–Lorraine* (Paris: 1917–19), I, pp. 59–67; II, pp. 185–89; "L'Université de Strasbourg." *Bulletin Alsacien-Lorrain du S.R. de Belfort* (Aug.–Sept. 1915), copy in Albert Thomas papers, AN, 210; France, Ministère de la Guerre, Service d'Alsace-Lorraine, Section d'Etudes de l'Instruction Publique, Sous-Commission de l'Enseignement Supérieur, Procès verbaux, 13 Sept. 1917–21 Feb. 1918, Albert Thomas papers, AN. 209; Pfister's draft, "Rapport sur l'Université de Strasbourg," BNUS; and Marc Bloch, "Christian Pfister, 1857–1933: Ses oeuvres," *RH*, 172 (1933): 569.

8 Pfister, "Rapport sur l'organisation future de la Faculté des Lettres de l'Université de Strasbourg," ADBR, 1045/176; John E. Craig, "France's First Chair of Sociology: A Note on the Origins," *Etudes Durkheimiennes* no. 4 (Dec. 1979): 8–13.

expelled across the Rhine.[9] In the meantime, the French Ministry of Public Instruction had appointed a commission of seventeen scholars, chaired by the physicist Paul Appell and again including Pfister, which arrived in Strasbourg in mid December. Fearing an exodus of the most talented Alsatian students, the Appell commission urged the immediate organization of a French university.[10] Off in Paris, where the government was preparing for the peace conference, the ministry decided to postpone a formal reopening but also to offer a limited number of courses in the main subject areas. Classes began on 16 January 1919. Among the small initial staff, consisting of selected professors on loan from other faculties, Alsatians held over from the German university, and officers stationed in the area, was Captain Marc Bloch.[11]

This provisional administrative arrangement resulted in chaotic instructional conditions, which were exacerbated by the distance between Strasbourg and Paris. The situation improved in March 1919 with the appointment of Alexandre Millerand as commissioner-general. Based in Strasbourg and reporting directly to the prime minister, he could make authoritative decisions at once.[12]

Marc Bloch, who after the armistice had remained on the intelligence staff,[13] was happy to be relieved of routine military duties and delighted to be assigned to the University of Strasbourg. Demobilized on 13 March, he finished the semester officially on leave from the faculty of the Amiens lycée. Bloch's initial teaching obligation also included instruction in introductory French, since

9 The expulsion and subsequent German protests in *New York Times*, 19, 21, 22 Apr. 1919; also Martin Spahn, "Die letzten Tage des Zusammenbruchs," *Süddeutsche Monatshefte* 29 (Dec. 1931): 224–31; Erich Klostermann, *Die Rückkehr der Strassburger Dozenten 1918–19 und ihre Aufnahme* (Halle: M. Niemeyer, 1932).

10 "Université de Strasbourg: Rapport de la Commission," ADBR, UStr.

11 Pfister, "La première année de la nouvelle université française de Strasbourg (1918–1919)," *Revue Internationale de l'Enseignement* (Sept.–Oct. 1919): 321–26; Procès verbal de l'Assemblée de la Faculté, 27 Jan. 1919, ADBR, AL 154 PI/2; Gustave Bloch to Jérôme Carcopino, 24 Feb. 1919, Carcopino papers, IF.

12 Pfister, "La première année," p. 338; cf. Alexandre Millerand, *Le retour de l'Alsace–Lorraine à la France* (Paris: Bibliothèque-Charpentier, 1923).

13 Bulletins de la Section de l'Information du D.Q.G., 5–17 Dec. 1918, "SG."

the student body of eight hundred Alsatians included some unable to work in that language. The facilities ranged from excellent to inferior. Bloch encountered poorly lit, inadequately heated rooms and a library of medieval history that ignored French history and lacked a single work by Fustel de Coulanges.[14]

Under Millerand's direction the structure and personnel of the new University of Strasbourg were established. Pfister, now acting dean, oversaw the selection of the permanent staff of the Faculty of Letters. It was on his recommendation that Marc Bloch was appointed an assistant lecturer (*chargé de cours*) in medieval history beginning on 1 October 1919.[15]

As soon as classes ended, Marc Bloch returned to Paris, where on 19 July he was married to the former Simonne Vidal. There was a religious ceremony four days later in the temple on the rue Buffault.[16] Simonne Bloch had been born in Dieppe in 1894. Her father, Paul Vidal (1869–1929), was Inspecteur-Général des Ponts et Chaussées under the Ministry of Public Works, a graduate of the Ecole Polytechnique and the Ecole des Ponts et Chaussées, and one of France's leading experts in internal navigation. Son and son-in-law of government engineers, with family roots in southern France and Alsace, Vidal between 1895 and 1912 had supervised the modernization of the port of Bordeaux and during the war had been responsible for navigation on the Seine and the provisioning of

14 Bloch to Ferdinand Lot, 11 Jan. 1920, Lot papers, IF; also Christian Pfister, "La première année," pp. 326–27, 332–33; Gustave Lanson, "La renaissance de l'université française de Strasbourg," *Revue Universitaire* 28 (1919): 323–36; Pierre Roussel, "L'Université de Strasbourg," *Le Flambeau* 2 (1919): 501–5.

15 Pfister to (Rector Jules) Coulet, 7 Mar. 1919, ADBR, W 1045/175; "Rapport de M. Pfister sur l'organisation future de la Faculté des Lettres de l'Université de Strasbourg," 19 Mar. 1919, ADBR, W 1045/176; Pfister to Coulet, 22 May 1919, ADBR, UStr.

  Because of the unique political situation of Alsace, Bloch's appointment had to be approved both locally and in Paris: Pfister's nomination, submitted to the Conseil Consultatif (5–6 June 1919) and to the Section Permanent du Conseil Supérieur de l'Instruction Publique (13 June 1919), was signed by Millerand on 28 July 1919 and approved by ministerial *arrêté* on 19 November. ADBR, W 1045/176.

16 Marriage certificate, dated 23 July 1919, EBC. There is an unsigned ketouba (religious certificate) in the archives of the Association Consistoriale Israélite of Paris, GG 241, Acte de mariage no. 9418.

14. Marc Bloch   15. Simonne Bloch

Paris. When his third child married Marc Bloch in 1919, Vidal left active service to teach at the Ecole des Ponts et Chaussées. In February 1923 he voluntarily returned during the Ruhr occupation to organize the complex transport operations along the navigable waterways. During the 1920s the Vidal residence, at 3, avenue Mozart in the sixteenth arrondissement, would be Bloch's home away from home on his research trips to Paris.[17]

Simonne Bloch had also done service in the Great War and been decorated for her work with prisoners and refugees between 1914 and 1918. By all accounts, she was a woman of tact and intelligence, gifted in music and foreign languages, who after the marriage also served as her husband's secretary, research assistant, travel companion, and friend. She shared many of his interests, read virtually everything he wrote, and also helped to create the well-ordered home that was indispensable to Bloch's happiness.[18] With

17 Biographical information on Paul Vidal in AN, F14 11619.
18 Lucien Febvre, "Marc Bloch et Strasbourg: Souvenirs d'une grande histoire," in *Mémorial des années 1939–1945*, Publications de la Faculté des Lettres de l'Université de Strasbourg (Paris: 1947), p. 172; Etienne Bloch, "Marc Bloch: Une vie complète," AN, 318 MI 1. Research notes in Simonne Bloch's handwriting abound; see, for example, AN, AB XIX 3846–48.

16. Simonne Bloch and Marc Bloch with their youngest children, Suzanne (b. 1930) and Jean-Paul (b. 1929)

a substantial dowry and ample servants, she was also renowned as a careful, thrifty housewife. The Blochs had six children, born over a decade in Strasbourg, in three groups: the older ones – Alice (7 July 1920), Etienne (23 September 1921), and Louis (26 February 1923); the middle child, Daniel (11 March 1926); and the two youngest, Jean-Paul (25 August 1929) and Suzanne (15 October 1930). Simonne Bloch was a devoted mother who, if less of a disciplinarian than her husband, was dedicated to the family's health, education and well-being.

Marc Bloch's household in Strasbourg retained close ties with the paternal and maternal grandparents in Marlotte and Paris and with the numerous aunts, uncles, sisters, brothers, and cousins; there were frequent reunions during the holidays. With the exception of a maternal grandmother, no links with Jewish orthodoxy remained. "Holidays" meant Christmas and Easter as well as the traditional French fetes. Although Marc Bloch read the Bible to his older children, they had no religious instruction and were raised, as he was, in a completely assimilated French home. With the early death of his brother Louis from cancer on 16 March 1922 and of his father on 2 December 1923, Bloch suddenly became the head of his family, responsible for his mother, two young nephews, and a widowed sister-in-law along with his own growing clan in Alsace.[19]

The French University of Strasbourg officially opened its doors in the fall of 1919. On 15 October the seven faculties met to elect their deans and representatives to the governing university council.[20] Classes began in early November. At 9 a.m. on 22 November the formal inaugural ceremony took place, exactly one year after French troops had arrived in Strasbourg. It was a colorful, patriotic occasion attended by President Poincaré, former premier Georges Clemenceau, and Marshal Ferdinand Foch, along with large numbers of French and foreign academics and statesmen. Opening and closing with the "Marseillaise," the proceedings were animated by the performance of orchestral works of César Franck, Camille Saint-Saens, and Georges Bizet by members of the new Strasbourg Conservatoire. There were four speeches, by the new rector, Sebastien Charléty, the proud and joyful Dean Pfister, the leader of the Francophile students during the German occupation, Pierre Bucher, and Poincaré, all emphasizing the Reich's failures, France's com-

19 In the file "Souvenirs sur les disparus," EBC, Bloch saved the violets from his brother's deathbed and the roses from his father's. When Paul Vidal died on 23 July 1929 after his wife's unexpected death, only one grandparent, Bloch's mother, remained. Draft letter, AN, AB XIX 3804; Bloch to Carcopino, 28 Aug. 1929, Carcopino papers, IF.

20 Attending his first meeting of the university assembly a day later, Bloch complained of a delay in receiving an important donation of copies of medieval documents because railway officials were unable to comprehend the addressee: "The Faculty of Letters of the University of Strasbourg." Procès verbal, 16 Oct. 1919, ADBR, AL 154 P 1/2.

mitment to excellence, and Strasbourg's special mission.[21] There were also three festive days of banquets, theater, musical performances, excursions, and the awarding of honorary degrees. Gustave Bloch, representing the Sorbonne, rejoiced in France's triumph and in his son's new position.[22]

Strasbourg appeared to be an ideal environment for Marc Bloch to begin his university teaching career. Here were spiritual links to a grand tradition. In the early 1860s his father's model and Pfister's teacher and idol Fustel de Coulanges had written the pioneering comparative study of Hellenic and Roman societies, *La cité antique*.[23] Two and a half centuries earlier, the rector of the University of Strasbourg, Jean Joachim Zentgraff, had investigated the healing rites of French kings, work that anticipated Bloch's research for *Les rois thaumaturges* (1924).[24]

At thirty-three, still without his doctorate, Marc Bloch had been named head of the Institute of the History of the Middle Ages, which replaced the German "Seminar."[25] He had an adequate budget, a modest library that he intended to expand, and access to

21 Fêtes de l'inauguration, 20–22 Nov. 1919, ADBR, w 1045/31, 32; program "Cérémonie de l'inauguration de l'Université de Strasbourg, 22 Nov. 1919," EBC; *New York Times*, 30 Oct., 2, 9 Nov. 1919, 2 Jan. 1920; Louis Madelin, "La journée de Strasbourg," *Revue des Deux Mondes*, 6th ser., 55 (1 Jan. 1920): 194–205; Roberto Michels, "L'Università di Strasburgo," *Nuova Antologia* 205 (2 Mar. 1920): 56–62; *Université de Strasbourg: Fêtes d'inauguration* (Strasbourg, 1920).

22 Gustave Bloch to Carcopino, 13 Nov. 1919, Carcopino papers, IF.

23 Henri Salomon, "Christian Pfister," *RH* 172 (1933): 560–63; F. Hartog, "Strasbourg et l'histoire ancienne en 1919," in *Au berceau des Annales*, ed. Charles-Olivier Carbonell and Georges Livet (Toulouse: Presses de l'Institut d'Etudes Politiques, 1983), pp. 41–43.

24 "Born in the free city, [he] became a subject of Louis XIV, delivered the eulogy on Henry of Navarre, and carved out a brilliant university career in his native city, which had become French. This present book figures among the publications of our revived Faculté des Lettres; and I am delighted thus to be able to continue in some measure – though with full awareness of the difference in spirit between our respective times – the work begun in former days by a Rector of the ancient University of Strasbourg." *RT*, p. 24.

25 Many of Bloch's research notes from this period were written on the back of the "Satzungen des historischen Seminars der Universität Strassburg" listing fifteen rules for the use of its facilities. See, for example, AN, AB XIX 3809.

the extensive university collection of documents, periodicals, and historical volumes.[26] The Faculty of Letters, handpicked by Pfister, was dedicated to research and pedagogic reform. As part of its mission of disseminating the fruits of French scholarship, Pfister's unit received subsidies to publish its own bulletin as well as a monograph series. There were opportunities for summer teaching and also generous subventions to encourage the faculty to lecture, write, participate in national and international organizations, and travel, especially abroad.[27] There was a program of inviting foreign dignitaries under which Henri Pirenne, who received an honorary doctorate, presented two classes and a public lecture and discussed his current work on economic history with the Faculty of Letters.[28]

There were also opportunities to cross the Rhine. Through the university's extension division Bloch delivered a lecture on French history to French officers directly across the river in Kehl.[29] In 1921, responding to the request of the French high commissioner in the occupied Rhineland, the Faculty of Letters established the Centre d'Etudes Germaniques in Mainz to provide specialized instruction to French army officers, journalists, and civil servants. Though not one of the regular faculty, Bloch gave occasional lectures in Mainz and twice served as external examiner for the *diplôme*. When the French army withdrew from the Rhineland in 1930, Bloch helped reestablish the Centre in Strasbourg.[30]

26 Bloch to Ferdinand Lot, 11 Jan. 1920, Lot papers, IF; also Bloch, "Institut d'Histoire du Moyen-Age." *Bulletin de la Faculté des Lettres de l'Université de Strasbourg* 1 (1922–23): 181–83. The budget for Bloch's institute, 2,500 francs, was identical in 1921 and 1929 (ADBR, AL 154 P1/2, P3/5).
27 Twelve members of the Strasbourg faculty attended the International Congress of Historical Sciences in Brussels in 1923; five attended the meeting in Oslo in 1928. ADBR, W 11045/42; AL 154 P2/4. Bloch attended and received subventions for both. Cf. Pfister, "La première année," pp. 345–52; Craig, *Scholarship and Nation Building*, pp. 233–37.
28 *Bulletin de la Faculté des Lettres de l'Université de Strasbourg* 2 (1923–24): 88–90.
29 "La légende monarchique française," 8 Nov. 1924, AN, AB XIX 3845.
30 On the Centre: ADBR, AL 98/354, 361; also Alfred Schlagdenhauffen, "Le Centre d'études germaniques de Strasbourg, 1921–1961," *Bulletin de la Faculté des Lettres de l'Université de Strasbourg* 40 (1960–61): 467–76; Etienne Vézian, "Le Centre d'études germaniques," *L'Alsace Française* 10 (9 Nov. 1930): 389–90; Bloch's participation in AN, AB XIX 3817.

Strasbourg, which became one of France's largest universities, was also recognized for its "spirit of synthesis."[31] Henri Berr admiringly noted the Faculty of Letters' ample staff, low faculty-student ratio, commitment to and time for research, and the novel Centres d'Etudes, which promised to break down the artificial compartments of traditional history. In contrast to most French universities, five faculties (Letters, Law, Roman Catholic Theology, Protestant Theology, and many of the sciences) were housed together in the Palais Universitaire, which made interdisciplinary work possible.[32] Contrary to the solitary habits of French academics, in the early years Strasbourg professors attended their colleagues' classes and taught courses together. Like pioneers on a new intellectual frontier, they produced individual and collaborative work.

The *réunions du samedi* of Strasbourg's Faculty of Letters began in January 1920.[33] Originally these were informal late-afternoon colloquia in the institutes of linguistics and the history of religion. When history was added, a three-week rotation began, and a more uniform format came about. Faculty members either presented their own research or commented on current writing in their field, followed by questions and discussions about literature, methodology, and theory. Such guests as Gustave Bloch and Henri Pirenne took part.[34] Through these often lively interdisciplinary *réunions* Bloch made the acquaintance of his mostly older colleagues: the geographer Henri Baulig (1877–1962), the historian of religion Prosper Alfaric (1876–1955), the Alsatian philologist of Romance languages Ernest Hoepffner (1879–1956), the archaeologist Albert Grenier (1878–1961), the Germanist Edmond Vermeil (1878–1964), the psychologist Charles Blondel (1876–1939), the socio-

31 Henri Berr, "L'esprit de synthèse dans l'enseignement supérieur: L'Université de Strasbourg," *RSH* 32 (Jan. 1921): 1–13.

32 The Medical Faculty, whose facilities were consolidated in the municipal hospital, had a special research laboratory for tuberculosis, which aided Bloch's research for *Les rois thaumaturges*. Pfister, "L'Université de Strasbourg" (17 Dec. 1921): 760.

33 *Bulletin de la Faculté des Lettres de l'Université de Strasbourg* 1 (1922–23): 106–7.

34 Résumés of the *réunions* between 1922 and 1939 are in the annual bulletins, which also contain book reviews, scholarly information, and course announcements; the most important meetings on social history took place in the early 1920s.

17. The University of Strasbourg, 1925

logist Maurice Halbwachs (1877–1945), the jurist Gabriel Le Bras (1891–1970), and, especially, his senior colleague in modern history, next-door neighbor and future collaborator Lucien Febvre (1878–1956), who had left a university position in Dijon – and possibly delayed his prospects of being called to Paris – to serve at Strasbourg.[35]

To secure a regular appointment at Strasbourg, Bloch had to obtain his doctorate. He benefited from a special government dispensation for war veterans, who were to be allowed to submit abbreviated works for the degree. After rushing to finish, Bloch returned to the Sorbonne on 4 December 1920. At 1 p.m. in the

35 Craig. *Scholarship and Nation Building*, p. 221; also Henri Baulig, "Lucien Febvre à Strasbourg," *Bulletin de la Faculté des Lettres de l'Université de Strasbourg* 36 (1957–58): 177–78; Georges Livet, "Lucien Febvre et Strasbourg: L'Institut d'histoire moderne de la Faculté des Lettres," in *Au berceau des Annales*, pp. 47–55.

The other members of Strasbourg's original history faculty – one of the largest in France – were: Eugène Cavaignac and André Piganiol in ancient history, Georges Pariset in contemporary history, Fritz Kiener in the history of Alsace, and Dean Pfister, who taught medieval and Alsatian history.

Salle du Doctorat, he defended his *thèse principale* and his *thèse complémentaire* before a six-member committee under the presidency of the senior professor, Charles Seignobos, and received the highest evaluation, "très honorable."[36]

The rules were greatly relaxed for the *thèse complémentaire*. Bloch was able to present an old published work, his 1912 article "Les formes de la rupture de l'hommage dans l'ancien droit féodal." Adhering to his original hypothesis on the existence and nature of the rite, he presented what he termed a "second edition" of the article: a list of additional sources and a defense of his methodology.[37] Almost two decades later, in Bloch's magisterial study of feudal society, the ceremonial disruption of the tie between lord and vassal returns as a significant detail.[38]

Bloch's principal thesis. "Rois et serfs," which was published at once with a subvention from the Sorbonne, established his credentials as a medievalist.[39] The work was a greatly reduced version of his original design, to study the rural population and the eradication of serfdom in the Ile-de-France. Because "circumstances" had "terribly delayed" the fulfillment of his ambitious plan, Bloch extracted one small, celebrated incident and probed it in considerable detail. He nevertheless admitted gaps in his research and advanced his hope someday to complete a more thorough investigation of serfdom in the entire Paris region.[40]

In *Rois et serfs*, Bloch chose to discuss two emancipation ordinances, by Louis X in 1315 and by Philip V in 1318, about which several historical fables had developed. Drawing on his skills in the criticism of evidence, Bloch demonstrated how their famous identical preambles, with their reference to man's "natural freedom," did not represent a royal endorsement of human liberty. They were, rather, a conventional formula, but one that also reflected the underlying tension in medieval political theory, between the ideal of

36 Preparations described in Bloch to Lot, 11 Jan. 1920, Lot papers, IF; defense in AN, AJ 16 4764X; see also Gustave Bloch to Carcopino, 29 Jan. 1921, Carcopino papers, IF.
37 "Thèse complémentaire: Soutenance," AN, AB XIX 3811; see above, Chap. 3.
38 *SF*, I, chap. xvi.
39 Full title: *Rois et serfs: Un chapitre d'histoire capétienne* (Paris: Champion, 1920); research notes in AN, AB XIX 3806, 3848, 3850.
40 *RS*, pp. 10–13.

natural equality and the reality of hierarchy, justified by man's Fall. Bloch punctured the myth that all the royal serfs were freed by the last Capetians. The celebrated orders applied only to two districts. Finally, he disproved their originality. Royal enfranchisement of serfs had begun over a century earlier. The edicts of 1315 and 1318 were modeled on the policies of Philip the Good, who in 1302 had made more extensive grants of freedom to his serfs.[41]

Like the *thèse complémentaire*, *Rois et serfs* anticipated Bloch's future work: his investigations of royalty, the functions and characteristics of royal officials, and the elusive history of the common people. Though of modest proportions, the book delineated the essential attributes of serfdom, traced a tentative pattern of royal, ecclesiastical, and seigneurial emancipation in the cities and countryside of the Ile-de-France, and contributed to the history of the Capetian monarchs, who, much like their successors during the next four centuries, chose to sacrifice their future income for immediate remuneration. Bloch combined two movements: royal emancipation (originally slow, cautious, and relatively liberal in its terms, which was transformed by the last impecunious warrior Capetians – those "resolute sellers of liberty" – into a regular source of revenue) and the serfs' urge for freedom, stirred in the twelfth century by the weakening of feudal bonds, the growing exactions of feudal lords, increased prosperity, and alliances between town and rural people. While the royals dominate the text, the serfs' condition underlies its theme.[42]

---

41 See Bloch's abbreviated summary, "Un aspect de la société médiévale: Rois et serfs," *French Quarterly* 3 (1921): 69–72.
42 Lucien Febvre, "Marc Bloch et Strasbourg," pp. 172–73; Charles-Edmond Perrin, "L'oeuvre historique de Marc Bloch," *RH* 199, no. 2 (1948): 164.

   Perrin was a Lorrainer, one year younger than Bloch, a former *normalien* (1908–11, ranking first in the *agrégation*), fellow of the Fondation Thiers, and front-line officer with six citations. In 1919 he obtained a temporary appointment to the University of Strasbourg followed by a year at the lycée Fustel de Coulanges, when he helped read the proofs for *Rois et serfs*.

   After seven years at the University of Grenoble, Perrin returned to Strasbourg in 1928 as Bloch's junior colleague in medieval history, where in 1935 he finally finished his 800-page doctoral thesis on the rural nobility of Lorraine. He was given a chair at Strasbourg in 1936 and then followed Bloch to Paris in 1937. Marc Bloch's report on Perrin's thesis, 19 Dec. 1935. ADBR, AL 154 P5/9; additional biographical information in AN, AJ 16 6115.

Bloch's style and method were manifested in *Rois et serfs*. There was no narrative. Instead, like a judicial investigator, Bloch conducted an examination of documents, posing stiff questions (which invariably led to others) and occasionally inserting a pithy commentary on the evidence itself. In several instances he introduced comparative examples to fill specific gaps in his sources and lend perspective to royal policy. *Rois et serfs* hints at Bloch's later virtuosity in combining legal, political, social, economic, and psychological factors to produce a more rounded and truer version of the past. It also revealed his emphasis on economic conditions,[43] his interest in form and ritual,[44] and his acute awareness of the need to separate the modern sensibility from the medieval.[45] Though but a sketch of a larger, never-completed design, *Rois et serfs* was a bridge between Bloch's prewar studies and his new life in Strasbourg, where he would now be free to expand his work and his horizons.

If their scholarship was distinctive, in the area of pedagogic reform the Strasbourg faculty made only modest gains. Bloch, more than most of his colleagues, was a severe critic of the rigidity of the French system, which emphasized preparing students for standardized examinations and forced professors to instruct according to a rigid curriculum set by the ministry.[46] Even with a larger variety of courses than universities in the interior, the junior and senior faculty of Strasbourg dutifully labored to meet the requirements for the *licence* and the *agrégation* set by committees composed primarily of Parisian professors. Artificial barriers – division into ancient,

---

43 *RS*, pp. 54, 166, 176.

44 *RS*, pp. 28, 41–42, 45–46.

45 *RS*, p. 161.

46 See Bloch's remarks to the Faculty Assembly, 10 June 1922, ADBR, AL 154 PI/2. Also: "Notre enseignement supérieur est garrotté par les programmes de licence et, beaucoup plus étroitement encore, dans les principales facultés, par les programmes d'agrégation, que le professeur reçoit tout faits des mains du jury." Marc Bloch, "Pour une histoire comparée des sociétés européennes," *RSH* 46 (Dec. 1928), repr. in *MH* I, pp. 37–38 n. 1. Pfister and his father had also felt the burdens of this system: Marc Bloch, "Christian Pfister," pp. 568–69; Jérôme Carcopino, "Gustave Bloch," in Ecole Normale Supérieure, Association Amicale de Secours des Anciens Elèves, *Annuaire* (Paris, 1925), p. 100.

medieval, modern, and contemporary – restricted the teaching of history; and many of the faculty continued to grind out "scholarly" books that were little more than course outlines for the *agrégation*.[47] On the other hand, even the most ardent Strasbourg reformers understood the constraints on them. In a provincial university where their students' abilities and horizons were limited, their own distinction would be measured not only by their scholarship but also by their candidates' achievements along the traditional stages in French academia.[48]

In a brilliant and articulate faculty, Marc Bloch stood out as a teacher. During his seventeen years at Strasbourg he had the opportunity to teach a wide variety of courses centering on the Middle Ages. By all accounts of his former students, these were carefully organized, methodically presented, filled with immense erudition and critical commentary, and also – like his writing – replete with occasionally long and invariably fascinating parentheses. Bloch was a demanding teacher. Student reports were judged severely; lack of perspective or rigor was especially unwelcome. Some of his students remembered Bloch as "glacial," caustic, and hypercritical. Though his method was fairly traditional, the new professor astonished his young students with his command of the literature, mastery of auxiliary disciplines, skill in languages, and insights.[49]

He opposed all doctrines – racial, economic, class, environmental. The historian's craft consisted of posing questions more than providing mere demonstrations of transcendent truths. Often he would repeat that historians were neither theologians nor moralists; their role was neither to condemn nor to absolve a particular institution,

47 On some of Bloch's attempts at reform: ADBR, AL 154 PI/D2; P4/7; also Bloch, "Sur les programmes d'histoire de l'enseignement secondaire," *Bulletin de la Société des Professeurs d'Histoire* (Nov. 1921): 15–17.
48 Paul Leuilliot, "Témoignage d'un 'fidèle'" and Alice Gérard, "A l'origine du combat des *Annales*: Positivisme historique et système universitaire," in *Au berceau des Annales*, pp. 72–73, 80–88.
49 Based on interviews in 1980–83 with Marc Bloch's former students: Henri Brunschwig, Philippe Dollinger, Jean Schneider, Jean Braun, André Hoeffner, Mme. Monfren, Fernand L'Huillier; also Roger Jaquel to author, 14 June 1982.

but to understand what circumstances had brought it into existence and what purpose it had served.[50]

Bloch's genius as a teacher was to follow a question through long, laborious paths of research, through time and space, reaching some tentative conclusions and posing new questions. He delighted in demonstrating the direction of his inquiry. Occasionally, in an attempt to stimulate his listeners' curiosity, critical spirit, or reflectiveness – or when he himself was uncertain of the answer – he concluded with a confession of "ignorance" (and often chided others for evading a similar admission).[51]

Bloch's teaching contrasted with the classical German *Bildungs-ideal*, the *alles wissen, alles tun* which in the nineteenth and early twentieth centuries produced a mutable balance between an idealized sense of personal autonomy and cultivation and the more pervasive reality of obedient and passive scholars, driven by a "nostalgia for synthesis." Bloch viewed education as a quest to situate oneself in relation to all parts of a whole one could not possibly master. One had to train the mind to develop the processes of critical thinking and analysis together with the goals of logical abstraction, generalization, and effective judgment, all the while remaining open to new ideas. For Bloch the process itself was important, the quality and judgment more significant than the accumulation of facts. In addition, the history Bloch conveyed to his students was a noble *jeu d'esprit*: a joyful, humane challenge.[52]

Fiercely proud of his cosmopolitanism, Bloch had a "horror of compartments (*cloisonnements*)" of either time or space. He enjoyed the role of the stern inquisitor of documents, always trying, according to one of his former students, "to prove the opposite." His courses represented preliminary statements. He offered no "method," no "grand plan," insisting that everyone had to develop his or her

50 From information provided by several of Bloch's students, in Robert Bou-truche, "Marc Bloch vu par ses élèves," in *Mémorial des années 1939–1945*, Publications de la Faculté des Lettres de l'Université de Strasbourg (Paris, 1947), p. 196.
51 "History is not a deductive science; it is based on gathering and interpreting facts we can only know imperfectly. Our basis is our sources; we must often utter the words: 'It seems...' and 'We do not know.'" AN, AB XIX 3930.
52 Interview with Henri Brunschwig (1980).

own way of understanding the texts. Some of his students found his teaching disconcerting, particularly his long reading lists in several languages and insistence that they be thorough, precise, and critical. One admitted he was often in despair about so "open" a master. One could be "lost" with the freedom that was imposed by Bloch. Yet over time this exigent master also assured them that while it was impossible to read and know everything, one could develop a technique of casting an eye "to the left and to the right."[53]

Bloch excelled in examining phenomena openly, concretely, and without prejudice. On one occasion he took a class out into the fields of Alsace to point out the characteristic elongated open fields of northern Europe that stretched from the Atlantic to the Elbe, in contrast with the irregular fields of southern Europe. France ("Alas!") was split in two. Bloch encouraged his students to learn German and was attentive to current German scholarship, but denounced its nationalist overtones. He ridiculed German medievalists who identified round-house villages as "Slavic" for their ignorance of similar architecture in southern France, and noted their imprecision and anachronisms.

Marc Bloch struck his young students as a forbidding figure: elegant, correct, and distant. Those who were invited for tea at his home were duly awed by the comfortably elegant surroundings.[54] But to those to whom he became a mentor, the cold, ironic, caustic Bloch became a generous, sensitive master, concerned about their well-being and their families as much as about their work in progress.[55] Bloch loved rural history and guided his students to do research in areas where there were solid documentation and useful questions. His guidance, however, never led to any form of dominance over their work or their ideas.

Because of their parallel interests, friendship, and future collaboration, Bloch and Febvre were long remembered as a gifted and ferocious team who flung open the doors between the medieval and

53 Interview with Philippe Dollinger (1980).
54 Interview with Fernand L'Huillier (1982).
55 Boutruche, "Marc Bloch," pp. 197–205; during his long directorship of Boutruche's thesis, Bloch wrote fifty-two letters to his student. Letters seen by courtesy of Mme. Boutruche, Montpellier.

modern seminar rooms and jointly proselytized for a better history. They added an additional year to the two generally required for the *licence* in history, insisting that their students first acquire a "solid historical background."[56] Both railed openly, occasionally viciously, against "traditionalists" who were too timid to range beyond established boundaries. There were, of course, significant temperamental differences between the reserved junior Bloch and the spirited elder Febvre. Nevertheless, this remarkable duo, with its force and its contrasts, left an indelible impression on young Alsatian historians.[57]

Like the Germans a half-century earlier, the new French professors were physically remote from the local community. The faculty tended to cluster near the university, generally residing in the handsome faubourg built by Reich architects. Bloch and his growing family occupied two houses on the Allée de la Robertsau, a broad, attractive, tree-lined boulevard of late-nineteenth-century villas leading from the Palais Universitaire to the Orangerie, and one on the Avenue de la Liberté, nearer the university. There was a considerable amount of socializing within the academic community, no doubt at the expense of local contacts.

There was a spiritual and political distance as well. Whether liberal or conservative, the Strasbourg faculty was committed to national assimilation. Good French patriots, they had little sympathy for the Alsatians' postwar "malaise," or for the ensuing autonomist movements among the students and the community.[58]

56 Interview with Jacques Godechot (1980); Godechot to author, "Souvenirs sur Marc Bloch." After a very formal orientation by Bloch and Febvre in 1924 about Strasbourg's exacting program, the seventeen-year-old Godechot decided to return to Nancy.
57 Philippe Dollinger, "Marc Bloch et Lucien Febvre à Strasbourg (Quelques souvenirs d'un de leurs étudiants)," François-Georges Pariset, "Du bon travail à Strasbourg...," and Paul Leuilliot, "Témoignage d'un 'fidèle,'" in *Au berceau des Annales*, pp. 65−74. Also, interviews with Brunschwig, Dollinger, Leuilliot (1980), André Hoepffner (1982), Godechot. Roger Jaquel to author, 14 June 1982.
58 Geneviève Baas, *Le malaise alsacien, 1919−1924* (Strasbourg: Développement et Communauté, 1972); also François-Georges Dreyfus, *La vie politique en Alsace, 1919−1936* (Paris: Presses de la Fondation Nationale des Sciences Politiques, 1969), pp. 9−72.

With the exception of a few professors of law and theology and the Alsatian holdovers in the Faculty of Letters, most stayed aloof from local politics. Pfister's group, with its Dreyfusard, anticlerical, left-center, and internationalist orientation, was labeled the "Jacobins." Ironically, these French humanists greatly resembled their German predecessors in conceiving their mission as the creation of an eminent national institution and not a showpiece of regional pride.[59]

The German language was banished, as French had been under the Second Reich. Vermeil refused to teach any of his literature courses in German. The Alsatian dialect was ignored.[60] Despite their Alsatian origins, neither Bloch nor Halbwachs investigated local subjects.[61] Fritz Kiener, the regional specialist, had constantly to defend his academic respectability and his championship of Alsatian particularism before his skeptical colleagues.[62]

There were a few attempts at accommodation. Sympathizing with its students' inadequate mastery of French, the Faculty of Letters maintained special summer language courses, and it adopted Marc Bloch's suggestion that students be offered scholarships and incentives to spend a year in the interior perfecting their French.[63] To

59 François-Georges Dreyfus, "Strasbourg et son université de 1919 à 1929," in *Au berceau des Annales*, pp. 14–18.
60 Craig, *Scholarship and Nation Building*, pp. 287, 306–7; Lucien Febvre, "Politique royale ou civilisation française? Remarques sur un problème d'histoire linguistique," *RSH* 38 (Dec. 1924): 37–53.
61 John Craig, "Maurice Halbwachs à Strasbourg," *Revue Française de Sociologie* 20 (1979): 273–92. Halbwachs, one of the most cosmopolitan members of the faculty, manifested sympathy for Alsatian localism in "Notre politique en Alsace–Lorraine," *Les Cahiers des Droits de l'Homme* 20 (20 Dec. 1920): 3–8, and for a short time after his arrival in Strasbourg did collect and publish data on the region. Afterwards he applied this material and directed his research toward more general social questions.
62 Charles-Edmond Perrin, "Fritz Kiener (1874–1942)," in *Mémorial des années 1939–1945*, Publications de la Faculté des Lettres de l'Université de Strasbourg (Paris, 1947), pp. 99–117.
63 Minutes of Conseil of the Faculty of Letters, 19 May, 24 Nov. 1928, ADBR, AL 154 P2/3; Bloch to Maugain, 12 July 1928, ADBR, AL 154/4. These deliberations followed the government's forceful action to suppress the autonomist movement in May 1928. Cf. Craig *Scholarship and Nation Building*, p. 312.

bridge the town-gown gap, several faculty members scheduled popular public courses, participated in the university's extension division and traveling lecturer series, and contributed to Bucher's moderate weekly periodical, *L'Alsace Française*. Bloch's sole article appeared in March 1930, in the issue commemorating the centenary of the birth of Fustel de Coulanges.[64]

These special efforts to some extent reinforced the feeling of being posted in a foreign colony, one which nonetheless exerted a potent influence on outsiders. In 1921, Bloch engagingly identified his one-year-old firstborn as a "grosse petite Alsacienne." When his children attended the local schools, they had to cope with the prescribed religious instruction and customs as best they could.[65] By mid decade, the "spirit of Locarno" stimulated a local revival of German theater, music, and art. Strasbourg after 1926 became more aggressively Christian and Alsatian, causing discomfort to the nonreligious and French speakers and to those like Marc Bloch who oriented themselves toward the nation's capital.[66]

French intellectuals in the postwar period can be divided into three groups. Between the ideologues and activists of the left and the right were those like Marc Bloch who out of conviction or personal necessity were *non-engagé*. Veterans of the Dreyfus Affair and four years of grueling trench warfare, they wearily withdrew to the sidelines of national politics. Bolstered by the idealism of Julien Benda, they guarded their principles, functioned as disinterested scholars, and stayed above the melee of partisan politics.[67] With the great political and military struggles seemingly decided, the Jacobins in Strasbourg joined their more conservative colleagues

64 *L'Alsace Française* (16 Mar. 1930): 206–9; Craig, *Scholarship and Nation Building*, pp. 279–82, which also describes two abortive projects designed to appeal to the lower-middle and working classes.
65 Interview with Etienne Bloch. Quotation in letter to Georges Davy, 28 Mar. 1921, AN, MI 318 1.
66 Craig, *Scholarship and Nation Building*, pp. 290, 304–5; growing native anti-Semitism is discussed in the Godechot contribution in *Au berceau des Annales*, pp. 32–33.
67 Julien Benda, *La trahison des clercs* (Paris: B. Grasset, 1927), esp. pp. 246–47. At the International Congress of Historical Sciences in Oslo in 1928, Bloch allusively termed comparative history a "purely scientific discipline. . . oriented toward knowledge and not toward practical results." Text of his communication reprinted in *RSH* 46 (1928): 15–50.

in renouncing political involvement. Like their compatriots in the interior, they read *Le Temps* each evening and voted regularly, but chose not to speak out on crucial public issues.[68]

Marc Bloch eloquently described the condition of his generation:

We emerged from the last war desperately tired, and after four years not only of fighting, but of mental laziness, we were only too anxious to get back to our proper employments and take up the tools that we had left to rust upon the benches. So behindhand were we with our work that we set ourselves to bolt it down in indigestible mouthfuls. . . .

Many of us realized at a very early stage the nature of the abyss into which the diplomacy of Versailles and the Ruhr was threatening to plunge us. We knew perfectly well that it would have the double result of embroiling us with our former Allies and of keeping open and bleeding our ancient quarrel with an enemy whom we had just, but only just, defeated. . . . We were not such fools as to believe that in a France impoverished, relatively undermanned, and capable of realizing only a very small industrial potential, a policy of the kind they contemplated was advisable.[69]

From his berth in Strasbourg Bloch early realized the dangers of the postwar reparations problem. It pitted France in an unequal struggle against hardline German nationalists like Hugo Stinnes, produced unrealistic, acrimonious debate over payments in goods, gold, or worthless Reich currency, and alienated America from its former ally. But when France invaded the Ruhr in 1923 to collect reparations he took a neutral stance. Though privately deploring an act of force that could and did provoke German defiance, he refused either to publicly oppose the government or participate in statements of support. He was against the idea of involving the local group of *Anciens combattants* on issues of either national politics or educational reform.[70]

68 P. N. Broadbent and J. E. Flower, "The Intellectual and His Role in France between the Wars," *Journal of European Studies* 8 (1978): 246–57; Craig, *Scholarship and Nation Building*, p. 278.

69 *ED*, p. 215.

70 Bloch to Davy, 28 Mar. 1921, AN, MI 381 1; Bloch to Gustave Cohen, 23 Feb., 2 Mar. 1923, AN, AP 59 2/3. Bloch's views were similar to the majority in France's huge veterans' organization, who were resolutely apolitical. See Antoine Prost, *Les anciens combattants et la société française* (Paris: Presses de la Fondation Nationale des Sciences Politiques, 1977), vols. II–III.

18. Bloch's study in Strasbourg, 1935

Paradoxically, the vibrant intellectual atmosphere at the University of Strasbourg reinforced the tendency of its professors to avoid partisan stands. In the meantime, in one decade, an exhausted France shifted from aggressive confrontation with its former enemies and allies to the elaborate defensive policy of the Maginot Line. One of the consequences of the university's sealing itself off into a closed, self-perpetuating institution of specialists was a public woefully ignorant of history and of the larger world. Bloch sensed that the ruling classes of France, and also of England, were now less educated than in Germany to meet the challenges of democracy.[71]

Bloch later explained that, "by a sort of fatalism" engendered by their disciplines, the professoriate were inhibited from "embarking on individual action." "We had grown used to seeing great impersonal forces at work in society as in nature. In the vast drag of these submarine swells, so cosmic as to seem irresistible, of what avail were the petty struggles of a few shipwrecked sailors?"[72]

71 Bloch to André Siegfried, 4 May 1931, Siegfried papers, Fondation Nationale des Sciences Politiques, Paris.
72 ED, p. 217.

In his angry retrospective analysis after the fall of France in 1940 Bloch blamed scholars for the debacle. He insisted that an integral part of the development of historical self-consciousness in modern civilizations was the persistence of the "individual mind" continually and fruitfully reacting with the "general mind":

For a man to form a clear idea of the needs of society and to make an effort to spread his views widely is to introduce a grain of leaven into the general mentality. By so doing, he gives himself a chance to modify it to some small extent, and consequently to bring some influence to bear upon the course of events that, in the last analysis, are dictated by human psychology. The real trouble with us professors was that we were absorbed in our day-to-day tasks. Most of us can say with some justice that we were good workmen. Is it equally true to say that we were good citizens?[73]

73 ED, pp. 217–18.

6. L'histoire humaine

The object of history is, by its nature, man.[1]

Behind the features of a landscape, or tools and machinery, or the most formal written documents, or the institutions that seem entirely remote from those who established them, are the men whom history seeks to grasp.[2]

The Great War had publicly tested historians' claims to an objective, scholarly discipline based on scientific fact gathering and rigorous criticism of the evidence. Beneath the scientific veneer of many practitioners a nationalistic spirit had been unleashed – more likely to apply scholarly prestige and resources to justifying the occupation of Belgium, eastern France, and the Russian Empire, or to advocating national liberation for the various client peoples of the Allies, than to drawing impartial conclusions from the "facts." In the war's aftermath historians were enlisted to attack or support the Paris treaties, which brought insufficient peace, security, and economic revival to Europe.[3]

Struck by the consequences of mass mobilization and a vast new range of technology, a small group of historians were determined to expand their discipline's range beyond its traditional preoccupation with politics, war, diplomacy, and great leaders, to transcend pure

1 Numa Denis Fustel de Coulanges, "Leçon d'ouverture de 1862," *RSH* 2 (1901): 243, quoted in *AH*, p. 35.

2 *AH*, p. 35.

3 Geoffrey Barraclough, *Main Trends in History* (New York: Holmes and Meier, 1979), p. 8; Klaus Schwabe, *Wissenschaft und Kriegsmoral: Die deutschen Hochschullehrer und die politischen Grundfragen des Ersten Weltkrieges* (Göttingen: Musterschmidt Verlag, 1969); Erich J. C. Hahn, "The German Foreign Ministry and the Question of War Guilt in 1918–1919," in *German Nationalism and the European Response, 1890–1945*, ed. C. Fink, I. V. Hull, and M. Knox (Norman: University of Oklahoma Press, 1985), pp. 43–70.

narrative with a strong analytic framework, to make history more complex, more accurate, and more "human." While the old guard of positivists still remained at their posts, writing and training their disciples, some of Marc Bloch's generation of war veterans, who had been weaned on the prewar social and behavioral sciences and on innovative works in economic, social, legal, and religious history, began establishing themselves in university faculties. They opposed not only the scientific pretensions of the French manual writers but also their rivals, the German historicists, who continued to insist on history's subjective and unique character.

The new *Histoire humaine* needed related disciplines in order to comprehend national and global issues and new economic and technological questions, and also to appeal to a larger international audience. The struggle against traditional history, already rooted in the United States, spread beyond Western Europe to Italy, Spain, the new states of Eastern Europe, and Japan. It was reinforced by the flowering of early Soviet and European Marxist historiography, by the brilliant work of Max Weber and the Frankfurt school, and also by such new journals as *Dziejow Spolecznych i Gospodarczych* (1926) in Poland; the *Economic History Review* (1927) in England; and the *Annales d'Histoire Économique et Sociale* (1929) founded by Bloch and Febvre, which will be discussed in the next chapter.[4]

The patron saint of this determined minority was Henri Pirenne. Already an eminent scholar, known for his prewar studies of early capitalism, medieval cities, and the history of Belgium, Pirenne saw his prestige enhanced by his resistance to German occupation policies and by his masterful work, written in captivity without his books or notes, on the foundations of Europe.[5] From their first

4 Barraclough, *Main Trends*, pp. 5–16; Georg G. Iggers, "The Transformation of Historical Studies in Historical Perspective," in *International Handbook of Historical Studies: Contemporary Research and Theory*, ed. Georg G. Iggers and Harold T. Parker (Westport, Conn.: Greenwood, 1979), p. 5.

5 *The Journal de Guerre of Henri Pirenne*, ed. Mary Lyon and Bryce Lyon (Amsterdam: North-Holland, 1976); F. M. Powicke, "Henri Pirenne," *English Historical Review* 51 (Jan. 1936): 79–89; James L. Cate, "Henri Pirenne, 1862–1935," in *Some 20th Century Historians*, ed. S. William Halperin (Chicago: University of Chicago Press, 1961), pp. 1–29; Bryce Lyon, *Henri Pirenne: A Biographical and Intellectual Study* (Ghent: E. Story–Scientia, 1974), pp. 227–76.

encounter in Strasbourg in 1919 Pirenne's influence on Marc Bloch was immense. The portly, exuberant, vivacious *maître*, who was the inspiration for the *Annales*, possessed an extraordinary combination of erudition and analytical imagination, patriotism and cosmopolitanism, devotion to the past and present-mindedness. Moreover, he was a champion of comparative history, which he considered the indispensable antidote to the catastrophe that had overwhelmed the profession during the Great War.[6]

In April 1923 Pirenne revived the International Congress of Historical Sciences and presided over its fifth convocation in Brussels. The organization dated back to 1 September 1898, when a group of diplomatic historians had summoned the first international history congress at The Hague, which was briefly reconvened in Paris during the exposition of 1900. Subsequently transformed into a broader, more universal institution with regular five-year meetings, the ICHS had assembled over a thousand historians in Rome (1903), Berlin (1908), and London (1913). The meetings consisted of plenary sessions and sections devoted to conventional time periods (ancient, medieval, modern) and subject matters (religious, legal, economic history).[7] These gatherings, which provided professional historians with the opportunity to meet their foreign colleagues face-to-face, also became prestige occasions for the host government and tended to underscore national rivalries. This was especially true among the medievalists, where German

---

6 "La convulsion par laquelle vient de passer le monde a été pour les historiens ce qu'un cataclysme cosmique serait pour un géologue." Henri Pirenne, presidential address, "De la méthode comparative en histoire," in Guillaume Des Marez and François Ganshof, eds., *Compte-rendu du Ve congrès international des sciences historiques: Bruxelles, 1923* (Brussels, 1923; Liechtenstein: Kraus Reprint, 1972), p. 23. Cf. Bryce Lyon, "Henri Pirenne and the Origins of *Annales* History," *Annals of Scholarship* 1 (1980): 69–84.

7 Lyon, *Pirenne*, pp. 198–99; for the early history of ICHS, see *The Nation* 67 (29 Sept. 1898): 238; 76 (7 May 1903): 371–72; *AHR* 8 (July 1903): 809–12; 14 (Oct. 1908): 1–8; 18 (July 1913): 679–91; Karl Dietrich Erdmann, *Die Ökumene der Historiker: Geschichte der Internationalen Historikerkongresse und des Comité International des Sciences Historiques* (Göttingen: Vandenhoeck and Ruprecht, 1987), pp. 13–96. It is not clear why Pirenne ignored the original Hague meeting and numbered Brussels the "fifth" (*Compte-rendu Ve congrès*, pp. 18, 22). The congress scheduled for April 1917 in St. Petersburg had, of course, not met.

scholarship was dominant despite Pirenne's efforts to promote the broader perspective of economic and social history.

After a lapse of ten years, the first postwar historical congress attempted to revive the spirit and structure of internationalism among historians. But much had changed. Less sumptuous than its predecessors – subsidized by King Albert, the Belgian government, and the Fondation Universitaire – the congress was held in a building lately used as a German field hospital. Many of the delegates had recently fought for the Allied cause. And, in spite of his universalist principles and denunciation of postwar rancor (*"l'esprit d'après-guerre"*), Pirenne personally blocked the admission of the leading German scholars. Nor were any delegates invited from Soviet Russia. Like the new League of Nations, the historians at Brussels were unready to welcome their former enemies or ideological opponents.[8]

Marc Bloch made his international debut at the Brussels congress of 1923. Part of a large delegation from the University of Strasbourg, he presented the fruits of his current studies of sacred royalty and feudalism to an audience of senior medievalists. Not surprisingly, he also engaged in a spirited debate over historical themes and methodology, denouncing his colleagues' preoccupation with "origins" and proposing that when sources were unavailable to uncover the meaning of a term, such as "fief," the wise historian would work backward from the classic period of feudalism as far as he or she was able to go.[9] This debut marked Bloch's transformation from the Parisian researcher to the Strasbourg savant.

Strasbourg, with its central Rhenish location, active faculty, and good library, was a promising workplace; but Bloch also traveled extensively to conduct research, attend conferences, and deliver

---

8 It was over Pirenne's tenacious opposition that the Austrian historians Karl Brandi and Alfons Dopsch were eventually named to the governing council of the International Committee of Historical Sciences he helped to found in Geneva in 1926. *Compte-rendu Ve congrès*, p. 20; Powicke, "Henri Pirenne," p. 87; Lyon, *Pirenne*, pp. 293–94.

9 "Une contamination de croyances: Les rois de France, guérisseurs d'écrouelles, saint Marcoul et les septièmes fils" and esp. "Qu'est-ce qu'un fief?" *Compte-rendu Ve congrès*, pp. 315–16, 102–4; notes on the latter presentation in AN, AB XIX 3812.

lectures. Bloch loved to travel. He avidly searched for his texts and materials at first hand. He also enjoyed meeting other scholars, and conducted an extensive correspondence with historians, librarians, and archivists. Because he was in a provincial university, Bloch early realized the importance of developing foreign contacts and forging cooperative relationships with other historians.

There were several distinctive characteristics in Marc Bloch's work. Unlike some of his contemporaries, he rejected vulgar present-mindedness, refusing to "insert Clovis or Charlemagne into the quarrels of contemporary Europe" or to emulate the pedants who used their parchments to decide the fate of whole peoples.[10] He was opposed to the system builders Oswald Spengler and H. G. Wells and also to Marxism's all-encompassing explanations. He rejected all forms of determinism, all grand and seductive theories: "Counterbalancing the complexity of nature is the complexity of human emotions and human reason."[11] Bloch continued to respect the work of Durkheim and paid tribute to his successors for re-founding the *Année Sociologique*. But as a historian, though not a chronicler, he insisted on the dimension of change over time, stressing subtle mutations and unpredictable lag as well as the surface ruptures that fascinated his contemporaries.[12] Finally, he maintained that regardless of the topic the historian's obligation was to understand his subjects, not judge them.[13] The honest craftsman remained above the immediate, the prosaic, and the partisan aspects of everyday life.

Having experienced the war's distortions of human consciousness and perceptions, Bloch also understood the propensity to adopt artificial conceptions, "certain pseudo-necessities": how easily navigable rivers had become national boundaries and how the illusorily

10 *RSH* 31 (1920): 152.
11 Review of Lucien Febvre, *La terre et l'évolution humaine: Introduction géographique à l'histoire* (Paris, 1922) in *RH* 145 (1924): 237; also lecture notes for course given in Strasbourg: "Les origines et la formation de l'état française et de la nation française," AN, AB XIX 3830.
12 Bibliographic note: "*L'Année Sociologique*, nouvelle série, t. 1 (1923–1924)," *RH*, 155 (1927): 176.
13 "Quelques contributions à l'histoire religieuse du Moyen Age," *RSH* 46 (1928): 160.

precise, abstract quality of maps had often influenced the political decisions of statesmen; how the concept of race had "haunted the thought of the nineteenth century"; and how abstract notions of gold, or its absence, distorted the historical reality of commercial exchange. In his research as in his teaching Bloch set himself up as a disciplinarian against the historian's instinctive "laziness" that made him prefer plausible abstractions over the arduous task of tracing a particular phenomenon back to its own unique source.[14]

Though he strove for a broader conception of history, Bloch's sensibility, like Pirenne's, was rooted in the *patrie*, in France and its people, as the basis of his investigations, the subject of all comparison. Immediately after the war, much of Bloch's teaching, writing, and reviewing was centered on the evolution of the French monarchy, the unification of the French nation, and the development of its civilization. He studied the old notables – Voltaire, Michelet, Guizot, Fustel, and Lavisse – and read the works of his contemporaries.[15] Following the completion of his thesis, *Rois et serfs*, he embarked on the immense research in France and in England for his first major monograph, *Les rois thaumaturges*.[16]

Conceived before the Great War and marked by the war's passions and outcome, *Les rois thaumaturges* was his "contribution to the political history of Europe in the widest and truest sense of the word."[17] To achieve this breadth, Bloch incorporated insights from medicine, psychology, and anthropology into his investigation of the origins, development, and durability of the gigantic *fausse nouvelle*, the belief in the royal miracle of the healing of scrofula that survived for more than eight centuries. But he resisted the vogue of confusing medieval European monarchs with either Poly-

14 See, e.g., *RH*, 145 (1924): 238–39.
15 See research notes in AN, AB XIX 3796, 3845, and esp. 3830, as well as Marc Bloch, "M. Flach et les origines de l'ancienne France," *RSH* 31 (1920): 150–52; review of Fritz Kern, *Gottesgnadentum und Widerstandsrecht im früheren Mittelalter: Zur Entwicklungsgeschichte der Monarchie* (Leipzig, 1914) in *RH* 138 (1921): 247–53.
16 The first edition appeared in the series Publications de la Faculté des Lettres de l'Université de Strasbourg, fasc. 19 (Strasbourg, 1924); most important research notes in AN, AB 3850, 3851.
17 *RT*, p. 21; also Jacques Le Goff, "Préface," *RT*, pp. i–xxxviii; Carlo Ginzburg, "Prefazione," *I re taumaturghi* (Turin: Einaudi, 1973), pp. xi–xix.

nesian or African magician-kings or with biblical or Roman rulers. He emphasized the unique characteristics of time and place that had produced the royal miracle in France and in England. He established the political motivations that lay behind the practice of touching for scrofula, a tuberculous inflammation of the neck glands. In France around the year 1000 Robert the Pious, the second Capetian king, exercised this power as a means of establishing the legitimacy and hereditary right of his still-precarious dynasty by endowing it with a supernatural character. A century later, according to Bloch, Henry I or Henry II adopted the practice as a means of claiming royal sanctity against the challenge of the Gregorian reformers in the English church.

Bloch demonstrated how popular reverence for the legitimate prince and the specifically Christian conception of the consecrated ruler coalesced in the robust legends of the wonder-working kings. In France and England, and nowhere else in Europe, royal power was manifested not only in military, legal, and institutional forms but also in this popular mystique, which helped princes compete with the church in their appeal to mass loyalty. Armed with their healing gifts and bolstered by their loyal officials, the French and English monarchs became quasi-priestly figures. Bloch, demonstrating an impressive mastery of conventional and novel sources, including iconographic evidence and royal roll books and exchequer account books documenting the numbers of people touched, traced the royal cures from the early Middle Ages through the age of religious wars, the development of absolutism, and the subsequent decline of credulity in the ritual and in divine-right monarchy in eighteenth-century England and nineteenth-century France.[18]

Les rois thaumaturges reinforced the prevailing proposition that royalty — its ambitions and vicissitudes — had dominated European history since earliest times.[19] Labeled a "curious subject" by his

18 In England the last touch was by Queen Anne on 27 April 1714; in France it was practiced by Charles X at Rheims on 31 May 1825, less than one hundred years before *Les rois thaumaturges* was written.
19 *RT*, pp. 18–19. Cf. Hans Schreuer, "Das deutsche Königtum: Eine germanistische Studie," *Schmollers Jahrbuch für Gesetzgebung, Verwaltung und Volkswissenschaft im Deutschen Reich* 42 (1918): 53–76; Louis Rougier, review of *Les rois thaumaturges* in *RSH* 39 (1925): 95–106.

republican father and his "gros enfant" by Bloch, the work unleashed his scholarly and creative energy and established his international reputation. *Les rois thaumaturges* contained a considerable amount of detail about the miracle. But Bloch's main question was very specific: how power had been acquired, used, and eventually lost.[20]

Because of Bloch's use of the Durkheimian term "collective consciousness" and his search for evidence in a wide variety of documents, *Les rois thaumaturges* has also been termed a forerunner of what is imprecisely termed the history of *mentalités*.[21] This was not a new interest for Bloch but was closely tied to his sensitivity to popular mental climates during the Dreyfus Affair and World War I and its aftermath. At Strasbourg his colleagues Maurice Halbwachs, Charles Blondel, Lucien Febvre, Gabriel Le Bras, and Georges Lefebvre were similarly exploring the terrain of cultural history and collective ideas.[22]

In his studies of various popularly held distortions and untruths Bloch simultaneously employed two techniques of demystification and analysis: applying critical method to the production and dissemination of *fausses nouvelles*, and also using these "collective representations" to penetrate the deeper realities of the epoch in which they were created and spread. Rejecting the premises of standard intellectual and political history – their artificial abstractions, their tendency toward anachronism, and especially their denial of psychological and material realities – Bloch's pioneering work in the history of *mentalités* introduced the possibility of linking

---

20 Almost three-fourths of the three-part work of 414 pages (pp. 87–405) is in chapter II with its Balzacean title "Grandeur et vicissitudes des royautés thaumaturgiques."

21 Jacques Revel, "Mentalités," in *Dictionnaire des sciences historiques*, ed. André Burguière (Paris: Presses Universitaires de France, 1986), pp. 450–56; Michel Vovelle, *Idéologies et mentalités* (Paris: Maspéro, 1982); also Burguière, "La notion de mentalité chez Marc Bloch et Lucien Febvre: Deux conceptions, deux filiations," *Revue de Synthèse* 3d ser., no. 111 (July 1983): 333–48; P. L. Orsi, "La storia delle mentalità in Bloch e Febvre," *Rivista di Storia Contemporanea* 14 (1983): 370–85.

22 *RT*, p. XL.

these two planes of research and reuniting the rational and emotional content of human reality.[23]

Bloch had plunged earlier into this problem in the article entitled "Réflexions d'un historien sur les fausses nouvelles de la guerre."[24] There he had lauded the young science of the "psychology of testimony" developed by criminologists, psychologists, and folklorists, whose pioneering laboratory experiments in perception and memory had advanced the understanding of the origins of falsification. He nonetheless maintained that to transcend the preoccupation with individual testimony and address the richer, more complex issue – how *fausses nouvelles* were disseminated – required a historian capable of probing not only the collective consciousness but also the process by which specific errors established themselves in a favorable terrain: how human prejudices, hates, fears, and other strong emotions transformed "a faulty perception into a legend."[25]

Bloch's "Réflexions" actually consisted of a review of four recent studies of rumors during the Great War and the tale of the notorious reservist from Brème. Bloch concluded that a *fausse nouvelle* always originated in "preexisting collective representations." Only its appearance was accidental. Indeed, it was the mirror in which the collective consciousness revealed itself. He exhorted his fellow historians to devote themselves to gathering similar evidence – it

---

23 Cf. Ginsburg, "Prefazione"; Revel, "Mentalités," pp. 450–51.
   For the development of Bloch's conceptions of this subject, see: Réunions du samedi, Strasbourg, 2 Dec. 1922, 20 Jan., 17 Mar., 24 Nov. 1923, 19 Jan. 1924, in *Bulletin de la Faculté des Lettres de l'Université de Strasbourg*, BNUS; also Bloch's reviews of M. Halbwachs, *Les cadres sociaux de la mémoire* in *RSH* 40 (1925): 73–83; E. Tonnelat, *La chanson des Niebelungen* in *RH* 151 (1926): 256–59; F. Schneider, *Rom und Romgedanke im Mittelalter: Die geistigen Grundlagen der Renaissance* in *RSH* 44 (1927): 168; J. Huizinga, *Herbst des Mittelalters: Studien über Lebens- und Geistesformen des 14. and 15. Jahrhunderts in Frankreich und in den Niederlanden* in *Bulletin de la Faculté des Lettres de l'Université de Strasbourg* 7 (1928–29): 33–35; Charles Blondel, *Introduction à la psychologie collective* in *RH* 160 (1929): 398–99; Maurice Halbwachs, *Les causes du suicide* in *AHES* 3 (1931): 590–92; Georges Lefebvre, *La grande peur de 1789* in *AHES* 5 (1933): 301–4.
24 *RSH* 33 (1921): 41–57; outline in AN, AB XIX 3845.
25 "Réflexions," p. 44.

was politically important, fast disappearing or forgotten, and should not be left to untrained or unscrupulous investigators.[26]

Bloch himself was unprepared to follow the whole of this assignment. Instead of analyzing the rumor-producing culture formed by the collective consciousness, he stayed with the first part, investigating errant witnesses, inadequate interpreters of texts, and, especially, misguided historians. He was intrigued by the deformed versions of the lives of saints and kings, which had been essential elements of the faith and culture of the Middle Ages. In Bloch's time there was a revival of popular and scholarly interest in these lives, which continued to be a fertile source of *fausses nouvelles*. For example, he unearthed the fortuitous political circumstances that had transformed the relatively unpopular monkish fourth-century bishop of Tours into the nationally beloved Saint Martin. But his main inquiry was devoted to analyzing contradictions in the sources, guesses and errors by the interpreters, and the presumably permanent gaps in our knowledge of an obscure though celebrated life. Similarly, in addition to examining the political background of the twelfth-century canonization of Edward the Confessor, he dwelt mainly and in considerable detail on the dating and accuracy of the sources relating the character, visions, and miracles of the last Anglo-Saxon monarch. He investigated the equestrian statue on the west facade of the cathedral at Senlis, traditionally identified as Philip VI, and discovered that the original subject, the Roman emperor Constantine, had in the sixteenth century for political or religious expediency been "reidentified" as the Valois king. Moreover, "Constantine," who was almost completely mutilated during the French Revolution, had undoubtedly been modeled on the philosopher Marcus Aurelius, a neat example of the process by which pagan iconography had been extensively absorbed by popular medieval culture. Finally, Bloch analyzed two dramatic medieval tales from England and France of King Solomon's punishment in the afterlife and the delay of his entrance into Paradise. Mustering vast amounts of material from centuries of Jewish, Muslim, Catholic, and Protestant theology, the folklore of the Latin and Slavic world,

26 Ibid. pp. 56–57.

and a host of iconographic examples, he concluded that these two odd myths of the suffering of David's profligate son were produced in a specific political or religious atmosphere created by a heightened concern with penitence.[27]

Relying on a mixture of texts and secondary sources and obviously relishing the hunt for confusion and contradiction as well as for confirmation, Bloch was deeply cautious about straying too far from his evidence and drawing sweeping conclusions about whole groups or societies. He appeared to enjoy his forays into areas charged with scholarly combat, not untainted with ideology and national rivalries.[28] For Bloch there was considerable distance, but not an unbridgeable gap, between a "modern" mentality, based on skepticism, criticism of evidence, and the ability to recognize contradictions, and the so-called primitive consciousness that clung to miracles and accepted the arbitrary and the supernatural as essential elements of existence. To be sure, human freedom depended on the expansion of reason.[29] As a historian he acknowledged both the Voltairean and the romantic interpretation of human phenomena:

> If an institution marked out for particular ends chosen by an individual will is to take its hold upon an entire nation, it must also be borne along by the deeper currents of the collective consciousness. The reverse is perhaps also true: For a rather vague belief to become crystallized in a regular rite, it is of some importance that clearly expressed personal wills should help it to take shape.[30]

Reviewers credited Bloch's intelligence and erudition and marveled at his energetic gathering of data; but some questioned his inter-

---

27 "Saint Martin de Tours: A propos d'une polémique," *Revue d'Histoire et de Littérature Religieuse* 7 (1921): 44–57; "La merveilleuse aventure de saint Martin," *L'Impartial Français* (26 Apr. 1927): 16; "La vie de saint Edouard le Confesseur, par Osbert de Clare, avec Introduction sur Osbert et les premières vies de saint Edouard," *Analecta Bollandiana* 41 (1923): 5–31; "Les vicissitudes d'une statue équestre: Philippe de Valois, Constantin, ou Marc-Aurèle?" *Revue Archéologique* 19 (1924): 132–36; "La vie d'outre-tombe du roi Salomon," *Revue Belge de Philologie et d'Histoire* 4 (1925): 349–77.

28 See, e.g., his "L'origine et la date de capitulaire de Villis," *RH* 143 (1923): 40–56.

29 See Bloch's interesting review of Guy de Tervarent, *La légende de sainte Ursule* in *RH* 171 (1933): 626–28.

30 *RT*, pp. 85–86.

pretations, attacked his skepticism, or challenged his singular preoccupation with sources.[31] When one critic asked bluntly whether Bloch understood "the spirit of the people of the Middle Ages," he refused to retreat. Though admitting a few errors and omissions, he defended the core of his research.[32] To the extent that he treated the structure of ideas and dealt skillfully with the psychological as well as political factors, Bloch can certainly be identified as an early contributor to the history of mentalities. Nevertheless, by the mid 1920s, while retaining an active interest in royalty, ritual, iconography, and the links between religion, social cohesion, and political power, Bloch sought new terrain. Perhaps the approach had revealed its limits, perhaps the reception was too cool, possibly he lacked sufficient material in Strasbourg to produce another *Rois thaumaturges*, and maybe he preferred the more concrete subjects to which he was beginning to turn.[33]

As a medievalist, Bloch found his particular nemesis in Simiand's "idol of origins": the legacy from nineteenth-century historians of pursuing politically charged investigations to serve national ends, leading to "discoveries" that certain races or tribes had "been there first." He adopted a middle position between those who believed in a distinct break between the world of the Roman Empire and that of the barbarian states which had destroyed and succeeded it, and those who stressed elements of continuity between Latin and Germanic civilization. He was similarly both attracted to and critical of

31 See, e.g., the reviews of *Les rois thaumaturges* by J. de Croy in *Revue des Questions Historiques* 7 (1925): 429–34; F. L. Ganshof in *Revue Belge de Philologie et d'Histoire* 5 (1926): 611–15; E. F. Jacob in *English Historical Review* 40, no. 158 (Apr. 1925): 267–70; and Lynn Thorndike in *AHR* 30 (1925): 584–85. Also H. Thurstin, "Critical commentary on the 'Biographer' of St. Edward the Confessor," *The Month* 141 (1923): 448–51; R. W. Southern, "The First Life of Edward the Confessor," *English Historical Review* 232 (Oct. 1943): 385–400; G. H. Gerould, review of "La vie d'outre-tombe du roi Salomon," *Speculum* 1 (1926): 243.

32 Review by R. Fawtier in *Le Moyen Age* 26 (May 1926): 238–44; Bloch's response, "La popularité de toucher des écrouelles," in 28 (1927): 34–41.

33 Le Goff, "Préface," pp. xxix–xxxii; H. Stuart Hughes, *The Obstructed Path: French Social Thought in the Years of Desperation* (New York: Harper and Row, 1966), pp. 34–37. Bloch's papers reveal a continuing interest in "the sacred"; see AN, AB XIX 3845.

Pirenne's thesis that Islamic expansion, "closing" the Mediterranean, had produced the essential characteristics of medieval Europe.[34] In studying medieval England he recognized that certain Victorian scholars and their successors had either exaggerated or blurred the distinctions between Anglo-Saxon and Norman political culture. They had also had a tendency to project their own ideological predilections onto the struggle between twelfth-century kings and barons or, at the other extreme, to ignore totally the political orientation of medieval actors.[35] He was especially alert to nationalist tendencies among German historians, particularly in their studies of the medieval emperors; to Bloch the "imperial mission" and the general trend of German thought since 1250 revealed "a fundamental will to power." He credited his neighbors' accomplishments in legal theory and their studies of population movements (*Siedlungskunde*), but — emphasizing that there had been little break with Wilhelmian historiography — he cautioned against their propensity to impose abstract systems and their indifference to comparison.[36]

Bloch was drawn into the discussion of the nature of European feudalism, a term inherited from eighteenth-century legalists that

34 Bloch, "La société du Haut Moyen Age at ses origines," *Journal des Savants* (1926): 403–20; "Observations sur la conquête de la Gaule romaine par les rois francs," *RH* 154 (1927): 161–78; reviews of E. Patzelt, *Die Karolingische Renaissance: Beiträge zur Geschichte der Kultur des frühen Mittelalters* in *RSH* 45 (1928): 148–49, and H. Pirenne, *Les villes du Moyen Age* in *Revue Critique d'Histoire et de Littérature* (1928): 203–6.

35 See, e.g., reviews of the French edition of vol. III of William Stubbs, *Histoire constitutionnelle de l'Angleterre*, of William A. Morris, *The Medieval English Sheriff to 1300*, of F. M. Powicke, *Stephen Langton* in *Le Moyen Age* 29 (1928): 72–76, 76–78, 341–42.

36 "L'empire et l'idée d'empire sous les Hohenstaufen," a Strasbourg course in 1927–28 for students preparing for the *agrégation* in German, published in *Revue des Cours et Conférences* 60 (1929): 481–94, 577–89, 759–68; also reviews of V. Ernst, *Die Entstehung des deutschen Grundeigentums* in *Revue Critique d'Histoire et de Littérature* (1927): 325–26; H. Brunner, *Deutsche Rechtsgeschichte*, II, ibid. (1928): 362. Also "Bulletin historique: Histoire d'Allemagne. Moyen Age" [review essay], *RH* 158 (1928): 108–58. Pirenne to Bloch (2 Nov. 1932, EBC) essentially concurred with Bloch's approach; see also Oscar J. Hammen, "German Historians and the Advent of the National Socialist State," *Journal of Modern History* 13 (1941): 161–88.

since the mid nineteenth century had dominated the study of the Middle Ages.[37] He distanced himself from both extremes: from those positing a unique and uniform feudal system between the tenth and thirteenth centuries and those who preferred to analyze particular aspects without striving for a more general synthesis. Bloch avoided the "ethnic dilemma" – whether feudalism was of Roman or Germanic origins – by insisting that it represented a "medley" of Celtic, Roman, and Germanic elements, that it "constituted an encounter and fusion of civilizations existing at very unequal stages of civilization."

He did venture to characterize the feudal system: In the absence of a strong state able to provide material and physical security, it was a regime based on personal and reciprocal ties of dependence; hierarchic and contractual in character, it was marked everywhere by "constraints, violence, and abuses." It varied throughout Europe (and there were places where it never took root, or was artificially planted), existed in more or less similar forms in other parts of the world, and underwent decline with the rise of towns, a money economy, and the establishment of national monarchies, leaving a powerful historical legacy in the notion of the political contract that counterbalanced and ultimately triumphed over the competing tradition of royal sanctity.[38]

Though not a pioneer in the "comparative method," which he adopted from Pirenne and also from the linguist Meillet, Bloch was an early and ardent practitioner who deemed it an "excellent tool" for the future of his profession.[39] There were various ways to

37 Bloch to Carl Stephenson, 3 Jan. 1928, Carl Stephenson papers, Cornell University, Ithaca, N.Y. Also Elizabeth A. R. Brown, "The Tyranny of a Construct: Feudalism and Historians of Medieval Europe," *AHR* 79 (Oct. 1974): 1063–88.

38 "Feudalism: European" in *Encyclopedia of the Social Sciences* VI (1931), pp. 203–10; also "Féodalité, vassalité, seigneurie: A propos de quelques travaux récents," *AHES* 3 (1931): 246–60.

39 "Mon titre? Le même toujours: 'Histoire comparée des sociétés européennes.'" Marc Bloch to Etienne Gilson, 28 Dec. 1933, archives of the Pontifical Institute of Medieval Studies, Toronto. Cf. Bloch, "Comparaison," *Bulletin du Centre International de Synthèse – Section de Synthèse Historique* 9 (June 1930): 31–39.

compare: One could search for universal phenomena in cultures and societies widely separated by either time or space, seeking similarities and continuities but also tending toward rather limited, narrow conclusions; or one could proceed historically, conducting a parallel study of neighboring or contemporaneous societies, a more limited approach that Bloch felt promised "richer results."[40] What better way to understand the enclosure movement in England than by searching for similar (though not identical) developments on the Continent, and vice versa? How better to comprehend the ostensible originality of the Carolingian state than by looking not at its predecessor, the Merovingian state, but by searching for possible historical links across the Pyrenees among the Visigoths? How better to grasp the origins of representative institutions in medieval Europe than to spread a broad compass around the Continent instead of concentrating on one specific example? Through skilled use of comparison, the historian could establish what was truly original and different: for example, how class and legal status differed in medieval England, France, and Germany (where "from the thirteenth century onwards the hierarchical idea developed with unparalleled vigor"). There indeed were problems: In the attempt to establish connections, one had to try out a variety of explanations with care and good judgment, but never discard the basic premise that comparison was necessary to free the researcher from artificial boundaries and anachronism. How to apply this prescription? Bloch invited scholars to formulate questionnaires that could be applied across regions and nations, to engage in collaborative works, and, above all, in whatever specialized work they produced "to base their plan, the treatment of the problems they raise, even the terms they use, on the knowledge gleaned from work carried out in other countries."[41]

Bloch himself applied the comparative method to a somewhat

---

40 "Pour une histoire comparée des sociétés européennes," *RSH* 46 (1928): 15–18.
41 Ibid., pp. 18–50. On Bloch's method, see William H. Sewell, Jr., "Marc Bloch and the Logic of Comparative History," *History and Theory* 6 (1967): 208–28; and the discussion by Allette Olin Hill and Boyd H. Hill, Jr., William H. Sewell, Jr., and Sylvia Thrupp in *AHR* 85, no. 4 (Oct. 1980): 828–57.

narrow case in his examination of the administrative classes of France and Germany. He compared the *sergent* with the *Dienstmann*. Both, owing to their skills and to the amorphous social situation of the tenth century, rose to occupy a middle position between the unfree and the powerful. Railing against his German colleagues for applying arbitrary, even anachronistic, classifications and chiding a Belgian historian for insufficient precision in his "verbal analysis," Bloch remarked on the similarity and contrasts in the evolution of this small group. Where in France many former serfs were able to attain freedom, on the other side of the Rhine the idea of class and the reality of class stratification remained more intractable and enduring.[42]

The duality between servitude and freedom was a recurring subject in Marc Bloch's work. Having inherited this problem from his staunchly republican father and, as a young researcher, having pored over numerous documents pertaining to emancipation, he returned to this theme in several of his studies.[43] As usual, he proceeded in a well-defined area, stressing technical questions, displaying his command of the sources and of linguistic development and variations. What were the origins of the popular if imprecise term *serf de la glèbe* (literally "serf of the earth")? How between the ninth and eleventh century in Europe did a group known as *culverts* − a word used to designate former slaves, persons neither fully emancipated nor serfs − constitute not only a distinct class

---

42 "Un problème d'histoire comparée: La ministérialité en France et en Allemagne," *Revue Historique de Droit Français et Etranger* ser. 4, 7 (Jan.−Mar. 1928): 46−91; also review of F. L. Ganshof, *Etude sur les ministériales en Flandre et en Lotharingie* in *Revue Critique d'Histoire et de Littérature* (1928): 207.

43 "Serf de la glèbe: Histoire d'une expression toute faite," *RH* 136 (1921): 222−42; "Les transformations du servage: A propos de deux documents du XIIIe siècle relatifs à la région parisienne," *Mélanges d'histoire du Moyen Age offerts à Ferdinand Lot* (Paris: E. Champion, 1925), pp. 55−74; "Collibertus ou Colibertus," *Revue de Linguistique Romane* 2 (1926): 15−24; "Servus Glebae," *Revue des Etudes Anciennes* 26 (1926): 352−58; "Les 'colliberti': Etude sur la formation de la classe servile," *RH* 157 (1928): 1−48, 225−63; and esp. "Liberté et servitude personnelles au Moyen Age, particulièrement en France: Contribution à une étude des classes," *Anuario de Historia del Derecho Español* 10 (1933): 19−115, repr. in *MH* I. pp. 286−355.

and social institution but also a mirror of the incongruities of medieval law and attitudes? What were the main differences between medieval serfdom and slavery, which survived the ruin of the ancient world and persisted for a long time on the borders of medieval Christian Europe? What human, economic, and accidental factors caused slavery and serfdom to end?

In his examinations of the condition of those without freedom, Bloch patiently investigated the definitions and distinctions established by medieval law and practice, all the minute, occasionally contradictory, frequently humiliating legal and customary gradations and restrictions, and the costly, cumbersome, sometimes coercive process of gaining freedom. He included the important role of the church in the feudal order alongside kings and the lay seigneury.[44] He stressed the difference between the politically anarchic ninth century, with its still-fluid conceptions of class and feudal obligations, and the twelfth, when with the revival of Roman law more intense attention was paid to status, obligations, and hierarchy. He concentrated mainly on France, indeed on northern France around Paris, though freely making contrasts with the south and with Spain, Italy, and Germany. Bloch's peasants were shadowy actors, who appear fleetingly in times of dispute and disruption; his seigneurs, lay and clerical, were also largely one-dimensional figures. What stands out in his didactic, sophisticated discussions, sprinkled with legal, linguistic, and literary examples, is a strong, modern voice mixing sympathy, irony, and outrage at the widespread exploitation and violence of medieval Europe. For example:

Like all feudal institutions, serfdom developed in a rough atmosphere replete with daily abuses of the law. . . . To give a too-well-ordered image of servile status summed up in a few articles in a code would mean that the historian had failed to communicate all the brutality and arbitrariness permitted in practice when one man had power over another.[45]

Bloch also maintained that then, as now, people are never "absolutely free." Language obscures the welter of claims on an individual, but its imprecision (either accidental or deliberate) was not an impedi-

44 See AN, AB XIX 3805: Bloch's notes on *servage*.
45 "Liberté et servitude personnelles," *MH*, I. p. 317.

ment to grasping the most essential distinctions as well as those forces tending to promote the human struggle for freedom.[46]

Despite his title at Strasbourg as well as the venerable divisions of history maintained at national and international conferences, Bloch refused to confine himself to the medieval arena. He sought themes and subjects well beyond its range. From his youth he was attracted to economic history for what he considered its concrete and specific qualities, affording the opportunity to gather and interpret statistical evidence.[47] Here he saw the possibility of working both with the unique and the general, combining politics, society, and material culture, breaking out of specific time periods, and also striving to resist the tendency toward "something mechanical, and too little human."[48]

Bloch had a passionate interest in the history of money, the instrument and measure of exchange which for him constituted a sensitive and permanent factor in economic life.[49] He distanced himself from then fashionable economic theories, preferring solid research over mechanistic interpretations of economic phenomena. Similarly he rejected the "historicizing straitjacket" of the positivist school: For him, understanding the beginnings of capitalism de-

---

46 In a rare personal example Bloch observed: "I consider myself to be a free man, but as a university professor, while I am 'free' for example vis-à-vis the state to use my vacation as I please, I am not free to fail in my teaching during the school year. When I have to interrupt that activity I must ask the competent authority to 'free' me from it." *MH*, I. p. 328.

47 See his reviews of W. T. Layton, *An Introduction to the Study of Prices* (London, 1912), and A. Walther, *Geldwert in der Geschichte* (Stuttgart, 1912) in *RSH* 25 (1912): 105–7, 244.

48 See esp. his review of J. H. Clapham, *An Economic History of Modern Britain: The Early Railway Age, 1820–1850* (Cambridge, 1926) in *RSH* 44 (1927): 157–59. Also Bloch to André Siegfried, 4 May 1931, Siegfried papers, Fondation Nationale des Sciences Politiques, Paris.

49 Bloch to Luigi Einaudi, 10 Oct. 1936, Fondazione Luigi Einaudi, Turin; Bloch, "Classification et choix des faits en histoire économique: Réflexions de méthode à propos de quelques ouvrages récents," *AHES* I (1929): 256–57, and "Une analyse de la vie économique," *RSH* 51 (1931): 254. Also John Day, "The History of Money in the Writings of Marc Bloch," in *Problems of Medieval Coinage in the Iberian Area* II, ed. Mário Gomes Marques and M. Crusafont I Sabater (Aviles, 1986): 15–27.

pended upon "a sufficiently precise knowledge of that institution in its *present state of continuous change*."[50] Keenly aware of Europe's economic dislocations after World War I and the crises preceding and following the crash of 1929, Bloch insisted on a scrupulous linkage between present and past that recognized continuity – similarities as well as differences – but also avoided the temptation of imposing on the past "opinions pillaged from imperfect descriptions of the present."[51]

Contrary to the tenets of classical economics, Bloch believed that an exchange economy lacked a self-regulatory mechanism capable of adjusting monetary supply to the state of trade. Simple balance-of-trade theory was incapable of explaining the very complex series of economic and political developments that had led, for example, to the abandonment of gold coins in Carolingian times. The prolonged monetary famine of the late Middle Ages ended only when overseas discoveries and conquest replenished Europe's treasuries. It recurred after 1620 because of the decline of metallic imports from the New World, and again receded in the century and a half before World War I with the discovery of new mines and especially with the development of modern banking systems in the West.[52] Bloch delved into the history of prices and into the mutations of currency. He studied general trends while also recognizing the importance of fortuitous, nonrational elements in economic life. Moreover, the history of money provided a rich opportunity for comparison: The colonial economies of the modern world to some extent clarified the imperfectly monetized economy of medieval Europe.[53]

Most of Bloch's interests and themes converged in the subject of rural history, a subject he pursued throughout his life. He had

50 "Quelques recherches sur les opérations de crédit dans le monde contemporain," *AHES* 1 (1929): 445–46 (emphasis added); also "La gestion financière," *AHES* 2 (1930): 452.

51 "Culture historique et action économique: A propos de l'exemple américain," *AHES* 3 (1931): 1–4; also "Le salaire et les fluctuations économiques à longue période," *RH*, 173 (Jan.–June 1934): 1–31.

52 "Publications diverses sur l'histoire monétaire et bancaire contemporaine," *AHES* 1 (1929): 617; "Le problème de l'or au Moyen Age," *AHES* 5 (1933): 1–34.

53 In "Economie-nature ou économie-argent: Un pseudo-dilemme," *AHS* 1 (1939): 7–16.

developed an early interest in field systems and especially in how rural life had been revolutionized by the process of enclosures: how open fields that had been planted, rotated, and grazed collectively had been transformed into compact fenced, hedged, or otherwise demarcated individual holdings.[54] Here was the physical counterpart to the gaining of personal freedom – an evolutionary process spurred by the spirit of individual enterprise, complemented by technological and scientific innovations and by the need for intensive farming to increase food production for an expanding urban population. Bloch looked to England, where, beginning in the sixteenth century and intensifying in the seventeenth and eighteenth, the growing power of the gentry in parliament, the zeal of reforming bureaucrats, and the development of legal, banking, and local administrative systems accelerated the enclosure of common lands as a correlate to the island kingdom's industrial revolution. He also recognized that enclosure, denounced by the powerful as well as by the poor and dependent, did despite its long-term benefits immediately contribute to rural poverty.[55]

The field of rural history had been dominated by foreign giants: the Germans Georg Hanssen, Georg Friedrich Knapp, August Meitzen, and Robert Gradmann and the English Frederich Seebohm, Frederick William Maitland, Paul Vinogradoff, and Richard Henry Tawney. Except for Fustel de Coulanges and Henri Sée (whose work Bloch drew on, expanded, and corrected), the principal French writers, Jules Sion, Lucien Febvre, Georges Lefebvre, and Paul Raveau, all concentrated on regional studies based largely on seigneurial records. Bloch had an open terrain to explore. Armed with his skills in languages, law, sociology, and economics, his enthusiasm for maps, his long fascination with the French countryside and its physical contours, his interest in collective consciousness, and his zest for comparison, he plunged into the investigation of types of rural habitations, village communities, agricultural tools, and, above all, the forms of agrarian life.[56]

54 "Note sur deux ouvrages d'histoire et d'économie rurales," *RSH* 27 (1913): 162–67.
55 Ibid., p. 165.
56 Bryce Lyon, "Foreword," *French Rural History* (Berkeley and Los Angeles: University of California Press, 1970), pp. ix–xv.

France, divided by different systems, geographical features, and peoples, was an ideal laboratory. In 1928 Bloch applied for and received a generous government stipend that allowed him during the next five years to make annual research trips during his spring vacations to selected French provincial archives, to make tracings, copies, and photographs of land divisions.[57] A year later he issued a call to French scholars of local history to consult hitherto-neglected land-registry maps dating from the First Empire as well as those that had survived from the Ancien Régime. He also called on foreign historians to share their findings on their nations' rural development.[58] For the rest of his life Bloch devoted himself to the retrieval and analysis of plans, which for him held the key to land use and control over the rural countryside.[59]

Les caractères originaux de l'histoire rurale française, Bloch's brilliant though tentative work of synthesis, appeared in 1931. It was a revised version of the lectures he had delivered in Oslo two years earlier at the Institute for the Comparative Study of Civilizations; realizing the remaining gaps in his data, he published it reluctantly. *Les caractères* was a typical Bloch work, with seven distinct though related chapters. Following a discourse on method, he discussed the main stages in the occupation of the soil; field patterns; the feudal regime during the Middle Ages; landlords and serfs during the two centuries preceding the French Revolution; types of village life; the agricultural revolution; and patterns of continuity between the past and the present. Bloch's terse, vigorous prose set a new standard for the genre. Drawing on older theoretical works and utilizing regional

57 Application and correspondence in Henry Omont papers, BN, NAF 13080; also AN, AB XIX 3844, for his application, budget, and expenses. Bloch received 5,000 francs from the Ministry of Public Instruction and 2,000 from the Ministry of Agriculture..
58 "Les plans parcellaires en France," *AHES* 1 (1929): 60–70, 390–98; "Les plans parcellaires: L'avion au service de l'histoire agraire – en Angleterre," *AHES* 2 (1930): 557–58; "Une bonne nouvelle: L'enquête sur les plans cadastraux français," *AHES* 4 (1932): 370–71; "Préface" in Jean Regné, *Répertoire des plans cadastraux parcellaires de l'Ardèche* (Annonay: Décombe, 1933). Copies of letters to Tawney in England and Vaclav Černy in Czechoslovakia in AN, AB XIX 3844.
59 See "Les plans cadastraux de l'ancien régime," *MHS* 3 (1943): 55–70, along with research notes in AN, AB XIX 3843, 3844.

and local histories as well as studies of geography, law, linguistics, archaeology, and the rural economy, Bloch plunged back from his own time to the prehistoric past in attempting to depict the essential characteristics of French agrarian history. Instead of a traditional study of land and peasants drawn principally from feudal documents and dominated by Roman-Germanic controversies, narrow regionalism, lifeless abstractions, antiquarianism, anachronisms, or discontinuities, Bloch's lectures presented rural history as a vibrant human interaction with the soil.

What were the original characteristics of French rural history? After a brief excursion back to the prehistoric past and to the Celtic, Roman, and Germanic settlements, Bloch began with solid documentation that described the dramatic land-reclamation projects of the eleventh and twelfth centuries, which, in contrast to those taking place at nearly the same time in Central and Eastern Europe, were performed by an army of internal colonists seeking to reconquer and repeople their ancestral lands and habitations. Like his compatriots, Bloch stressed the continuity of French agrarian civilization, but he also emphasized its diversity. Bloch now divided France into three rural orders: the regime characteristic of northern Europe, of flat lands and long, parallel open fields, which used the wheeled plow and triennial rotation, entailing extensive communal laws and responsibilities; the regime of southern, Mediterranean Europe, of rugged, mountainous lands, irregular fields, the wheelless plow, and biannual crop rotation that involved less-developed communal habits; and the scattered regime of western and central France, of wooded, hilly land, poor soil, sparse settlement, and intermittent and intense cultivation with or without the plow, where there were enclosed fields and distinctive habits of individual autonomy. Striking a contrast to Meitzen's "racial" theories, Bloch insisted that these variations (what he characterized simply as "types of civilizations") were the result of a host of factors: the intermixture of climate, soil, technology, the economy, religion, habits of thought, and especially the human process of adaptation.[60]

60 These considerations were further developed in Bloch's presentation to some of France's leading historians, sociologists, and legal scholars: "Le problème des régimes agraires," *Bulletin de l'Institut Français de Sociologie* (1932) (Séance du 15 mars 1932): 45–92.

In his two densest chapters Bloch traced the transformations of rural authority. The landlord's withdrawal from actual control over the land in the twelfth century led to the decline of serfdom; but the inflation of the sixteenth century in some places resulted in the refeudalization of the countryside and more onerous claims on, and control over, the peasantry. The *manse*, France's most ancient rural organization, mysteriously disappeared between the ninth and eleventh centuries, possibly because of new royal tax policies or new seigneurial practices. Following a short period of stabilization, the emerging rural communities began struggling for independence but also witnessed growing class stratification from within. France under the Ancien Régime was characterized by its "timidity" in failing to end archaic communal practices and promote the consolidation of landholdings and enclosure.[61] Even after the Revolution, France lagged behind England and other parts of Europe in capitalist development of its agriculture and in rural productivity. Paradoxically, it was a nation that venerated individual property rights while maintaining some communal farming obligations. There remained until Bloch's time a remarkably diverse range of rural properties, from extremely large to tiny.

In *Les caractères originaux* Bloch painted with broad strokes. He described how ages of war, plague, and reduced planting and harvests, which had often produced improvements in the lives of rural people, had alternated with more tranquil and prosperous times that had imposed stiffer physical and legal restraints on the peasants. He demonstrated his dexterity with toponymy, his interest in monetary developments, and his zest for comparing France with the rest of Europe and the outside world. Few individuals inhabit his text, because his subject was France and how its people had etched their history on its soil.

The book drew a large positive response from Europe and abroad. Foreigners hailed this worthy successor to Fustel, and praised

---

61 In "La lutte pour l'individualisme agraire dans la France du XVIIIe siècle," *AHES* 2 (1930): 329–83, 511–43, 543–56, Bloch recounted the struggles of a handful of enlightened reformers against the forces of tradition; the bitter administrative infighting; the gradual gains; and the widespread regional, legal, and economic variations on the eve of the Revolution.

Bloch's objectivity, virtuosity, and provocative suggestions as well as the telling maps and illustrations of land use he had reproduced.[62] French reviewers agreed, although some carped at details (his imperfect knowledge of southern France; his omission of the development of rural industry; his ignoring the factor of rural demography) and at some of his premises, like the emphasis on monoculture and the absence of ecological considerations.[63] Bloch had been vague, perhaps deliberately, on the issue of communal behavior: Did this apply to planting alone, or could one actually generalize about the rural population's attitude toward mutual defense as well as political control? Was such behavior a cause or an effect of physical necessities, technological constraints, or external coercion? Bloch was ambivalent about the results of the process that promoted economic individualism. He was ambivalent in human as well as in economic terms about the benefits and costs of large versus small holdings. Writing at the height of Stalin's onslaught on the Russian peasant and against the backdrop of the prolonged and widespread suffering of postwar Western cultivators, Bloch was no doubt aware that despite elements of distinctiveness, French rural life reflected a pertinent and compelling human drama to which the historian could contribute a still tentative but instructive synthesis.

62 See reviews of HRF by F. M. Powicke in *History* 17 (1932): 157–59; J. H. Clapham in *English Historical Review* 47 (1932): 655–57; R. H. Tawney in *Economic History Review* 4 (1933): 230–33; Alfons Dopsch in *Zeitschrift für die gesamte Staatswissenschaft* 94 (1933): 115–21; Carl Brinkmann in *Zeitschrift der Savigny-Stiftung für Rechtsgeschichte* 52 (1932): 538–40; James Lea Cate in *Journal of Modern History* 5 (1933): 517–18; Charles H. Taylor in *AHR* 37 (1931–32): 736–37; Jan Rutkowski in *Kwartalnik Historyczny* 46 (1933): 155–57; John Frödin in *Ymer* (Stockholm) 52 (1932): 283–86; Svend Aakjaer in *Historisk Tidsskrift* (Copenhagen) ser. 10, 2 (1932): 146–47; Gino Luzzatto in *Nuova Rivista Storica* 17 (1934): 503–5.
63 See, e.g., reviews by Lucien Febvre in *RH* 169 (1932): 189–95; A. Demangeon in *Annales de Géographie* 41 (1935): 535–40; Albert Mathiez in *Annales Historiques de la Révolution Française* 9 (1932): 72–74; Robert Boutruche in *Journal des Savants* (1933): 200–9, 250–60; Henri Hauser in *Revue Critique d'Histoire et de Littérature* N.S. 98 (1933): 543–45; Philippe Arbos in *Revue de Géographie Alpine* 20 (1932): 609–14; and Jules Sion in *Revue de Synthèse* 3 (1933): 25–37.

7. *The* Annales

At the foundation of our enterprise is a sort of minor intellectual revolution.[1]

The development of the modern historical profession in the mid nineteenth century required a regular and timely means of communication, the scholarly journal, whose purpose was to disseminate information and knowledge, generate further research, and establish norms and standards of writing and criticism. Descendant of the seventeenth-century periodicals that had circulated the results of scientific experiments and of the eighteenth-century publications of various local and regional learned societies, the professional journal served to define and underline the discipline's autonomy and importance, establish a system of ranking and evaluation of its practitioners, connect the capital and its elite teaching and research institutions with the provinces, and address current social and political questions in a scholarly manner.

In 1859 the *Historische Zeitschrift*, the first scholarly historical periodical to survive to the present, was founded in Munich by Heinrich von Sybel.[2] Established according to the nineteenth-century Rankean creed of rigorous scientific scholarship, it soon stimulated the creation of French, English, and American counterparts: the *Revue Historique* (1876), the *English Historical Review* (1886), and the *American Historical Review* (1895). The apparatus of these publications was fairly similar, generally consisting of original contributions based on analysis of documentary sources (*articles au*

1 Marc Bloch to Lucien Febvre, 20 Sept. 1929, AN, MI 318 1.
2 Two journals had preceded the *Historische Zeitschrift*: the *Historisch-Politische Zeitschrift* (1832–34), founded by Leopold von Ranke; and the *Zeitschrift für Geschichtswissenschaft* (1844–48), edited by Adolf Schmidt. Margaret F. Stieg, *The Origin and Development of Scholarly Historical Periodicals* (University, Ala.: University of Alabama Press, 1986), pp. 4–6, 20–38.

fond), review essays of scholarly literature grouped by subject, abbreviated reviews of specific works, and bulletins of interest to the profession. The reigning national journal, each with its eminent editor and advisory board, concentrated largely on its nation's political and diplomatic history and reflected mainstream ideological and patriotic values.

During the two decades before World War I, which coincided with Marc Bloch's early training as a historian, there was a marked proliferation of scholarly journals in France and throughout Europe. These included specialized publications devoted to specific time periods, methodologies, or subsections of the disciplines: periodicals representing the new social sciences, like the influential *Année Sociologique*, a handful of reviews like the *Vierteljahrsschrift für Sozial- und Wirtschaftsgeschichte* that tried both to bridge national boundaries and to expand history's subject matter, and pioneering journals like the *Revue de Synthèse Historique* that promoted a broad, interdisciplinary approach. This infusion of new scholarly journals challenged the older publications, some of which made significant modifications in their format and coverage.[3]

Bloch and his future collaborator Lucien Febvre were thus able to observe their mentors, Vidal de la Blache, Durkheim, and Berr, as aspiring and combative editors: their fervent manifestos as well as their sometimes acrimonious scholarly debates (on which influence and faculty positions often depended). As young historians they were part of the division into collaborators and rivals, competing for more distinctive articles and more critical reviews, and countering the "German challenge" with a more vital French historical profession.[4]

In January 1929, seventy years after the appearance of the *Historische Zeitschrift* and ten years after their arrival in Strasbourg,

---

3 Stieg, *Scholarly Historical Periodicals*, pp. 33–37; also Alain Corbin, "Matériaux pour un centenaire: Le contenu de la *Revue Historique (1876–1972)*," *Cahiers de l'Institut d'Histoire de la Presse et de l'Opinion* (1976): 161–202.

4 André Burguière, "Histoire d'une histoire: La naissance des *Annales*," AESC 34, no. 6 (Nov.–Dec. 1979): 1350–52.

After 1905 Febvre was responsible for the section on regional history of the *Revue de Synthèse Historique*, where Bloch in 1912 published reviews as well as his first major article, "L'Ile-de-France."

Bloch and Febvre jointly introduced their new journal, the *Annales d'Histoire Economique et Sociale*, which, with a series of title changes, continues to this day.[5] Shortly after their appointments to Strasbourg they announced their intention of establishing a journal dedicated to social and economic history. The traditional French historical profession and its periodicals, with their positivist, largely political orientation, appeared insufficiently equipped to examine and analyze the welter of postwar economic, financial, and social problems. French social science appeared to bog down after 1918, and no heirs took up the mantle of Vidal de la Blache or Durkheim. The economists were largely isolated within faculties of law, which were dominated by practical and theoretical concerns. The pioneering path of historical synthesis, charted by Henri Berr, needed revitalization and expansion.[6]

The *Annales'* model and rival was the *Vierteljahrsschrift*, with its quartet of Austrian, German, and Swiss editors and its board of Swedish, British, and Italian historians, which had been founded in 1903 as an international enterprise but which after the war tended, somewhat predictably, to exclude French subjects and writers.[7] One of its editors and major contributors was Georg von Below (1858–1927), twenty-eight years Bloch's senior, a skilled practi-

---

5 The journal kept its original title through 1938, was renamed the *Annales d'Histoire Sociale* in 1939, became the *Mélanges d'Histoire Sociale* between 1942 and 1944, was once again *Annales d'Histoire Sociale* in 1945, and from 1946 to the present has been called *Annales: Economies, Sociétés, Civilisations*.

6 Berr, who retired from his teaching post in 1925, became the director of the Centre International de Synthèse, a publicly and privately financed interdisciplinary research institution that also included the natural sciences. In 1931 his journal was renamed the *Revue de Synthèse*, reflecting interests that transcended history. Berr was also devoted to a project launched after World War I: the editing of, and introductions to, a hundred-volume collection, "L'évolution de l'humanité," to which Bloch and Febvre both contributed. Henri Berr, "Au bout de trente ans," *Revue de Synthèse* 1 (1931): 5; also Lucien Febvre, "De la *Revue de Synthèse* aux *Annales*," *AESC* 7 (July–Sept. 1952): 289–92.

7 In volume 20 (1927) of the *Vierteljahrsschrift für Sozial- und Wirtschaftsgeschichte* none of the seven articles or thirteen review articles dealt with French history, and of seventy-two reviews only one treated a book in French: the *Mélanges d'histoire offerts à Henri Pirenne* issued on the fortieth anniversary of his appointment at Ghent.

tioner of medieval and economic history, who also represented the sort of narrow national vision the *Annales'* editors hoped to transcend.[8]

In 1921 Bloch and Febvre had decided to create a new international journal. They requested advice from Pirenne, to whom they offered the post of director; but their esteemed *maître*, burdened by writing and teaching responsibilities and unwilling to gain honorary credit for others' labors, declined an editorial post.[9]

At the international historical congress in Brussels in 1923 Febvre brought his proposal to the economic history section, where it provoked considerable discussion and debate, particularly over the participation of German historians, whom Pirenne had excluded from the congress. The Dutch led the fight to give any new journal a "truly international character," and the Poles made alternative suggestions for the journal's format.[10] Febvre's controversial proposal was referred to a special commission, which had no German member, where for the next four years it foundered and eventually expired. As its leading advocate, Pirenne tried unsuccessfully to interest the League of Nations in the project; he battled on the commission against those members who wished to reinstall political over comparative history.[11]

The Locarno agreements of 1925 signaled the political and economic eclipse of France. Together with the prolonged crisis of

8 Marc Bloch, "Un tempérament: Georg von Below," *AHES* 3 (1931): 553–59; also Below's autobiographical *Die Geschichtswissenschaft der Gegenwart in Selbstsdarstellungen* I (Leipzig: F. Meiner, 1925) and Jürgen Fröchling, "Georg von Below – Stadtgeschichte zwischen Wissenschaft und Ideologie," *Die Alte Stadt* 6, no. 1 (1979): 54–85.

9 Bryce Lyon, "Henri Pirenne and the Origins of *Annales* History," *Annals of Scholarship* 1 (1980): 69–84.

10 *Compte-rendu du Ve congrès international des sciences historiques: Bruxelles, 1923* (Brussels, 1923; Liechtenstein: Kraus Reprint, 1972), pp. 292–304.

11 Another important factor may have been the insistence of the Rockefeller Foundation, the chief expected source of funding, on including a German member on the board of the international review of economic history. Waldo Leland to Pirenne, 4 Mar. 1924, Leland papers, Library of Congress, Washington, D.C.

On the proposal's treatment, International Committee of Historical Sciences, *Bulletin* 1 (1926–29): 189, 192–94, 337–44; 2 (1929–30): 355, 403–10.

the franc, this spilled over into the intellectual realm. France was generally perceived to have fallen behind England and a revived Germany. Febvre became discouraged and sought his way back to Paris. It was Bloch who rescued the journal project and cast it in a new direction. By 1928 he and Febvre decided to abandon their original plan of creating an international review in favor of founding a distinguished national journal.[12]

That summer Bloch journeyed to Oslo to attend the Sixth International Congress of Historical Sciences, where he delivered two well-received presentations, on comparing medieval societies and on French agrarian systems.[13] In addition, armed with brochures, he announced the inauguration of the *Annales*: "a national review with an international spirit." With Pirenne's loyal support he was able to bury the stillborn international project in committee. At Oslo Bloch communicated personally with potential collaborators and conducted delicate negotiations with probable French and European rivals on behalf of the fledgling journal.[14]

Bloch was disappointed in the Oslo meeting itself. It was the last congress he would attend. In the half-decade since Brussels little had been accomplished within this earnestly cosmopolitan institution toward reducing professional history's divisions into arbitrarily narrow classifications. At Oslo there were too many papers on too limited subjects, and too few major themes. By its commitment to a "problem-oriented" history, a history based on both rigorous research and attention to present-day concerns and probing large, significant questions, the *Annales* hoped to redeem the dashed hopes of the postwar period for "rapprochement and organization," in

12 Paul Leuilliot, "Aux origines des 'Annales d'histoire économique et sociale' (1928): Contribution à l'historiographie française," *Mélanges en l'honneur de Fernand Braudel*, II (Toulouse: Privat, 1973), pp. 317–18; Leuilliot to author, 29 Apr. 1983.

13 "Pour une histoire comparée des sociétés médiévales" and "Le problème des systèmes agraires: Envisagé particulièrement en France," in VIe congrès International des Sciences Historiques, *Résumés des communications présentées au congrès* (Oslo, 1928), pp. 119–21, 264–65.

14 Bloch to Febvre, 22 Aug. 1928, AN, MI 318 1; International Committee of Historical Sciences, *Bulletin* 2 (1929–30): 105; also Leuilliot, "Origines," pp. 322–23.

short for a better history. It was just afterwards, on their side trip to Stockholm, that Pirenne made the memorable suggestion to Bloch that they begin their sightseeing with the new city hall, explaining: "If I were an antiquarian, I would have eyes only for old things. But I am a historian. That is why I love life."[15]

The practical work of founding the *Annales* challenged Bloch and Febvre's ingenuity and patience, but in the end proved possible. Wary of any form of outside control exerted by a publisher, they finally signed with Armand Colin, publisher of the *Annales de Géographie* and other important serials and books in the arts, humanities, and social sciences. Colin's director Max Leclerc (1864–1932) was a firm and exacting chief. Dubbed "the emperor," he was a man of vision who throve on details and was brusque but also realistic and flexible. He shared their sense of mission, and until his death intervened in almost every aspect of the publication.[16]

Why "*Annales*"? Leclerc insisted on a short, clear title. They had to avoid colliding with the most visible competition, the faltering *Revue d'Histoire Economique et Sociale*; they also countered a last-minute maneuver to merge the two ventures. By happy agreement Bloch and Febvre were able to share the designation *Annales* with the geographers, thanks to their friend and future collaborator Albert Demangeon, the editor of *Annales de Géographie*. To some ears "*Annales*" struck an ironic note, conjuring up an undigested yearly chronicle. On the other hand, more than "*Revue*," the name *Annales* corresponded with the directors' purpose. It was to be a working manual, continually updated, written in contemporary, occasionally combative prose, and serving as a vehicle of communication with their readers, a platform for intellectual exchange, and a point of orientation for their penetration of the discipline of history. Pirenne is credited with the selection of "*Annales d'Histoire Economique*" over the more ambiguous "*Annales Economiques*." History was thereby re-

15 Marc Bloch, "Les congrès: Sciences historiques," *AHES* 1 (1929): 71–73; Bloch to Febvre, Stockholm, 22 Aug. 1928, AN, MI 318 1; Bloch to Pirenne, 30 Aug. 1928, HP. Pirenne quotation in *AH*, p. 47.

16 Febvre to Pirenne, 27 May 1928, HP; Febvre to Bloch, n.d. (before Feb.), 13 June 1928, and Bloch to Febvre, 11 May, 4 July, 28, 31 Oct. 1928, AN, MI 318 2, 1; also Bloch and Febvre, "Max Leclerc," *AHES* 4 (1932): 337–38; Paul Leuilliot to author, 29 Apr. 1983.

cognized as the unifying, if not preponderant, element of the human sciences. *"Sociale"* was added, in a reversal of the title of the *Vierteljahrsschrift für Sozial- und Wirtschaftsgeschichte*, to assert the new journal's complementary interest in broad social questions, its ties with sociology, and its essentially interdisciplinary nature.[17]

The selection of the editorial committee reflected Bloch and Febvre's aspiration to form a liaison between the disciplines as well as within the historical profession plus Leclerc's cautions against an enterprise that was "trop universitaire." In addition to Demangeon (1872–1940), who was professor of economic geography at the Sorbonne, the original committee of eight included the Strasbourg sociologist Maurice Halbwachs (1877–1945); the economist Charles Rist (1874–1955), a former deputy governor of the Bank of France and professor of political economy at the Faculty of Law in Paris; the influential political writer André Siegfried (1875–1959), a member of the Institut de France and professor at the Ecole des Sciences Politiques in Paris; and four diverse historians: Strasbourg's professor of ancient history André Piganiol (1883–1968); the *chartiste* Georges Espinas (1869–1948), *archiviste honoraire* at the Ministry of Foreign Affairs; Henri Hauser (1866–1945), who held France's only chair in economic history at the Sorbonne; and Pirenne (1862–1935), the only foreign member, whose interests ranged from medieval Europe to the modern history of Belgium. Practically all mature, well-established individuals, their average age in 1929 was fifty-six. In addition to Demangeon, several members had significant connections with other journals: Pirenne had been on the original board of the *Vierteljahrsshrift* and after World War I had aided the founding of the *Economic History Review*; Halbwachs had helped to revive the *Année Sociologique*; Rist was on the board of the *Revue d'Histoire Economique et Sociale*; Piganiol and Hauser were advisors to the *Revue de Synthèse Historique*. Unlike most editorial committees, with their passive role, this one was intended to be a working group that would help shape the *Annales*. Except for Rist and Siegfried,

17 Leuilliot, "Origines," pp. 320–31; Febvre to Bloch, n.d. (before Feb.), 28 Mar. 1928, and Bloch to Febvre, 11 May 1928, AN, MI 318 1. Bloch to Pirenne, 17 Mar. 1928, HP.

each of the eight contributed articles and reviews and recruited authors for the journal.[18]

Bloch and Febvre drew upon their Strasbourg base to staff the journal. Their former student Paul Leuilliot, *agrégé* in history and geography at the University of Strasbourg, became the journal's secretary. The "faithful Leuilliot" performed a myriad of technical functions and wrote a considerable number of book reviews. Georges Lefebvre, historian of the French Revolution, Eugène Cavaignac, the Roman historian, and Henri Baulig, the geographer, were other key Strasbourg collaborators. The co-directors also relied upon their Paris connections. Febvre's *normalien* friend Albert Thomas, the first director of the International Labor Office, recruited technical writers for the *Annales*.[19]

No doubt there were risks in appointing an apprentice historian as their secretary and especially in soliciting a mixture of colleagues and outsiders to write for their journal. Bloch and Febvre searched for authors with "interesting" themes and points of view. They also planned to ask specialists to write even outside their own fields. Experienced and prepared, they were confident in their judgment and resources as well as their ability to lead, communicate, and collaborate.[20]

The two directors were also restive and ambitious. It was not a coincidence that on the eve of the first issue in late 1928 both Bloch and Febvre announced their availability as candidates for positions at the Collège de France.[21] Though the *Annales* was conceived in the reconquered eastern borderland, it undoubtedly represented a signal to the Paris intellectual world, to which the journal's reformist message was directed. Strasbourg's resources, faculty, and spirit had no doubt nurtured many of the original ideas and goals of the

18 Pirenne to Bloch, 17 Nov. 1930, EBC. Leuilliot (to author, 29 Apr. 1983) noted however that formal committee meetings gradually disappeared and that the basic operation was managed by Bloch and Febvre.
19 Lucien Febvre, "Albert Thomas historien," *AHES* 4 (1932): 381–84.
20 Febvre to Bloch, n.d. (summer), n.d. (before 4 July), n.d., 11 Sept., 23 Sept. 1928, and Bloch to Febvre, 27 Sept., 28 Oct. 1928, AN, MI 318 2, 1.
21 Bloch to Director, 15 Dec. 1928, CdF, G-iv-j-36d; also G-iv-j-35c, G-iv-j-36o.

Annales, of a pioneering collaboration in some way directed against the establishment and espousing international cooperation.[22] But as Bloch and Febvre approached the end of their first decade in Alsace they had become disenchanted with Strasbourg's provincialism and restive at their distance from the capital's libraries, archives, and book dealers, its publishers, foundations, and governmental sources of funding, its elite institutions, intellectual leaders, and the foreigners who graced its cultural life. To a considerable extent the journal represented a joint strategy, not so much aiming at "hegemony" or "preeminence" but, as a forthright presentation of their professional credentials, preparing the return of two gifted historians to the place they aspired to.[23]

One of the leitmotifs of the history of the *Annales* is the intellectual and personal relationship between Bloch and Febvre.[24] Indeed, there are few contemporary or even historical parallels with the loyal and productive friendship between these two scholars, well documented in their copious correspondence, which lasted for fifteen years. Their collaboration breathed life into the *Annales* and shaped its distinctive characteristic as a joint enterprise. From the outset there were important similarities and differences in the lives, work, and temperaments of the two founders.

Febvre, eight years Bloch's senior, was born in Nancy in the same decade as the Franco-Prussian War and still in its shadow. His father, a *normalien* and lycée professor of French grammar, came from Franche-Comté, and his uncle was a professor of history. An adored, precocious only child, Febvre passed his youth and early studies in the small provincial garrison town of truncated Lorraine and left for Paris at age eighteen. After preparing at Louis-le-Grand

22 Useful background in *Au berceau des Annales*, ed. Charles-Olivier Carbonell and Georges Livet (Toulouse: Presses de l'Institut d'Etudes Politiques de Toulouse, 1983), pp. 7–77.
23 The term "hegemony" is André Burguière's in "Histoire d'une histoire," p. 1353.
24 See H. Stuart Hughes, *The Obstructed Path: French Social Thought in the Years of Desperation* (New York: Harper and Row, 1966), pp. 19–55; Fernand Braudel, "Personal Testimony," *Journal of Modern History* 44, no. 4 (Dec. 1972): 448–67; Paul Leuilliot, "Témoignage d'un 'fidèle,'" in *Au berceau des Annales*, pp. 70–74; Marleen Wessel, "De persoonlijke factor: Nieuw licht op Marc Bloch en Lucien Febvre," *Skript: Historisch Tijdschrift* 7, no. 4 (Dec. 1985): 251–62.

and performing his one year of military service, he entered the Ecole Normale Supérieure in 1899. Preceding Bloch by five crucial years, Febvre lived at the prereformed Ecole at the climax of the Dreyfus Affair and at the time of its most vibrant intellectual and political activism. Here he formed his closest friendship, with the psychologist, physician, and philosopher Henri Wallon (1879–1962). In addition to several historians Febvre's close circle also included Halbwachs, the geographer Jules Sion (1878–1940), the psychologist Charles Blondel (1876–1939), the Germanist Ernest Tonnelat (1877–1948), the linguist Jules Bloch (1880–1953), and the literary and intellectual historian Paul Hazard (1878–1944).

In his search for a career Febvre followed an indirect path to history. He rejected what he termed "history according to the defeated of 1870," the prudent, methodical, fact-based writings of Albert Sorel and Emile Bourgeois and also the revisionist work of the *sorbonnard* Charles Seignobos. Originally attracted to literature, Febvre claimed to have chosen his profession as a result of the challenge and inspiration of his *normalien* professors Gustave Bloch, Monod, and Pfister. Like Marc Bloch's, Febvre's was a history enriched by the work of Vidal de la Blache, Durkheim, Meillet and the philosopher-anthropologist Lucien Lévy-Bruhl, as well as by Pirenne's simple and ingenious formulations and especially by Berr's "spirit of synthesis." In some respects Febvre's early career anticipated Marc Bloch's. *Agrégé* in history and geography in 1902, he too obtained a fellowship at the Fondation Thiers (1903–6). However, he taught at lycées near his birthplace, in Bar-le-Duc (1902–3) and Besançon (1907–12) and did not make the study trip to imperial Germany. In contrast to the Parisian Bloch, Febvre was an avowed provincial, deeply rooted in the culture and history of eastern France, by origin if not by birth "from the land of Courbet, Pasteur, and Proudhon."

At age thirty-three, in 1911 Febvre completed his doctorate, a study of the history, geography, economy, and society of Franche-Comté during the age of Philip II, and a year later he was appointed to the Faculty of Letters of the University of Dijon, where among his colleagues was his fellow Franc-Comtois the historian of the French Revolution Albert Mathiez. During World War I he served almost four and a half years at the front, like Bloch rising from sergeant to

137

captain, but in command of a machine-gun company. Also like Bloch, he was wounded once and received four citations and the military Legion of Honor.[25]

In October 1919 – also thanks to his connection with Pfister – Febvre was named a tenured professor of modern history at the new University of Strasbourg. Opening his inaugural lecture two months later with the challenging query, What is the place of history "in a world in ruins?", Febvre characterized himself as a vigorous "combatant." He called for a "useful" history, not engaged in idle fact gathering, not placed in the service of politics, ideology, or the national cause, not arranged according to artificial or "false" laws by those wishing to "realize a synthesis before having finished the analysis." He advised his audience that the restless and critical mind was "the best and surest safeguard for our national ideal, for our civilization, for our independence and our will to peace and freedom."[26]

If his fourteen-year sojourn in Alsace delayed Febvre's return to Paris, Strasbourg was nonetheless a good environment. In 1921 he married, at age forty-three, and fathered three children. Febvre was highly successful at the university. An imaginative, colorful lecturer and teacher, occasionally flamboyant or caustic, he personally designed his Institute of Modern History to include not only the works of the literary giants of the sixteenth century but also the research of contemporary economists and sociologists as well as historians of art, music, language, and religion. His courses were infused with the

25 Biographical information in CdF, C-XII: Lucien Febvre; also biographical references in Febvre, *Combats pour l'histoire* (Paris: Colin, 1953), pp. v–ix, 44–49; Robert Mandrou, "Lucien Febvre, 1878–1956," *Revue Universitaire* 66 (Jan.–Feb. 1957): 3–7; Hans-Dieter Mann, *Lucien Febvre: La pensée vivante d'un historien* (Paris: Colin, 1971), pp. 15–20; Fernand Braudel, "Lucien Febvre," *International Encyclopedia of the Social Sciences* v (1968), pp. 348–50; Palmer A. Throop, "Lucien Febvre 1878–1956," in *Some Twentieth-Century Historians*, ed. S. William Halperin (Chicago: University of Chicago Press, 1961), pp. 277–98.
26 "L'histoire dans le monde en ruines: Leçon d'ouverture du cours d'histoire moderne de l'Université de Strasbourg," *RSH* 30 (1920): 1–15.

interplay of ideas and economic and social structures and the tension between individuals and the collectivity.[27]

Febvre's friendship with Marc Bloch, which began in 1920, was fruitful for both. In addition to sharing students and university concerns, their neighboring offices and residences gave them the opportunity to exchange ideas. Their closeness developed into a joint mission of renewing the craft of history by loosening their elders' control over the levers of power, breaking down artificial barriers, banishing pedantry and anachronism, and establishing history's prime goal of "understanding" (*comprendre*). Febvre encouraged his younger colleague's labors on *Les rois thaumaturges* and *Les caractères originaux de l'histoire rurale française*, and with his support Bloch revived and assisted in Febvre's long desire to found a new journal.

Febvre nonetheless was always the senior partner. He had stronger connections with the older generation and more considerable professional credentials. Moreover, despite his wide-ranging interests and reformist zeal, Febvre was the more specialized historian, rarely straying from the sixteenth century, less driven than his younger collaborator to explore new methods and new terrains, less inclined to follow Pirenne's footsteps from the medieval world to the present. Though both were interested in comparative history, it was Bloch who actually practiced this craft. Both stayed abreast of the work of Durkheim's successors, but Bloch dealt more consistently and proficiently than Febvre with economic phenomena, social groups, and institutions and was also the more severe critic of sociology's unhistorical tendencies. Neither wrote strictly narrative history. Each in his distinctive way treated the past didactically, often with virtuoso displays of wit and brilliance and disdain for more prosaic scholarship. Both tended to pose questions aimed at penetrating what they considered the human reality of the past, and their texts were generously sprinkled with suggestions for further research. Both scolded particular scholars for their deficiencies, but Febvre more than the polymathic Bloch used these as points of departure for

27 Henri Baulig, "Lucien Febvre à Strasbourg," *Bulletin de la Faculté des Lettres de l'Université de Strasbourg* 36 (1957–58): 175–84.

his own work. For example, Febvre's brief popular study of Luther, published in 1928, was an attack upon the rudimentary psycho-analytic exposé of the reformer by the Catholic historian Father Heinrich Denifle, and his more extensive later work on Rabelais originated in and was shaped as a refutation of Abel Lefranc's assertion, in a book published in 1922, of Rabelais's atheism.[28] Both Bloch and Febvre were products of pre-World War I French training that emphasized literary culture, linguistic skills, and Cartesian logic. But while Febvre, who rarely did research in archives, based his critical analyses on a sophisticated, often intuitive, humanist consciousness, his more erudite partner, the historian's son who was also fascinated with the natural and social sciences, arrayed his work with a vast number and variety of scholarly citations.

Given their similarities and differences, each no doubt influenced the other. In fact, on the eve of the *Annales*' birth it appeared that they had exchanged their main focus. With his Luther book, Febvre seemed to have abandoned his earlier emphasis on geography and begun concentrating on the history of *mentalités*, just as Bloch, after completing *Les rois thaumaturges*, had plunged into his explorations of rural France.[29] But this is an oversimplification, reinforcing the quasi-mythic representation of the Bloch-Febvre relationship and of the famous "spirit of Strasbourg." Both men before the Great War had amassed a significant personal inventory of subjects and interests. Febvre's plunge into the history of ideas, which probably originated in his youthful fascination with philosophy and psychology and his friendships with Berr and Wallon, had almost no connection with the specific qualities of the criticism of testimony, which Bloch in fact had never entirely abandoned. And Bloch's interest in peasant emancipation and in land apportionment and use in rural France dated from his research for his doctoral thesis and his exploration of the Ile-de-France. It is enough to say that although

28 Febvre, *Un destin: Martin Luther* (Paris: Rieder, 1928); *Le problème de l'incroyance au XVIe siècle: La religion de Rabelais* (Paris: Albin Michel, 1942).
29 Noted in Hughes, *Obstructed Path*, p. 36; Braudel, "Febvre," p. 349; André Burguière, "The Fate of the History of 'Mentalities' in the 'Annales,'" *Comparative Studies in Society and History* 24 (1982): 426.

they shared an interest in certain subjects, recognized points of intersection, acknowledged the other's expertise, and occasionally even withdrew on the other's behalf, the richness of their collaboration was achieved without sacrifice, or even significant modification, of their own multifaceted individual development.

Their personalities were to some extent complementary. Bloch and Febvre, two articulate, cultivated, self-assured, and energetic individuals, were traditional bourgeois in their tastes, manners, and appearance. Although the interruption of their careers caused by their war service and the Strasbourg detour placed them under continuing pressure to produce, their obligations toward their growing families, their concern over their own and their families' health, and their occasional bouts of fatigue and lethargy served as restraints on their considerable ambition. Embarking on their new enterprise, each possessed a strong sense of fairness in dealing with the other that kept the issue of harmonizing and balancing their mutual contributions to the fore.[30]

Both were sincere though not chauvinist patriots and both were "unpolitical." Yet neither professor's son, neither member of a profession so closely linked with French and European politics, and neither war veteran, teacher, and father was apolitical. There were old ties to Jaurès, to the Dreyfusards, and to the republic, if not to its current leadership. A distinct sense of optimism, not uncharacteristic of French intellectuals at the time, permeated their expressions of loyalty and social responsibility, which were at the base of the *Annales*. Underlying Bloch and Febvre's distaste for conventional political and diplomatic history and their zest for a "new" social and economic history were their shared experience of mechanized total war and their joint hope that good scholarship by good citizens would set guideposts for those in power to combat oppression, class antagonism, and ruinous national rivalries.

In the *Annales'* first issue the directors made their mission explicit.[31] Why launch still another addition to the considerable list of French, European, and international journals, and why another

30 The correspondence is replete with examples; see, e.g., Febvre to Bloch, 28 Mar., 2 July 1928, and Bloch to Febvre, 5 July 1928, AN, MI 318 2, I.
31 "À nos lecteurs," AHES I (15 Jan. 1929): 1–2.

periodical devoted to "economic and social history"? In a candid, hearty declaration to their prospective readers, the two historians announced their threefold aim. First, they intended to heal the schism dating from the beginning of the century between historians and social scientists by providing a forum for the dissemination of contrasting methodologies and approaches. Second, they sought to break down or at least attenuate the compartmentalization of history into the fields of ancient, medieval, and modern, and to obviate such artificial distinctions as "primitive" versus "civilized" societies. Finally, while respecting "legitimate specialization," they aimed at lowering the walls between disciplines and creating a community of the human sciences, essential prerequisites to the development of economic history, and of history itself. In a tone that would be characteristic of the journal's first decade, the directors concluded: "Our enterprise is an act of faith in the exemplary virtue of work that is honest, conscientious, and solidly constructed."

The first decade of the *Annales*, 1929 to 1938, coincided with an extraordinarily bleak era in European and world history. It spanned the onset of the Great Depression, Japan's invasion of Manchuria and Italy's attack on Ethiopia, the Spanish Civil War, and the extinction of Austrian and Czechoslovak independence, and it was punctuated by the eruption of religious, nationalist, and anticolonial violence in India and in the Middle East, the first five-year plan and Stalinist purges in Soviet Russia, and political and racial persecutions in Fascist Italy, Nazi Germany, and parts of Eastern Europe. While the large and small democracies, divided internally and battered by the prolonged economic crisis, lost confidence and hope and more or less abandoned any semblance of unity, the League of Nations foundered. For France, the painful efforts to preserve the costly victory of 1918 collapsed in the wake of Germany's revival. Lacking the allies, manpower, domestic concord, and financial resources necessary to maintain itself as a Great Power, the Third Republic reeled through ten years of political unrest from Poincaré to Daladier.

For both Bloch and Febvre this eventful period consisted of individual and joint achievements and setbacks, of harmonious cooperation and occasional friction, of insularity as well as the impact of the troubled world outside. Even as they moved forward with their own careers, the *Annales* occupied a central position in their personal and professional lives. It made major demands on their energies with its publication deadlines. Perhaps their most significant sacrifice was that during this period both had to delay the completion of their *chefs d'oeuvre*: Bloch's *Société féodale* (1939–40) and Febvre's *Problème de l'incroyance* (1942).[32] On the other hand, this first decade of the *Annales* is itself generally considered a significant chapter in twentieth-century historiography.[33]

The journal's first year, 1929, was its testing ground. Despite the substantial and varied contributions of French and foreign writers and the positive response from their ardent supporter Pirenne, there were disappointments over certain authors and articles. Too, Bloch and Febvre had trouble shuttling between Strasbourg and Paris, coordinating editorial chores and staff work, and submitting to the close scrutiny of their exacting publisher, Armand Colin, over their editorial policy and practices. In a limited, competitive market, with growing financial exigencies, they needed to increase their contributors and subscribers. And they had to reach beyond a purely academic audience, to archivists and librarians, regional and local historians, and to the large number of literate nonspecialists who could benefit from the *Annales*' perspective.[34]

Toward the end of their first year Bloch and Febvre reassessed their journal and made fundamental decisions on its orientation, direction, and format. The main characteristic of the *Annales* was established: its emphasis on economic history over an unusually extended time frame, from the ancient world to the present. But the *Annales*' originality was in its stress on current issues. At a time

---

32 Bloch to Febvre, 11, 14 Dec. 1934, AN, MI 318 1; also Leuilliot to author, 29 Apr. 1983.
33 See, e.g., Geoffrey Barraclough, *Main Trends in History* (New York: Holmes and Meier, 1979); L. Allegra and A. Torre, *La nascita della storia sociale in Francia della Commune alle "Annales"* (Turin: Einaudi, 1977); M. Cedronio, F. Diaz, and C. Russo, *Storiografia francese di ieri e di oggi* (Naples: Guida, 1977); Georg Iggers, *New Directions in European Historiography* (Middletown, Conn.: Wesleyan University Press, 1975); and esp. Massimo Mastrogregori, *Il genio dello storico: Le considerazioni sulla storia di Marc Bloch e Lucien Febvre e la tradizione metodologica francese* (Rome: Edizioni Scientifiche Italiane, 1987).
34 See, e.g., Febvre to Bloch, 6, 26 Aug. 1929, AN, MI 318 2.

when contemporary world history was relegated to a minor or isolated place in French universities and journals and when bankers and businessmen rarely read scholarly periodicals, the *Annales* featured topical questions in almost all of its issues. This contemporary aspect was not simply the result of its pragmatism nor of some unrealistic idealism. It reflected a conviction that the interdependence of the present and the past was, in fact, "the main justification for the study of history."[35]

Both editors appreciated the difficulty of recruiting competent analysts of the present and of writing contemporary history. But exactly as they had heaped criticism on their fellow historians for the sin of anachronism, Bloch cautioned would-be practitioners of contemporary history against mechanically forging links between the present and the past by merely tracing "roughly similar" precedents. The "case approach" favored by military history and adopted by the newly emerging field of business history risked, according to Bloch, the production of pedestrian studies and, at the worst extreme, of misleading analogies – ignoring the dictum that history was the science of change.[36] According to their aim of promoting a profound and useful history – neither ignoring the present nor aspiring to play a preceptorial role – Bloch and Febvre took the position of independent, socially involved scholars.[37]

The *Annales'* direction remained a joint one. When the first setbacks forced the editors to curtail their ambitious program, Febvre began to falter. But Bloch, who remained confident in their collaboration and in their mission, persuaded him not to withdraw.[38] To survive and flourish, Bloch insisted, they must emphasize the journal's uniqueness. There was no question of producing

35 "Cette solidarité du présent et du passé qui, à aller au fond des choses, est la justification véritable de l'histoire." Bloch, "Pour mieux comprendre l'Europe d'aujourd'hui," *AHES* 10 (1938): 61.

36 Bloch, "Culture historique et action économique: A propos de l'exemple américain," *AHES* 3 (1931): 1–4.

37 Febvre to Bloch, 26 Aug. 1929, AN, MI 318 2; also Olivier A. Dumoulin, "'Profession historien' 1919–1939: Un 'métier' en crise?" (thèse pour le doctorat de 3ème cycle, Ecole des Hautes Etudes en Sciences Sociales, 1983), pp. 268–71.

38 Febvre to Bloch, 24 Sept. 1929, and Bloch to Febvre, 29 Sept. 1929, AN, MI 318 2, 1.

an "improved version of the *Revue Historique*," whose *sorbonnard* directors could choose among the best scholarly articles, bestow favor on selected reviewers, and thereby put out the unrivaled standard-bearer of the profession. The *Annales* was a small, new provincial enterprise, whose editors would have to "knock on many doors" to expand its influence and prestige. Bloch and Febvre agreed not to abandon the search for a few illustrious authors and more interesting subjects. But Bloch correctly foresaw that the essence of the *Annales*, the source of its spirit and the basis of its survival, would be not only its editors' active direction but their signatures in most of its sections and issues.[39]

At the end of its shaky first year the *Annales* was redesigned to have a six-part structure, consisting of the three traditional sections and three that reflected its own stamp. It regard to the first, the number of articles was drastically reduced and limited to original studies, there were extended book reviews ("Questions de fait et de méthode"), and there were short book reviews ("Courriers critiques") covering a broad international range, which pointed out strengths and weaknesses in terse, modern prose. On the other hand, the heart of the *Annales* was the rest: the news of the profession ("La vie scientifique"), which, instead of containing an undigested chronicle and assorted documents, was streamlined, focused, and laced with critical commentary; the directed investigations ("Enquêtes") launched by Bloch, which were spread over a number of issues; and the brief, general essays ("Problèmes d'ensemble"), which became a key element of the *Annales*' critical mission.[40]

In its first year, the *Annales*, much like its older counterparts,

---

39 Febvre to Bloch, 26 Aug., 3, 9 Sept., end Dec. 1929, and Bloch to Febvre, 29 Sept. 1929, AN, MI 318 2, 1.
40 Febvre to Bloch, 6 Oct. 1929, AN, MI 318 2. Bloch and Febvre, "Au bout d'un an," *AHES* 2 (1930): 1-3. During the first three years (1929-31), the *Annales* appeared in four issues; there were five between 1932 and 1937; and in 1938 four were resumed. The price of an annual subscription in France rose from 50 francs in 1929 to 60 francs in 1932 to 90 francs in 1938. Armand Colin published 2,500 copies in the first year, reduced this to 1,100 in 1930, to 900 by the middle of 1934, and to 800 between 1935 and 1938, with subscriptions never rising much above 300. Figures supplied by Colin, 15 Mar. 1983, 1 Dec. 1988.

had featured a balanced selection of seventeen original articles on ancient, medieval, modern, and contemporary history by notable French and foreign writers, both scholars and nonspecialists. Then came some significant modifications. The average number of articles dropped to eleven. Ancient history almost disappeared, medieval history declined, and the emphasis shifted to modern and especially to contemporary European and world history. Between 1929 and 1932 about one-third of the *Annales'* articles were contributed by foreigners: American and British social scientists, officials of the International Labor Office, and specialists in medieval and modern history recruited by Bloch and Pirenne. After 1933 the list of authors contained fewer eminences and became less international. An overwhelming proportion of original studies in the *Annales* emanated from French historians, social scientists, bankers, and colonial administrators.[41]

The majority of articles in the *Annales* were of standard length and contained all the conventional scholarly apparatus of traditional journals – footnotes, appendixes, and bibliography. But the contemporary studies, written largely by nonhistorians or nonscholars, which constituted almost 40 percent, were frequently shorter and less formal in their format and presentation. This contrast gave the *Annales'* article section its distinctive tone, balancing Bloch's penchant for extensive documentation with Febvre's distaste for ostentatious displays of erudition. Moreover, while dispensing with the standard practice of publishing editions of original documents, the *Annales* tended to incorporate more tables, charts, and graphs than most journals, which greatly increased the costs of production.[42]

There were several noteworthy articles among the almost one hundred published during the decade. The legal scholar Robert

41 Between 1929 and 1938, 8% of the *Annales'* articles were in ancient history, 16% in medieval, 33% in modern, and 38% in contemporary history, with 6% covering miscellaneous subjects.
42 Dumoulin ("Profession historien," p. 297) possibly overemphasizes the non-scholarly aspect of the *Annales* by comparing it with other journals as to the number of articles in the decade 1929–38 with no citations: *Annales*, 17.6%; *RH*, 6.4%; *Revue d'Histoire Moderne*, 10.9%; *Revue d'Histoire Economique et Sociale*, 6.6%.

Besnier traced the history of the concept of private property, its various forms and limitations, from ancient Rome to the present. Foreigners Pirenne and Fritz Rörig (the *Annales'* only German author) contributed original studies of medieval commerce; Roberto Lopez, of the origins of Genoese capitalism; and G. I. Brătianu, of Balkan and Byzantine serfdom. In 1933 Bloch sketched the outlines of a revisionist monetary history, made direct references to the current world crisis, and called for more work to develop the basis of a "human" history of medieval money.[43]

Almost all of the articles covering the sixteenth century through the early twentieth dealt with the evolution of modern capitalism: industry and agriculture, currency and credit, banking and the stock market, the building of railways and canals. They ranged over a large geographic horizon to North and South America, Africa, the Middle East, and Asia. The American economic historian Earl J. Hamilton documented the spectacular price revolution in sixteenth-century Castille, and Henri Hauser called for investigation of the political and economic role of banks in early modern Europe. Preceding Bloch's meticulous study of agrarian individualism, Georges Lefebvre reappraised the impact of the Revolution on rural France; and André-Emile Sayous, a prolific economist and generous supporter of the *Annales*, reexamined Strasbourg's economic and urban development under the Second Reich.[44]

43 Besnier, "De la loi des douze tables à la législation de l'après-guerre," *AHES* 9 (1937): 321–42; Pirenne, "L'instruction des marchands au Moyen Age," 1 (1929): 13–28, and "Un grand commerce d'exportation au Moyen Age: Les vins de France," 5 (1933): 225–43; Rörig, "Les raisons intellectuelles d'une suprématie commerciale: La Hanse," 2 (1930): 481–98; Lopez," Aux origines du capitalisme génois," 9 (1937): 429–54; Brătianu, "Servage de la glèbe et régime fiscal: Essai d'histoire comparée roumaine, slave et byzantine," 5 (1933): 445–62; Bloch, "Le problème de l'or au Moyen Age," 5 (1933): 1–34. Age," 5 (1933): 1–34.

44 Hamilton, "En période de révolution économique: La monnaie en Castille (1501–1650)," *AHES* 4 (1932): 140–49, 242–56; Hauser, "Réflexions sur l'histoire des banques à l'époque moderne (de la fin du XVe à la fin du XVIIIe siècle)," 1 (1929): 335–51; Bloch, "La lutte pour l'individualisme agraire dans la France du XVIIIe siècle," 2 (1930): 329–83, 511–43, 543–56; Lefebvre, "La place de la Révolution dans l'histoire agraire de la France," 1 (1929): 506–23; Sayous, "L'évolution de Strasbourg entre les deux guerres (1871–1914)," 6 (1934): 1–19, 122–32.

Articles about the post-1914 period added demography, sociology, and human geography: Halbwachs produced two lively critical articles analyzing the urban fabric of "Greater Berlin" and "ethnic Chicago."[45] Major economic, financial, and political questions were treated in a nontheoretical, moderately nationalist tone. On the eve of the Great Depression Maurice Baumont documented the strengths and weaknesses of Weimar Germany's remarkable industrial recovery; Demangeon presented the physical and economic impediments to European union; ILO official Georges Méquet pinpointed the population and agrarian problems of Soviet Russia; émigré scholars Franz Borkenau and Lucie Varga probed contemporary socialism and the roots of Italian and German fascism; financier Jacques Houdaille appraised the work of the Bank for International Settlements and weighed the progress of the U.S. New Deal; and, as signaled by Febvre's ambivalent response to the Colonial Exposition of 1931, various administrators and academics based overseas wrote insightful and informative but Eurocentric studies of the French Middle East, North Africa, and the Sudan.[46]

The *Annales'* peak year of exciting articles and active contributors was 1933; then the decline began. Pirenne was overburdened, and stalwarts such as Baumont, Halbwachs, and Lefebvre began con-

---

45 "Chicago: Expérience ethnique," *AHES* 4 (1932): 11–49, and "'Gross Berlin': Grande agglomération ou grande ville?" 6 (1934): 547–70.

46 Baumont, "L'activité industrielle de l'Allemagne depuis la dernière guerre," *AHES* 1 (1929): 29–47; Demangeon, "Les conditions géographiques d'une union européenne," 4 (1932): 433–51; Méquet, "Le problème de la population en URSS," 1 (1929): 48–57, "Le problème agraire dans la Révolution Russe," 2 (1930): 161–92, and "La collectivisation agricole dans l'URSS," 10 (1938): 1–24; Borkenau, "Fascisme et syndicalisme," 6 (1934): 337–50, and "Un essai d'analyse historique – La crise des partis socialistes dans l'Europe contemporaine," 7 (1935): 337–52; Varga, "La genèse du national-socialisme – Notes d'analyse sociale," 9 (1937): 529–46; Houdaille, "La Banque des Règlements Internationaux," 3 (1931): 321–48, and "Essor et vicissitudes de l'expérience Roosevelt," 8 (1936): 321–33; Febvre, "L'histoire économique et la vie: Leçons d'une exposition," 4 (1932): 1–10; e.g., Henri Labouret, "Irrigations, colonisation intérieure et main-d'œuvre au Soudan français," 1 (1929): 365–76, and J. Berque, "Sur un coin de terre marocaine: Seigneur terrien et paysans," 9 (1937): 227–35.

centrating on their own publishing endeavors.[47] In response to external political events – more compelling and more menacing than in 1929 – the editors drew different conclusions. Bloch sought better historical articles for the *Annales*, younger authors, and a wider range of subject matter. He looked for recruits among his students and Strasbourg colleagues as well as from archivists and local savants. Febvre, with a different perspective, preferred short, unusual, and provocative articles and added nonhistorians and nonuniversity people to the roster. He was now in Paris at the Collège de France, editor of the *Encyclopédie française,* and still connected with the *Revue d'Histoire Moderne* and with Berr's *Revue* and Centre de Synthèse. With more contacts, more responsibilities, and more outlets for his ideas than Bloch, Febvre viewed the *Annales* in a more restricted perspective.

Pirenne's death in October 1935 marked the onset of seemingly permanent doldrums.[48] Issues were continually delayed, raising questions about the journal's robustness and ability to survive. Despite their mounting burdens, Bloch urged that the editors themselves revitalize the journal. The result was a special issue devoted to the history of technology. In his brief introduction Febvre urged that this new discipline incorporate all the uneven, accidental, and human elements of science and invention. Bloch brilliantly traced the long history of the water mill – its invention in the ancient world, its disappearance and revival in medieval Europe, and its survival into the industrial age – linking it with problems of resources and manpower as well as an array of political and legal factors.[49] Bloch also prevailed upon Febvre to issue a joint article on

47 Pirenne to Bloch, 1 Jan. 1933, EBC; Bloch to Pirenne, 29 Sept. 1933, HP; Bloch to Febvre, 15 Feb., 11 May 1934, EBC, and 7 Oct. 1934, AN, MI 318 1; Febvre to Bloch, 19 Jan., n.d. (before 31 May), 4 July, n.d. (between 26 June and 10 July) 1934, AN, MI 318 2.
48 See Febvre's obituary, "Henri Pirenne, 1862–1935," *AHES* 7 (1935): 529–30; "corrections" in Bloch to Febvre, 11 Nov. 1935, AN, MI 318 1. Also Bloch to Pirenne, 29 May 1935, HP; Bloch, "Henri Pirenne (23 déc. 1862–24 oct. 1935)" *RH* 176 (1935): 671–79.
49 Bloch to Febvre, 6 June 1935, EBC, and n.d. (ca. 30 Oct. 1935), AN, MI 318 1; Febvre, "Réflexions sur l'histoire des techniques," *AHES* 7 (1935): 531–35; Bloch, "Avènement et conquêtes du moulin à eau," ibid., pp. 538–63.

the *agrégation*. This was just a portion of his larger, long-pending crusade to reform the teaching of history. Viewing the examination system, originally designed to maintain standards and ensure fairness, as now ossified and oppressive, the editors advocated higher standards and a broader scope within areas of specialization. Bloch's voice rang out clearly in the article's jibes at such mundane examination subjects as "The First Four Capetians" and in its complaint that in teaching the preparatory course in "French Feudal and Seigneurial Society" one was prevented by the examiners' narrowness from bringing in English or German examples. For Bloch if not for Febvre, the subject of educational reform was not a minor cause but a symptom of a "larger drama of consciousness" troubling France and Europe.[50]

As personal and political tensions mounted between 1934 and 1938, article selection inevitably provoked friction between the two directors. Each projected his opinion of worthwhile subjects and acceptable writing styles; and each coped with the restrictions imposed by his partner's predilections as well as the actual availability of fresh material.[51] The *Annales*' articles never attained a uniform profile, but there were some common features. There were, for example, a fairly high percentage covering long time periods, but very few dealing primarily with the question of origins. Economic history remained dominant in all periods. There were virtually no articles on biography, church, political, diplomatic, or military history, or the history of ideas, and very few devoted to social or cultural history. The Reformation and the Enlightenment received scant attention, and the French Revolution – itself the subject of a separate journal – was treated exclusively by Lefebvre.[52]

The *Annales*' profile was reflected in the titles of its articles, which generally followed three forms: the simple declarative statement

50 Febvre to Bloch, 4 Mar. 1937, and Bloch to Febvre, 13 May 1938, AN, MI 318 2, 1; Bloch and Febvre, "Pour le renouveau de l'enseignement historique: Le problème de l'agrégation," *AHES* 9 (1937): 113–29; Bloch to Febvre, 16 Feb. 1934, EBC, and 13 May 1938, AN, MI 318 1.
51 Bloch to Febvre, 9 Sept. 1935, AN, MI 318 1, and 13 Dec. 1935, EBC; also Febvre to Bloch, n.d. (ca. Mar.–Apr.) 1938, and Bloch to Febvre, 13 May 1938, AN, MI 318 2, 1.
52 Dumoulin, "Profession historien," passim.

("La politique ferroviaire du Second Empire," "Les zones pionnières de l'état de São Paolo"), the widely prevalent scientific-sounding case study ("Un grand chapitre de l'histoire du fer: Le monopole suédois," "En Syrie et au Liban: Village communautaire et structure sociale"), and the characteristic *problème*: "Le problème de l'or dans le monde antique," "Le problème de la population en URSS," "Les problèmes de l'or aujourd'hui." *Histoire-problème* – the representation of the past as open to fresh, probing investigations – bridged the contrasting temperaments and perspectives of the two editors.

The traditional book- and article-review section ("Courriers critiques") covered a considerable amount of French and foreign literature, but concentrated on Western Europe and economic history. As could be expected, the main burden fell on Bloch, Febvre, and Leuilliot, who between 1933 and 1938 averaged sixteen, fourteen, and eight titles a year respectively. The remainder were solicited either from loyal collaborators – Demangeon, Espinas, Halbwachs, and Jules Sion – or from occasional or one-time contributors. There were chronic problems of recruitment, of timely book distribution, and of review deadlines which – scarcely different from other journals then and now – frayed tempers.[53] But there was also the opportunity for the editors, especially for Bloch, who covered by far the broadest range of subject matter, to greatly expand their reading, their libraries, and their influence with a freedom and independence beyond that granted by other journals.[54]

Grouped into thematic or geographic categories and headed by bold descriptive titles, the *Annales'* short reviews were generally one to three paragraphs in length, timely, and informative.[55] A large variety of literature was included, from teaching manuals to scholarly articles, specialized monographs to collected essays, atlases to archival

---

53 Bloch to Febvre, 24 Mar. 1933, AN, MI 318 1, and 11 May 1934, EBC; n.d. (summer), 7 Oct., 23 Nov. 1934, 12 Aug. 1935, AN, MI 318 1, and Febvre to Bloch, n.d. (ca. 4 July), 8 July 1934, AN, MI 318 2.
54 Bloch's review subjects covered ancient, medieval, and modern history; England, France, Germany, Scandinavia, Spain, Italy and Eastern Europe; economic, urban, and social history. Remarks on Jewish history in *AHES* 1 (1929): 304; 5 (1933): 99; 6 (1934): 309–10.
55 See Febvre to Bloch, 29 Mar. 1929, AN, MI 318 2.

collections. Bloch and Febvre's reviews were sprinkled with criticisms and corrections, exhortations to explore new avenues of inquiry, encouragement of promising ventures, and vigilance against the demon of national bias, especially in German literature.[56]

As a reviewer Bloch developed an elegant directness, as in this commentary on an article by a renowned Austrian medievalist:

> The *Tijdschrift voor Rechtsgeschiedenis* asked M. Alfons Dopsch to summarize his theses on the origins of medieval society and economy. This exceptionally lucid statement will serve as a useful guide to his rather expansive works. The author has included a selection of criticisms of his ideas, primarily to maintain his position rather than bolster it with any additional evidence. Nothing is more typical of the ordinary development of a science. A system of interpretation, or rather a group of working hypotheses, invariably provokes challenges by the research that it has stimulated. Indeed, the creation of a work of synthesis is rarely ever the achievement of the pioneering scholar.[57]

More extended reviews were grouped in a special section, "Questions de fait et de méthode" and were written largely by Bloch and Febvre, with the assistance of a few collaborators and a long list of mostly French guest writers. This section covered important theoretical works or subjects of modern and contemporary interest. However, there were frequently lags averaging one to two years before these reviews appeared.[58]

This review section served two purposes, to promote works by the "*Annales* group"[59] and, by using the literature, to stimulate discussion of topical issues. Halbwachs discoursed critically on the

---

56 See, e.g., Febvre's review of Hans Simmer, *Grundzüge der Geopolitik* in *AHES* 1 (1929): 129–30.
57 "Aux origines du Moyen Age," *AHES* 7 (1935): 102; cf. Bloch to Febvre, 15 Feb. 1934, EBC.
58 Hauser's discussion of John Nef's article "The Progress of Technology and the Growth of Large Scale Industry in Great Britain," *Economic History Review* 5 (1934), appeared two years later: "La première 'révolution industrielle' anglaise," *AHES* 8 (1936): 71–74.
59 See, e.g., Bloch's and Baulig's reviews of Febvre and Demangeon's collaborative study of the Rhine in *AHES* 5 (1933): 83–85, 85–86; Bloch's reviews of Halbwachs's *Les causes du suicide*, 3 (1931): 590–92, and of Lefebvre's *La grande peur de 1789*, 5 (1933): 301–4; and Febvre's review of Georges Friedmann's *Problèmes du machinisme en U.R.S.S. et dans les pays capitalistes*, 6 (1934): 397–99.

structure of modern advertising and Georges Friedmann on the Stakhanovite phenomenon in the Soviet Union; Lefebvre dissected monographs on the *cahiers* preceding the French Revolution and on the social and economic origins of German heavy industry. In their reviews of works on West Africa and the Middle East, Bloch and Febvre each urged their colleagues to delve deeper into these exotic subjects. Bloch pleaded for a colonial history with fewer "heroic stories" and more attention to the structure of native societies. Febvre implored his colleagues to cease "collecting" ancient or strange customs and become critical scientists equipped to extend the range of human history.[60]

If the standard journal fare of articles and book reviews took on a new vibrancy in the *Annales*, the other half – the professional news ("La vie scientifique"), directed investigations ("Enquêtes"), and thematic essays ("Problèmes d'ensemble") – manifested both its originality and the limits of its editors' ambitions. Relying on themselves and a small group of loyal collaborators, Bloch and Febvre tried to establish new standards, larger goals, and a more critical perspective.

True to its practical mission, the *Annales* presented a more extensive, better-organized professional news section than most comparable journals, providing exceptional coverage of foreign as well as domestic items. The initial effort to fulfill a timely function with a mélange of birthdays, retirements, *Festschriften*, deaths, recent publications, and works in progress was soon abandoned in favor of more structured and substantial documentation and commentary.[61] There were full listings of facilities: archives and libraries, museums and expositions, research centers and institutes, local, national, and international congresses, periodicals and assorted research tools including serials, atlases, encyclopedias, texts, and manuals. If their original hope to publish complete annual bibliographical lists had to be abandoned, Bloch and Febvre gave scholars and nonprofessional historians a valuable instrument for research.

The journal also promoted certain of its favorite themes. Each

---

60 Bloch, "L'Afrique occidentale: Problèmes de pratique et expériences historiques," *AHES* 5 (1933): 397–98; Febvre, "En terre arabe: Régionalisme nationaliste ou panarabisme unitaire," 7 (1935): 194–96.
61 Bloch to Febvre, 9 Aug., 29 Sept. 1929, AN, MI 318 1.

issue contained announcements of the publication of statistical data from a wide variety of sources – private and public, scholarly and commercial, domestic and foreign – covering a broad range of economic, social, and theoretical questions. Outnumbering historical subjects, most were of contemporary concern, such as League of Nations reports on international trade and finance, migrant labor, and refugees, and annual governmental reports on colonial affairs and on prices, salaries, employment, and public health.[62] A special section, "Cartography and Social Realities," inserted in 1934 and again in 1937 and 1938 gave Bloch and Febvre the opportunity to campaign against the cult of *Geopolitik*. Pointing out technical and historical errors, they urged mapmakers and atlas publishers to interact more fully with the human sciences: to improve their methods of graphic representation, frequently oversimplified in accordance with a narrow conception of geography and politics; and to integrate such factors as language, work, habitation, and culture.[63]

For a number of years an unusual section entitled "Economists, Historians, and Men of Action" featured biographies of deceased major figures, such as Max Weber, François Simiand, F. W. Maitland, and Albert Thomas – and also Walther Rathenau and John Jacob Astor.[64] Febvre used these occasional abbreviated essays – part homage, part critique – to link the *Annales* with sympathetic, independent individuals who had not graced its pages. Bloch's biographical portraits (a relatively uncharacteristic genre for him) were straightforward, critical evaluations of the aspirations and achievements of his elder colleagues.[65]

62 See, for example, the announcement of the population, agricultural, and manufacturing statistics for Jewish Palestine in 1936 in *AHES* 10 (1938): 59.
63 Bloch, "Réflexions sur un atlas historique scolaire," *AHES* 6 (1934): 495–97; Febvre, "Noir–blanc: Un atlas scolaire allemand," ibid., p. 582; also Febvre, "La représentation cartographique des faits économiques et l'Atlas de France," 9 (1937): 382–84; Bloch, "Une erreur" (review of Joseph Calmette, ed., *Atlas historique* II: *Le Moyen Age*), ibid., pp. 384–85.
64 Bloch to Febvre, 26 July 1929, AN, MI 318 1.
65 See, e.g., Febvre, "Albert Mathiez: Un tempérament, une éducation," *AHES* 4 (1932): 573–76, and "François Simiand (1873–1935)," 7 (1935): 391; Bloch, "George Unwin, sa vie et les idées directrices de son oeuvre," 1 (1929): 241–47, and "Un tempérament: Georg von Below," 3 (1931): 553–59.

The section for news of the profession gave Bloch and Febvre the chance to call attention to their own outside ventures, announce the work of their collaborators, promote subjects like the study of folklore, and encourage private and official initiatives in favor of economic and social history. They also editorialized against archaic methods of writing history texts and manuals, and against cumbersome restrictions on researchers. Upon returning from a research trip to England where he savored the services of the British Museum, Bloch savagely attacked the regulations and procedures of the Bibliothèque Nationale.[66]

After the hopes stimulated at Brussels in 1923, the *Annales* scrutinized the succeeding international congresses held at Oslo (1928), Warsaw (1933), and Zurich (1938) and deplored the same overloaded schedules, traditional division of the discipline, and absence of overall plan and direction.[67] However, its own bulletin board became increasingly local and national. With the exception of statistics, the *Annales'* foreign news coverage was drastically reduced after 1933. "La vie scientifique" centered on the French world, its issues, institutions, and research tools. It nonetheless remained an important part of the journal, reflecting Bloch and Febvre's early positivist training, their crusade to banish pedantry, and their dedication to communicate useful, significant, digestible items to their local and (shrinking) foreign audience.[68]

The *Annales'* investigations ("Enquêtes"), detached from their original place in "News of the Profession," were to be the journal's link with the larger world of analysts and contemporary issues. In the first five years the *Annales* published groups of studies of Europe's banking and agricultural crises. Bloch and Febvre's wider purpose, to associate present problems with the past, led to collab-

66 Bloch, "Clio," and "Un siècle d'histoire moderne," and Febvre, "Pour comprendre l'Europe contemporaine," *AHES* 6 (1934):378–82; Bloch and Febvre, "Nous n'avons pas mérité cela," 8 (1936): 151–52; Bloch, "La grande pitié des lecteurs" (on the BN), 10 (1938): 54–55; also Bloch to Febvre, 12 May 1936, EBC.

67 Bloch to Febvre, 27 Dec. 1933, AN, MI 318 1; also Bloch and Febvre, "Pour préparer le prochain Congrès International des Sciences Historiques," *AHES* 8 (1936): 44–48.

68 Bloch and Febvre, "Au lecteur," *AHS* 1 (1939): 6.

orative studies of the history of prices, the problem of gold, the history of transportation and technology, and the identification of source materials for the study of economic history from the archives of private industry.[69]

The historical investigations were essentially Bloch's personal mission, a means of linking the solitary scholar with his colleagues, pooling the resources of various specialists, and achieving genuine comparative history. The first extended *enquête*, and for Bloch perhaps the most important, was centered on *plans parcellaires*. This involved the retrieval and interpretation of village maps and registers of landholdings that had been drawn up for tax purposes during three separate periods: under the seigneurial regime, during the half-century after the French Revolution, and just prior to World War I. Widely scattered in local, regional, and national depositories, of uneven accuracy and completeness, they nonetheless provided crucial evidence of patterns of settlement, ownership, and cultivation, and of change and continuity. Bloch for several years had systematically combed French local archives to scrutinize and copy these neglected *plans*. Here were the essential data for his analysis of the contrasting features of French rural life and the growth of agrarian freedom.[70]

At Oslo Bloch had invited contributions from foreign colleagues in order to promote the sharing of technical and archival data, set standards, and guard against the sort of "flights of imagination" and nationalist bias that had marred the pioneering studies of August Meitzen.[71] The *plan-enquête* ultimately spanned seven years. In addition to Bloch's opening résumé, the *Annales* published contributions from Czechoslovakia, Denmark, England, Germany, Sweden, and North Africa (but, despite Bloch's hopes, not from Italy).

69 Febvre to Bloch, 20 Sept. 1930, AN, MI 318 2; Bloch to Febvre, 29 Sept. 1929, AN, MI 318 I.
70 Bloch, "Peuplement et régime agraire," *RSH* 42 (1926): 97–99; also AN, AB XIX 3844, on Bloch's own research, including one of the first fruits: his lectures in Brussels in January 1932 on the French agrarian system; Bloch to Jean Regné, 31 July 1932, reproduced in preface to Regné, *Repertoire des plans cadastraux parcellaires de l'Ardèche* (Annonay: Décombe, 1933).
71 Bloch to Febvre, 15 July, 8 Sept. 1929, AN, MI 318 I; Bloch and Febvre, "Nos enquêtes collectives," *AHES* I (1929): 58–59.

There were notices on the use of aerial photography for mapping terrain and reminders of archival gaps and errors. As the initiator and animating spirit, Bloch continued to applaud local and national accomplishments, fretted over the human delays, and noted the financial problems of cataloguing and providing access to this precious group of sources, which would remain one of his prime causes almost to the end of his life.

Bloch also launched the next historical inquiry, on the nobility. It was linked not only to his research for *La société féodale* but to the *Annales'* other mission, Pirenne's plea for attention to "social" questions.[72] Bloch set the main topics for the investigations, recruited the French, English, Italian, and Austrian writers, and supervised the editing and translations. The result was less successful than earlier efforts, less cosmopolitan and original. For unlike privately endowed or officially sponsored research, the *Annales'* investigations were based on informal cooperation among French and foreign scholars. Bloch could not assign questionnaires, select a uniform body of sources, impose regulations, or provide significant remuneration for authors. The *enquêtes* were an example of humanists' attempting to emulate the sciences by "organizing research."[73] They also reflected Bloch and Febvre's personal commitment to collaborative work. Despite their shortcomings, they kept international scholarship alive at a time of increased nationalism, and they produced several ongoing studies useful to scholars and nonspecialists alike.

The section of general problems ("Problèmes d'ensemble") was even more experimental and risky. Here the emphasis was on a few significant topics, historical or contemporary. A handful of writers evaluated one or several pieces of literature within a larger context of methodology and interpretation.[74] Espinas wrote several detailed

---

72 Bloch and Febvre, "Les noblesses," *AHES* 8 (1936): 238–42; Bloch to Febvre, 11 May, 12 Aug. 1934, 10 Oct. 1935, 30 May 1936, EBC, and 13 Apr., 11 Sept. 1935, 2, 12, 30 Mar. 1936, AN, MI 318 1. Bloch to R. H. Tawney (20 Mar. 1936, Tawney papers, London School of Economics) indicates the importance of this inquiry.

73 Dumoulin, "Profession historien," pp. 200–4.

74 "For many years this has been the most lively, the most novel, the most 'us.'" Bloch to Febvre, 14 May 1933, AN, MI 318 1; also 22 Mar. 1934, ibid.

essays on urban history from the Middle Ages to the present; Houdaille contributed critical studies of contemporary banking, currency, and general economic problems. There were a few isolated subjects: the technical aspects of gothic architecture, the origins of cultivated plants, and the nature of Norwegian communes. There were also essays of scholarly significance: Georges Lefebvre's integration of price history into the history of the French Revolution (1937); theoretical importance: Georges Friedmann's critical evaluation of Taylorism in the industrial process (1935); and topical concern: ILO official Imre Ferenczi's study of the condition of foreigners in the contemporary world (1936) and Henri Mougin's analysis of the economic causes of Nazism (1937).[75]

This section provided another platform for the editors. Febvre crusaded against the application of such terms as class and gentry to remote times or inappropriate situations. He railed against "the primacy of politics," especially the exaggerations of the political dimension of national identity. He also attacked the methodology of political economy practiced by French law faculties that produced stultified, superficial interpretations of economic realities.[76]

Febvre also embroiled the *Annales* in the notorious "Jassemin affair."[77] Henri Jassemin, an archivist at the Archives Nationales who had graduated in 1917 from the Ecole des Chartes, was awarded the *doctorat d'état* from the Sorbonne in 1933 for a highly praised thesis on the Paris Treasury Office (Chambre des Comptes de Paris). The published version received accolades from French and foreign scholars and was nominated for a major prize.[78] An outraged Febvre could not "resist the pleasure of exposing its elegance." Like a

---

75 Bloch to Febvre, 9 Oct. 1935, AN, MI 318 1.

76 Febvre, "Histoire, économie et statistique," *AHES* 2 (1930): 581–90, "Fondations économiques, superstructure philosophique: Une synthèse," 6 (1934): 369–74, "De la France à l'Europe: Histoires, psychologies et physiologies nationales," 4 (1932): 199–207, and "De l'histoire-tableau: Essais de critique constructive," 5 (1933): 267–81.

77 Febvre to Bloch, 19 Jan., 14 Apr., n.d. (Apr.–July), n.d. (ca. 31 May), n.d. (26 June–10 July) 1934, AN, MI 318 2.

78 Henri Jassemin, *La Chambre des Comptes de Paris au XVe siècle, précedé d'une étude sur ses origines* (Paris: Picard, 1933); reviews by J. Viard in *Bibliothèque de l'Ecole des Chartes* 94 (1933): 366; B. Pocquet du Haut-Jusse in *Revue des Questions Historiques* 118 (1933): 499; E. C. Lodge in *English Historical Review* 49 (1934): 344–45.

typical *chartiste*, Jassemin had "examined the fifteenth-century Chambre des Comptes without once asking how computations were made (*comment on comptait*)" – for many centuries tokens were used to calculate deniers, sous, and livres – thereby demonstrating "one of the magnificent qualities of 'realism' in our studies."[79]

In his ferocious review Febvre ridiculed Jassemin's impeccable presentation, identical to what *chartistes* had applied indiscriminately for almost a half-century to all sorts of medieval institutions, and he also faulted Jassemin for gaps in research, technical imprecision, and the absence of comparison. Jassemin's clever response, published in the next issue, termed it the "old debate" between the *érudit* and the popularizer: one who produced serious works of scholarship, the other who spouted scintillating theories to dazzle university students. The incident left a bad taste. Febvre believed that the Ecole des Chartes was the seedbed of the French right. He had targeted a well-placed victim, challenged his credentials as a historian, and termed his work "in this year 1934 . . . useless." Although the directors denied Jassemin's complaint of an unfair attack upon a venerable institution and its corps of archivists (on whose collaboration and support the *Annales* depended), they had provoked a latent resentment of their journal for its imperious, partisan tone.[80]

Bloch, similarly if less brutally combative, promoted his own conceptions. He insistently demanded broader, more meaningful historical training and championed collaborative work. For rural studies he challenged the historian to "think more like an economist," urged writers of local history to conduct more painstaking research, and stressed that every investigation of ancient settlements required the help of linguists, geographers, and archaeologists to explain human penetration of and response to the physical environment.[81] While assailing the prevailing myth that the Middle Ages

79 Febvre to Bloch, n.d. (end Sept.) 1933, AN, MI 318 2.
80 Febvre to Bloch, 19 Jan. 1934, AN, MI 318 2; Bloch to Febvre, 28 Apr., 3 July 1934, EBC; Febvre, "Comptabilité et Chambre des Comptes," *AHES* 6 (1934): 148–53; letter by Jassemin, ibid., pp. 333–36; note by Bloch and Febvre, "Correspondance," ibid., pp. 332–33.
81 "La vie rurale: Problèmes de jadis et de naguère," *AHES* 2 (1930): 96–120; "Sur quelques histoires de villages," 5 (1933): 471–78; "Réflexions d'un historien sur quelques travaux de toponymie," 6 (1934): 252–60; "Régions naturelles et groupes sociaux," 4 (1932): 489–510.

had been stagnant in regard to inventions, Bloch tirelessly campaigned against Lefebvre des Noëttes's "curious" theory that the advent of the harness had marked the end of medieval slavery. He also challenged one of his rivals, the medievalist Louis Halphen, author of the volume covering the eleventh through the thirteenth century in the series "Peuples et civilisations," for failing to transcend a purely political chronicle.[82]

In these "editorials" Febvre often got bogged down in polemics over the interaction between past and present, the comparability of "modern" and "primitive" societies, and the interchangeability of words and institutions. Bloch, on the other hand, searched for better tools, more erudition, fewer rules and restrictions, more breadth and curiosity. Returning to his favorite methodology, Bloch proposed that the study of peoples outside the mainstream (*sociétés d'exception*) might well stimulate and enlarge the discipline of comparative history, "serving as a marvelous reflection of influences to which they had not submitted."[83] Exceptions, mutations, lag, and precocity – untimely, unplanned, uneven development – these were embedded in Bloch's experience and consciousness as well as in the *Annales*' first decade.

The year 1939 marked an abrupt change. The journal, reduced to four annual issues and published by the directors themselves, was renamed *Annales d'Histoire Sociale*. This came in the wake of several years of mounting difficulties with the firm Armand Colin over technical, personnel, and editorial questions, culminating in the final dispute over the special issue on Nazi Germany in November 1937. Bloch persuaded Febvre to proceed independently using their own resources and gaining control over the enterprise. In the first issue of the *Annales d'Histoire Sociale* the editors reassured their readers of continuity of format, personnel, and content. The abbreviated title represented only a minor alteration, reflecting the new

82 A propos Lefebvre des Noëttes: "Les 'inventions' médiévales," AHES 7 (1935): 634–43, and, earlier, "Problèmes d'histoire des techniques," 4 (1932): 482–86, and "Technique et évolution sociale: A propos de l'histoire de l'attelage et celle de l'esclavage," RSH 41 (1926): 91–99; Halphen: "Manuels ou synthèses?" AHES 5 (1933): 67–71; Bloch to Febvre, 4 Oct. 1933, EBC.
83 Bloch, "Une expérience historique: La Sardaigne médiévale," AHES 10 (1938): 50–52.

legal status of ownership but no substantial shift of policy or orientation.[84]

Yet a serious internal crisis had preceded the creation of the new *Annales*. Though Bloch had finally reached Paris in 1936, both he and Febvre, burdened with a myriad of professional and personal obligations, found consultation and coordination as difficult as when they were physically separated. Serious disagreements arose over specific articles and reviews, and there were procedural debates over decision making and control. In a larger sense, the directors' personal and professional differences had been magnified by their extraordinary decade of collaboration.[85] As another world war approached and each labored to complete his delayed *chef d'oeuvre*, they also evaluated their *Annales*. Febvre, who turned sixty in 1938, had finally acquired a permanent country residence, "Le Souget," in the village of Saint-Amour in his native Franche-Comté. Under his own cedars, surrounded by his entourage of disciples and close friends, he lamented the journal's "loss of influence," its "dullness" and "center-left academic conformism."[86] Bloch, at age fifty-two, now the youngest member of the *Annales* board,[87] harped on practical matters: the absence of regular meetings, delayed book reviews, inadequate communication with authors, and poor liaison between the two chiefs.[88]

Before agreeing to continue, they openly acknowledged their differences. Febvre above all desired a "journal of ideas." As the *Annales'* "*sourcier*" (spring-finder), he sought younger authors and a more lively format; as its chief *combattant* he targeted the Paris

---

84 Bloch and Febvre, "Au lecteur," *AHS* 1 (1939) 1–3. The difficulties and break with Colin: Bloch to Febvre, 20 Sept. 1937, 25 May 1938, AN, MI 318 1. Max Leclerc had died in 1932.
85 Bloch to Febvre, 13 May 1938, AN, MI 318 1.
86 Febvre to Bloch, n.d. (Mar.–Apr.), 8 May, 18 June 1938, AN, MI 318 2.
87 The next youngest member, Piganiol, now professor of ancient history at the Sorbonne, resigned at the end of 1937. The ten-member editorial committee now included Joseph Cuvelier (member of the Royal Academy of Belgium, replacing Pirenne), Demangeon, Espinas, Halbwachs, Hauser, Lefebvre, Gaétan Pirou (professor in the Faculty of Law of Paris), Rist, Paul Rivet (professor and director of the Museum of Ethnography), and Siegfried.
88 Bloch to Febvre, 9 May 1938, AN, MI 318 1.

establishment with renewed stridency and relentlessness.[89] Bloch, nearing the pinnacle of his professional life, now less deferential toward Febvre, less specialized, and admittedly the more learned, defended their creation for its "seriousness and intelligence." The success of the *Annales* resided precisely in its "solid, fastidious, precise, and unpretentious information."[90] Their private sparring having run its course, both admitted their unwillingness to direct the journal alone or precipitate its demise. In the pre-Munich summer of 1938 they soothed each other's hot tempers and hurt feelings and submerged their differences. With its congenital problems the *Annales* would continue, preserving its essential format but also opening itself to some new blood.[91]

In the twilight of the Third Republic and the last months of peace the *Annales d'Histoire Sociale*, with its sprinkling of new names and small modifications, was a moderately robust offspring. The year's entire list of articles numbered only five. Bloch attacked the "sclerosis" of the slogans "natural economy" and "closed economy" used by the German medievalists Bruno Hildebrand and Alfons Dopsch, insisting that the widespread barter system of the Middle Ages never entirely replaced a monetary standard of value.[92] The sociologist Georges Friedmann analyzed the contemporary paradox of a skilled-labor shortage existing simultaneously with widespread unemployment; the Austrian refugee Lucie Varga wrote on the fate of peasant folklore in northern Italy under the fascist regime; and Bloch and Febvre's former Strasbourg student Henri Brunschwig described economic conditions in Nazi Germany on the eve of war. In the section for short book reviews there were several topical issues, including the New Deal, "Jewish problems," and the Third Reich.

In the longer essays the two directors took center stage: Bloch, in a long-delayed critique of Friedrich Meinecke's *Entstehung des*

89 Febvre to Bloch, 18 June 1938, AN, MI 318 2.
90 Bloch to Febvre, 22 June 1938, AN, MI 318 1.
91 Bloch to Febvre, 29 Oct., 12 Nov. 1938, AN, MI 318 1.
92 "Economie-nature ou économie-argent: Un pseudo-dilemme," *AHS* 1 (1939): 7–16.

Historismus, faulted the former editor of the *Historische Zeitschrift* for glorifying the state and ignoring new, non-German currents of historical scholarship.[93] Febvre, who contributed on a strikingly large range of subjects, from Erasmian thought to National Socialist ideology, savagely attacked a work by the old Sorbonne master Charles Seignobos "as the negation of what I call history."[94]

The *Annales'* new autonomy intensified two of its characteristics: the stress on the contemporary and the in-group quality. Within the abbreviated sampling of professional news, "La vie scientifique" published a somber account of the international historical congress held in Zurich at the height of the threatening summer of 1938. On the other hand, there was a communication from a retired primary-school director, A.-V. Jacquet, linking the *Annales* with the masses of intelligent, nonprofessional readers who savored it in their local libraries.[95] The *enquêtes* continued, with several new authors writing on prices, technology, and the nobility. There was the new subject of capitalism. "Problèmes et bilans," a much-reduced version of "Problèmes d'ensemble," contained short discussions on land distribution in the Ottoman Empire, the French economy on the eve of the Revolution, and the transformation of the world banking system after World War I. Febvre lauded their new collaborator André Varagnac's scientific study of folklore, and Bloch linked the "spirit of the *Annales*" with Hauser's meticulous work on the history of prices.[96] The year's final issue appeared after war had begun. With Bloch mobilized and most of their collaborators at the front, Febvre had to manage the journal alone. In the wake of another German

---

93 "'Historisme' ou travail d'historiens?" *AHS* 1 (1939): 429–30. Meinecke had dedicated this book "to the memory of the University of Strasbourg in the days before the war."

94 "Un essai d'histoire européenne," *AHS* 1 (1939): 293–95. Febvre to Bloch, n.d. (June), 18 June 1938, AN, MI 318 2; Bloch to Febvre, 22 June 1938, AN, MI 318 1.

95 Ch.-Edmond Perrin, "Les historiens au congrès de Zurich," *AHS* 1 (1939): 307–9; Jacquet, "L'histoire économique et sociale intégrée aux mathématiques: Réflexions d'un éducateur," ibid., pp. 298–306.

96 Febvre, "Folklore et folkloristes: Notes critiques," *AHS* 1 (1939): 152–60; Bloch, "L'histoire des prix: Quelques remarques critiques," ibid., pp. 141–51.

invasion, he evoked the memory of the *Annales'* original guide, Pirenne; inspired by the departed *maître's* courage and stoicism, he pledged that the new *Annales* would go on.[97]

When during the late 1960s and 70s the *Annales'* successor attained international preeminence, the journal's first decade was accorded almost legendary status. The struggles and achievements of the founders, and also the reaction of their opponents, tended to be magnified by those who had a stake in establishing a "long duration" for their very successful form of "new history."[98] What in fact was accomplished during this first decade, to which Bloch devoted so much of his time, spirit, and energy?

More than other journals of its day, the *Annales* represented "living history," broad, immediate, useful history, informed by other disciplines and, concerning human phenomena, animated by a relentless sense of curiosity, nuance, and comparison. Its articles were often fresh and provocative, its reviews intelligent, its research projects ambitious; and it filled the role of a review by covering a vast range of scholarship. Frankly eclectic in its orientation, it rejected Marxist dialectics, German historicism, and all forms of determinism. With limited resources and ambition, it created no coterie or school but radiated its own spirit of openness.

Out of their positivist roots which they sought to improve and enrich, Bloch and Febvre promoted scientific rigor, exacting criticism, and local, regional, national, and international collaboration. Later myths notwithstanding, they achieved only a modest measure of recognition in a shrinking, competitive academic world and in a dark and troubled age. There were critics and opponents of their strident tone; but the *Annales'* greatest enemy was not simply the

97 Febvre, "A nos lecteurs, à nos amis" (10 Oct. 1939), *AHS* 1 (1939): 353–54; cf. Febvre to Bloch, n.d. (before May) 1939, AN, MI 318 2.
98 See esp. Braudel, "Personal Testimony," pp. 461–67; Jacques Le Goff et al., eds., *La nouvelle histoire* (Paris: C.E.P.L., 1978). Also Lynn Hunt, "French History in the Last Twenty Years: The Rise and Fall of the *Annales* Paradigm," *Journal of Contemporary History* 21 (Apr. 1986): 209–24; Jacques Revel, "The *Annales*: Continuities and Discontinuities," *Review* 1 (1978): 9–18; Traian Stoianovich, *French Historical Method: The Annales Paradigm* (Ithaca, N.Y.: Cornell University Press, 1976); Maurice Aymard, "The *Annales* and French Historiography," *Journal of European Economic History* 1 (1972): 491–511.

indifference of the Sorbonne but also the distance from their colleagues across the Rhine, the Channel, and the Atlantic.

In its creation and survival, the *Annales* was one of Marc Bloch's major accomplishments. It gave him and Febvre a place in the world of scholarship. It fulfilled his hope of creating an accessible, innovative, distinguished French journal that addressed and responded to the world outside.

8. Paris

I have too much work on the drawing board to succumb to the poison of discouragement.[1]

When the Allied troops evacuated the Rhineland in June 1930, five years ahead of the schedule foreseen in the Versailles treaty, France had ceased to play a dominant role in Europe. The costly victory of 1918 had been eroded by the dissolution of Allied unity, by Germany's rapid recovery, and by the failure of successive French governments to enforce the treaty clauses. On the eve of the Great Depression power had shifted across the Rhine, where in September 1930 Hitler's Nazi party scored a spectacular electoral victory that accelerated both the economic crisis and the final destruction of the Versailles peace.[2] The Third Republic, France's longest regime, now entered its last tormented decade, marked by political instability, economic misery, colonial unrest, and international decline.

For Marc Bloch the decade of the 1930s was punctuated by a striking interaction among personal, professional, and outside political events. In the more peaceful, optimistic twenties he had remained relatively uninvolved in politics and contemporary events. This was no longer possible after 1930. With the Nazi menace across the Rhine, Strasbourg represented an unsafe environment. He sought a post in Paris at a time of shrinking resources and mounting anti-Semitism. Once there, he faced a darkening international situation under a controversial Popular Front government. And after

1 Bloch to Pirenne, 15 Jan. 1935, HP.
2 Sally Marks, "The Misery of Victory: France's Struggle for the Versailles Treaty," *Historical Papers/Communications Historiques* (Winnipeg: Canadian Historical Association, 1986): 117–33.

only three years at the Sorbonne, upon the completion of his magisterial work, *La société féodale*, Bloch, again in uniform, awaited France's second invasion in twenty-five years.

Like his father's long tenure in Lyon, Bloch's in Strasbourg was not originally expected to be permanent. Despite congenial conditions and the university's extraordinary financial support, from the mid 1920s there was a steady flow of departures to Paris. The early euphoria stimulated by Strasbourg's unique mission was soon dissipated. The local Alsatian students tended to be limited and careerist, and, despite the faculty's prestige, the university failed to attract many students from the interior or from abroad. The overall decline of interest in studying history in the interwar period was reflected in the sharp diminution of degree candidates. During Bloch's seventeen-year tenure at Strasbourg he directed only one completed doctoral dissertation.[3]

As its most ambitious students and faculty sought to escape the city and the university's parochialism, Strasbourg became increasingly recognized as the anteroom to Paris. Indeed, the initial hopes for the *Annales* were predicated on both editors' prospective relocation to the capital. Within the Faculty of Letters, where unusually close ties had been forged among the founding professors, there were both a keen sense of loss at each departure for the Sorbonne or the

3 D.E.S. soutenus à la Faculté des Lettres de Strasbourg, ADBR, w 1045/141. Two other candidates, André Deléage and Robert Boutruche, finished later.

The student, William Mendel Newman (1902–77), was an American Jew, born in Missouri, who came to Strasbourg from Toulouse in 1930 to study medieval history with Marc Bloch. Highly intelligent but extremely introspective, Newman suffered in a foreign culture from loneliness and minor health problems as well from misunderstandings with Bloch and practical difficulties with his subject. His principal thesis (which Bloch had suggested), "Le domaine royal sous les premiers Capétiens (987–1180)," was officially accepted on 28 October 1936, successfully defended on 13 February 1937, and accorded the grade "très honorable." Newman's diary, which is in the custody of Professor Giles Constable, Institute for Advanced Study, Princeton, N.J., includes several negative references to Bloch's courses and to his aloof, occasionally caustic personality, along with a grudging admiration, especially in his later years, for Bloch's scholarship. Perrin and Bloch to Maugain, 21, 25 Oct. 1936, ADBR, w 1045/134, for evaluation of Newman's thesis.

Collège de France and a tendency to maintain the contacts that encouraged and promoted further defections.[4]

There was an even more pronounced exodus in the 1930s, the result of a number of factors including the diminishing numbers and growing political radicalism of the students, budgetary reductions, threats of a lowered special supplement to the faculty's basic salaries, the difficulty in recruiting able replacements for lost faculty, and, out of the cumulative sense of disappointment in a provincial institution, the desire to advance at least personally. The local environment, envenomed by autonomist and Nazi propaganda, manifested an intensified anti-Semitism and German influence that reduced the tenuous links between professors and the Alsatian community. Now in a border city, the University of Strasbourg's administration planned as early as 1934 for an evacuation to Clermont-Ferrand in the event of another war. The *réunions du samedi* sharply decreased. A dozen of the most eminent members of the Faculty of Letters departed between 1933 and 1937. Some prudent, ambitious academics even considered locations other than Paris to escape the mounting tensions on the Rhine.[5]

The attractions of Paris were obvious. Its faculties commanded the highest salaries and prestige and, with the best students, colleagues, and work facilities and easy access to the major libraries, archives, research institutes, ministries, and governmental and private foundations, as well as the scholarly journals, publishers, and the press, they could exert significant influence over their disciplines. Balancing its higher cost of living, the capital offered richer, more varied living conditions and the reestablishment of the family and

4 Christian Pfister to Gustave Cohen, 20 Sept. 1925, AN, Gustave Cohen papers/3; Bloch to Febvre, 28 Aug. 1929, AN, MI 318 1; "Zehn Jahre französische Universität in Strassburg," *Elsass-Lothringische Mitteilungen* 12 (1930): 68–69.
  Good discussion of the exodus in John E. Craig, *Scholarship and Nation Building* (Chicago: University of Chicago Press, 1984), pp. 245–48, 320–26.
5 Jacques Godechot, "Georges Lefebvre, historien du Directoire, du Consulat et de l'Empire," in *Hommage à Georges Lefebvre (1874–1959)* (Nancy: G. Thomas, 1960), pp. 23–24; interview with Jacques Godechot, 1981. On German propaganda among the university students: ADBR, AL 98/361. Evacuation plans: Direction de l'Instruction Publique à Strasbourg, "Plan de mobilisation, 1934," ADBR, Université de Strasbourg.

personal ties of a predominantly Parisian-born or -trained faculty.[6]

For Bloch, Paris represented a pressing personal as well as professional goal. The heavy toll of parental deaths in the twenties had made him the senior member of two families. A return to the capital would reunite his Strasbourg clan with his widowed mother in Marlotte and his widowed sister-in-law and two nephews in Paris, and with his wife's three sisters and brother.[7] After over a decade of hurried research trips, made possible by stays at the residence of his wife's deceased parents, he now needed his own place in the capital. Moreover, he wanted his six children, especially those approaching secondary school age, to have access to better and more demanding instruction. There was a first step in 1930, when Bloch used the inheritance from the Vidals to purchase a country home in the tiny village of Fougères in the Creuse, ending his family's itinerant vacations in Alsace. Despite its relative isolation, sombre landscape, and rural poverty, the Fougères property gave Bloch his place in the interior. He acquired the stable urban-to-rural alternation that had nourished his father and most Parisian intellectuals.

As he entered his forties, Bloch's health dictated some relief from Strasbourg's damp, dark climate and cold winters. He suffered from a crippling form of rheumatoid arthritis, which began in October 1914 in the Gruerie, occasionally paralyzed his hands, and forced him to take painful spa cures at Aix-les-Bains. Though leery of exchanging one provincial place for another, Bloch, when his body and spirit ached, like some of his colleagues toyed with the idea of "retiring" to a southern university, to Aix-en-Provence, or even to

6 As of 1 January 1933 a professor in the Faculty of Letters at the Sorbonne occupying the highest rank was paid 20,000 francs more than his Strasbourg counterpart, though at the second rank the difference was only 10,000, and at the third, 7,000. Cf. Enseignement Supérieur/Lettres, "Table de classement du personnel enseignant et des assistants au 1.1.1933," ADBR, AL 154 P4/7. Strasbourg's *première classe* salary, unchanged for three years, was 70,000 francs. Bloch, who in 1936 was finally promoted to that rank, left Strasbourg with a salary of 62,000 francs.

7 After the deaths of his mother-in-law and father-in-law only fifteen months apart: "Que des deuils, ces deux parts, depuis notre mariage" (Bloch to Febvre, 26 July, 9 Aug. 1929, AN, MI 318 1). On his mother: Bloch to Febvre, 24 April 1934, EBC.

19. Fougères: Bloch's country home

Montpellier, where however a rival medievalist, Augustin Fliche, was ensconced. The Paris climate was only slightly more salubrious than Strasbourg's, but its other attractions helped.[8]

For eight years the principal focus of Bloch's Paris quest was the Collège de France. Located in the heart of the Latin Quarter, it had been founded in 1530 with six professors for the purpose of advancing humane studies and the "spirit of the Renaissance." Four hundred years later it remained a small, exclusive research-oriented institution with only forty-seven professors. Subject to direct ministerial authorization for its budget, the Collège was totally independent of the French university structure. The professors, who received permanent appointments, were not required to possess any academic credentials or prepare students for state examinations.

8 Bloch to Febvre, 18 Oct. 1934, 19 June 1935, EBC and 4 Aug. 1936, AN, MI 318 1. Bloch to Pirenne, 29 Sept. 1933, 30 Aug. 1934, 29 May, 21 July 1935, HP. On the debilitating and sometimes lonely spa routine: Marc Bloch to Etienne Bloch, Aix, 3, 8, 13 Sept. 1933, 26 June 1934 (EBC), also containing strong doses of advice and encouragement to his older son.

Their lectures, free and open to the public, covered any subject that interested them and could be arranged according to their own schedule.[9]

Access to this privileged existence depended on a combination of intellectual prestige, professional connections, and good fortune. Vacancies created by deaths or retirements were decided by the faculty, who were not constrained to establish or maintain chairs in specific disciplines. The faculty assembly's deliberations, often prolonged and dramatic, were influenced as much by the candidate's personality as by the Collège's internal environment and outside political factors. Candidates underwent a grueling test that involved not only a formal presentation of their credentials and their main subject in lesson form but also a series of personal interviews with all the electors, men of widely diverse temperaments and professional specializations. The public deliberations were carefully prepared. Each candidate normally had a sponsor who drew on his own personal and scholarly credits as much as his oratorical skills. There were two votes, each requiring an absolute majority of those present. The first assigned a specific field to a vacant chair; the second selected a candidate. The Collège's elections were therefore a small but significant barometer of the intellectual and political climate. In expansive times its procedures occasionally rewarded novelty and innovation, but in shrinking circumstances they favored convention and caution. As the relatively large 1914 generation of academics competed to succeed their still-vigorous elders in a shrinking number of posts, the Collège, despite its formidable entrance procedures, was a prized goal.[10]

Bloch and Febvre first signaled their candidacies for the Collège de France when a vacancy occurred in 1928. Bloch opened his campaign for a chair in comparative history, announcing himself

9 Theodore Zeldin, "Higher Education in France, 1848–1940," *Journal of Contemporary History* 2, no. 3 (July 1967): 77; cf. A. Lefranc, P. Langevin et al., *Le Collège de France, 1530–1930* (Paris: Presses Universitaires de France, 1932).
10 See Febvre to Pirenne, 5 Jan. 1929, HP, on his impending week in Paris "climbing stairs" to court fifty diverse electors. On "la porte étroite," Olivier A. Dumoulin, "'Profession historien' 1919–1939: Un 'métier' en crise?" (thèse pour le doctorat de 3ème cycle, Ecole des Hautes Etudes en Sciences Sociales, 1983), pp. 87–94.

as virtually the only practitioner in France. He then prudently withdrew from the large field of almost a dozen contestants in favor of his senior collaborator, who had declined the "comparative" label and presented himself in modern history. Rather than force the electors into an "embarrassing choice" between them, Bloch agreed that Lucien Febvre would go first.[11]

Febvre, who had turned fifty in 1928, had always intended to return to Paris, where he could exert greater influence as a scholar and teacher. But he was turned down by the Sorbonne in 1926 and decided against a candidacy for the Ecole Pratique des Hautes Etudes, which, although considered an anteroom to the Collège and the Sorbonne, provided inadequate financial support for a family with three young children. Febvre between 1929 and 1933 aimed his efforts forcefully and singlemindedly toward the Collège de France. His assets were an impressive list of publications, including his recent work on Luther, the newly launched *Annales*, and his excellent connections from the Ecole Normale Supérieure, the Fondation Thiers, and the University of Strasbourg, which had sent several of its faculty members to the Collège. Against him were his field, modern history, which had been ignored for almost four decades, and his physical distance from the capital. Most candidates for the Collège were already ensconced in Paris institutions, making them more visible and giving them easy access to the electors.[12]

In the 1920s there had been a steady infusion of new professors into the Collège in the sciences and the liberal arts – but an even greater multiplication of candidates. During Febvre's four-year waiting period, there were in fact twelve appointments. Almost all of these elections were highly competitive and occasionally tinged with political and religious considerations as well as reflecting the traditional rivalries between scientists and humanists. Twice

---

11 Bloch to Febvre, 23 Nov. 1928, AN, MI 318 I; Assemblée des professeurs, 18 Nov. 1928, and Bloch to Croiset, 15 Dec. 1928, CdF, G-iv-j 35C, 36D.

12 Christophe Charle and Christine Delangle, "La campagne électorale de Lucien Febvre au Collège de France, 1929–1932: Letters à Edmond Faral," *Histoire de l'Education* 34 (May 1987): 49–50. Febvre to Faral, 7 Dec. 1929, ibid., pp. 51–53. Febvre's three-part formal presentation (vita, bibliography, and *projet d'enseignement*) in CdF, C-XII 491.

directly defeated, in January 1929 and in March 1932, and once beating a tactical withdrawal, Febvre cautiously waited for his rivals either to win or withdraw while maintaining his core of devoted supporters inside the Collège.[13]

Febvre's fortunes improved in 1932 with the appointment of Anatole de Monzie (1876–1947) as minister of national education. Monzie gave a new chair to the Collège, and he also appointed Febvre *secrétaire-général* in charge of the new *Encyclopédie française*, a major civic as well as intellectual undertaking designed to rival the Italian and Soviet projects. Finally it was Lucien Febvre's turn at the Collège. On 13 November 1932 the electors voted to restore the chair in modern history, whereupon Febvre on 8 January 1933 was unanimously elected and on 19 February was formally admitted through the narrow door at Place Marcelin Berthelot.[14]

Febvre interpreted his victory as a vindication of the *Annales* as well as a revival of the grand tradition of modern history instruction long absent from the Collège. But his triumph scarcely reflected an antiestablishment vote. The *Encyclopédie* appointment was persuasive enough. Moreover, his supporters, although noting Febvre's fruitful alliance with the social sciences, had strongly emphasized his reestablishing the Collège's venerable ties with Michelet, Monod, Lavisse, and Denis. In his inaugural address Febvre paid generous tribute to his supporters and also to Bloch. Perhaps misreading the signals, Febvre confidently assured his collaborator, "You now will follow."[15]

13 Charle and Delangle, "Campagne électorale," pp. 53–69; CdF, Assemblée des professeurs, ser. G IV–K (1929–32).
14 Assemblée des professeurs, 8 Jan. 1933, CdF, G IV-K-14D; Décret, signed by the president of the republic and Monzie, in CdF, C-XII (L. Febvre). Cf. Febvre to Bloch, 20 Aug., 8 Sept., 13 Nov. 1932, AN, MI 318 2; Febvre to Pirenne, n.d. (end Apr. 1933), HP; Charle and Delangle, "Campagne électorale," pp. 53–69; Louis Planté, *Un grand seigneur de la politique: Anatole de Monzie (1876–1947)* (Paris: Clavreuil, 1955), pp. 200–2.
15 Febvre to Bloch, 13 Nov. 1932, AN, MI 318 2. Inaugural lecture, "De 1892 à 1933: Examen de conscience d'une histoire et d'un historien," published in *Revue de Synthèse* (1934), reprinted in his *Combats pour l'histoire* (Paris: Armand Colin, 1953), pp. 2–17; Bloch's appreciation in Bloch to Febvre, 1–2 Aug. 1934, EBC.

Bloch, now forty-seven, was eager to follow. Febvre's absence left a terrible void, and Pfister's illness and death marked the close of an era at Strasbourg. It was therefore timely to revive his candidacy.[16] *Les caractères* had received positive reviews. Bloch had been commissioned to write two volumes on the economic history of the Middle Ages and another on feudal society for Henri Berr's series on the evolution of humanity. He had lectured in Ghent and in Madrid and had been invited for the following year to present three lectures at the London School of Economics.[17] Like Febvre, he was determined to enter the Collège directly, which was one of the reasons he declined a colleague's proposal to offer his candidacy for a vacant position in the Fifth Section of the Ecole Pratique des Hautes Etudes.[18]

Febvre entered the Collège just as darkness was descending on the other side of the Rhine. The aging generation of French intellectuals needed replacement. The death in April 1933 of the Germanist Charles Andler, Gustave Bloch's close friend and fellow Dreyfusard, stirred Marc Bloch into action. With his credentials as a comparative historian he sought to win Andler's chair at the Collège.[19]

Bloch's spontaneous inclination toward *Sturm und Drang* was tempered, on Febvre's strong advice, to a "prudent," exploratory letter-writing campaign. The responses were not encouraging. Less than three months after the Nazi seizure of power in Berlin, the Collège could scarcely dispense with a Germanist.[20] Bloch decided to withdraw before the vote in anticipation of a more suitable occasion, the seemingly imminent departure of the classical archaeol-

---

16 Bloch to Febvre, 14 May 1933, AN, MI 318 1.
17 Bloch to Febvre, 28 Jan. 1932, AN, MI 318 1; Bloch to Lot, 26 Feb., 26 Oct. 1933, Lot papers, IF; Bloch to Maugain (Pfister's successor as dean of the Faculty of Letters), 30 June 1933, ADBR, AL 154 P4/7.
18 Bloch to Le Bras, 7 June 1932 (EBC), identifying himself as a "virtual candidate at the Collège." Bloch (to Febvre, 17 Aug. 1941, AN, MI 318 1) recalled the vacant position, which involved instruction in the religious history of the Middle Ages.
19 Bloch to Febvre, 2 Apr. 1933, AN, MI 318 1.
20 Bloch was correct: On 18 June 1933, the Assemblée voted to retain the chair in Germanic languages and literature, and on 19 November 1933 Bloch's Strasbourg colleague Ernest Tonnelat was elected: CdF, G IV-K16C, 17A.

ogist Camille Jullian, whose chair of national antiquities seemed more likely to be converted.[21]

Having announced his candidacy, Bloch found it enervating to join the line of assorted talented, ambitious, and equally impatient aspirants, which included several friends and colleagues as well as rivals, waiting for deaths and retirements at the Collège. He welcomed but also feared his impending opportunity. He had learned that he needed unequivocal support inside the Collège, and that that could be vitiated by a variety of factors. The intense competition for chairs during the preceding four years had left a legacy of wounds, hopes, and remembered and resented strategies. Febvre, though sympathetic, was greatly preoccupied by his new *Encyclopédie* tasks and, moreover, was still a political novice. Could a small elite institution absorb Bloch as well as Febvre, thus permanently establishing an assertive duo in its midst? Bloch's Jewish background had for the first time become a factor. The long shadows of German anti-Semitism had penetrated French academic life, threatening to reduce the Jews' access to higher positions. Could the Collège, with its Jewish faculty numbering almost 15 percent, add a Bloch? Febvre was disquieted. One anxious Jewish professor strongly counseled him to avoid the brouhaha associated with another Jew's recent candidacy and conduct a "calm" campaign without zealous pursuit of the electors.[22] But Bloch's cause required aggressive promotion and self-promotion. His novel "comparative history" label, reminiscent of the unsuccessful candidacies of his father, the somewhat unconventional ancient historian, and also of Berr, the tireless crusader for *synthèse*, placed him at a disadvantage in any foreseeable contest against practitioners of established fields.

21 Bloch to Febvre, 4, 12, 19, 27 Apr. 1933, AN, MI 318 1. Jullian was the last professional historian elected to the Académie Française in the interwar years, a sign of the gap between scholarship and the grand public. Henri Dubief, *Le déclin de la IIIe République, 1929–1938* (Paris: Seuil, 1976), pp. 141, 143. Later, in *ED*, p. 203, Bloch quoted the right-wing novelist Paul Bourget, who named the Académie Française, the British House of Lords, and the German General Staff as the "three citadels of Conservatism."
22 Febvre to Bloch, n.d. (after 16 Apr. 1933), and Bloch to Febvre, 24 May 1933, AN, MI 318 2, 1. On Sylvain Lévi's earlier apprehensions, see Febvre to Faral, 4 Feb. 1932, in Charle and Delangle, "Campagne électorale," pp. 59–60.

Bloch's candidacy affected his professional life. The more absorbed he became in the Collège's affairs, the more he distanced himself from Strasbourg. Some of his duties, including responsibility for the preparatory courses and the direction of the Institut d'Histoire du Moyen-Age, were filled by his junior colleague Charles-Edmond Perrin.[23] There was a spillover into his publications. In one important instance he reluctantly wrote for the *Revue Historique* an extended evaluation of the work of François Simiand, once one of the chief critics of the positivist historians, who too had succumbed to the limitations of his method, but was also one of the Collège's leading figures. Bloch's tone was appreciative but also critical. His prose was dense with examples, analysis, and comparisons, for he knew that his text would be carefully measured by attentive electors.[24]

This pivotal year, 1933, was also punctuated by severe illness, family concerns, and Bloch's first painful sojourn to heal his almost paralyzed hands in Aix-les-Bains. The threatening events across the Rhine obligated Bloch in late May to attend a brief reserve officers' training course in Strasbourg, his first since the demobilization.[25] With their first prolonged separation came the first signs of strain between the *Annales'* co-directors. Febvre's removal to Paris and the

---

23 Bloch to Maugain, 24 May 1933, 7 Jan., 12 Nov. 1934, ADBR, AL 154 P4/7, 8. In addition to covering Bloch's classes and students, Perrin took up his senior colleague's long crusade for better heating in the Palais Universitaire, a condition that aggravated Bloch's arthritis and, at temperatures below 16 °C, impeded teaching: See Bloch to Maugain, 5 Nov. 1933, ADBR, AL 154 P4/7; Perrin to Maugain, 20, 30 Nov. 1933, P4/7, and 28 Oct. 1935, P5/9. At the height of his Paris campaign in 1934–35 Bloch announced in the bulletin of the Faculty of Letters that he would not hold regular office-hours, but gave his local address and telephone number. (P5/9).

24 "Le salaire et les fluctuations économiques à longue période," *RH* 173 (Jan.–June 1934): 1–31. On its delicacy: Bloch to Febvre, 9 May 1933, AN, MI 318 1, and 16 Nov. 1933, EBC; also Eugen Weber, "About Marc Bloch," *American Scholar* 51 (1981–82): 80.

25 Ministère de la Guerre, Dossier Marc Bloch, SHV. Assigned to the Strasbourg group of subdivisional areas, Bloch received an official commendation for his grasp of the group's functions. Bloch to Pirenne, 30 June, 29 Sept. 1933, HP; Bloch to Alice Bloch, Aix, 6, 9 Sept. 1933, and to Etienne Bloch, 3, 8, 13 Sept. 1933, EBC.

establishment of the journal's secretariat in the capital relieved Bloch of many of the routine responsibilities, but also impeded easy communication and prompt decision making. Bloch's visits to the capital, hurried and strenuous, taxing his health and necessitating absences from his family and his classes, created threefold pressure: They required delicate negotiations with the Strasbourg administration; they had to be prudently interwoven with the Collège's deliberations; and they were constrained by his editorial tasks and the requirements of the *Annales'* flagging publication schedule. Travel became associated with dread as much as with opportunity, and Paris, the ultimate destination, became a fatiguing combat zone.[26]

When Camille Jullian died in December 1933, Bloch began his campaign by soliciting the support of his former Strasbourg colleague Etienne Gilson, recently elected to teach the history of medieval philosophy at the Collège de France. After careful reflection he was still determined to present himself as a specialist in the "comparative history of European societies," refusing to substitute "medieval" for "European" to make his label more acceptable. He carefully selected the venerable Gilson as his patron. Febvre and a few other supporters stood in the background.[27]

Bloch's formal presentation to the Collège, an extended résumé of his intellectual development, was blunt and combative. He appealed to an institution that had a tradition of "welcoming intellectual innovation." He stressed the *Annales'* dedication to social and

26 "J'ai la flemme, oui une flemme intense de promener inutilement dans Paris mes pauvres jambes de rhumatisant." Bloch to Febvre, 20 Mar. 1933[4], EBC. On scheduling difficulties and complications, 5 May 1933, AN, MI 318 I; 9, 16, 28 Oct., 16, 22, 28 Nov., 1 Dec. 1933, EBC. Bloch went to Paris in mid May (after the Collège voted to retain the German chair) and in early December (after the vote to replace Andler with Tonnelat) on *Annales* business and in January 1934 as an announced candidate.

27 Bloch to Gilson, 28 Dec. 1933. Gilson collection, Library of the Pontifical Institute of Medieval Studies, Toronto. Bloch to Febvre, 24, 27 Dec. 1933, EBC. Febvre strongly counseled Gilson to stress Bloch's "traditional" skills, erudition, editing of texts, and close contact with scholars of local history, in undated letter in annex to J. Ambrose Raftis, "Marc Bloch's Comparative Method and the Rural History of Medieval England," *Medieval Studies* 34 (1962): 366–68.

economic inquiry over conventional methodologies and announced his determination to "shatter" (*briser*) antiquated, falsely convenient categories. A self-professed medievalist, Bloch renounced that title's handy "symmetry" on a faculty roster in favor of the freedom to consult all possible sources and range across all possible time lines. He pledged to "continue to passionately study the Middle Ages" but not restrict it to an "empire within an empire," and to attract young, lively scholars who had been repelled by its "falsely frozen appearance." He proposed to teach a European history that stressed the continent's unity and contrasts and laid out general principles but also encouraged detailed research. Comparative history promised to renew historical scholarship, spread its influence beyond France's borders, and exercise a salutary influence over the "rigid framework of our universities."[28]

There were two historian claimants for Jullian's chair, Bloch and the archaeologist Albert Grenier. Grenier, a Strasbourg colleague and contributor to the *Annales*, was considerably older than Bloch and expected to follow in Jullian's steps. Bloch's task was to convince the electors that he had all the scholarly qualifications to fill and enlarge a post in this venerable discipline.[29]

Bloch opened his campaign in early January 1934 with a brief trip to Paris to pay courtesy visits to the principal electors,[30] followed by his much-anticipated voyage to England, his first in thirteen years. He departed with his wife on 28 January amid the disquieting news of riots connected with the revelations of the Stavisky scandal.[31]

Bloch spent a memorable fortnight in England. At the London School of Economics he delivered, in French, three lectures on comparative history entitled "Seigneurie française et manoir anglais." Seeking collaborators for the *Annales*, he spoke with R. H. Tawney, Eileen Power, and Michael Postan. He spent a weekend at Oxford, where he met Sir Maurice Powicke and the refugee scholar Ernst

28 *Projet d'un enseignement d'histoire comparée des sociétés européennes* (Strasbourg: Dernières Nouvelles de Strasbourg, [1933]), which includes "Etat des travaux de M. Marc Bloch" (bibliography up to 31 Dec. 1933) and "Etat des services de M. Marc Bloch" (his curriculum vitae); copy in BN.
29 See Bloch to Febvre, 9 Mar. 1934, EBC.
30 Bloch to Maugain, Paris, 7 Jan. 1934, ADBR, AL 154 P4/8.
31 Bloch to Febvre, 27 Jan. 1934. EBC. "Les manifestations sont visiblement plus que tolerées. Au fond c'est la grosse crise du fonctionnarisme à laquelle nous assistons."

Kantorowicz, and at Cambridge, where he saw G. G. Coulton and J. H. Clapham, who invited him to contribute to *The Cambridge Economic History of Europe*. He also passed several happy hours working in the British Museum. In contrast with his bleak view of the current state of the French academic establishment, Bloch admired the charms and comfort of English university life.[32]

While Bloch was away, on the evening of 6 February 1934 a vast throng of right-wing demonstrators and veterans' organizations gathered at the Place de la Concorde threatening to cross the Seine, storm the Chamber of Deputies, and topple the new Radical government. They accused the government of abetting the notorious Jewish swindler Serge Stavisky (who had died recently under mysterious circumstances) and denounced it for firing a right-wing police official. In the ensuing struggle between the demonstrators and the small numbers of police who had cordoned off the bridge, fifteen people were killed and an estimated fifteen hundred were injured on both sides, making it one of Paris's bloodiest incidents since the Commune. And when a day later the Radical Premier Edouard Daladier resigned to make way for a broad "national union" ministry to combat the disorders, for the first time in the Third Republic's history a government had been overthrown by street violence.[33]

Across the Channel, Bloch experienced the anguish of his remoteness together with the burden of explaining the events to his distressed English hosts. He was struck by the manifestation of rightist

32 "Seigneurie française et manoir anglais: Quelques problèmes d'histoire comparée," AN, AB XIX 3834. Bloch to Gilson, 15 Feb. 1934, Gilson collection, Library of the Pontifical Institute of Medieval Studies, Toronto. Bloch (to Febvre, 15 Feb. 1934, EBC) reported that "the London School of Economics was interested in sending students to us, if the gods wish to let me work with you," but also noted his unpromising efforts to uncover English authors, reviewers, and subscribers for the *Annales*.

33 Julian Jackson, *The Popular Front in France: Defending Democracy, 1934–39* (Cambridge: Cambridge University Press, 1988), pp. 1–2. Gordon Wright, *France in Modern Times*, 3d ed. (New York: Norton, 1981), pp. 380–82, estimates the number of wounded on both sides at 1,500; Dubief, *Le déclin de la IIIe République*, pp. 76–78, gives a figure of over 2,000; Joel Colton, *Léon Blum: Humanist in Politics*, 2d ed. (Durham, N.C.: Duke University Press, 1987), pp. 92–96, gives 1,000. All agree that the 6 February incident was the catalyst for the alliance of the left that eventually produced the Popular Front.

violence emerging from the French middle classes, reminiscent of 18 Brumaire. Returning directly home to Strasbourg nine days later, he remained appalled and mystified: "At the bottom of all this disorder I perceive a horrible and puerile mixture of flabbiness, superficial cliques, poor work habits, and a total lack of intelligence."[34] Febvre, profoundly shaken by the spectre of a French fascism, which he suspected was being nurtured by the most venerable institutions of higher learning, chastised his collaborator. As a result of a brief message Bloch had sent from London during the crisis, he characterized his younger colleague as the incarnation of one of Benda's aloof, disinterested *clercs*.[35]

Bloch and Febvre had indeed moved apart. Febvre for over a year had been established in the capital, residing comfortably with his family on the fifth floor of 1, rue du Val de Grace facing the Val's handsome dome. He had added a rich variety of social and professional contacts, tasks, and travels to his obligations to the *Annales*, the *Encyclopédie*, the *Revue de Synthèse*, and the Société d'Histoire Moderne. Bloch chided his colleague for having become "very Parisian," at the risk of squandering his energies, deserting the historian's laboratory, and neglecting the *Annales*, which was falling ever further behind schedule and was desperate for authors and articles. Bloch, on the other hand, was still a supplicant, calculating his movements, dependent upon his friends, and forced to neglect his own work. Having renounced a second trip to Paris on the eve of the Collège's deliberations, he had further distanced himself from the inflamed political atmosphere that Febvre had absorbed.[36] In such circumstances he was naturally more restrained and objective, but also more vulnerable to Febvre's accusation of indifference.

But Bloch was scarcely indifferent. Privately he expressed concern not only over the extreme nationalist, antirepublican Ligues and the right-wing sympathies of high police officials, magistrates, and municipal officials, but also over the glaring inadequacies of the

---

34 Bloch to Febvre, 15 Feb. 1934, EBC.
35 Febvre to Bloch, 19 Jan., n.d. (9–14 Feb.) 1934, AN, MI 318 2.
36 "I do not intend to come to Paris on the 18th. I await the sentence here." Bloch to Febvre, 9 Mar. 1934; also 15, 20 Feb., 5 Mar. 1934, EBC; also Bloch to Gilson, 15, 20 Feb., 5 Mar. 1934, Gilson collection, Library of the Pontifical Institute of Medieval Studies, Toronto.

moderates and the left, over governmental corruption and parliament's weakness. No, he was not so obsessed with his candidacy that he ignored the omnipresent danger, exacerbated by the disorder of the universities and the "intellectual poverty of so many of our statesmen."[37] Neither Bloch nor Febvre was prepared to mount the barricades in defense of the timid Daladier or prod his aged compromise successor Gaston Doumergue. Both reluctantly signed the 5 March "Manifesto to the Workers" composed by Alain (E. Chartier, 1868–1951), Paul Langevin (1872–1946), and Paul Rivet (1876–1956), three prominent left-wing intellectuals and veterans of the Dreyfus era who helped found the Comité de Vigilance des Intellectuels Antifascistes (CVIA).[38] Both directors of the *Annales* had misgivings about the tone of the manifesto and the CVIA's leadership, and placed little confidence in the value of mass appeals. Torn between his sense of duty ("Ma bonne volonté est toute prête") and inaction ("Elle est, comme beaucoup d'autres, sans emploi"), Bloch was nevertheless opposed to combating the threat of domestic fascism by imitating its demagogic methods.[39] He

37 "Ne croyez pas que toutes mes pensées soient centrées sur le tout petit morceau de France que sont les dix pieds carrés de votre salle de réunion. Je suis profondément troublé par tout ce que je vois, entends, lis, ou devine. La menace est partout: dans le fascisme de M. Frot ou du Colonel La Rocque, dans les indignations vertueuses de Chiappe et de l'Hôtel de Ville, dans les sottes élucubrations de Léon Blum et le 'pas d'histoire' des vieux manoeuvriers parlementaires qui prétendent être notre Comité de Salut Public." Bloch to Febvre, 20 Mar. 1933[4], EBC. See also 16 Feb., 14 Apr. 1934, EBC. Bloch was even more scathing on the weakness of France's parliamentary regime in *ED*, pp. 199–205.

38 Bloch to Febvre, 16 Feb., 20 Mar., 13 Apr. 1934, EBC. Bloch signed a day after the meeting on Jullian's chair (which was at least a month before the next), hoping to avoid the impression of flattering Paul Langevin, professor of physics at the Collège de France and a key elector (Bloch to Febvre, 14 Jan. 1934, EBC).

39 "Je me refuse obstinément à faire le jeu de tous les fascismes en emboîtant les pas derrière MM les Postiers." Bloch to Febvre, 19 May 1934, AN, MI 318 1. Febvre to Bloch, 19 Jan., n.d. (after 12 Feb.), n.d. (early Mar.) 1934, AN, MI 318 2. On "les hommes de bonne volonté" (the archtypical *normaliens* of Jules Romains's novel, who in the interwar period moved from the professoriate to public service) on the one hand and the CVIA on the other, see Pascal Ory and Jean-François Sirinelli, *Les intellectuels en France, de l'Affaire Dreyfus à nos jours* (Paris: Colin, 1986), pp. 78–79, 98–99; also David Caute, *Communism and the French Intellectuals, 1914–1960* (New York: Macmillan, 1964), pp. 113–14.

was reluctant to enter a hypercharged, politicized atmosphere, led by a motley combination of libertarians, pacifists, socialists, and communists.[40]

One day before Bloch signed the manifesto, on 18 March, the deliberations of the electors of the Collège de France ended in a shocking setback. Bloch's supporters, led by Gilson, proposed a chair in the comparative history of European societies. Grenier's adherents, led by Abbé Breuil, insisted on the maintenance of national antiquities. After he had spoken on Grenier's behalf, the chemist Camille Matignon fell unconscious and died, and the debate was suspended for two months.[41] In gathering testimonies and pondering the deeper reasons for the debacle, Bloch was chagrined by Febvre's passive role during the public deliberations and even more by his own inactivity after returning from London, which undoubtedly had weakened his cause. Determined to revitalize his campaign and make additional trips to Paris, he appointed Febvre "secretary" of the "Bloch syndicate" to keep his name before the electors.[42]

Bloch's renewed campaign was soon aborted. In less than a month, on 12 April 1934, the Doumergue government published its budget-cutting decrees that severely curtailed university expenditures. The 10 percent reduction mandated for the Collège de France meant that Jullian would not be replaced.[43]

Bloch, who had seen this possibility, was disappointed but not entirely without hope. If access to the Collège was blocked, he turned his attention to the Sorbonne, where several retirements in medieval and economic history were expected within the next two

40 Commenting on an article submitted to the *Annales* by a Polish medievalist, Bloch objected to the substitution of "Gdansk" for the proper historical name Danzig. Bloch to Febvre, 19 May 1934, AN, MI 318 1.

41 Febvre to Bloch, n.d. (before 18 Mar.), 18, 19 Mar. 1934, AN, MI 318 2; also CdF, Assemblée des professeurs, 18 Mar. 1934, G IV-K-18K.

42 "Il y a, comme naguère un Syndicat Dreyfus, qui fit beaucoup parler de lui, aujourd'hui un Syndicat Bloch. Permettez-moi de vous en constituer secrétaire." Bloch to Febvre, 9 Apr. 1934, EBC; see also Bloch to Gilson, 20 Mar. 1934, Gilson collection, Library of the Pontifical Institute of Medieval Studies, Toronto. Bloch to Febvre, 20, 22 Mar. 1934, AN, MI 318 1.

43 CdF, Assemblée des professeurs, 20 June 1934, G IV-K-19B.

years. There Bloch entered another keen competition and a new, wearying round of entreaties for a less prestigious, more demanding post. Either place in Paris was worth all his efforts. He was determined to leave Strasbourg, which he increasingly regarded as a cold, remote "hole," suffering its own budget cuts, staff losses, internal bickering, and declining morale, and where his promotion had been delayed.[44] Added to his mounting health and family concerns, the difficulties over the *Annales*, and the slow progress of his work were the menacing international and national developments of mid 1934: the brutal Nazi intervention in Austria, Hindenburg's death, and troubling signs of French weakness. Like Febvre, Bloch sought in his work an antidote to discouragement and in the *Annales* a critical if not powerful voice in the politics of the day. During the summer of 1934 Bloch recouped his energy and spirits alone at Aix, with his family in Fougères, and on an idyllic trip to Venice. There was another tough round of combat ahead.[45]

In the fall the Collège was granted a single chair to replace the four recently vacated, but additional contestants entered the competition. Bloch's rivals now included two more Strasbourg colleagues and Febvre's oldest friend, the psychologist Henri Wallon.[46] Dutifully visiting Paris to test the waters and work on the *Annales*, he returned ill, fatigued, and disgruntled that he had missed an exposition on aerial photography that would have been useful for his research. He was absorbed with his family and laden with work. Among his projects at this time were a multivolume series on the history of the peasantry for Gallimard, a chapter on feudalism for the *Cambridge Economic History*, the article on the water mill for the *Annales*' special issue on technology, the "Alimentation" entry for

44 Bloch to Febvre, 20, 22 Mar., 9, 12, 14, 24, 28 Apr., 3, 11 May 1934, AN, MI 318 I. Budget cutbacks in Strasbourg detailed in Craig, *Scholarship and Nation Building*, pp. 320–23.

45 See Bloch to Pirenne, Fougères, 30 Aug. 1934, HP. Also Febvre to Bloch, 14 Apr., n.d. (before 31 May), n.d. (26 June–10 July) 1934, AN, MI 318 2; Bloch to Febvre, Aix, 26 June, n.d., Fougères, 24 Aug. 1934, AN, MI 318 I; Aix, 9 July, Fougères, 14, 29 July, 1–2, 12, 23 Aug. 1934, EBC; to Alice Bloch, Aix, 25 June, 5 July 1934, and to Etienne Bloch, Aix, 26 June 1934, EBC.

46 Bloch to Febvre, 18, 21 Oct. 1934, EBC; Febvre to Bloch, n.d. (Oct.–Nov.) 1934, AN, MI 318 2.

the *Encyclopédie française*, and his usual stack of reviews of works in many languages and on a wide variety of subjects. Bracing himself for another disappointment, Bloch plunged into his work as a shield against the next judgment. Considering himself a far less facile writer than Febvre, he found refuge in the slow, meticulous technique where he sought an "inner freedom" from the narrow confines imposed by his candidacy.[47]

The blow did indeed fall on 15 January 1935. Two days before, voters in the Saar had overwhelmingly approved reunification with the Third Reich.[48] At the Collège on that fateful day the five contenders for the one chair were arranged for presentation in the following order: national antiquities, statistics, chemistry, experimental psychology, and comparative history of European societies. As Bloch expected, psychology drew a substantial number of votes away from him, and the scientists gravitated toward Grenier. By the fourth ballot the venerable national antiquities had achieved the requisite majority of twenty-two. Psychology, with nineteen, had established a strong claim to the next chair, and Bloch, with one, had been openly defeated.[49]

Bloch appraised his defeat philosophically, informing Pirenne he had too many irons in the fire to succumb to the poison of discouragement.[50] Febvre, trying to console Bloch and himself, scratched the wound of his own inexplicable silence and of rumored anti-Semitism among the Collège's faculty.[51] Whatever its deeper causes,

47 Bloch to Febvre, 21 Oct., 21, 23, 30 Nov. 1934, EBC; also 23, 28 Nov., 11, 14 Dec. 1934, AN, MI 318 1; to Dean Maugain, 12 Nov. 1934, ADBR, AL 154 P4/8.
48 In Moscow the purge trials of former leading Bolsheviks had resumed, and France under Pierre Laval had commenced a policy of cautious overtures to Italy, Germany, and Russia. Jean-Baptiste Duroselle, *Politique étrangère de la France: La décadence, 1932–1939* (Paris: Imprimerie Nationale, 1979), pp. 124–42.
49 CdF, Assemblée des professeurs, 13 Jan. 1935, G-IV-K-210. Bloch's case was presented by André Siegfried and supported by Alexandre Moret and Antoine Meillet; see "Proposition de création d'une chaire d'histoire comparée des sociétés européennes au Collège de France," ibid. G-IV-K-21A; Grenier's formal election, 8 Dec. 1935, G-IV-K-26K.
50 Bloch to Pirenne, 15 Jan. 1935, HP.
51 Febvre to Bloch, 13, 30 Jan., 2 Feb. 1935, AN, MI 318 2; also Febvre to Pirenne, n.d. (Mar. ?) 1935, HP.

Bloch's failure was a blow to his ego, his long-held plans, and his future prospects of entering the Collège, and it forced him to divert his attention toward the Sorbonne.[52]

Hope was rekindled when François Simiand died unexpectedly in April 1935. Bloch, who was depressed by international events, and the news of Nazi Germany's renunciation of the disarmament clauses of the Versailles Treaty and introduction of universal conscription, sought an escape from his bleak thoughts in a "new adventure," the attempt to succeed to Simiand in the chair of the history of labor at the Collège. This approach had the advantage of avoiding competition with the popular psychologists. But once again a supplicant, "the eternal candidate," he had to depend heavily upon his friends, and especially Febvre, for support.[53]

To be safe, Bloch, anticipating Henri Hauser's retirement, at the same time also worked diligently to gain France's only chair in economic history at the Sorbonne.[54] He was not optimistic over either prospect, or about the future. Pirenne's death in October 1935 was a severe loss. His relations with Febvre were, at best, prickly. Their personal and editorial debates grew heated, and the *Annales* continued to fall further behind schedule. Contemplating the next International Congress of Historical Sciences scheduled for August 1938, Bloch speculated whether within the next three years he might find himself in a concrete bunker or in a concentration camp.[55]

Cautious until the end, he nevertheless hoped to assemble enough support to succeed Simiand. However, he quickly recognized that there was significant opposition in the Collège to a historian's occupying Simiand's chair. Suddenly, in early February 1936, the Faculty of Letters of the Sorbonne unexpectedly voted to retain Hauser's chair, with Bloch's candidacy in view. Unwilling to pursue two candidacies simultaneously, Bloch chose the more likely and

---

52 Bloch to Febvre, 15 Mar. 1935, EBC.
53 Bloch to Febvre, 13, 18 Apr. 1935, AN, MI 318 1, and 1 May, 11, 19 June, 15 Sept, 31 Oct., 2, 5 Nov. 1935, EBC. On 3 November the Collège voted to retain Simiand's chair: CdF, G-IV-K-24S.
54 Bloch to Febvre, 4 July 1935, EBC, and 9 Sept. 1935, AN, MI 318 1; to Ferdinand Lot, 4 Aug., 4 Sept. 1935, Lot papers, IF.
55 Bloch to Febvre, 20 Dec. 1935, AN, MI 318 1.

withdrew once and for all from contests at the Collège. In a surprising twist, his Sorbonne rival Emile Coornaert, who since 1930 had been a professor at the Ecole Pratique des Hautes Etudes, was elected on 29 March to fill Simiand's chair.[56]

Bloch's formal election to the Sorbonne was unexpectedly delayed. In the meantime German troops had entered the formerly demilitarized Rhineland. By foreclosing the possibility of French military support for its East European allies, the Third Reich had completely altered the European balance of power. Until it became clear that France and Britain would not respond to this treaty violation, Bloch, at the border in Strasbourg, was anxious about the safety of his family.[57] It was not until 18 June that the Sorbonne's Faculty of Letters voted unanimously to offer him the position in economic history. His official appointment was signed by the new minister of national education, Jean Zay, on 28 July 1936.[58]

Bloch's postmortem was blunt and unsparing. This was, after all, the first major setback of his career, and it had been accompanied by

56 Bloch to Febvre, 27, 28 Jan., 7 Feb. 1936, EBC; Bloch to Administrator Bedier, 11 Feb. 1936. CdF, G-IV-K-29H; Febvre to Bloch, n.d. (29 Mar.) 1936, AN, MI 318 2; Bloch to Febvre, 30 Mar. 1936, AN, MI 318 1. Coornaert was elected on the third round by a vote of 23 to 13. CdF, Assemblée des professeurs, G-IV-K-29X.

57 Bloch to Febvre, 12 Mar. 1936, AN, MI 318 1. Interpretations of the Rhineland crisis in Barry R. Posen, *The Sources of Military Doctrine: France, Britain and Germany between the World Wars* (Ithaca, N.Y.: Cornell University Press, 1984), pp. 104–6, 126–7; Stephen A. Schuker, "France and the Remilitarization of the Rhineland, 1936," *French Historical Studies* 14, no. 3 (1986): 299–338.

58 Bloch's initial appointment was as *maître de conférences* (lecturer), which was upgraded to *professeur sans chair* on 4 Jan. 1937 and to a (transformed) chair of economic history on 1 Nov. 1937 (AN, AJ 16 4757).

On his candidacy: Fawtier to Lot, 5 Jan. 1936, Lot papers, IF; Bloch to Febvre, 19 Apr. 1936, AN, MI 318 1, and 12 May 1936, EBC.

The recommendation of the selection committee (he was the sole candidate) consisting of Pagès, Carcopino, and Roussel – "Il n'est pas douteux que la large compétence de M. Bloch, son expérience professionnelle incontestée le mettent en état de diriger très brillamment à la Sorbonne les études d'histoire économique" – was adopted unanimously by the Faculty Council, 18 June 1936 (AN, AJ 16 4757); notice from Dean of the Faculté des Lettres to Rector, Université de Paris, 19 June 1936, ibid.

an uncomfortable combination of professional and personal nonacceptance. In the past he had overcome the ostracism of certain medievalists by creating his own professional identity with his writing, teaching, lectures, and journal. But he had failed to convince the Collège's electors that they should reward his personal achievement. On the other hand, he recognized a serious recrudescence of anti-Semitism, a "curious social phenomenon" that had penetrated the frontier from the east, aimed not specifically against himself but at his name and his ancestry. According to Bloch, there were two types of anti-Semites, those who wished to "exterminate" or expel the Jews, whose excessive and repugnant manner rendered them less dangerous than the second, the "numerus clausus" types, who established a fine, impenetrable quota on outsiders. This second category included many assimilated Jews, eager to guard the gate for their own self-aggrandizement and self-defense. In contributing to his exclusion both had imposed an external limit on Bloch's aspirations, not unconnected with his intellectual nonconformism, but nevertheless more intractable, painful, and generalized in its implications.

Bloch also interpreted his setback as a symptom of the corruption of French academic and political life.[59] Viewing his Sorbonne election as a vindication, he pledged to strive there to bring in "fresh air." To be sure, the responsibilities of his new position would limit his horizons. He would not enjoy the freedom of the chair he had envisaged for the Collège, and would have to continue his seventeen-year struggle against the constraints of the *agrégation*. But he intended, together with Febvre, to carry on the task of change.[60]

The Paris he had reached was in considerable ferment, reminiscent of his youth during the Dreyfus Affair. After the bitterly fought legislative elections of April-May 1936 produced a Popular Front majority, Léon Blum on 4 June formed a Socialist-Radical

59 Four years later, in criticizing the powerful quasi-public corporations that had sapped the vitality of the Third Republic for their "bureaucratic tendencies, routine mentality, and professional arrogance," Bloch included those venerable academic institutions that filled their vacancies "by a system of co-option that was not without its dangers when the need for new blood arose." *ED*, pp. 202–3. An even later postmortem in Bloch to Febvre, 28 May 1943, EBC.
60 Bloch to Febvre, 30 Mar., 19 Apr. 1936, AN, MI 318 1.

cabinet supported by the communists in the Chamber. Faced with mass strikes, the new government moved vigorously to settle the nationwide labor disputes, and in its first ten weeks sent parliament a spate of social legislation, a historic collective bargaining act, nationalization measures, and a bill dissolving the right-wing Ligues. Anti-Semitism had flared at once. At the opening session of the new Chamber, the rightist deputy Xavier Vallat (who four years later would be appointed commissioner-general for Jewish affairs under Vichy) announced: "Your arrival in office, M. le Président du Conseil, is incontestably a historic date. For the first time this old Gallic-Roman country will be governed by a Jew."[61]

Target of immense hatred and lacking the charisma and following of Jaurès, the humanist-socialist Blum at age sixty-four faced enormous tasks. France was beset by right and left radicalism and by threats abroad. When the Spanish Civil War erupted in July 1936, his nonintervention policy alienated the communists. The right was hostile toward his social policies. Mounting budget deficits, prices, and unemployment led to capital flight and alienated workers. Bloch returned to the capital at a time of malice and calumny: "Overnight there was a crevice in the stratum of French society, separating social groups into two blocs."[62]

But Paris was still a major intellectual and cultural center. Under the Popular Front, scholarship received increased official support. The Centre National de la Recherche Scientifique (CNRS) was created in 1936 and the Musée de l'Homme a year later.[63] In literature,

61 *Journal Officiel, Chambre des Députés, Débats parlementaires, compte-rendu sténo-graphique*, 6 June 1936. Edouard Herriot, who had just defeated Vallat by a vote of 377 to 150 for president of the Chamber, tried futilely to interrupt him, but Vallat continued: "I have the special duty here...of saying aloud what everyone is thinking to himself: that to govern this peasant nation of France it is better to have someone whose origins, no matter how modest, spring from our soil than to have a subtle Talmudist." Herriot censured the speaker but gave the furious Blum no opportunity to respond. Colton, *Blum*, pp. 144–45.

62 *ED*, p. 209; cf. Dubief, *Le déclin de la IIIe République*, pp. 171–207. Bloch's hopes for academic reform by the Popular Front: Bloch to Febvre, 12 May 1936, EBC; concern over Spain: 4 Aug. 1936, AN, MI 318 1.

63 But one of Bloch's "decent" bourgeois acquaintances had obstinately refused to set his foot inside the universal exposition of 1937, despite the "incomparable display of the glories of French art," because "a detested minister had officiated at the opening ceremony"; others justified their abstention by the demands of the trade unions. *ED*, pp. 209–10.

20. Paris: the Panthéon and rue Soufflot, ca. 1936

painting, music, dance, theater, and film, Paris's rich atmosphere, in shining comparison to its eastern and southern neighbors, remained a magnet for creative spirits, especially those seeking refuge from totalitarianism.[64]

Bloch settled into a spacious apartment on the upper two stories

64 On the cultural policy of the Popular Front, Ory and Sirinelli, *Les intellectuels*, pp. 102–3; Jackson, *Popular Front*, pp. 113–45.

of 17, rue de Sèvres, which contained a private study and library for his work, comfortable quarters for his large family, and handsome areas to entertain his friends, colleagues, and students.[65] At fifty, he was a distinguished-looking figure, small, compact, well-groomed, and elegantly attired. His age was revealed in his balding, somewhat wrinkled countenance. A thick, bushy mustache stretched between his rather large nose and exceptionally narrow lips. His most striking feature was his pale eyes, which stared intensely from behind thick glasses, generally creating a serious expression but on occasion producing smiles of irony or genuine warmth. Bloch was a demanding but devoted husband and father. A heavy smoker, severely self-disciplined and nervous, in the privacy of his home Marc Bloch sometimes succumbed to sudden fits of anger which he ascribed to his "nasty character."[66]

Bloch savored the joys of Parisian bourgeois life: good cuisine, the company of his old friends from the Ecole Normale, concerts, exhibitions, the theater, and film. For relaxation he read voraciously in science and literature and, like many middle-class Europeans of his generation, his favorite murder-mystery authors, Agatha Christie and Dorothy L. Sayers, in the original English.[67]

Bloch was a popular, admired professor at the Sorbonne. There with his colleague Maurice Halbwachs he co-founded the Institute of Economic and Social History and devoted himself to its development.[68] He also taught courses at the Ecole Normale Supérieure

65 The elegant and well-organized domestic atmosphere of the rue de Sèvres is described in an essay by his oldest son, Etienne Bloch, "Marc Bloch: Une vie complète," pp. 11–13, AN, MI 318 1, and also in interveiws with Etienne, Alice, Louis, and Daniel Bloch as well as with several of his former students.
66 Etienne Bloch, "Marc Bloch," p. 11.
67 Ibid., pp. 13–16.
68 Bloch, "A l'ombre de la Sorbonne (Note sur l'Institut d'histoire économique et sociale)," *AHES* 10 (1938): 53.
      Established by the Assembly of the Faculty of Letters on 12 February 1938 and approved by Minister Jean Zay on 10 June, the Institute was set up "to develop, coordinate, and promote studies on the history of *faits économiques* in themselves and in their relationship with the history of ideas as well as of social structures." With its own working library – not duplicating any existing collection – it was to fill a definite lacuna in the scholarly resources of Paris. Bloch, who was officially named director of the Institute on 28 November 1938, received a subvention of 16,000 francs in January 1939. AN, AJ 16 2597, 4758.

21. Sarah Bloch, Marc Bloch, and his nephew Jean Bloch-Michel

and the *Écoles Normales* of Saint-Cloud and Fontenay. Among his students were the future historians Michel Mollat, François Chevalier, and Pierre Goubert, and the future government official Pierre Sudreau. Bloch was a devoted, natural teacher, whose courses were memorable experiences for young scholars and whose kindness, wit, and brilliance left an enduring impression.[69]

Now in the nation's center, Bloch was available to participate in a rich variety of professional activities. He helped set up the International Congress of Folklore held in Paris in the summer of 1937, took part in the Commission des Recherches Collectives of the *Encyclopédie française*, the *journées* of Berr's Centre de Synthèse, the Comité Français des Sciences Historiques, and the Société des Professeurs d'Histoire et de Géographie. He served on the national commissions on the history of law, toponymy and anthrotoponymy, and the economic history of the French Revolution.[70] For two years he compiled the bibliographies of French economic history for the *Economic History Review*. During this busy, challenging period Bloch was also able to organize a memorable work trip and family journey through the English countryside in September 1937.[71]

It was a remarkably productive time. Now officially titled an economic historian, Bloch plunged into the discipline with his characteristic energy, resourcefulness, and critical perspective. In January 1937, addressing an audience of *polytechniciens*, he asserted the essential characteristic of his new trade, the need to establish

69 Interviews with Pierre Goubert (1980) and Georges Livet (1982) (Bloch's students at Saint-Cloud); François Chevalier (Ecole Normale Supérieure) (1981); Pierre Sudreau (Sorbonne) (1982).

See also Bloch to Brunschwig, 11 June 1939 (Courtesy of Professor Brunschwig), a ten-page letter (with five endnotes) giving his former Strasbourg student detailed criticisms and suggestions on his thesis, "La crise prussienne à la fin du XVIIIe siècle et la genèse de la mentalité romantique," which was being prepared under the supervision of another professor.

70 See Bloch's article "Alimentation" in *L'encyclopédie française* XIV (*La civilisation quotidienne*) (Paris, 1954), 14-40-2, 3. Also "Au visiteurs," Bloch's introduction to the BN exhibition *Les travaux et les jours dans l'ancienne France* (Paris, June–Sept. 1939). Bloch's other activities are detailed in his file "Collaborations diverses," EBC.

71 Bloch to Febvre, London, 20 Sept. 1937, AN, MI 318 1.

long patterns of analysis, to understand contemporary phenomena not in terms of "yesterday" but by reaching back to their furthest, most pertinent traces.[72] According to Bloch, the historian of economic as of all human questions must tear away the "convenient screen" of the immediate past to perceive those "distant truths of history" that might once again manifest themselves.[73] On the other hand Bloch refused to neglect political realities. In his course at the Sorbonne on the economic aspects of the reign of Louis XIV, Bloch attributed France's economic decline under the Sun King, as compared with the prosperity of its Dutch and English neighbors, to an absolutist system that had systematically expropriated capital, stifled initiative, and impoverished the peasantry.[74]

Bloch still considered it his duty to scrutinize German scholarship. In 1938 he finally ended his arduous surveys for the *Revue Historique* with strongly critical remarks against the infiltration of the Nazi ideology into German medieval historiography, separating the Third Reich from Europe.[75] In his review of Friedrich Meinecke's two-volume opus *Die Entstehung des Historismus*, he offset his appreciation of an incontestable intellectual achievement with vigorous criticism of its underlying premises: the virtual "deification of the

---

72 "What would you think of an astronomer who attached much more importance to the study of the moon than the sun on the lovely pretext that the distance between the star at the center of our planetary system and the earth is approximately 390 times superior to that which separates us from our satellite?" "Que demander à l'histoire?" lecture, 29 Jan. 1937, *Centre Polytechnicien d'Etudes Economiques* 34 (1937): 15–22, reprinted in X-Crise, Centre Polytechnicien d'Etudes Economiques, Son Cinquantenaire 1931–1981, *De la récurrence des crises économiques* (Paris: Economica, 1982), pp. 138–49. My thanks to Ambassador René Brouillet, who attended Bloch's lecture, for an interview and a copy of the text.

73 Three years later, in *ED*, p. 169. Bloch also criticized oceanographers "who refuse to look up at the stars because they are too remote from the sea, and consequently are unable to discover the causes of the tides" (pp. 197–98).

74 *Aspects économiques du règne de Louis XIV* (Paris: Les Cours de Sorbonne, 1939).

75 *RH* 184 (1938): 190. Bloch, who had virtually lost contact with his German colleagues, commented to Febvre on 20 Sept. 1937 (AN, MI 318 1) on the "odious" behavior of the Third Reich's representatives at the folklore congress in Paris.

state"; the insistence that historical thought had reached its climax in the period between Goethe and Ranke; the negation of the efforts in the twentieth century, admittedly timid, uncertain, and outside Germany, to integrate history into a larger human science; and, finally, the pretension of examining the *esprit* of historical scholarship while resolutely ignoring questions of technique, as if studying the theory of physics but neglecting what actually happened in the laboratory. Bloch recognized the ancient rivalry between *idée* and *Begriff* and, after looking conscientiously across the frontier, concluded that neither side had an exclusive claim on defining the truth.[76]

As an investigator of *mentalités* Bloch was sensitive to the popular appeal of Nazism, its deft use of symbols and rituals to mobilize the masses. Just before the debacle of 1940 Bloch praised a book by a French ethnologist who had underlined the resurrection of pre-Christian myths and gods in the Third Reich.[77] Shortly afterward he ruefully noted that by virtually abandoning those national rituals that exalted and united the people, the Third Republic had "left it to Hitler to revive the paeans of the Ancient World."[78]

To be sure, Bloch's principal subject and primary preoccupation during these last years before World War II was his long-delayed study of feudal society. He had sketched an outline earlier in 1931, in his article in the *Encyclopedia of the Social Sciences*. He further developed his ideas in the lectures he had delivered in London in 1934; in his chapter on seigneurial institutions in the first volume of *The Cambridge Economic History of Europe*, which he completed in 1937;[79] and in the three lectures he presented at Cambridge in May 1938 entitled "Some Economic and Psychological Aspects of

76 "'Historisme' ou travail d'historiens?" *AHS* 1 (1939): 429–30.
77 Review of Georges Dumézil, *Mythes et Dieux des Germains* (Paris, 1939), in *RH* 188 (Apr.–June 1940): 274–76. Bloch's review has recently stirred controversy. See Carlo Ginzburg, "Mythologie germanique et nazisme: Sur un ancien livre du Georges Dumézil," *AESC* no. 4 (1985): 695–715, and Georges Dumézil, "Science et politique: Réponse à Carlo Ginzburg," no. 5 (1985): 985–89.
78 *ED*, pp. 210–11.
79 Chap. VI, "The Rise of Dependent Cultivation and Seignorial Institutions," trans. J. H. Clapham, *The Cambridge Economic History of Europe* I (1941), pp. 224–77; see Clapham to Bloch, 12 Sept. 1937, 3 Mar. 1938, EBC.

Feudalism."[80] Finally, in 1939 and 1940, his long-delayed two-volume masterpiece *La société féodale* appeared.[81]

Here was the culmination of Bloch's training as a medievalist and the clearest manifestation of his strategy in the *Annales*. In *La société féodale* Bloch combined all his skills, in languages, law, literature, iconography, toponymy, geography, and psychology, to produce a brilliant representation of the social structure of Western and Central Europe between the middle of the ninth and the beginning of the thirteenth century. But this was no static tableau. Bloch's design, open-ended, included economic and political analysis as well as a cogent description of mental climate. He defined two feudal periods, one born of invasion and devastation, the second marked by economic expansion and intellectual revival, and used one to define the other. Employing the problem approach of the *Annales*, he not only examined the various autochthonous feudal systems of France, Germany, and Italy, but compared these with imposed systems (England), noted places (Ireland, Scandinavia, Frisia) where feudalism did not take root, and leaped abroad to Japan to underline specific characteristics of the European experience.

Bloch's text, less taut and disputatious than in his earlier works, was often eloquent. There were memorable aphorisms concerning the uncertain medieval concept of time and the ways language had served both to unite and separate peoples; startling ironies, like the relatively easy conversion to Christianity of the warlike Vikings and the widespread multiple loyalties of vassals; revealing cultural clues, such as the function of the heroic epic, the often distorted, falsified texts which nonetheless were an essential element of the medieval European imagination; strong descriptive writing about the violent world and character of the nobility and the distinctive landscape of rural villages; fascinating parentheses on the historical importance of the stirrup and on changes in family structure in the thirteenth century; and an elegant conclusion, that feudalism had introduced in the West a contractual basis for freedom and the right of resistance.

In *La société féodale* Bloch transcended the old legalistic, schematic

---

80 Text in AN, AB XIX 3813; plans and preparations in EBC.
81 Vol. I: *La formation des liens de dépendance* (Paris: Albin Michel, 1939); vol. II: *Les classes et le gouvernement des hommes* (Paris: Albin Michel, 1940).

descriptions of feudal institutions and his predecessors' arguments over their Roman or German origins. With his penchant and facility for classifying vast amounts of disparate information, he conveyed most of the essentials of the complex reality of a living society without succumbing to the pitfalls of pedantry or oversimplification. To be sure, there were gaps and there were shortcomings. Bloch's "Europe" was limited to the boundaries of the Carolingian world; he was unbalanced in evaluating the Vikings; he virtually ignored two classes – the clergy and the bourgeoisie; and his insistence on the medieval roots of modern nationalism, national antipathies, and Franco-German differentiation seems excessive.

Through the inauspicious timing of its appearance, *La société féodale*, though written for the broad audience of Berr's series "L'évolution de l'humanité," received a delayed and limited response, and that primarily from specialists.[82] Curiously, the sole major criticisms came from his colleague Febvre, who complained in the *Annales* about the book's arbitrary categories, schematic character, absence of individual portraits, and limited view of "civilization." On the other hand, French, Belgian, and even German medievalists welcomed and praised Bloch's synthesis, which to this day, despite many scholarly revisions, represents a signal contribution to both the scholarly and lay audience.[83]

82 Bloch to Ferdinand Lot, 28 Nov. 1941, Lot papers, IF.
83 Febvre's reviews in *AHS* 2 (Jan. 1940): 39–43; 3 (1941): 125–30. Bloch's response, 8 May 1942, AN, MI 318 1. Important contemporary reviews by William A. Morris in *AHR* 45 (1940): 855–56; 46 (1941): 617–18; F. M. Powicke in *English Historical Review* 55 (1940): 449–51; F. L. Ganshof in *Revue Belge de Philologie et d'Histoire* 20, nos. 1–2 (1941): 183–93; Ch.–E. Perrin in *RH* 194 (1942–44): 23–41, 114–31; Ferdinand Lot in *Journal des Savants* (Jan.–Mar. 1943): 12–32, 49–58; Theodor Schieffer in *Deutsches Archiv für Geschichte des Mittelalters* 4 (1940–41): 278–79.
   Later appreciations and criticism by Lawrence Walker, in *History and Theory* 3 (1963): 247–55; Bryce Lyon, "The Feudalism of Marc Bloch," *Tijdschrift voor Geschiedenis* 76 (1963): 275–83; G. Picasso, *Le istituzioni della società feudale nell' opera di M. Bloch* (Milan: Celuc, 1971). Recent critical writing by Elizabeth A. R. Brown, "The Tyranny of a Construct: Feudalism and Historians of Medieval Europe," *AHR* 79, no. 4 (Oct. 1974): 1063–88; Constance B. Bouchard, "The Origins of the French Nobility: A Reassessment," *AHR* 86, no. 3 (June 1981): 501–32. Editions of *La société féodale* have been published in Italy, Japan, Mexico, Great Britain, the United States, Hungary, Argentina, Sweden, Portugal, Spain, Israel, and Germany.

But just as he was completing his *chef d'oeuvre*, the domestic and international situation deteriorated, and before the appearance of the second volume Bloch would be back in uniform.[84] After Blum resigned on 22 June 1937, the Popular Front, though governing until April 1938, expired in spirit if not in form, a victim of its adherents' blunders and equivocations and of its enemies' obstruction and contempt.[85] As the franc fell ceaselessly and government expenditure and trade deficits mounted, French diplomacy became distinctly passive. Poincaré's spirit had been exorcised by Messrs. Mussolini, Hitler, and Laval. In the face of the Rome-Berlin axis and the anti-Comintern pact, of Franco's advances and the Japanese invasion of China, Paris's alliances had evaporated. Belgium reverted to neutrality; the Little Entente ceased to function; and Britain under Chamberlain initiated a vigorous, largely independent policy of appeasing the dictators with France trailing distractedly behind.[86]

Bloch was convinced that France had succumbed to "decadence," much noted at home and abroad.[87] Soon he would catalogue its manifestations. A sensationalist press and stultifying educational system had failed to stimulate critical thought. A succession of coalition governments had planted incompatible personalities and ideologues in positions of power. An atavistic diplomacy had been based obstinately on yesterday's "faded ghosts." The political parties on the left and the right had been notorious for their narrowness and contradictions. The trade unions had been marked by sectarian and

---

84 In his foreword to the English edition, *Feudal Society* (London, 1961), p. xi, Michael Postan recalled receiving his copy "de la part de l'auteur aux armées." Bloch's private papers, EBC, contain a list of the individuals and journals to receive copies of *SF*.

85 *ED*, pp. 209–12; cf. Dubief, *Le déclin de la IIIe République*, pp. 219–22.

86 Bloch to Febvre, London, 20 Sept. 1937, AN, MI 318 1. Cf. Duroselle, *Politique étrangère:* "La pâle année 1937," pp. 314–25.

87 "At the time when Belgium had just rejected the offer of an alliance in favor of a neutrality that unhappily turned out to be fallacious, a friend of mine in Brussels said: 'You've no idea of the amount of damage done to the French cause by your great Weeklies. They declare in every issue that France, as a nation, is in an advanced stage of putrescence. Well, I'm afraid we believe them. How can you expect us not to?' I'm afraid we believed them only too well." *ED*, p. 211. See the debate over "decadence" in "Fall of France: Causes," proceedings of a conference, 10 May 1980, Center for European Studies, Harvard University (Cambridge, Mass., 1980).

kleinbürgerlich considerations that constricted urgent production. The bourgeoisie had been tinged by arrogance and contempt for the masses. And the army had been dangerously isolated from the world of ideas. Plagued by the permeating fatalism of its aged rulers, France, unlike Germany, clung to the world of the old while rejecting the new. Though after 1937 there was some economic restructuring, and arms production accelerated, France failed to construct enough modern engines, tanks, and planes, to adequately train its army and reservists, and to develop the requisite diplomacy, tactics, and strategy to deter the fascist threat.[88]

When Nazi Germany annexed Austria in March 1938, Blum, rebuffed in his efforts to form a Union Nationale, was still in the process of organizing the last Popular Front cabinet, which survived only one month. The Anschluss occurred at the moment when some Frenchmen were reciting "Better Hitler than Blum!" There were unmistakable signs of flaccid resistance by the democracies to the Third Reich's treaty violation and lack of concern over its absorption of an additional 183,000 Austrian Jews. Bloch and Febvre had long been concerned about the fate of Austria, about the spread of Nazism in its academic circles and the suppression of the left. In the wake of the Anschluss and the ensuing persecutions of Austrian scholars, Bloch decided to withdraw his contribution to the volume honoring the illustrious Austrian medievalist Alfons Dopsch. Suspecting that this scholarly homage would be restricted to supporters of the new order and would lack the "intellectual freedom and healthy scientific confraternity" essential to such an enterprise, he felt that someone of "his nationality, his ideas, and his name" ought not be a collaborator in a work published in Vienna.[89]

The Eighth International Congress of Historical Sciences met in

88 *ED*, pp. 176–214 passim. On rearmament and its shortcomings, see also Duroselle, *Politique étrangère*, pp. 445–58, and Robert Allan Doughty, *The Seeds of Disaster: The Development of French Army Doctrine, 1919–1939* (Hamden, Conn.: Archon, 1985), pp. 178–90.
89 Bloch to Erna Patzelt, 13 Apr. 1938, courtesy of Professor Patzelt. Earlier correspondence: 9 Dec. 1936, 23, 29 Sept. 1937. Bloch did, however, contribute an article for the Italian historian E. Besta: "De la cour royale à la cour de Rome: Le procès des serfs de Rosny-sous-Bois," *Studi di storia e diritto in onore di E. Besta* (Milan: A. Giuffré, 1938), II, pp. 149–64. Correspondence, EBC.

Zurich between 28 August and 3 September 1938 under even darker clouds than Bloch had predicted three years earlier. The war scare provoked by Hitler's claims against Czechoslovakia appeared about to erupt into hostilities.[90] War was averted when the Allies capitulated at the Munich conference on 30 September. In July Bloch had taken part in a three-day training course at group subdivisional headquarters in Strasbourg. After seventeen and a half years as a reserve officer, he was still a captain assigned to staff duties. He had neglected to attend any formal refresher courses that would have qualified him for a promotion. Called up on 25 September at the height of the international crisis over Czechoslovakia, Bloch joined thousands of reservists who descended on Strasbourg during that anxious weekend. From this exposed border he glumly observed the defects of "Operation 41": The arriving reservists found insufficient supervisory personnel and inadequate matériel and provisions, which compounded the confusion, fear, demoralization, and opposition that accompanied France's first real demonstration of force.[91] There were scant echoes of 1914. After grimly preparing for bombing and invasion, France ecstatically greeted Daladier's return from Munich and largely ignored its own desertion of a tiny democratic ally.[92]

Munich bought peace at a considerable price. Bloch consoled himself that young lives had been spared and the land not destroyed. However, his relief was tinged with dismay and bitterness as he reflected on France's political and moral deterioration from Versailles and the Ruhr to the time of Spain and Munich. He was finally demobilized on 6 October, and, as usual, the antidote to gloom and disgruntlement was his work, into which he plunged with renewed energy.[93]

90 See above, note 55. Ch. –Edmond Perrin, "Les historiens au congrès de Zurich," *AHS* I (1939): 307–9.
91 Bloch, "Témoignage: Observations sur les opérations d'application de la mesure 41, 26–27 sept. 38," AN, AB XIX 3852. Also Ministère de la Guerre, Marc Bloch dossier, SHV; *ED*, pp. 26–27.
92 Duroselle, *Politique étrangère*, pp. 355–66. French sentiments of fear and relief evoked in Jean-Paul Sartre, *The Reprieve*, trans. Eric Sutton (New York: Knopf, 1951).
93 Bloch to Febvre, 3 Oct. 1938, AN, MI 318 I. Cf. J. H. Clapham (editor of *The Cambridge Economic History of Europe*) to Bloch, 21, 22 Sept. 1938, EBC.

But in the garden of work other problems loomed. This was a time of considerable tension between the *Annales*' co-directors, who had just completed their first decade of collaboration. Before and after the Munich crisis there were heated exchanges relating to alterations in the journal's title, staff, and direction.[94] Febvre's views largely prevailed. He introduced the new personnel and the new slant of the *Annales d'Histoire Sociale*. With his permanent place at the Collège de France and with the completion of over half the volumes of the *Encyclopédie*, the expansion of his circle of disciples, and the resumption of his much-delayed *Rabelais*, Febvre remained the senior partner, well accustomed to his secure position in French academic life.[95] Bloch, on the other hand, worn down by his labors to establish himself as an expert economic historian, was still searching for his stronghold. To be sure, the completion of *La société féodale* represented an important milestone in his long, arduous climb.[96]

Suddenly at the end of 1938 another candidacy loomed, the directorship of the Ecole Normale Supérieure. The philosopher-sociologist Célestin Bouglé (1870–1940), vice-director from 1928 to 1935 and director since 1935, was approaching retirement, and there was due concern over his succession. Bouglé was an admired administrator, greatly appreciated by the *normaliens* for his concern for their welfare.[97] His career had manifested the special combination of scholarly commitment and political engagement, the effort to reconcile humanism and social justice, that marked his 1890s group of *normaliens*. *Agrégé* in philosophy in 1893, he had gravitated

94 See Chapter 7.
95 In November 1938 Febvre was appointed to represent the Collège de France on the council of Bloch's Institute of Economic and Social History. During the preceding spring under the shade of "his cedars" in Le Souget, Febvre, who had turned sixty, reflected on "his public, his work, and his concerns." Febvre to Bloch, 18 June 1938, AN, MI 318 2.
96 Bloch to Febvre, 5 Dec. 1938, AN MI 318 1.
97 During Bouglé's tenure a few women (including Simone Weil) were for the first time admitted to the Ecole. Robert Smith, *The Ecole Normale Supérieure and the Third Republic* (Albany: State University of New York Press, 1982), pp. 76–78, 101, 136; a dissenting opinion on Bouglé's administration in his successor Jérôme Carcopino's *Souvenirs de sept ans* (Paris: Flammarion, 1953), p. 189.

cautiously toward Durkheim's ideas. As a lycée professor at Saint-Brieuc during the Dreyfus Affair he had helped found the local Ligue des Droits de l'Homme and eventually became its vice-president. Bouglé, a lifelong adherent of the Radical party, had been a candidate in legislative elections in Toulouse and Paris, was for thirty years a bimonthly contributor to *La Dépêche*, and in 1924 had been a strong supporter of the Cartel. On his visits to the United States in 1926 and 1938 he had delivered lectures at Harvard and Columbia. Tied both to the liberal democratic philosopher Elie Halévy and to the leftist Durkheimians, Bouglé was committed to the virtues of *culture générale* as well as to the necessity of organized research in sociology and the other social sciences. As director of the privately funded Centre de Documentation Sociale, which was located in the Ecole, he had overseen research and intellectual exchange important in the development of interwar sociology. In short, the directorship had been filled by an open, liberal spirit committed to the Ecole's mission of leadership in the world of ideas and action.[98]

Bloch was reluctant to seek such an exalted position, one that would curtail his activities as a scholar and expose him to bureaucratic, ceremonial, and political pressures. On the other hand he believed he had adequate credentials to be an administrator and was concerned about the survival of the Centre. Moreover, as a war veteran he considered himself better qualified than his expected rival, a noncombatant with ostensibly left-wing, pacifist views.[99] In

98 See esp. Célestin Bouglé, *The French Conception of "Culture Générale" and Its Influences upon Instruction* (New York: Bureau of Publications, Teachers College, Columbia University, 1938). Also "Célestin Charles Alfred Bouglé: 1870–1940," *American Journal of Sociology* 45 (Mar. 1940): 770; W. Paul Vogt, "Un durkheimien ambivalent: Célestin Bouglé, 1870–1940," *Revue Française de Sociologie* 20, no. 1 (Jan.–Mar. 1979): 123–40; Ory and Sirinelli, *Les intellectuels*, p. 46.

On the radical and socialist traditions of the Ecole Normale, "two branches of the same political tree rooted in the Enlightenment," see Smith, *Ecole Normale*, pp. 114–26.

Materials on the Centre de Documentation Sociale in AN, 61, 67 AJ 97, and in RFA.

99 Bloch to Febvre, 5 Dec. 1938, AN, MI 318 1, referring to Maurice Halbwachs, Bouglé's old collaborator and potential successor, who was supported by Lucien Febvre.

the aftermath of Munich he felt it was essential for intellectuals to come forth and promote "vigilance" against the forces that menaced France.[100] Nevertheless, in the shadow of Blum's coup de grace Bloch was prepared for the burden of his name. Uncowed by the growing condemnation all around him of Jewish anti-Fascist militancy and "warmongering," he made ready to assert his principles and point to his complete and long-standing citizenship.

According to his decade-long custom, Bloch consulted Febvre about the potential candidacy at their alma mater. Febvre, who favored someone else, was decidedly negative. On personal grounds, he cautioned that Bloch's "inflexible" temperament might provoke the assertive *normaliens*. On professional grounds, he warned his already overburdened colleague that jealous rivals might charge him with unbridled ambition. But above all, there was the overriding issue of anti-Semitism. Given the current tense atmosphere, he feared that Bloch might be stripped of his dignity and subjected to all the abuses being heaped collectively upon the Jews.[101]

Although still undecided over whether to become a candidate, Bloch refused to accept any of Febvre's objections.[102] Acknowledging both the existence of anti-Semitism and the danger of ignoring it, he declared that "courage" was the best response. According to the law he was a French citizen, and that fact, he insisted, surpassed everything else. In the face of a distressing political atmosphere and undoubted personal risk, Bloch invoked the almost vanished, self-effacing value system of 1915 and 1916. When a task was necessary, it must be pursued "jusqu'au bout." Bloch neither backed down nor considered an assistant directorship.[103]

It was now a quarter of a century since Marc Bloch as a young

100 In the winter of 1938 Bloch joined the Amis de la Vérité, a former pacifist organization which now adopted a violently anti-Munich platform. See Etienne Bloch, "Marc Bloch," AN MI 318 1.
101 Febvre to Bloch, n.d. (6 Dec.) 1938, AN, MI 318 2, written under the letterhead of the Comité de l'Encyclopédie Française, which reported that students at Strasbourg had recently threatened violence if Zay, the minister of national education, visited the university.
102 Bloch to Febvre, 7 Dec. 1938, AN, MI 318 1.
103 Bloch to Bouglé, 18 May 1939, AN, MI 318 1. Bouglé died in office on 25 January 1940, when Bloch was already in uniform, and was replaced by Gustave Bloch's protégé Jérôme Carcopino.

historian had exuded pride in his country and an unquestioned sense of membership in the French nation. Tried in battle, exalted by victory, and marked by two decades of personal, professional, and political growth and upheaval, Bloch in 1939 was still an ardent patriot, though not uncritical of his country.[104] The scholar had learned to examine the key features and regional peculiarities of his own society and compare it with others within the larger context of Europe. He had demonstrated the value of history in ferreting out remote, complex, and obscure links with the present. The citizen, however, had occasionally been lax, too cautious or too distracted to respond to signals of danger to himself and his homeland. As he himself aged, Bloch's love of France was cast into a new relationship: the "mother," once vigorous, accomplished, and celebrated, now frail, occasionally incompetent, and subject to betrayal by her brood, vis-à-vis the illustrious, exigent "son," who had served her in his work and whose trials and achievements over the twenty-five years had cemented the bond. In the meantime the ranks of the pre-1914 rivals and antagonists had swelled – those who gloated over France's feebleness and corruption and openly awaited a "punishment."[105] As his beloved seemed to shrink before the final challenge, Bloch's became an increasingly isolated voice, insisting on the ancient high standard, ignoring his vulnerability and emphasizing his responsibility.[106]

The international scene grew darker in 1939. Franco toppled the Spanish Republic in February. One month later Czechoslovakia was dismembered and Nazi Germany seized Memel. Ironically, for Bloch March 1939 was an exceptionally rich month, with lectures at the Institut des Hautes Etudes in Brussels called "Monetary Mutations in France under the Old Regime" and at an Anglo-French conference in Cambridge entitled "The Problem of Classes in France and England in the Middle Ages."[107] In the midst of the new

104 Lecture notes, AN, AB XIX 3796, 3831.
105 *ED*, p. 214.
106 The image of the weak mother and the disappointed, berating lover is strong a year later in *ED*, pp. 167, 197.
107 Brussels text: AN, AB XIX 3824; Cambridge text, AN, AB XIX 3834. In connection with his Brussels lecture, see Stenghers to Bloch, n.d., and Bloch to Stenghers, 29 Mar. 1939, courtesy of Professor Jean Stenghers.

international crisis, Bloch was recalled hastily from Cambridge to reserve duty in Strasbourg, where he was briefed on "modifications to the 1938 mobilization plans."[108]

France, now completely surrounded by fascist and small neutral states, essentially clung to its twin pillars of the Maginot Line and the English alliance. At this point an aroused Britain offered daring but essentially unfeasible guarantees to Hitler's next probable targets, Poland and Romania. In that last spring of the Third Republic, France's mood was permeated by somber visions of Verdun and Dachau, Guernica and Prague. "Why die for Danzig?" taunted the right.[109]

Bloch spent the summer quietly at his country home in Fougères. He made a short motor trip with his wife to work in Paris, with its strained mixture of glitter and fearful expectancy. They also went to Geneva to view an exhibition of paintings from the Prado Museum. Bloch interpreted the absence of Goya's depiction of the 3 May 1808 executions as possibly too painfully evocative of "more recent massacres."[110]

On 23 August Berlin and Moscow startled the world with their nonaggression pact, which gave Germany a virtually free hand in the east. With mounting Nazi threats against Poland, the Western democracies had to decide between further capitulation and war. Marc Bloch was ready for war and ready to defend France.[111] On 24 August 1939 he was called up for the third and last time. Except for some brief visits during the next four and a half years, he had left Paris for good.[112]

108 Ministère de la Guerre, Marc Bloch dossier, SHV; Marc Bloch to Alice Bloch, 6 Apr. 1939, EBC; *ED*, p. 27.
109 Marcel Déat in *L'Oeuvre*, 4 May 1939.
110 Marc Bloch to Etienne Bloch, 12 Aug. 1939, EBC.
111 Interview with Raymond Aron, 1982, and in his *Mémoires* (Paris: Julliard, 1983), p. 161. Marc Bloch to Etienne Bloch, 12, 24 Aug. 1939, EBC. EBC.
112 *ED*, p. 27, gives his call-up date as 24 August; Bloch's military records (Ministère de la Guerre, Marc Bloch dossier, SHV) as the 25th.

9. Strange Defeat

It is useless to comment on the events. They surpass in horror and in humiliation all we could dream in our worst nightmares.[1]

In 1914 most of Europe was permeated by a warm atmosphere of idealism and patriotism. The mood a quarter of a century later was somber and resigned. Except for the Poles, who were joined resolutely in defense of their homeland, World War II did not begin as a popular war. Two days after the 1 September German invasion of Poland, when Hitler refused to withdraw, the Allies grimly honored their commitment and declared themselves in a state of war with the Third Reich. Once more Italy at the outset of hostilities announced its neutrality; this time Stalin's Russia stood by its nonaggression treaty and awaited its own advantage; and twenty-one other Continental nations waited fearfully on the sidelines, attempting to protect themselves from domination or destruction.[2]

In France national unity on the eve of another great war had been eroded by at least a decade of economic distress and political and ideological cleavage. This was an imposed war. But there was no clear and imminent danger, no Alsace-Lorraine to liberate, no precise war aims. Personal loyalty to the nation and its honor was tempered by the doleful awareness of Marc Bloch and many others that for them this was, after all, the "second time."[3]

1 Bloch to Febvre, 8 July 1940, AN, MI 318 1.
2 Gordon Wright, *The Ordeal of Total War, 1939–1945* (New York: Harper and Row, 1968), pp. 7–12.
3 Bloch to Febvre, 17 Sept. 1939, AN, MI 318 1. Cf. Frederick Seager, "Les buts de guerre alliés devant l'opinion (1939–1940)," *Revue d'Histoire Moderne et Contemporaine* 32 (Oct.–Dec. 1985): 618–38, Jean-Pierre Azéma, *From Munich to the Liberation, 1938–1944,* trans. Janet Lloyd (Cambridge: Cambridge University Press, 1984), p. 19, and D. Barlone, *A French Officer's Diary (23 August 1939–1 October 1940),* trans. L. V. Cass (Cambridge: Cambridge University Press,

Bloch was again posted to Strasbourg, where his first duties involved the evacuation of the exposed civilian population behind the shelter of the Maginot Line. The expected immediate German bombing and shelling of Strasbourg did not materialize. The evacuation was completed without too much difficulty in a "strangely poignant calm." Across the Rhine the enemy displayed a surprising and clever benignity. For example, he declined the opportunity to fire on such easy targets as two depots for recruits close to the river bank that curiously had not been relocated when the Kehl bridgehead was remilitarized in 1936.[4]

Despite continuing alerts, the panic of the war's opening days was quickly dispelled by the enemy's inactivity, at least on the western front. Parisians after the first false air-raid alarms soon put aside their gas masks, and the city regained a semblance of composure and normality. Bloch nevertheless had already decided to install his family in an apartment in Guéret, the Creusois departmental seat, about twenty-nine kilometers from Fougères, well removed from the *atmosphère d'alerte* that might at any moment descend on the capital, and safely distant from any imaginable battle zone.[5]

Bloch admitted afterwards that his experience during the first days of mobilization had given him a "considerable shock." As could be expected, the new system of depots, replacing the old corps organizations, produced all sorts of delays and difficulties. The

---

1942), pp. 1–5. Barlone, a World War I veteran and captain in the 2d North African Division of the First Army who later joined the Free French forces, though in a command-post rather than a staff position, produced a work that complements Bloch's *ED*.

4 *ED*, p. 42; also Marc Bloch to Philippe Wolff, 4 Jan. 1940, courtesy of Professor Wolff; Marc Bloch to Alice Bloch, 31 Aug. 1939, EBC; Bloch to Febvre, 5 Sept. 1939, AN, MI 318 1. Cf. Alistair Horne, *To Lose a Battle: France 1940* (Harmondsworth: Penguin Books, 1979), pp. 126–27. The Germans apparently wished to promote the notion of their benevolence by obligingly turning on their searchlights from the other side of the river while Strasbourg was being evacuated (p. 134). Despite the smoothness of the procedure, many Alsatians were less than eager to be moved. SHV, 31 N 142.

5 Bloch to Febvre, 17 Sept., 4 Oct. 1939, AN, MI 318 1. Bloch to Mollat, 4 Dec. 1939, courtesy of Professor Mollat. Bloch's mother stayed with his family through the winter.

procedure for obtaining supplies was haphazard and inefficient. The officers waded through cryptic numbered "measures" set long in advance,[6] and there was "appalling confusion" in setting up units and commands. On 5 September Bloch's subdivisional group headquarters moved back from Strasbourg to Molsheim, a main transit route in the foothills of the Vosges, where they devoted themselves to setting up provisions, communications, base, and transit facilities for the Sixth Army. At first Bloch, busy with "paperwork and details," relished being "in the thick of things" and having the chance to mingle with "different types of people." Discouragement eventually set in when the Sixth Army at last established its own organization and took over these chores. His tasks reduced to menial duties, Bloch contained his boredom behind a calm demeanor, but he yearned to serve in a more useful capacity.[7]

Despite local mishaps and difficulties France's mobilization was judged to have proceeded unexpectedly smoothly and thoroughly. At the outbreak of hostilities there were 67 French divisions on a war footing plus the first contingent of 5 British Expeditionary Force divisions that were beginning to arrive in the north, against an overall total of 107 German divisions, over three-quarters of which were committed to the east.[8] Nevertheless, while Poland rapidly succumbed first to the Nazi onslaught and then to the Soviet occupation, the Western democracies remained relatively inactive. Conforming to its obligation, France launched a minor attack on the Saar and daily fired a few rounds from the Hochwald bastion of the Maginot Line but, fearing retaliation, vetoed British proposals to

6 Later Bloch recalled that one insufficiently understood message led to the "premature massacre of all the carrier pigeons" of Alsace and Lorraine. *ED*, pp. 91–92.
7 Marc Bloch to Alice Bloch, 31 Aug., 14 Sept. 1939, EBC; Bloch to Febvre, 5 Sept. 1939, AN, MI 318 1; *ED*, pp. 27–28, 92–93. Bloch's small party consisted of five persons, a general of brigade, a lieutenant-colonel, two captains, and a lieutenant, who spent their time sitting in their schoolroom office "longing for a runner to arrive unexpectedly with some official form that would provide us with an excuse for filling up still further forms." On mobilization: SHV, 31 N 139, 144.
8 Horne (*To Lose a Battle*, pp. 127–28) notes that mobilization was too efficient, occasionally denuding vital war industries of manpower; it also (Bloch to Febvre, 3 May 1940, AN, MI 318 1) seriously reduced the number of civilian doctors.

float mines down the Rhine. Britain, also fearing reprisals, refused to bomb the Ruhr, and only dropped innocuous propaganda leaflets over Germany. More might have been done. France could conceivably have penetrated the weakly defended Siegfried Line and fought its way toward Berlin. But there was never any intention of risking a major offensive for Poland, despite almost universal admiration for its short, futile struggle against overwhelming odds. While acknowledging the Poles' courage, Bloch shared the widespread, longstanding French disapproval of their "artificially" enlarged and indefensible borders set after World War I and of Warsaw's unreliable leadership. When Poland capitulated on 28 September, he endorsed the "prudence" of France's strategy, on the one hand its massive preparedness to avert German "surprises" and on the other the avoidance of a prodigious squandering of human blood as in 1914.[9]

Although the original *casus belli* had disappeared with the destruction of Poland, Daladier refused to respond to Hitler's peace offer of 6 October, thus accepting the inevitability of an armed struggle in Western Europe. Marc Bloch foresaw a protracted and geographically extended conflict in which the Allies' superior material resources would ultimately vanquish the more aggressive, audacious foe. He also dreaded another round of postwar "misunderstanding" between Britain and France.[10] In the meantime there were serious areas outside Allied control: Stalin's plans, Mussolini's calculations, and, closer to home, the neutrals' display of jealous independence. Bloch fretted over their secrecy and their unwillingness to coordinate their defense plans.[11] In addition he lacked confidence in Daladier's resolve and was critical of the internal

9 Bloch's critical words on the Poles in letters to Etienne Bloch: 14, 28 Sept., 5 Oct. 1939, EBC.
10 Bloch to Etienne Bloch, 22 Oct. 1939, EBC, with comments on George Bernard Shaw's "eccentric" politics, on the remnants of pacifism among the English left, and on his fears of a postwar recrudescence of Poincarism.
11 Bloch's harsh words on the neutrals: "Très prompts à crier au secours quand ils ont la frousse, mais désireux, par dessus tout, de ne pas se faire casser la figure: ce qui est humain et un peu lâche; car quel serait leur sort, en cas de victoire allemande, par bonheur bien improbable..." Bloch to Etienne Bloch, 14 Feb. 1940, EBC.

policies of his cabinet of National Defense. Despite the French communists' lack of "moral courage," Bloch disapproved of their proscription when no comparable steps had been taken against the equally subversive radical right.[12]

In his painful enforced leisure Bloch weighed the personal repercussions of the impending conflict. He urged his two oldest children who were impatient to serve to complete their studies, for it would be a "long war."[13] To Febvre he glumly predicted new hopes and disappointments, and the heroism and slaughter that would inevitably engulf the young. He confessed his own "bad conscience": After four years of horror between 1914 and 1918 he and his generation had "sold their souls" for some repose and intellectual freedom, unwittingly entrusting power to inadequate leaders and standing by mute while they wrecked Europe with a faulty, mismanaged peace settlement.[14]

But during his autumn of disgruntlement Bloch the historian was never bored. As usual, he was fascinated by the "human spectacle" around him. In between his meager chores he read a bit, purchased a notebook, and began to write.[15] To "exorcise the demons of the present" he planned a history of the French people, not excluding politics, wars, or great individuals, but to be primarily a history of the "profound realities" of one distinctive and cherished national group within the broader context of European civilization. It would be dedicated to Pirenne, "who, at the time his country was fighting

12 Bloch to Etienne Bloch, 14 Sept., 27 Oct., 3 Nov. 1939, EBC. French communist deputies had initially voted in favor of war credits, but on 20 September, following the directives of the Comintern, the PCF endorsed the partition of Poland, denounced the "imperialistic war," and urged an end of hostilities. A week later the government declared the dissolution of the party. Azéma, *Munich to the Liberation*, pp. 26–27; Horne, *To Lose a Battle*, pp. 145–48.
13 Marc Bloch to Etienne Bloch, 11 Sept. 1939, and to Alice Bloch, 14, 20 Sept. 1939, EBC.
14 Bloch to Febvre, 17 Sept., 10 Oct. 1939, AN, MI 318 1. Cf. *ED*, pp. 215–16: "J'appartiens à une génération qui a mauvaise conscience....Puissent nos cadets nous pardonner le sang qui est sur nos mains!"
15 Marc Bloch to Etienne Bloch, 14 Sept., 5 Oct. 1939, and to Alice Bloch, 29 Sept., 9 Oct. 1939, EBC; Bloch to Febvre, 8 Oct. 1939, AN, MI 318 1. Cf. *ED*, p. 28.

beside mine for justice and civilization, wrote in captivity a history of Europe." Separated from his notes and his library, Bloch commenced with the introduction, a nine-page discussion of criticism of sources, indicating the joy as well as the toil of his suspended craft.[16]

On 10 October he was moved to a new group headquarters in Saverne to perform "equally dreary tasks," but he stayed only two days. After weeks of entreaties Bloch was rescued by a well-placed friend. He joyfully left Alsace, reassigned to First Army headquarters in Picardy.[17]

Now Bloch moved away from the area of France's heavy eastern defense fortifications to the north facing Belgium, where more than three years after the Brussels government's declaration of neutrality the Maginot Line had not been completed. Since the mid twenties French strategy had been based on a continuous impregnable line of defense. But instead of extending its concrete emplacements to the sea, France had devised the "Belgian maneuver": German troops, thwarted by the Maginot Line, were again expected to pour through the Low Countries, whereupon French and British forces were to move quickly over the border, link up with the Belgians, and establish a short, tight line that would halt the invasion. This was a predominantly political plan, to demonstrate French resolve to defend a small neutral country, to reinforce Britain's commitment, and this time to keep the struggle off French soil as well as to add more manpower to the Allied defense.[18]

16 "Histoire de la société française dans le cadre de la civilisation européenne," Molsheim, 22 Sept. 1939 (EBC), which was the germ of Bloch's *Apologie pour l'histoire*. Cf. Lucien Febvre, "Comment se présentaient les manuscrits de 'Métier d'historien,'" *AH*, pp. 161–62.

17 Marc Bloch to Alice Bloch, 9 Oct. 1939, EBC; *ED*, p. 28. Determined to use his skills as a liaison with the British Expeditionary Force, Bloch appealed to his colleague Gabriel Le Bras, assigned to the 2d Bureau (Intelligence), to his fellow *normalien* Edouard Herriot, and also to one of Gamelin's aides: Bloch to Febvre, 5, 17 Sept., 8 Oct. 1939, AN, MI 318 1. It is not certain which "high-ranking officer" effected Bloch's transfer. *ED*, p. 28.

18 "La mission en Belgique," Opérations de la 1ère Armée, SHV (cf. *ED*, pp. 52–53); Robert Allan Doughty, *The Seeds of Disaster: The Development of French Army Doctrine, 1919–1939* (Hamden, Conn.: Archon, 1985), pp. 62–69; Barry R. Posen, *The Sources of Military Doctrine: France, Britain, and Germany between the World Wars* (Ithaca, N.Y.: Cornell University Press, 1984), pp. 105–40.

There were serious drawbacks to this plan. By deferring to the neutrals' scruples, it gave the enemy a precious time advantage. The offensive side, requiring much advance preparation, entailed considerable risks of rapid movement: disarray of commands, communications, and provisions; depletion of reserves; inability to anticipate weak points; and also the relinquishing of the human and material advantages of defending the homeland. Moreover, France's defensive planning was also defective. Lulled by the ostensible protection of the Maginot Line, it ignored the vast potential of German *Blitzkrieg* both as a model to emulate in developing more effective armored forces and as a caution against complacency once the onslaught began.

Bloch, a historian devoted to the science of change, concurred with the doctrine of his superiors, that the old predominantly offensive strategy of Napoleon and Foch was obsolete: "le feu tue" (literally, "fire kills"). He was convinced that the most minutely planned attacks could be impeded by solidly entrenched defensive positions bolstered by improved firepower and automatic rifles, modern antitank weapons, and railroads that facilitated the rapid deployment of reserves. Thus in the exposed north, a sector passively waiting to respond to a Nazi strike through the Low Countries, he experienced the debilitating effects of France's flawed strategy.[19]

A circuitous route via Paris brought Bloch to First Army headquarters at Bohain in Picardy, where he was greeted by a "lovely northern sunlight." In response to his repeated requests, he was assigned by General Headquarters to the Intelligence Branch as liaison with the British, but he immediately discovered that as one of three appointees for the same task he would have to share the duties. He was placed in the 4th (Quartermaster-General's) Bureau and again involved with transport, labor supply, and rations. After a hurried study of English military vocabulary and army organization Bloch had his first encounter with his Q Branch English counterparts on 23 October.[20]

He soon perceived the shallowness of Allied collaboration. There were two separate armies occupying nearby districts without real contact or understanding. The British reputedly worked more dili-

19 Marc Bloch to Etienne Bloch, 27 Oct. 1939, EBC.
20 Bloch to Febvre, 15 Oct. 1939, AN, MI 318 1; to Etienne Bloch, 16, 22 Oct. 1939, and to Alice Bloch, 17, 22 Oct. 1939, EBC; cf. *ED*, p. 29.

211

gently at their chores. But, according to Bloch, they also offended French sensibilities with their soldiers' looting and lechery and their officers' detachment and snobbery. Through his efforts a British officer was attached to First Army Intelligence, but neither side succeeded in surmounting personal and national distrust and prejudices. Even more damaging, Bloch was unable to persuade his superiors to appoint a permanent French liaison at Lord Gort's headquarters. Without daily contact, comradeship and closeness failed to develop. Discouraged by the meager results of his intermittent and mainly perfunctory visits, and with his chiefs' tacit consent, Bloch finally quit traveling the road to Arras.[21]

A new challenge had developed when Bloch was asked to replace the officer in charge of petrol supplies. Overnight he became "the mighty Fuel King of the most heavily motorized army on the whole of the French front"[22] who, at a few hours' notice, would have to support its rapid forward motion. With the help of a sympathetic fellow officer he underwent a crash course on fuel and soon learned to "count petrol tins and ration every drop." His apprenticeship over, Bloch like "everyone else slipped back into the unexciting existence of the military bureaucrat," in which stages of calm were followed by periods of frenetic activity. Because of the gap in crucial information on the organization of fuel supplies in Belgium, Bloch managed to conduct one successful, if unauthorized, inquiry into petrol dumps on neutral territory.[23]

"Let us hope," Bloch wrote his wife as he began learning the fuel-trade, "that Hitler decides to go slow for a week or two."[24] Indeed, the Führer had originally intended to strike the west soon after Poland fell. In October he ordered the attack for as early as 12 November. But this was Europe's coldest winter in a half-century. Faced with weather delays and fierce disagreement among his generals over a plan for decisive victory and not another war of attrition in the west, a vacillating Hitler finally postponed the assault until

21 *ED*, pp. 99–103, 108–13. Cf. Barlone, *Diary*, p. 35; Horne, *To Lose a Battle*, p. 138.
22 *ED*, p. 29.
23 Bloch to Febvre, 12 Nov. 1939, AN, MI 318 1; Bloch to Le Bras, 15 Nov. 1939, EBC; *ED*, pp. 29–31, 114–16, 133–38. Bloch to his fourteen-year-old son Daniel (16, 26 Apr. 1940, EBC), gives detailed descriptions of his tasks.
24 *ED*, pp. 29–30.

spring.[25] As both sides dug in for eight long months, observers labeled it a "queer kind of war," a "phony war" (*la drôle de guerre*), a *Sitzkrieg*.[26]

This was a new war for Bloch, who stood before a peaceful frontier, feverishly wondering when it would ignite. He lived at staff headquarters among younger men, all seemingly competent professionals but with ingrained prejudices and extremely limited intellectual horizons, who revealed a profound ignorance of French society. It was a world far removed from the "spirit of the *Annales*." Feeling useless and ill-used, he feared that his sacrifice of his family was in vain. Bloch missed his wife and fretted over her burdens. He was pained by the death of his close Creusois friend the savant Louis Lacrocq, who had looked after his family. Although he had declined to apply for a release based on his large number of dependents, he worried incessantly about his children, left fatherless in an isolated, provincial town, and especially about the older ones' education, careers, and future.[27]

Overall French morale began deteriorating rapidly at the onset of winter. There were shortages of guns, antitank weapons, and planes. While officers were deluged with paper, the soldiers of the First Army in freezing temperatures laid barbed wire, dug shallow antitank ditches and minefields, and constructed concrete block-houses before the border that were obviously incapable of supporting heavy bombardment.[28] Winter's cold plus inertia and boredom took their toll, along with false rumors, false alerts, and the periodic barrages of enemy and official propaganda.[29] There were instances of

---

25 H. A. Jacobsen, *Fall Gelb* (Wiesbaden: F. Steiner, 1957); Gen. W. Warlimont, *Inside Hitler's Headquarters, 1939–1945* (London: Weidenfeld and Nicolson, 1964); Posen, *Military Doctrine*, pp. 86–88. Bloch (to Alice Bloch, 29 Jan. 140, EBC) predicted that a "prudent" Hitler would avoid defeat in the Low Countries, which would be a "mortal blow' for the Nazi regime.

26 Horne, *To Lose a Battle*, pp. 133–36.

27 Bloch to Ferdinand Lot, 3 Nov. 1939, Lot papers, IF; to Etienne Bloch, 22 Oct. 1939, EBC; to Febvre, 12 Nov. 1939, AN, MI 318 1; to Alice Bloch, 20, 22, 28 Jan. 1940, EBC.

28 Barlone, *Diary*, pp. 26–29; "Le secteur de la Ière Armée," Opérations de la Ière Armée, SHV.

29 Bloch to Etienne Bloch, 3 Nov. 1939, EBC; Barlone, *Diary*, pp. 21–26; Horne, *To Lose a Battle*, pp. 138–44.

insubordination, pillaging, alcoholism, and unauthorized leaves. Resentments built up against the Belgians, the British, and the home front, and against those in comfortable staff quarters. Mail was slow, erratic, and crudely censored. At the beginning of the war some front-line troops remained for six weeks without news of their families. Most important, no one had yet answered the question "Why are we fighting?" The General Staff tried to divert the troops and raise their spirits with sports and light entertainment, which only reinforced the strangeness of their condition. As frigid Arctic air blanketed the immobilized western front under steely gray or sometimes bright, clear skies, Bloch meditated on the psychological problem of a "nation at arms that does not fight, a mobilized army lacking all sense of danger."[30]

Temporary escape was possible. During his idle time at the front Bloch devoured his English mysteries and also read Montaigne. He savored music from radio broadcasts. On 10 January from Berlin came a very academic performance of Beethoven's Eighth Symphony, and from London a well-played Mozart quartet. He made two trips to Paris, where he met his wife, who was working again as a hospital volunteer, visited relatives, and saw Febvre and also his friend Paul Etard, the librarian of the Ecole Normale. While observing the war's marks on life behind the front Bloch was also able to enjoy small pleasures: a sandwich in a café, Stravinsky's *Les noces*, and several good films.[31]

The Russo-Finnish war reinforced Bloch's despair. Again the Allies offered no aid and managed only to expel Soviet Russia from the League of Nations. On 12 March 1940 one more small country succumbed to its neighbor's aggression and the Western powers suffered another moral defeat.[32] Bloch at that moment was hospitalized with severe bronchitis in a military clinic in Paris. Afterward

30 Bloch to Philippe Wolff, 4 Jan. 1940, courtesy of Professor Wolff; cf. Barlone, *Diary*, pp. 28, 43, 82.
31 The "excellent American film, *Mr. Smith Goes to Washington*" and the overly "sentimental, but well-acted *Goodbye Mr. Chips*," but also the extremely disturbing French drama with Erich von Stroheim on the war clouds and mobilization of 1939–40, *Menaces!*. Bloch to Alice Bloch, 11, 22, 27 Jan., 1, 6, 12 Feb. 1940, EBC.
32 Bloch to Etienne Bloch, 14 Feb. 1940, EBC. Barlone, *Diary*, pp. 27–31.

he had an extended convalescence, first in his apartment in Paris and later in the Creuse.[33]

In the wake of Finland's defeat, the wavering Daladier was replaced by the more vigorous Paul Reynaud. Late in March the Western Allies adopted Churchill's scheme for mining Norwegian territorial waters, which precipitated a German lightning attack on Denmark and Norway. The Allied expedition to Narvik to cut the iron-ore route and preserve a free Norwegian enclave was a fiasco, leading paradoxically to Chamberlain's resignation and Churchill's appointment as prime minister. Bloch, because of his Norwegian experience and contacts and his yearning to serve, had earlier contemplated volunteering for the expedition. Following the debacle he deplored its "poor preparation" and its "bad impression" on the neutrals.[34]

Bloch, still fatigued from his illness, returned to the front in a black mood over the seven-month-long "war of nerves." Little had changed despite the toppling of the men of Munich. He grumbled over the officers' "garrison mentality," which eroded the troops' morale; the cruel dark spring, "which has not decided to give us our legitimate portion of sun and greenery"; and the "waiting" for something undefined and perhaps quite terrible, which at least gave purpose to their "absurd existence." Bloch railed against the neutrals, though he understood their aloofness in view of the Allies' lax conduct since Munich. He suspected that the diehard appeasers, Bonnet, Déat, and company, and the right-wing press – seemingly in the ascendancy – would sap France's already reduced fighting spirit. Again he complained about his own paper-pushing idleness, symptomatic of the plague of "peacetime" habits and attitudes that permeated the immobile front. If he did not find more useful work Bloch, despite considerable misgivings, contemplated requesting

---

33 Bloch was evacuated to a temporary hospital housed in the Belgian pavilion of the Cité Universitaire. Simonne Bloch to Alice Bloch, Paris, 5 Mar. 1940, and to Etienne Bloch, 12 Mar. 1940; Marc Bloch to Alice Bloch, 8, 12, 16 Mar. 1940, EBC; Bloch to Febvre, 20 Mar. 1940, AN, MI 318 1; Lucien Febvre, "Marc Bloch: Témoignages sur la période 1939–1940: Extraits d'une correspondance intime," AHS (1945), "Hommages à Marc Bloch" – I: 17, n. 3.
34 Bloch to Alice Bloch, 1 Feb. 1940, and to Etienne Bloch, 5 Apr. 1940; Simonne Bloch to Alice Bloch, 13 Apr. 1940, EBC.

permission to return to the Sorbonne on "special assignment" for the *rentrée* that fall.[35]

In those last days before the German onslaught, Bloch searched for France.[36] His combat experience in the Great War had given him the opportunity to mingle with the "people," the brave miner from Pas-de-Calais and the shopkeeper from the Bastille quarter who had both died for France, one literally on his shoulder. His strained existence during the *drôle de guerre* exposed him continually to France's "other side," a group of polite, marginally educated, narrow-minded, and often petty and selfish middle-class reservists and career officers separated by numerous expressions of taste, manners, language, and ideology from the real France of its people. Bloch recognized that the fissure had deepened, perhaps irretrievably, in June 1936, with the advent of the Popular Front, whose enemies still wanted revenge. On the eve of his second invasion, with no Jaurès to champion the people and no Clemenceau to lead, he understood that a divided France was in danger as much from within as from without.[37]

Nevertheless, France's appearance of complacency persisted. In early May, despite beautiful spring ("Goering") weather and clear indications of a German offensive elsewhere than expected, General Gamelin restored normal leave throughout the army. On 9 May there was "complete calm" at the front and no suspicion that the recent German movements amounted to anything other than an episode in the war of nerves.[38] Bloch departed on a routine errand

35 Bloch to Febvre, 6 Apr. 1940, AN, MI 318 1. Cf. Bloch to Etienne Bloch, 28 Mar. 1940, and to Alice Bloch, 31 Mar. 1940, EBC. *ED*, p. 31.

36 As did the slightly younger Barlone, who in *Diary*, pp. 34–35, contrasted the "rottenness" of the politicians with the "heart of France...clean, honest, brave," his men who were "the true France. All of them, humble folk, country folk, artisans, workpeople, small business proprietors – how patriotic, upright, and worthy they are in every sense of the word. And how contemptible are those Deputies who get elected to serve their own ends, and for what they can get out of the people."

37 Bloch to Febvre, 3 May 1940, AN, MI 318 1; *ED*, pp. 205–10. Also, Barlone, *Diary*, p. 45.

38 Opérations de la Ière Armée, SHV. In early May General Billotte replied to the complaints of his corps commanders about arms deficiencies: "Why bother yourselves? Nothing will happen before 1941!" Horne, *To Lose a Battle*, p. 237.

216

and met his wife in a still peaceful and relatively cheerful Paris, although that night their sleep was interrupted by occasional sirens and antiaircraft fire. Reynaud had just offered his resignation, and Churchill was about to take the reins in London. At 4:30 a.m. on 10 May Guderian led the 1st Panzer Division across the Luxembourg border, followed by Rommel and his 7th Panzers across the Belgian frontier. Shortly after sunrise the Luftwaffe bombed Holland, Belgium, and France. On that morning at General Headquarters in Meaux, Bloch got a cold reception for his request for the petrol coupons that he used to keep check on the fuel consumption of his various units. Upon learning of the previous night's events, he raced back to the station, crossed Paris, and struggled to board an "incredibly overcrowded train" to get back to his battle post.[39]

Now the real war had begun, the war Bloch named the "great tragic campaign of the North."[40] France's original Plan E called for a short advance into Belgium, to the Escaut (Scheldt) River. This conservative plan allowed sufficient time to prepare fortified positions and maintain liaison among the forces. However, it abandoned to the enemy the capital as well as two-thirds of Belgium's territory, its main industrial plant, and the bulk of its army. Plan E anticipated a war of attrition similar to World War I, in which French troops were more or less protected against encirclement. On 15 November 1939 General Gamelin adopted the more ambitious Plan D, which called for a much longer advance to the Dyle River, thereby protecting Brussels, linking up with more Belgian forces, and creating a shorter defensive line but also "increasing the probability of encounter battles and reducing the time available to prepare defensive positions."[41] The Dyle plan also raised acute problems of transport and intelligence, especially in regard to the secretive Belgians, and posed the challenge of conducting aerial and tank warfare and defense on foreign soil.

In accordance with the Dyle plan, General Blanchard's First Army was supposed to enter Belgium immediately after the German

39 ED, pp. 31–32; Simonne Bloch to Alice Bloch, 13 May 1940, EBC.
40 ED, p. 32.
41 Posen, Military Doctrine, p. 91; ED, pp. 65–67; Barlone, Diary, p. 33; Horne, To Lose a Battle, pp. 157–65; L. F. Ellis, War in France and Flanders, 1939–1940 (London: H. M. Stationery Office, 1953), pp. 17–38.

invasion. Moving between the B.E.F. and Corap's Ninth Army, this highly motorized and equipped army was to advance about one hundred kilometers in six to eight days to the Gembloux plateau, a region almost entirely devoid of natural obstacles. By adopting the Dyle plan and adding the even more daring and controversial Breda variant in March 1940, which sent the French Seventh Army into Holland, the General Staff jeopardized its basically defensive principles. By failing to adequately fortify the weak hinge of the Allied advance defending Sedan and the Ardennes forest and by sending its elite units so far so quickly without adequate preparation, it offered an opportunity for the swift mechanized German formations to break through, surround, and destroy them.[42]

On 10 May at 9 a.m. the first soldiers of the First Army crossed the frontier, and the bulk followed at noon. Returning hastily from Paris, Bloch moved from Bohain to the new temporary staff headquarters on the border at Valenciennes, where he had his first glimpse of the effects of a German bombing attack. In accordance with his "nomadic instinct," not prized by his superiors, and in order to obtain precious first-hand information on Belgian fuel supplies, Bloch bargained aggressively with a friendly adjutant to the local supply-group commander and traded petrol for a car. On 11 May he set out for Mons and a day later went on to Nivelles, Fleurus, and Charleroi. In this handsome green, rolling countryside, where Marshal Ney's army had once fought and where now Belgian miners, enjoying a brilliantly sunny Pentecost holiday, stood at their doors to welcome the French motorized columns, Bloch observed a grim aspect as well. The roads were crowded with masses of refugees coming from the opposite direction, carrying and pushing their piles of possessions away from the battle districts around Liège.[43]

---

42 "La mission en Belgique," Opérations de la Ière Armée, SHV; also Gen. R. Prioux, *Souvenirs de guerre* (Paris: Flammarion, 1947), pp. 29–35; Posen, *Military Doctrine*, pp. 91–94.

43 Disbanded Belgian soldiers and ugly rumors of treachery added to the somber aspect of Bloch's fact-gathering tour. *ED*, pp. 32–33, 97–98. Also "Ière phase," Opérations de la Ière Armée, SHV; Barlone, *Diary*, pp. 46–47. On 13 May Bloch wrote hurriedly to his son Daniel ("Je vais bien. J'ai beaucoup de travail. Je t'embrasse."), EBC.

The news was indeed grave. The Eben Emael fortress had fallen, and the Germans were rapidly moving westward virtually unopposed. At noon on 11 May General Prioux sent back an alarming report of his exposed position on the Gembloux gap, which his cavalry corps had occupied that morning. The Belgians, with whom the French had had almost no prior contact, had done little to fortify this vital open plain against the imminent German attack. Prioux pleaded for an immediate reconsideration of the Dyle plan, urging withdrawal and the establishment of a solid defensive line along the Escaut. Blanchard conveyed this message to First Army group commander General Billotte, who that night in person delivered his response to Prioux. Since the Seventh Army and the B.E.F. were already moving toward their objectives, the Dyle plan must go forward, with the advance of the First Army speeded up from seven to four days. Its heavily mechanized units had to move in daylight, under constant and practically unopposed attack by the Luftwaffe, leaving much of their artillery behind.[44]

On 11–12 May on the Hannut plateau, midway between Liège and the Dyle, the first full-scale tank battle between the French and the Germans took place. Both sides sustained heavy losses. Though outnumbered over two to one, the French held out and, after a brief respite, were able to maintain their positions until the fifteenth. But news had already arrived on the thirteenth that Rommel had crossed the Meuse.[45]

Suddenly the fatal weakness of the Dyle plan became manifest. It was based upon a poorly prepared entry into Belgium, with weak amounts of air cover, inadequate organization for offensive tank warfare, and limited coordination with the British and Belgians, as well as a profound ignorance of Germany's ability to fight an unimaginable war. Knowing the direction of Allied forces, Hitler had adopted the daring Manstein plan, which reconcentrated an important group of his armored forces from Belgium and Holland for a breakthrough in the lightly fortified Ardennes and a daring

44 *ED*, p. 66. Also Opérations de la Ière Armée, SHV; Barlone, *Diary*, p. 48; Prioux, *Souvenirs*, pp. 66–69; Horne, *To Lose a Battle*, pp. 278–79, 283.
45 *ED*, pp. 66–67; Erwin Rommel, *The Rommel Papers*, ed. B. H. Liddell Hart (London: Collins, 1953), pp. 7–14.

crossing of the sharply escarped valley of the Meuse. While Prioux was holding firm near Gembloux the terrifying news had arrived of the collapse of Huntzinger's Ninth Army and the opening of a sixty-kilometer breach between Namur and Sedan, which threatened the rear of the First Army. But not until 15 May did General Blanchard order a three-stage, fifty- to seventy-five-kilometer retreat to the frontier, weakly coordinated with the British, on roads still clogged with refugees and with French planes virtually absent from the skies.[46]

Thus began the series of piecemeal – Bloch also called them "niggling" – retreats that allowed German planes and tanks to chase the French back to the sea without any prospect of another Marne miracle.[47] Averaging between twenty and thirty kilometers, these displacements, barely a half-hour's journey by car, rarely stayed ahead of the enemy's fire. Indeed, the French rarely knew the enemy's precise location, direction, and material resources, owing not only to faulty intelligence reports but also to their own misjudging of distance, their slow movement, and their lethargic reactions. For example, a "safe" rear headquarters set up on 22 May in Merville was actually closer to the battle zone than the more advanced group at Estaires.[48] The Germans turned up unexpectedly, everywhere, dampening the troops' morale and causing discouragement and muddled thought from the bottom up to the top.[49] Instead of there being an organized "disengagement" far enough back to reestablish a solid defensive line, "small groups of reinforcements were continually dribbled into every breach as it occurred, with the inevitable result that they were cut to pieces."[50]

Bloch complained that although "the whole rhythm of modern

46 "Ière phase (15 mai)," Opérations de la Ière Armée, SHV; ED, pp. 67–68; Barlone, Diary, pp. 48–49; Ellis, War in France, pp. 59, 63, 76.
47 ED, p. 64; cf. "Ière phase (16–20 mai)," Opérations de la Ière Armée, SHV.
48 ED, p. 71.
49 "Certain breakdowns...occurred mainly because men had been trained to use their brains too slowly. Our soldiers were defeated and, to some extent, let themselves be too easily defeated, principally because their minds functioned far too sluggishly." ED, p. 75.
50 ED, p. 64.

warfare had changed its tempo...the metronome at headquarters was always set at too slow a beat."[51]

The ruling idea of the Germans in the conduct of this war was speed. We, on the other hand, did our thinking in terms of yesterday or the day before. Worse still, faced by the undisputed evidence of Germany's new tactics, we ignored, or totally failed to understand, the accelerated rhythm of the times. So true is this that it seemed as though each of the two opposing forces belonged to an entirely different period of human history. We interpreted war in terms of the assagai versus the rifle which we had experienced over long years of colonial expansion. But this time it was we who were cast in the role of the natives.[52]

The Dyle plan in ruins, could its mistakes be rectified? The great Field Marshal von Moltke had asserted, *"One* fault only in the initial deployment of an Army cannot be made good during the whole course of the campaign."[53] Bloch characteristically disagreed: "Early mistakes," he wrote, "become tragic only when the men in charge are incapable of putting them right."[54] Allied leaders proved incapable of preventing a setback from becoming a catastrophe.

On 19 May General Gamelin was replaced by the seventy-three-year-old General Maxime Weygand, who had been recalled hurriedly from Syria. Appraising France's heavy losses, the gaping hole, and precious lost time, Weygand journeyed to Ypres, where a counteroffensive was agreed upon for 23 May. But in the wake of sudden key French staff changes, Allied disarray, and the inexorable advance of German forces, the Weygand plan disintegrated. Fearing encirclement, Gort's army on 23 May evacuated Arras and headed for the Channel, blowing up bridges, cutting phone lines, and leaving a legacy of bitterness on the French side. The seeds of distance, doubt, and distrust between the Allied armies that Bloch

---

51 *ED*, pp. 68, 69.
52 Also the chiefs "showed a mulish determination to maintain a salient in the direction of Valenciennes and Denain, the only consequence of which was that, when finally it was decided to retreat to the coast, the divisions left to hold these advanced positions could not be withdrawn in time." *ED*, p. 64.
53 Quoted in Horne, *To Lose a Battle*, p. 658.
54 *ED*, p. 68.

had detected during the phony war bore their bitter fruit at Arras.[55]

Meanwhile Bloch was following the dreary itinerary of General Blanchard's retreating headquarters through the ugly bomb-scarred landscapes that complemented the "growing mood of depression," in a series of memorable lodgings. On 18 May, they were in a schoolhouse in the suburbs of Douai that was under heavy bombardment; on the nineteenth in a nursery school in Lens, where the flames of Arras lit the distant horizon and which itself was soon ablaze from an incendiary raid; on the twenty-second in an inn in Estaires-sur-Lys, a traffic center and prime target of German pilots; and on the twenty-third in a graceless ornate chateau set in a lovely park in Attiches, where bombs fell continually around them, knocking out power plants, electricity, and radio.[56]

Bloch retained vivid memories of this desolate retreat in Flanders. On 20 May in Lens he located on the school wall map the current German position at the mouth of the Somme, and several times he was unable to reach General Headquarters by telephone. Suddenly he felt the sense of abandonment produced by the fatal words "an army surrounded."[57] The historian who had often read and narrated accounts of war and battles for the first time suffered this "terrible, sickening reality."[58]

On 22 May he had his "baptism" of aerial bombardment. Unlike machine-gun fire and shells, whose menace could be calculated and endured with a sort of "cold fear," these first bombs induced a

---

55 "IIIe phase (21–24 mai)," Opérations de la Ière Armée, SHV; *ED*, pp. 103–9; Ellis, *War in France*, pp. 172–76.

Later Bloch recognized the need for the British army to avoid being "pounded to pieces on the European continent." He faulted Gamelin for unpardonable vanity toward the British, citing an instance during the Norwegian campaign ("Procès-verbal du Comité de guerre, 26 avr. 1940," *Les documents secrets de l'Etat-Major général français* [Berlin: Deutscher Verlag, 1941], p. 98) when the general allegedly said: "It is up to the British to find the bulk of the troops. But it is *for us to give them moral support, to organize the strategy of the campaign, and to supply the necessary planning and inspiration,*" quoted, with Bloch's emphasis, and "Helas!" in his addenda of July 1942 to *ED*, p. 106.

56 *ED*, pp. 33–39; Simonne Bloch to Alice Bloch, 30 May 1940, EBC.

57 *ED*, pp. 34–35; "IIe phase (20 mai)," Opérations de la Ière Armée, SHV.

58 *AH*, p. 48.

paralyzing "terror" because of their perceived power and the victim's sense of defenselessness:

The noise is hateful, savage, and excessively nerve-racking, both that of the built-in hissing sound as they descend...and that of the actual burst, which shakes every bone in one's body. It seems to crush the very air with unparalleled violence, and conjures up pictures of torn flesh....A man is always scared of dying, but particularly so when to death is added the threat of complete physical disintegration. No doubt this is a peculiarly illogical manifestation of the instinct of self-preservation, but its roots are very deep in human nature. Had the war lasted longer it is probable that our men would have acquired...some of the contempt bred of familiarity....Reason would have convinced them that, no matter how terrible it might be, its material effects were no worse than those of other forms of attack.[59]

Along the way he continued to function as Fuel King. Plagued by the memory of communication breakdowns during the last war, Bloch during the quiet months had developed a system of "bypassing" to maintain direct contact with the various sections of his fuel-supply group, which persisted "under more active conditions." No matter how often headquarters and the supply park moved, he "always knew where to find both" and was always "sure of passing on urgent instructions." His agile motorcyclists were able to locate every company and senior supply officer, and his four brave supply officers maintained constant links with the corps. Between 11 and 31 May Bloch claimed never to have used "official channels" to communicate with subordinate units, but all orders and requests reached their destination:

Never once, so far as I know, did the fighting troops run short of petrol which our "Mickeys" (this was the army nickname for the mobile tanks, with their small, sprightly Mickey Mouse insignias) so heroically delivered, often over considerable distances. Nor did we ever abandon to the enemy any of our depots in a fit state to operate. The whole line of our retreat from Mons to Lille was lit by more fires than can ever have been kindled by Attila.[60]

59 *ED*, pp. 85–86; also pp. 82–83.
60 *ED*, pp. 95–96; cf. Marc Bloch to Sarah Bloch, 9 June 1940, EBC.

During the retreat Bloch meditated on the human side of the catastrophe. He witnessed dramatic instances of hope and despair, courage and cowardice. He was especially critical of those staff officers who, "expecting that everything would happen as the manuals said," lost heart when the Germans "refused to play the game according to Staff College rules." Thinking that all was lost, they "acquiesced in the loss."[61] The rigid orderliness of peacetime produced indecisiveness and chaos under war conditions. Bloch insisted that they were "very badly supplied with information" by the intelligence staff. Information was withheld, errors were not corrected, and the famous "Intelligence Bulletins," circulated in a series, often contained inaccurate, contradictory, and therefore misleading statements and analyses.[62]

Because no necessary pruning of officers was undertaken during the long *drôle de guerre*, after 10 May there were too many elderly and incompetent figures in responsible posts. A particularly inept colonel was left in charge of organizing staff cars.[63] Bloch was infuriated by the airtight doors separating the various bureaus, especially between intelligence and supply, that impeded prompt and alert action.[64]

In the immediate search for scapegoats there were widespread rumors of listlessness in the ranks. Bloch's experience was otherwise. He applauded his colleagues, mostly modest soldiers and reservists, who had sped along dangerous roads to fill petrol drums and at considerable personal risk ignited fires to deny fuel to the enemy. If discipline had occasionally broken down, Bloch faulted the leaders more than the men.[65]

The leaders of 1940, according to Bloch, were too passive and inflexible. Expecting to remain safe in the rear, they were surprised by the enemy's audacity and intimidated when withdrawal, even before the enemy's arrival, turned into headlong flight. This shak-

61 *ED*, pp. 154–55; cf. Marc Bloch to Sarah Bloch, 9 June 1940, EBC.
62 "Il faut bien le dire...que nous fûmes donc mal informés!" *ED*, pp. 115–22. Earlier, Bloch to Le Bras, 15 Nov. 1939, EBC.
63 *ED*, pp. 127–28.
64 *ED*, pp. 132–38.
65 *ED*, pp. 141–42.

iness permeated the most responsible circles. The ravages of age, sleeplessness, piles of paper, and insufficient personal orderliness manifested themselves at the highest reaches.[66]

Bloch was severe in his judgment of General Blanchard, who at Lens was reportedly urged by a corps commander, "Do anything you like, sir, but for Heaven's sake do something!" At the chateau of Attiches Bloch observed this usually elegant figure sitting "in tragic immobility, saying nothing, doing nothing, but just gazing at the map spread on the table between us, as though hoping to find on it the decision which he was incapable of taking."[67] On the night of 25–26 May Bloch accidentally overheard Blanchard make the unutterable prophecy of "capitulation," a word no true leader ought even to have thought. It represented the "triumph of the spirit of Bazaine," the old political general who, besieged by the Prussians in Metz in October 1870, had capitulated without a fight.[68] On 25 May the timorous Blanchard was appointed First Army group commander replacing Billotte, who had died in an automobile accident. Thus he was able, according to Bloch, to escape the immediate consequences of a disaster for which he had shared a full measure of responsibility.[69]

On 26 May Bloch moved into this last headquarters northwest of Lille, a charming villa in Steenwerck. The house next door was occupied by the new First Army commander, General Prioux, who had the doleful duty of presiding over an army in disintegration. Masses of British, French, and Belgian troops were heading toward Dunkirk for embarkation. As expected, Leopold III capitulated on 28 May, exposing Prioux's forces to encirclement by Rommel's fast-

66 *ED*, pp. 142–45, 149–50.
67 *ED*, p. 52. It was also at Attiches that Bloch observed "one of the most degrading spectacles of human weakness" he had ever witnessed: a dull-eyed, chain-smoking cashiered former general of one of the most brilliant divisions, reportedly deprived of his command for drunkenness (p. 37).
68 *ED*, pp. 144–49; Barlone's more critical comments in *Diary*, p. 72.
69 *ED*, p. 39. Later in Normandy Bloch reencountered the general, who infelicitously congratulated him for having survived the "Flanders adventure," in which Blanchard's own part was to have lost more than half his army and abandoned his successor to capture by the enemy (pp. 51–52).

moving forces.[70] With the enemy drawing nearer, Bloch pressed tenaciously to destroy the important Lille fuel dumps, braving official indecisiveness and inertia and risking one of his messengers. He succeeded. All the dumps and electric power stations were decimated before the Germans arrived. He also secured Prioux's agreement to abandon his mobile tanks, although this deprived the army of its last few remaining gallons of petrol.[71]

To his confused and despondent men Prioux announced on 28 May that he would remain with only one or two officers at the head of his trapped troops awaiting the enemy's arrival, and he released the rest of his staff to escape to the coast. Bloch developed great compassion for this unfortunate, brave cavalry general. In the garden in Steenwerck he also experienced a rare comradeship with his recently named chief, a tall, fair-haired captain of gunners, who had volunteered to stay with Prioux. Bloch was struck by the metamorphosis of this conscientious and sincere but formerly inflexible, vulgar, and prejudiced officer into a real leader and a great man. This was the privilege of the "true man of action." "When the critical moment comes," Bloch wrote soon afterwards, "blemishes of character are effaced, while virtues, till then only potential, appear in an unexpectedly vivid manner. . . . Faced by a genuine test, his obsession with trivialities ceased and his contentious manner disappeared."[72] According to Prioux's instructions, Bloch spent most of 28 May burning all his records, including his diary and personal correspondence, retaining only a few precious or useful objects for his journey. That night he set out in a long, slow automobile column moving across the Belgian countryside, for the French roads were already cut.[73]

During the next twenty-four hours there were many stressful

70 "IVème phase (25–29 mai)," Opérations de la Ière Armée, SHV; *ED*, pp. 37–39; Barlone, *Diary*, pp. 55–56; Prioux, *Souvenirs*, pp. 118–20; also *Rommel Papers*, chap. ii: "Closing the Trap," pp. 29–43.

71 *ED*, p. 98; Barlone, *Diary*, p. 56.

72 *ED*, p. 55–57. "T" had planned to shoot Germans rather than be taken captive, but he was freed to depart by the arrival of the commander of the trapped 4th Corps, whose exhausted liaison officer, a member of Bloch's group, agreed to stay in his place.

73 *ED*, pp. 39–40.

moments. By daybreak they had barely covered ten kilometers. Evading the German motorized scouts by wheel and on foot, Bloch reached Hondschoote around noon. With his colleague Captain Lachamp, he searched out his main fuel column, which had preceded them to Bray-les-Dunes, but, stopped at Furnes by blown bridges and an incredible traffic jam, he returned to Hondschoote.[74] At nightfall, taking a more direct route, Bloch set out on foot on a "hideous" journey in dense, confusing motor traffic. At Bray, which was swollen by thousands of abandoned English and French vehicles and other equipment, he found his column and an empty house to rest in. Because there was no fresh water in the coastal area, he had only champagne to quench his considerable thirst.[75]

Between 24 and 27 May the German panzers had halted to regroup and prepare the next assaults, thus enabling four British and a number of French divisions to escape to the Dunkirk area and set up a perimeter defense.[76] By the evening of 27 May almost 8,000 Britons had been evacuated. Two days later Weygand finally ordered the debarkation of French troops. During the next four days, between 27 and 31 May, the Royal Navy, joined by French warships reinforced by a vast improvised armada of small private boats and aided by massive sorties by R.A.F. fighters, carried 165,000 men across the Channel.[77]

After Prioux's surrender, the First Army had virtually ceased to exist. Though now without staff duties, Bloch continued to assume responsibility for his men, virtually unarmed and packed together on the beaches anxiously awaiting rescue, captivity, or death. As the Germans crept closer and the shells and bombs grew more destructive, they watched the English depart for safety. Bloch observed one especially poignant incident involving a French interpreter who "after long months of intimate companionship in billets and on the

---

74 Where he had a brief encounter with his former student Maurice Rey, who, in the midst of their panicky withdrawal, made Bloch smile with his enthusiastic comments about *La société féodale*, which he had just finished reading. Rey to author, 17 Sept. 1979.

75 *ED*, pp. 39–41.

76 Horne, *To Lose a Battle*, pp. 598–603; cf. Alan Bullock, *Hitler: A Study in Tyranny* (New York: Harper and Row, 1964), pp. 584–86.

77 Horne, *To Lose a Battle*, pp. 618–20; Ellis, *War in France*, pp. 218–20.

battlefields. . . found himself left to his own devices on the sands, forbidden to set foot on the ship which he saw steaming away with his former friends lining the rails." It required "superhuman doses of charity not to feel bitter" as "ship after ship carried their foreign companions to safety."[78]

Bloch got busy on 30 May trying to insert his men's names on the official evacuation lists. During his wanderings he served briefly as a traffic-control officer on the clogged streets of Bray-les-Dunes and visited the Perroquet café on the Belgian frontier, which for a few hours was the zone commander's temporary headquarters. Finally Bloch found his main Quartermaster Branch comrades at Malo-les-Bains, where he spent that night bivouacking on the dunes. Their sleep was punctuated by German shells aimed methodically toward only one place, thus sparing them from a massacre "in their sandy dormitory among the sea grasses."[79]

The departure was not smooth. Early the next morning, 31 May, Bloch was assured that his men would be boarded. However, their ship was bombed; most were rescued. He was now free to make his own arrangements, but his chief showed no eagerness to help. That afternoon Bloch fortunately found a cavalry corps commander who gave him and two of his friends an official movement order. Because of a bungled message, they had twice to cross Dunkirk, now a "ruined town with its shells of buildings half-visible through drifting smoke," its streets cluttered "less with human bodies than human debris."[80] Amid the destruction and chaos, a chance meeting with a former student from Strasbourg who was also awaiting debarkation gave Bloch the opportunity to express his confidence in the "destiny of France."[81]

Marc Bloch's last minutes on the Flanders coast were accompanied by the cacophony of bombs crashing, shells bursting, machine-gun fire, and the noise of antiaircraft batteries. But other images supplanted the horror and danger: a lovely summer night, a sky of pure

78 *ED*, p. 102.
79 *ED*, pp. 41–42. Barlone also arrived in Malo on 30 May: "As usual, no guides, no military traffic control, not even a direction arrow placed by the High Command." *Diary*, p. 59.
80 *ED*, pp. 42–43.
81 Interview with Jean Braun, 1982.

22. Dunkirk: French troops on the beach

gold, a mirrorlike sea, and the marvelous patterns of smoke from the burning refinery. He took pleasure in the name of his vessel, the *Royal Daffodil*, which came from an Indian fairy tale. Above all, he savored a soldier's sense of relief in having escaped captivity.[82]

The eight-day evacuation was amazingly effective. By 3 June, the day before Dunkirk fell, some 200,000 British and 130,000 French troops had been taken off the beaches, although all their equipment was lost and the Wehrmacht took 50,000 prisoners. The "miracle of Dunkirk" occupies a special place in contemporary history.[83] There is the still resilient, though largely discredited, myth of Hitler's forbearance in allowing the evacuation as a means of preparing for peace with Britain. More accurately, Dunkirk revealed the weakness of the seemingly invincible Luftwaffe, the difficulties of coordinating

82 *ED*, p. 43. The *Royal Daffodil*, a passenger ferry steamer, that day carried 1,600 Frenchmen to England. Arthur D. Divine, *The Nine Days of Dunkirk* (New York: Norton, 1959), p. 197.
83 Divine, *Nine Days*; also Horne, *To Lose a Battle*, pp. 617–20; Ellis, *War in France*; H.A. Jacobsen, *Decisive Battles of World War II: The German View* (London: Deutsch, 1965).

the Wehrmacht's swift-moving armored divisions, and significant cracks in the war leadership of the Third Reich. For Britain, Dunkirk's success transformed a despondent people into Hitler's well-led, staunch, tenacious opponents. For France, tasting defeat and bitterness toward its ally, it meant the rescue of a battered army from the inferno.[84] Nevertheless, they and all their precious jettisoned war supplies – rifles, artillery, tanks, antitank guns, and antiaircraft guns – would be sorely missed when the enemy unleashed his next offensive on the southern front.[85]

Bloch had only a brief stay in England. Landing by morning at Dover, he spent the whole day traveling by train across southern England. He later recalled a sense of "long torpor" interrupted by "chaotic sensations and images" that rose intermittently to the surface of his consciousness: devouring ham and cheese sandwiches handed through the train windows by "girls in multicolored dresses" and clergymen "who looked as solemn as though they were administering the sacrament"; the "faint sweet smell of cigarettes showered on us with the same generous profusion; the acid taste of lemonade and the flat taste of tea with too much milk in it; the cosy green of lawns; a landscape made up of parks, cathedral spires, hedges, and Devonshire cliffs; groups of cheering children at level crossings..." Bloch contrasted the spontaneous warmth and kindness of the civilians' reception with the coldness and excessive suspicion of the British authorities. Certain transit camps "had almost a penal air." Certain officials, obsessed by the need to maintain discipline over motley foreign troops, behaved in a "clumsy" manner, leaving "lasting traces in men's memories."[86]

That evening from Plymouth they returned to France, to an even less auspicious reception. Arriving at Cherbourg at dawn on 2 June, they waited in the harbor for the 9 a.m. arrival of the dock officials. Now in the rear zone of a nation at war, instead of cheering crowds, sandwiches, and cigarettes they encountered a formal, dry, and slightly mistrustful welcome. Following a short stay in a squalid,

84 Cf. Maxime Weygand, *Mémoires: Rappelé au service* (Paris: Flammarion, 1953), p. 132.
85 *ED*, pp. 79–80; Barlone, *Diary*, pp. 64, 72.
86 *ED*, pp. 44, 102–3.

inhospitable rest camp, brightened by a few female Red Cross volunteers, they embarked on a bumpy 120-kilometer train ride. They arrived in Caen ungreeted in the middle of the night, but were at least able to find lodgings in good hotels.[87]

There was also a joyful reunion in prospect. At Cherbourg Bloch had telegraphed his wife, who joined him soon after he was settled in Caen. Simonne Bloch found her husband, after all his adventures, "sunburned and thinner," but also "bustling, energetic, making himself useful in many capacities, and admired and appreciated by his men and fellow officers." With his car he was able to tour the zone in Normandy occupied by the former Army of the North, which had been abruptly transferred to the rear without leaders, plan, or organization.[88]

On 9 June Bloch wrote his eighty-two-year-old mother, who was now experiencing her third invasion: "We must hold out; and if we do, even with a few setbacks, we will surely prevail. The Germans have overextended themselves. In any event, afterwards there will be many scores to settle."[89]

It was too late. Fresh from their northern victory, the German panzers, completely reorganized and redeployed, were preparing the final blow. From the sea to the Meuse, a front of some 280 kilometers, the Germans had some 104 fully armed divisions against, at best, some 60 Allied divisions behind the Somme and the Aisne. With 90 percent of France, including the capital and the major cities, still unoccupied, Weygand had space and room to maneuver if he wished and could devise a new strategy to overcome France's deficiencies in arms, air power, and manpower. But despite the lessons of the previous campaign the aged marshal stubbornly adhered to the principle of the continuous front. There were no fallback plans for regrouping or resistance. There were no schemes for trading space for time. If the Somme-Aisne front did not hold, Weygand for political as well as military reasons preferred a decisive, even unsuccessful, battle over organizing a complicated

---

87 *ED*, pp. 44–45.
88 Simonne Bloch to Alice Bloch, 2, 6 June 1940, and to Etienne Bloch, 5 June 1940, EBC; Marc Bloch to Sarah Bloch, 9 June 1940, EBC.
89 Bloch to Sarah Bloch, 9 June 1940, EBC.

strategic retreat back to Brittany or even North Africa.[90] The proponents of a new kind of warfare, of matching the Germans' speed and armor with well-sited mobile pockets of resistance, were stilled.[91] The army whose collapse seventy years earlier had led to the birth of the Third Republic, and which because of, or despite, its long privileged role had set itself apart from French democracy, preferred defeat to a popular uprising, a *levée en masse*.

One day after the fall of Dunkirk, on 5 June, the Reich's final westward and southward offensive began. After some initial French resistance, the Germans broke through in every direction. On 10 June, with Paris surrounded on three sides, the government fled. German troops marched into the capital on 14 June. That day Rommel captured Le Havre. One day later Verdun fell.

Though considered to be in a rear zone, the remnants of the First Army in Normandy were only 150 kilometers from the Somme-Aisne front. While Rommel sped closer, moving incredible distances each day, they were slowly being reorganized and reequipped. Bloch, impatient and critical of their exposed location and dilatory procedures, also observed the ravages of continual internecine strife and a bullying commander, which sapped the morale of an already shaken band of escapees.[92] The panzers fanned out eastward toward the Maginot Line; southeastward toward the Alps to join the troops of Italy, which declared war on 10 June; and southwestward to the Atlantic coast. In the meantime Bloch once more endured a painful series of piecemeal withdrawals to successive Norman chateaux, again moving at "too slow a beat." He believed that had they been removed promptly to the Charente, if not to the Garonne, they might still have been deployed before the Germans had time to surround whole French armies in the east and in the south.[93]

The First Army had its last posting in Brittany. After two weeks

90 Barlone, *Diary*, p. 77; William Shirer, *The Collapse of the Third Republic* (New York: Simon and Schuster, 1969), pp. 757–60; slightly different interpretation in Horne, *To Lose a Battle*, pp. 621–24.

91 *ED*, pp. 78–79.

92 *ED*, pp. 124–26, 138.

93 Reporting another move of just a dozen kilometers, Bloch complained that, knowing less and less of their fate they were far from the battlefield and "forgotten in a corner." Bloch to Sarah Bloch, 13 June 1940, EBC; *ED*, p. 69.

of relative inactivity, the remains of Bloch's headquarters staff were assigned to a newly constituted group charged with the last-ditch defense of the western peninsula. On 15 June they received their last orders, to report to Rennes by car or by train. After he had helped with the evacuation, Bloch's own departure was delayed until the next morning because of a lieutenant-colonel who was willing to brave the capture of a group of officers rather than suffer the inconvenience of arriving in Rennes after dark! Though there were no dire consequences, for Bloch this was symptomatic of the lethal combination of imprudence and languor that had plagued the entire French campaign.[94]

Rennes, packed with refugees, was the next target of the German advance. A heavy air raid on 17 June left two thousand killed and nine hundred injured. From the shelter of his office in the upper town Bloch shuddered at the now familiar deadly sounds but derived a "purely animal sense of relief" from his relative safety.[95] That day they learned that Marshal Pétain, who had replaced Reynaud the night before, had asked for an unconditional armistice. Deserted by France's leaders and knowing the end was near, the troops had little incentive to risk their lives.[96]

On 18 June Hoth's Armoured Corps, which had captured Caen and broken through the thin line sealing off the Brittany peninsula, swept into Rennes, capturing several generals. Anticipating their arrival, Bloch had sought out his batman to prepare for his departure. On remounting the hill leading to his office, he discovered a German column debouching on the boulevard and moving between him and his destination. "Not a shot was fired. A number of French soldiers, including a few officers, just stood and watched."[97]

Bloch had to decide what to do. Long before, he had "ferociously resolved" to "take any step to avoid capture." If he had believed he still could be useful, he might have mustered the courage to stay at his post. But there was no organized resistance and therefore no

94 *ED*, pp. 45, 70–71.
95 On the Rennes bombing: *ED*, p. 45; Jacques Benoist-Méchin , *Sixty Days That Shook the West*, trans. Peter Wiles (New York: Putnam, 1963), p. 379.
96 *ED*, p. 148. Reynaud had remained in office almost six weeks during the emergency.
97 *ED*, pp. 45–46.

point in carrying on with his duties. He concluded that the only way he could continue to serve his country and his loved ones was by "escaping before the trap should finally be sprung."[98]

But how? Fleeing westward, he would probably have been rounded up sooner or later in the cul-de-sac of the Brittany peninsula. He could have headed south, to Nantes (which, he later learned, the Germans did not occupy for another day), but he was pessimistic about his chances of crossing the Loire. He pondered a flight to Brest and slipping across to England, but rejected the idea of "deserting his children and going into exile for an indefinite period."[99]

Thus was born the "professor's solution." Returning to his quarters, Bloch changed into civilian dress and, with the help of a colleague at the local university, booked a hotel room under his own name. His gray hairs and academic mien were sufficient to allay any suspicion by the German military authorities that they were looking at an escaped French officer. Indeed, because of their easy triumph the new masters of Rennes were rather blasé on the subject of taking prisoners.[100]

Bloch stayed about ten days in Rennes, constantly jostled by German officers in the streets, in restaurants, and even in the hotel, and torn on each occasion by the "agony of seeing the cities of his country given over to the invader," the "surprise at his peaceful cohabitation with persons who, a few days before, he would only have encountered at the point of a revolver," and, finally, the "malicious pleasure of pulling a fast one on these gentlemen."[101] Though deception was alien to Bloch's nature, he amazed himself with his performance.[102]

On 22 June Germany compelled France to sign a humiliating armistice in the forest at Réthondes, in the same railroad car where the Reich had capitulated on 11 November 1918. Though the sovereignty of the French state and its empire remained intact, its army and navy were demobilized and two-thirds of the country – the

98 *ED*, p. 46.
99 *ED*, p. 46.
100 *ED*, p. 47.
101 Ibid.
102 "J'ai horreur de mensonge." Bloch to Etienne Bloch, 11 Nov. 1939, EBC.

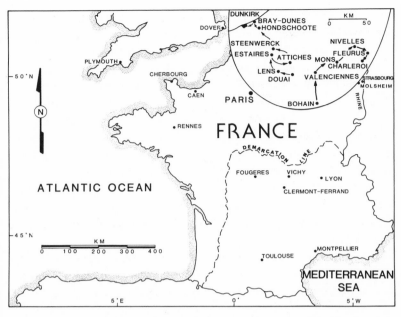

23. Map of France, 1940, with details of Bloch's movements

land north of the Loire valley and the entire Atlantic coast – was to be occupied by German troops, with France paying all the costs. In principle a temporary agreement pending a final peace settlement, its harsh terms also included stipulations for handing over German refugees, collaboration with German military authorities in the occupied zone, and the dispatch of a million and a half prisoners of war as hostages.[103]

Once the fighting was officially over, France slowly came back to life. As soon as the railways were operating, Marc Bloch set out for the south, stopping in Angers on 28 June, where he had friends and relatives.[104] Following a roundabout route, he reached Guéret on 4 July and found four of his children, who had lived under bombardment during the last days of hostilities. The joyful reunion was

103 "Ce honteuse armistice..." Simonne Bloch to Alice Bloch, 4 July 1940, EBC; *ED*, p. 148; Azéma, *Munich to the Liberation*, pp. 45–49.
104 Bloch to Sarah Bloch, 29 June 1940, EBC.

to some extent marred by his wife's absence and fear for his two nephews (his brother's sons), who were both prisoners.[105]

Simonne Bloch had undergone her own frightful odyssey. On 13 June she had left with her son Louis to retrieve her mother-in-law in Marlotte. But on the return journey, also carrying two of Sarah Bloch's elderly friends, they were halted by the great Parisian exodus. Under intermittent bombing, two million civilians and retreating soldiers together with a mass of assorted vehicles clogged all the roads south. This poorly organized flight from the Germans reinforced France's sense of shock and helplessness. It produced a fertile environment for *fausses nouvelles*, misinformation and distortion, and for urban-rural, north-south enmity, as well as a widespread resentment of the beaten republic that had failed to protect its people.[106]

Simonne Bloch and her charges stayed for three days in the countryside, with almost no food and no news, sleeping in the car not far from the fighting. Finally, on the twenty-fourth, they drove to Paris, where they stayed for over a week. Once Simonne Bloch was able to secure travel permission from the Militärbefehlshaber Paris to cross back into the unoccupied zone, the weary group finally reached Guéret on 7 July, three days after Marc Bloch's arrival.[107] Lucien Febvre and his family had remained in their Jura country home until 17 June, when the Germans were only fifty kilometers away. Rescued in an empty military truck, they underwent a dismal flight along clogged, undefended roads, halting in Lyon, where they witnessed the victors' jubilant arrival.[108]

In France in July 1940 there was a need to revive the semblance of normal life to offset the recent horror and humiliation. The Bloch

105 Bloch to Febvre, 8 July 1940, AN, MI 318 1.
106 J. Vidalenc, *L'exode de mai–juin 1940* (Paris: Presses Universitaires de France, 1957). H. R. Kedward, "Patriots and Patriotism in Vichy France," *Transactions of the Royal Historical Society* 5th ser., 32 (1982): 180–88, sees the misery of the *exode* as crucial to the triumph of Pétainism.
107 Simonne Bloch to Alice Bloch, 4 (Paris), 8 (Guéret) July 1940, "Zulassungsbescheinigung," 5 July 1940, EBC.
108 Febvre to Faral, 8 July 1940, CdF, C-XII 47; Fernand Braudel, "Présence de Lucien Febvre," *Eventail de l'histoire vivante: Hommage à Lucien Febvre* (Paris: Armand Colin, 1953), pp. 2, 7–8; Mme. Richard (Febvre's daughter) to author, May 1982.

family remained for a time in Guéret, where the two older sons prepared to take the *baccalauréat* later that summer. Because the town was crowded with refugees, it was difficult to feed and lodge nonresident candidates. Bloch, awaiting his demobilization, volunteered to serve as an external examiner. Anxious about his children's prospects, he weighed the importance of the *bac* against the totality of their "uncertain future."[109]

Almost immediately after his arrival in Guéret, Bloch set to work writing his testimony of the last ten months. Just as he had taken the first opportunity to jot down his combat impressions a quarter of a century before, Bloch now hastily recorded those recollections that were "still fresh and living in [his] memory." This time, however, there was a debacle to recount and to explain. Bloch called it a "platonic" piece of work, intended to remain hidden in his files until France was again free and its citizens could examine the reasons for the "most terrible collapse in our history." By September he had completed the manuscript, which was published six years later, after the Liberation and his death, under the title *L'étrange défaite* (Strange Defeat).[110]

Written in a "white heat of rage," *L'étrange défaite* is a cranky, querulous, self-revelatory work. The most lyrical phrases are reserved for Bloch's reveries of the Great War and his memories of individual feats of courage by common soldiers. The most biting are reserved for slackers, especially in high places, who shrank before the challenge of "clenching their teeth, hanging on, imparting to others their self-confidence," and displaying a "ruthless heroism," when the country was in danger. Bloch was the aggrieved patriot who spared himself and his beloved France no pain. "It is a harsh duty that compels a man to make a public show of his mother's weakness when she is in misery and despair." The book crackles with the tension of a "vexed lover," who accuses himself and others. There is a dogged

109 Bloch to Febvre, 8 July, 8 Sept. 1940, AN, MI 318 1. Febvre (who had similarly volunteered, in gratitude to his Lyon colleagues who had sheltered him and his family) to Faral, 8 July 1940, CdF, C-XII 47. On the efforts to return to normal: Robert O. Paxton, *Vichy France: Old Guard and New Order, 1940–1944* (New York: Norton, 1972), pp. 17–19.
110 Bloch to Febvre, 8 July 1940, 26 July 1942, AN, MI 318 1; Simonne Bloch to Alice Bloch, 16 July 1940, EBC; *ED*, p. 23.

honesty over his personal quirks, his fear of boredom and hatred of "slovenliness," his "nomadic spirit" and his mordant wit, his impatience with dullness and his zest for military life, his hyper-critical sensibility but also his abiding faith in young people, the men and women on whom France's fate depended. The book rings with his acute burden of personal responsibility and unwillingness to shed guilt. He considered a sin no less heavy because confessed to.[111]

Bloch's design was intelligible in this three-part work with its distinctive structure of a courtroom trial. First he presented himself in the witness box, the historian-soldier-patriot of Jewish ancestry. Though admitting the limits of his personal observations and of the second-hand information he had accumulated, Bloch insisted he was a credible witness. "From a comparison of particular sincerities, truth will eventually emerge."[112] Next came the "testimony by one of the vanquished," over half the book, consisting of shrewd, insightful analysis of the military side of the disaster. Finally, the "examination of conscience by a Frenchman," which addressed the deeper roots of the debacle in French politics and society. To create a useful document Bloch had scrupulously sifted and ordered his impressions for an unseen judge, for his children, and for future researchers. Instead of undigested reminiscences or a fluent adventure narrative, he built a well-wrought study on three interconnecting levels of autobiography, military analysis, and political inquiry. Overcoming "weariness and discouragement," he followed a "harsh and exacting" path, as witness and analyst.[113] As the conscientious historian he sought behind the great abstractions "the only concrete realities: human beings."[114]

Why had France's military leaders failed to draw the correct lessons from the Polish campaign, which Germany had virtually duplicated in the campaign of the north? Bloch concluded, as many

111 *ED*, p. 218.
112 *ED*, p. 48.
113 *ED*, pp. 21–22.
114 *ED*, p. 51. Cf. Bloch to Etienne Bloch, 25 Apr. 1940, EBC: "Le métier d'historien...est un beau métier....Pour être bien fait il exige beaucoup de travail, beaucoup de connaissances diverses et une réele force intellectuelle: curiosité, imagination, ordre dans l'esprit; la faculté, enfin, d'exprimer avec clarté et justesse les pensées et les façons de sentir des hommes."

have since, that they had read history wrong, reaching back to the lessons of the Great War, making "yesterday's wisdom tomorrow's folly."[115] Age and timidity were allowed to prevail over youth and intelligence. Bloch insisted:

The world belongs to those who are in love with the new. That is why our High Command, finding itself face-to-face with novelty, and being quite incapable of dealing with it, not only suffered defeat; but, like boxers dulled by overweight and thrown off balance by the first unexpected blow, they accepted it.[116]

Bloch sought the reasons why the republic had failed to mobilize its people against the Nazi menace. He faulted his fellow citizens, the workers and middle class, parliamentarians, journalists, and especially teachers. The regime that for Bloch had once been at the vanguard of human freedom and creativity had succumbed to softness, selfishness, and a reactionary form of nostalgia. Rejecting the comforting certainties of right and left orthodoxy for a confident, critical rationalism, Bloch insisted, unsurprisingly, that education must be the mainstay of any future French democracy:

We must choose: either [like the Germans] make our people into a sounding board which responds automatically to the magnetism of a few leaders...; or we educate them to be able to collaborate fully with the representatives they themselves have chosen. At the present stage of civilization there is no halfway solution to this dilemma.... The masses no longer obey. They follow either because they have been hypnotized or because they know.[117]

And Bloch recognized that democracies had to guard themselves against drill-routine professions of loyalty, recalling Condorcet's famous report on public education: "No group of our citizens should ever be forced to regard either the French Constitution or even the Declaration of Rights as Tables of the Law sent down from heaven, to be treated with adoration and unquestioning belief."[118]

115 ED, p. 161.
116 ED, p. 164; also Barlone, Diary, p. 64. Cf. Azéma, Munich to the Liberation, p. 64: "The French High Command was stupefied by the successes of enemy strategy."
117 ED, p. 187.
118 Quoted in ED, pp. 195–96.

Though more hurriedly conceived and executed, *L'étrange défaite* can be seen as a realization of *Les rois thaumaturges*. In 1940 Bloch attempted to apply the study of individual and mass psychology to the present disaster. He characterized Nazism's victory over France as a "triumph of intellect." Germany's considerable but not unlimited human and material resources had been reinforced by Hitler's "methodical opportunism," his gift for action and improvisation, and his clever reading of the foe's psyche. France's defeat was the result of a gigantic false perception: the misreading of its people, the enemy, and history itself.[119]

Almost a half-century later Bloch's military analysis stands up, as does much of his political commentary.[120] But there were some significant limits to his book. In both wars Bloch curiously ignored the importance of Russia, its contribution to France's salvation in 1914 and its fateful neutrality in 1940. Bloch was unjustly severe with Poincaré and uncritically sympathetic to the Weimar Republic.[121] Despite his professional training and personal experience Bloch barely acknowledged the significance of the financial, industrial, and demographic weaknesses of interwar France. Like Polybius, he preferred human over determinist reasons for the catastrophe.[122] In Marc Bloch's darkest moment he defined the choice in *L'étrange défaite*: between Hitler's dark vision of human vice and the ethos of virtue represented by Montesquieu and by the French Revolution. Though virtue and freedom were risky causes, in them he had defined his own destiny.[123]

119 Bloch (to Febvre, 26 July 1942, AN, MI 318 1): "Les historiens que nous sommes avaient eu d'autres expériences que celles des chartes."
120 Two years later Bloch annotated *ED* with newly published documents but allowed the original manuscript to remain unchanged. See John C. Cairns, "Some Recent Historians and the 'Strange Defeat' of 1940," *Journal of Modern History* 46 (Mar. 1974): 60–85; "Fall of France: Causes," proceedings of a conference, 10 May 1980, Center for European Studies, Harvard University (Cambridge, Mass., 1980).
121 *ED*, pp. 198–99, 215–16. Cf. Sally Marks, "The Patriot as Historian: Marc Bloch and *Strange Defeat*," paper delivered to the Southern Historical Association, Nov. 1986.
122 Bryce Lyon, "Marc Bloch: Did He Repudiate *Annales* History?" *Journal of Medieval History* 11 (Sept. 1985): 189.
123 *ED*, p. 220.

10. Vichy

Indeed, I live in Dark Times!
— Bertolt Brecht, *To Posterity*

The older we become, the more humane we should become.[1]

France's military collapse in May 1940 led to the creation of a new regime that ended the Third Republic. Like the restored monarchy of 1814, Pétain's government not only sought accommodation with the victor and occupier but also represented the triumph of the outgroup of the previous years. In the summer of 1940 the traditionalist antirepublicans were ready to substitute *Travail, Famille, Patrie* for *Liberté, Egalité, Fraternité*.

Numbed by the debacle, France offered little resistance and even gave a certain amount of support to the "New Order." Indeed, there were now two Frances. Two-thirds of the country[2] was under German military administration, the Militärbefehlshaber in Frankreich. The "free," or unoccupied, zone was ruled from the spa town of Vichy. A third France, the forces in exile that de Gaulle, in London, sought to unify, was yet to be formed or recognized by the French people or its former allies. On 10 July 1940 by a vote of 569 to 80, parliament gave Pétain full power to abandon the 1875 constitution. Under the grandiose slogan of "National Revolution," the tough leadership of Vice-Premier Pierre Laval, and the soothing mystique of the marshal, Vichy France in its first hundred days, before the imposition of immediate and vigilant German supervision, was

1 Bloch to Febvre, 18 May 1942, EBC.
2 With the exception of Alsace and Lorraine, which, contrary to the armistice, were annexed de facto by the Third Reich, and the northeastern *Sperrzone*, the départements of Nord and Pas-de-Calais, which until June 1941 were attached to the military administration in Brussels.

transformed into a right-wing, collaborationist, authoritarian state.[3]

The prevailing waves of shock and condemnation of the defeated republic, self-scrutiny, and faintly hopeful resignation were recorded in the private diaries of intellectuals; André Gide reread Zola's account of the debacle of 1870–71 but also selections from Goethe (in German) and Kafka's 1914 masterpiece, *The Trial*.[4] In both zones there were only a handful of "resisters of the first hour," who produced scattered demonstrations and a small clandestine press. For example, in Paris an intelligence-gathering network of anthropologists was formed at the Musée de l'Homme. On the other hand, the communists were paralyzed by the Hitler–Stalin pact and by the mass arrests of October 1940, and the radicals and socialists were discredited by the debacle.[5]

France's sudden collapse created an immediate danger for the 310,000 Jews within its borders. Approximately 150,000 were foreign-born: the pre-1939 refugees from Central and Eastern Europe and the 1940 wave from Holland, Belgium, and Luxembourg, half of whom were stateless. Menaced directly by the terms of the armistice and by Vichy's internment policies, they immediately sought refuge or further emigration. Native French Jews on both sides of the demarcation line experienced a "special anxiety." Anguished by the nation's calamity, they expected to share the general suffering but retained full confidence in France's protection. Nevertheless, with few illusions about Nazi racial policies, they dreaded the special acts of discrimination that might be "imposed" by the conqueror.[6]

3 See esp. Robert Paxton, *Vichy France: Old Guard and New Order, 1940–1944* (New York: Norton, 1971), pp. 1–50; also Gordon Wright, *France in Modern Times*, 3d ed. (New York: Norton, 1981), pp. 406–9; Jean-Pierre Azéma, *From Munich to the Liberation, 1938–1944*, trans. Janet Lloyd (Cambridge: Cambridge University Press, 1984), pp. 50–55; Henri Michel, *Année 40* (Paris: R. Laffont, 1966).

4 *The Journals of André Gide*, trans. and ed. Justin O'Brien, IV (New York: Random House, 1957), June–Sept. 1940.

5 Paxton, *Vichy France*, pp. 38–41.

6 Yerachmiel (Richard) Cohen, "A Jewish Leader in Vichy France, 1940–1943: The Diary of Raymond-Raoul Lambert," *Jewish Social Studies* 43 (Fall 1981): 307 n. 23, quoting entry of 15 July 1940.

It was with that threat in mind that Marc Bloch decided to seek shelter for his family in the United States, the "land of liberty and welcome."[7] Soon after his arrival in Fougères, on 25 July 1940 he wrote to four American colleagues, soliciting their aid in securing an academic appointment in medieval, economic, or comparative history. Seeking a temporary position for one or several years, Bloch indicated that his wife and six children would accompany him and perhaps also his eighty-two-year-old mother.

For the time being Bloch expected to return to his home in Paris and to his professorship at the Sorbonne. He had taken the precaution of obtaining leave with full salary after his demobilization, for the period from 12 July through 31 August 1940.[8] There were obvious difficulties in returning to the Nazi-occupied zone with his entire family, which had already undergone a prolonged separation, the recent bombardment, and considerable anxiety about the future. The "altered political situation" convinced him of the prudence of leaving his three oldest children in the unoccupied zone to continue their higher education. As to the younger children, he weighed his anxiety over their being exposed in Paris to racial persecution and other hardships against the prospect of his returning alone and another lengthy separation.[9]

In the end he did not return. In early September Bloch went to Vichy for consultations at the Ministry of National Education, where he was advised of the dangers he as a non-Aryan would face and of the government's inability to protect him. A sympathetic official in charge of higher education recommended that Bloch solicit an appointment in the unoccupied zone, which he promptly proceeded to do, at the University of Strasbourg-in-exile in

7 Bloch to Professor Earl Hamilton, 25 July 1940, RFA, Rec. group 1.1, ser. 200, box 48, folder 550. Identical letters were sent to the Director of the American Council of Learned Societies, W. G. Leland, and to Professors Payson Usher and N. B. Gras of Harvard University. Cf. Bloch to Febvre, 8 July 1940, AN, MI 318 1.
8 AN, AB XIX 3825; leave granted in Arrêté, 7 Aug. 1940, AN, AJ 16 4758.
9 Soon after Bloch's return, when his eleven-year-old son Jean-Paul had suddenly stopped playing and burst into tears "because of all that has happened," he wondered if he should not leave his wife and the three youngest in Fougères or in Clermont: Bloch to Febvre, 8 Sept. 1940, AN, MI 318 1.

Clermont-Ferrand. His satisfaction over this development was tempered by his other concerns over possible difficulties connected with rejoining the Alsatian university, and by having to abandon his apartment, his books, and most of his notes. Above all, there was the first realization of his powerlessness as he endured the slow progress of formal approval of his Clermont appointment through the entire month of September.[10]

To Febvre Bloch confided his mood of cautious optimism. "Camped" in the countryside, separated from his irreplaceable dossiers, and suspended between his lost world and an uncharted new one, Bloch experienced a not unpleasant sense of "detachment" that had begun almost four months before in Steenwerck when he had "begun to scatter his worldly goods," and which might well end in an exile where all would be left behind. Like Febvre's Comtois, Bloch's Creusois neighbors had confirmed his confidence in the rural people's resources ("our last hope"). Too, a recent communication from a former fellow officer had displayed a beautiful "stoicism." Bloch recalled that the Hundred Years' War had not ended at Crécy, or even at Poitiers, although the poor idiots who had fought did not live to see the happy outcome.[11] Survival in these dark times called for traits Bloch could endorse: self-deprivation, self-discipline, and tenacity.[12]

On 3 October 1940 the Vichy government issued the Statut des Juifs, the culmination of a spate of laws since the middle of July curtailing the civil rights of French Jews in the unoccupied zone and regulating and restricting their participation in national life. On 4 October Vichy made its assault on foreign Jews, authorizing their internment or police surveillance, and three days later, on 7

---

10 Bloch to Febvre, 8, 26 Sept. 1940, AN, MI 318 1. Febvre and Paul Etard were eventually able to retrieve Bloch's dossiers and have them sent to him: Lucien Febvre, "Marc Bloch: Témoignages sur la période 1939–40: Extraits d'une correspondance intime," *AHS* (1945), "Hommages à Marc Bloch" – 1: 26.

11 Bloch to Febvre, 26 Sept. 1940, AN, MI 318 1.

12 Bloch to Etienne Bloch, 30 Sept. 1940, EBC: "Nous avons tous besoin de nous tenir perpétuellement en laisse et surtout en ce moment, de vivre constamment en état d'ascèse au sens étymologique du mot – c'est à dire 'd'exercise': exercise de discipline, de volonté, de stoïcisme."

October, it revoked the citizenship of Algerian Jews. Contrary to the widespread belief of Jews and non-Jews at the time and since, these edicts were neither the result of a German *Diktat* nor a shield to preempt worse German actions. Nor were they a reaction to popular pressure. The exclusionary laws of October 1940 drafted by high Vichy personnel implanted anti-Semitism as official French policy. They were "autonomous acts taken in pursuit of indigenous goals."[13]

Despite Pétain's soothing assurances, especially to the foreign press, French Jews were jolted by the Statut. Its racial definition of their identity denied their long-standing adherence to France. At a stroke they were excluded from government, the military, the press, education, and cultural institutions and were threatened with future erosion of their citizenship.[14] At the very time the Statut was being drafted, Marc Bloch was anxiously awaiting official notification of his appointment to Clermont-Ferrand. On 23 October the ministry "provisionally" placed him at the disposal of the Faculty of Letters of the University of Strasbourg-in-exile.[15]

At the outbreak of war in September 1939 the University of Strasbourg, in its twentieth year, was, according to earlier plans, evacuated to Clermont-Ferrand. Retaining its autonomy, the faculty shared quarters with the local university in the recently completed Cité Universitaire, which offered sufficient space and facilities for the transplanted Alsatians. Flanked on three sides by mountains with only a narrow plain opening to the north, Clermont appeared to offer physical protection as well. Though considerably reduced

13 Quotation is from Michael R. Marrus and Robert O. Paxton, *Vichy France and the Jews* (New York: Basic, 1981), p. 13; see also all of chap. 1 ("First Steps") and chap. 2 ("The Roots of Vichy Anti-Semitism"). Text of the Statut in *Journal Officiel*, 18 Oct. 1940.

14 "C'était un coup à la tête, au coeur": Georges Friedmann, *Fin du peuple juif?* (Paris: Gallimard, 1965), p. 8. "A new revocation of the Edict of Nantes": Cohen, "Jewish Leader," p. 294, quoting from Raymond Lambert's diary, 10 Oct. 1940; also entries of 2, 9, 19 Oct., 6 Nov., 20 Dec. 1940. Cf. J. Lubetzski, *La condition des Juifs en France sous l'occupation allemande, 1940–1944: La législation raciale* (Paris: Centre de Documentation Juive Contemporaine, 1945), pp. 11–12, 28–63.

15 Bloch's salary was to be paid by the Faculty of Letters and reimbursed by the ministry. Letters dated 2, 14, 24 Oct., EBC.

in size by the absence of its mobilized faculty and students, the University of Strasbourg-in-exile had opened in November 1939.[16]

With a population in 1940 of approximately one hundred thousand, Clermont-Ferrand was France's seventeenth-largest urban center and the regional capital of the Auvergne. It was rich in history. On its southern Plateau de Gergovie the Gallic chieftain Vercingetorix had temporarily stopped Julius Caesar in 52 B.C., in its center Pope Urban II had launched the First Crusade in 1095, and on the western Puy-de-Dôme Blaise Pascal had conducted experiments in 1648 proving that the atmosphere had weight. A university town since the Napoleonic era, known primarily in the twentieth century for its Michelin plant, Clermont was suddenly awakened in the summer of 1940 from its isolated provincial character. It was briefly occupied by the Germans between 21–28 June. Then, for the first two days of July, Clermont was the temporary seat of the French government between its hasty departure from Bordeaux, which was to be in the German zone, and its permanent establishment in Vichy, only sixty kilometers to the north. Like most cities in the unoccupied zone, Clermont's population swelled and later only partially receded from the massive influx of refugees in the summer of 1940, which strained its limited housing and social services and created social and political tensions.[17]

The University of Strasbourg added to the city's burdens when in the summer of 1940 demobilized faculty and students descended on Clermont. With the end of hostilities, the majority of the 850,000

16 Faculté des Lettres, Assemblée, 18 Nov. 1939, ADBR: AL 154, no. 2; also Jean Plagnieux, "Chronique de la faculté repliée à Clermont-Ferrand (1939–1945)," *Revue des Sciences Religieuses* 43 (1969): 289–90; Gabriel Maugain, "La vie de la Faculté des Lettres de Strasbourg de 1939 à 1945," in *Memorial des années 1939–1945*, Publications de la Faculté des Lettres de l'Université de Strasbourg (Paris: Belles Lettres, 1947), pp. 3–13.

17 John F. Sweets, *Choices in Vichy France: The French under Nazi Occupation* (Oxford: Oxford University press, 1986), pp. 3–7. This is a fine local study of Clermont-Ferrand, written as a supplement and corrective to Marcel Ophuls's acclaimed film *The Sorrow and the Pity* (1971) based on Clermont. Also interview with Mme. Monfren (Bloch's former student in Clermont-Ferrand), 1982.
    On the choice of Vichy: Paxton, *Vichy France*, pp. 18–19.

Alsatians evacuated to the interior the year before now returned to their homes under German rule. The occupier announced its intention of reopening a National Socialist university in Strasbourg. The Clermont exiles thus felt compelled to maintain their French Alsatian institution despite their isolation, the sundering of family ties, and their delicate position vis-à-vis the Germans and Vichy. Though some returned to their homeland, most of the students attending in 1939–40 remained in Clermont, their numbers reinforced by some two to three hundred new refugees, making approximately one thousand Alsatian students, who were generally known for their ardent patriotism. Despite financial and material hardships and equivocal support from Vichy, the exiled university opened its doors again in late October 1940.[18]

Bloch and his family, along with his mother and a niece, settled in Clermont. They rented a small first-floor apartment whose dining room served as Bloch's study and bedroom. Despite all their privations, at least they were together. And despite the absence of his notes and his library and the mediocre resources in Clermont, Bloch was heartened by the friendly greeting of his former colleagues.[19] As his friends returned to Paris for the *rentrée*, he commenced his new teaching assignment, taking over two of the preparatory courses for the *agrégation*: "Medieval Cities" and "Italy, Germany, and the Papacy, 1056–1152."[20] But the future was highly uncertain.

In the United States Bloch's overture made its way slowly

18 Responding to German demands, the administration was eventually forced to return its library collections and laboratory equipment. The Vichy government hesitated to allow it to fill its vacant professorships. Maugain, "Faculté," pp. 20–21; John E. Craig, *Scholarship and Nation Building: The Universities of Strasbourg and Alsatian Society, 1870–1939* (Chicago: University of Chicago Press, 1984), pp. 329–31. On the students: Jean Lassus, *Souvenirs d'un cobaye* (Colmar: Alsatia, 1973), pp. 55–61; Sweets, *Choices*, pp. 10, 171, 191.
19 Bloch to Febvre, 26 Sept. 1940, AN, MI 318 1.
20 Boutruche to Bloch, 21 Oct. 1940, AN, AB XIX 3837; "Medieval Cities" in ibid. In a report by two officials of the Deutsches Institut, Dr. Bremer and Dr. Rabuse, to the German Foreign Ministry on French universities in the unoccupied zone (Paris, 21 May 1941) Bloch's presence in Clermont was noted: a Jew teaching "economic history [sic]...unwilling or unable to return to Paris." NARS, Germany AA T-120 K1634/4744/K402927.

through academic and institutional channels as the New World braced for a fresh influx of endangered scholars. Even before the fall of France, Alvin Johnson, the energetic and resourceful president of the New School for Social Research in New York City, which had already established the University in Exile for European refugee intellectuals in the 1930s, had called upon the Emergency Rescue Committee and the Rockefeller Foundation to prepare for a new exodus. Offering the New School's services for administrative apparatus and sponsorship, Johnson succeeded in obtaining the promise of funding from the foundation for the rescue of a hundred "scholars of the first rank," who were to be placed either at major universities or at the New School itself. Though pitted against the growing resistance of aid agencies and the State Department to bringing more Jewish and possibly left-wing intellectuals to America, and constrained by his own institution's financial difficulties, Johnson nevertheless set a plan in motion that between September 1940 and December 1941 brought fifty eminent European scholars to North America, including the anthropologist Claude Lévi-Strauss.[21]

Bloch's case was handled meticulously. His appeal was turned over to the Rockefeller Foundation as that of a notable figure whose family was endangered by his Jewish origins. Johnson personally solicited letters of support from major American scholars, and the responses were overwhelmingly positive. Bloch was termed one of France's most brilliant historians of medieval economic and social history, "a scholar of the first rank," highly original and productive, lucid, and precise.[22] On 25 October 1940 the Rockefeller Foundation agreed to support Bloch's rescue, earmarking a sum of

21 Peter M. Rutkoff and William B. Scott, *New School* (New York: Free Press; London: Collier Macmillan, 1986), pp. 128–30; Alvin Johnson, *Pioneer's Progress: An Autobiography* (New York: Viking, 1952), p. 337. Bloch was acquainted with Johnson, who was associate editor of the *Encyclopedia of the Social Sciences*.
22 See the immediate enthusiastic responses by Austin P. Evans, Lynn Thorndike, and H. H. Byrne of Columbia University, 14, 15, 16 Oct. 1940, James Lea Cate and Einar Joranson of the University of Chicago, 14, 25 Oct. 1940, James W. Thompson of Berkeley, 16 Oct., N. S. B. Gras of Harvard, 14, 18 Oct. 1940, RACEP.

$6,000 to permit the New School to invite him to the United States.[23]

On learning of the foundation's assent, Bloch secured the informal agreement of his superiors at Vichy that he could accept a temporary appointment in the United States. But he urged speed on his American helpers because of the "quick pace" of events in Europe and "the possibilities that new obstacles to traveling may spring up." He also added a request that his mother, "marvelously young for her age," be included in their emigrant group.[24]

The New School obliged with a cable and letter dated 19 November appointing Bloch Associate Professor of Medieval History for a two-year term beginning 1 January 1941 or on his arrival in New York, at an annual salary of $2,500. Bloch accepted at once, and set to work on their passage, permission to leave, and visas.[25] Job-like he waited for "deliverance."[26]

The first obstacle was revealed on 13 December, when Bloch visited the American consulate in Lyon. From the clerk in charge of visas and Consul General Walter Sholes, he learned that nonquota visas could be issued immediately to himself, his wife, and four minor children, but that his mother, a daughter aged twenty, and a son aged nineteen would not be eligible. Their cases would be handled in "chronological order" according to routine procedures, which included close scrutiny of the adequacy of their financial resources. Although the French immigration quota was scarcely filled, by mid December 1940 there was already a list of over five hundred applicants awaiting processing. The consulate in Lyon was severely understaffed. In addition to representing Belgian and British interests, it now handled on behalf of the United States a

23 Thomas B. Appleget to Alvin Johnson, 25 Oct. 1940, RACEP. The foundation had received letters of support directly from Usher, Hamilton, Gras, and John Ulrich Nef; see, e.g., Gras to J. H. Willits, 30 Sept. 1940, RFA.
24 Bloch to Leland, 31 Oct. 1940, RFA.
25 Johnson's 19 Nov. 1940 cable and letter; Bloch's cable (22 Nov. ?) ("Accepte remerciements") and 10 Dec. letter, RACEP.
26 Describing his situation on 19 November 1940: "Expecto donae veniat immutatio mea" (All the days of my appointed time will I wait, till my change come) (Job 14: 14). Bloch, notebook "Mea," EBC.

myriad of political, economic, and personal questions in France's "Second Capital," the financial, industrial, and communications center of Vichy. Hence there was no prospect of a decision before May or June.[27]

Bloch's hopes for an immediate flight with his loved ones were paralyzed. He could not leave Sarah Bloch, at age eighty-two, alone in Clermont-Ferrand. As a Jew she was prohibited by German regulations from crossing the demarcation line either to return to her home in Marlotte or to go to her daughter-in-law's residence in Paris. Even if he reluctantly left his oldest son temporarily in France, he could not leave his daughter behind. Moreover, his next son would turn eighteen on 26 February 1941. With considerable apprehension Bloch contemplated the alternatives of delaying his departure for six months or making a detour to Martinique, where they might obtain the three nonquota visas more rapidly but might also have to leave three family members for an indeterminate time. He asked Johnson to do all in his power to "alleviate our difficulties."[28]

In the meantime Bloch had to secure permission to continue teaching under the Statut des Juifs. According to its provisions, within three months of its issuance, or by the beginning of January

27 Walter Sholes, "Some Aspects of Consular Work and Conditions at Lyon, France during 1940–41" (confidential), Basel, 5 Sept. 1941 (NARS, USDS RG 84 [American Consulate, Basel], Confidential Files 1941 123-L, covering the period 9 June 1940–30 Apr. 1941), details the especially "arduous" period between the beginning of October and the beginning of January, when his small, overburdened, untrained staff handled visa control along with "requests of every character and description from the Embassy and the hundreds of Americans and aliens daily crowding our small and unsuitable consular quarters." Though help arrived at the end of December and in early January, there were several complaints in 1941 over dilatory visa handling. On 10 February 1941, with an enlarged staff of one vice-consul and two clerks, the Lyon consulate expected to process 45 immigration visas and 15 transit visas monthly and had a backlog of 5,000 applications. Sholes to H. Freeman Matthews, Secretary of U.S. Embassy Vichy, 10 Feb. 1941, ibid.; Leahy to Secretary of State, 12 Feb. 1941, NARS, USDS FW 811.111 Refugees/959. My thanks to Richard Breitman for these documents.

28 "Impossible partir sans mère enfants." Radiogram, Bloch to New School (received 15 Dec. 1940); Bloch to Johnson, 14 Dec. 1940, RACEP.

1941, he would lose his position and his livelihood. Article 8 of the Statut empowered the government to grant exemptions to those who had rendered "exceptional services" to the French state. Of 4,000 Jewish university professors, 125 applied to the Ministry of Education based on their literary, scientific, and artistic credentials and on their military records.[29]

Vichy intended to act cautiously in bestowing exclusions to its own racial laws, reserving these for outstanding individuals in important posts.[30] Bloch's personal connections proved helpful. In December 1940 he was able to make a trip to Paris to discuss his case.[31] At the Sorbonne the dossiers and exemption requests of the Jewish professors were assembled, ranked, and forwarded to Vichy by the acting rector, Jérôme Carcopino. A former protégé of Gustave Bloch and devoted friend, Carcopino strongly supported Bloch's case.[32] Vichy's minister of education was Jacques Chevalier, a *normalien*, philosophy professor, former dean at Grenoble, and Pétain's godson and confidant involved in unofficial negotiations with the British. He was also the father of one of Bloch's most gifted students. Chevalier gave a strong endorsement to Bloch's exemption, based on his scholarly eminence in France and abroad and also his distinguished military record.[33] The Conseil d'Etat, crediting the

29 Figures in Militärbefehlshaber in Frankreich, Verwaltungsstab, Aktennotiz, 16 Apr. 1941, AN, AJ 40 555.
30 Two Jewish officers, General Darius-Paul Bloch and Chief of Artillery Squadron Pierre-Solomon-Isaac Brisac, were granted *dérogations* on 10 December 1940: *Journal Officiel*, 13 Dec. 1940, 1 Jan. 1941, CDJC, XCV, 100.
31 The December visit to Paris is mentioned in Bloch to Febvre, 27 Sept. 1941, AN, MI 318 1; Bloch to René Baehrel, 30 Aug. 1942, quoted in "Deux lettres de Marc Bloch," AESC 2, no. 3 (July–Sept. 1947): 366. Bloch to Maugain (8 Dec. 1940, ADBR, AL 154 P8/15) cites a "return" and an expected "absence."
    Bloch saw his friends Febvre and Etard and was also able to retrieve some essential books from his apartment.
32 Jérôme Carcopino, *Souvenirs de sept ans, 1937–1944* (Paris: Flammarion, 1953), pp. 247–51, 254–57. Carcopino, who had succeeded Bouglé as director of the Ecole Normale Supérieure, had hosted Pétain's visit to the rue d'Ulm in September 1940.
33 "Avis du Secrétaire d'Etat à l'Instruction Publique," 2 Dec. 1940, Archive, Conseil d'Etat, 224.032, with thanks for permission to see Bloch's file.
    On Jacques Chevalier, once the disciple of Henri Bergson but now considered

latter more than the former, concurred.[34] On 23 December 1940 Carcopino and Chevalier were granted an interview by Pétain at the Hôtel du Parc in Vichy, where, among other things, they discussed the Statut.[35]

Slightly after the deadline, on 5 January 1941, Pétain, with the concurring advice of the ministers of education, interior, and youth and the family as well as the Conseil d'Etat, issued a decree exempting ten Jewish professors from exclusion from their professions. One was Marc Bloch.[36] Of the ten, seven were originally from Paris, although only two had remained there. There were three humanists: Bloch, his rival medievalist at the Sorbonne, Louis Halphen, and the linguist Jules Bloch from the Collège de France; two scientists, the chemist Paul Job (Sorbonne) and the biophysicist René Wurmser (Ecole des Hautes Etudes, Paris), and five medical professors: André Mayer and Robert Debré (Paris), and Paul Reiss, Max Aron, and Marc Klein (Strasbourg). The language of Bloch's citation was striking. Echoing Vichy's Christian and nationalist orientation, he was specifically cited as a medievalist and for his work on France's kings, rural history, and feudal society. His work

an ultraconservative (who immediately introduced compulsory religious instruction in public education), see Paxton, *Vichy France*, pp. 88–89, 151, 159, 160; Robert Aron, *The Vichy Regime*, trans. H. Hare (Boston: Beacon, 1969), pp. 128–29, 234–36.

His son, François Chevalier, who later became an outstanding historian of colonial Spanish America, studied rural history in Bloch's seminar (1937–38) at the Ecole Normale Supérieure. After his demobilization, when he was considering continuing his studies in Spain, he visited Marc Bloch in Clermont-Ferrand on 25 November 1940. In the course of their meeting they discussed the themes of the recently published *Société féodale*, and Bloch helped Chevalier with his research subject, methodology, and literature as well as suggesting professional contacts in Spain. Letter from François Chevalier to author, 14 May 1979; interview, 1981.

34 17 Dec. 1940, Archive, Conseil d'Etat, 224.032.

35 Carcopino, *Souvenirs*, pp. 250–57, which stresses his effort to include military service in claims for exemptions.

36 No requests by technical, secondary school, or primary school teachers were granted. "Dérogations accordées par décret en Conseil d'État en application de la loi du 2 oct. 1940," CDJC, cxv 100; Militärbefehlshaber in Frankreich, Verwaltungsstab, "Aktennotiz," 16 Apr. 1941, AN, AJ 40 555.

24. Vichy: Pétain and Darlan reviewing a parade of the 152d Infantry Regiment in front of the Hôtel du Parc, 1941

on comparative history, economic history, and the *Annales* was not mentioned.[37]

On learning that he had been spared, Bloch could scarcely hide his chagrin at the great injustice inflicted on his countrymen. The less fortunate, young and old alike, had been condemned to ostracism and penury. Only a day before the exemption decree, one of France's greatest philosophers, Henri Bergson, had suddenly died. "What," Bloch asked Carcopino, "would have been Bergson's fate had the Statut been issued when he was a young lycée professor in Clermont?"[38]

When Carcopino took the helm of the Ministry of National Education in February 1941 he devoted himself to easing the plight

37 The citation, signed by Pétain and Chevalier on 5 January, read: "...Marc BLOCH, professeur à la Faculté des Lettres de l'Université de PARIS, a fait preuve dans ses ouvrages d'histoire médiévale, non seulement de la plus solide érudition, mais d'idées nouvelles et fécondes qui se sont affirmées notamment dans ses travaux sur le caractère sacré qui s'attachait à la personne des rois de FRANCE et d'ANGLETERRE, sur la stabilité des formes de la propriété rurale en FRANCE depuis les temps les plus anciens et sur l'organisation de la société féodale." Text in NARS, Germany AA T-120 K1633/4742/K401844.
38 Bloch to Febvre, 16 Apr. 1941, AN, MI 318 1. Chevalier read a eulogy for his former *maître* on the radio but missed the memorial service in Paris: Carcopino, *Souvenirs*, p. 260.

of some of his expropriated colleagues. During the next year there were a number of instances of ministerial laxness in enforcement. In addition, the faculties of Strasbourg, Lyon, Montpellier, and Toulouse were openly reluctant to collaborate in the persecution of their Jewish colleagues, and the charity of fellow scholars saved a few proud families from starvation.[39] Bloch, while recognizing and appreciating these gestures, remained outraged over the Statut and keenly aware of being among the "rare survivors."[40]

The exemption decrees of 5 January represented an isolated, controversial phenomenon. Vichy's extreme sensitivity on this issue was indicated by the absence of publication of the decrees in the *Journal Officiel* and by the requirement that they be renewed periodically. The German Military Government, informed officially on 24 January, objected strenuously to applying the decrees in the occupied zone and sought the removal of Halphen and Mayer. The German embassy in Paris deprecated the prestige of the others as simply "creations of Jewish propaganda," artificially promoted under the ministry of Jean Zay. It protested an act that obliterated the "clear distinction between Jewish and non-Jewish Frenchmen" and suspected Vichy's zeal in implementing its own racist laws.[41] It was not until 20 February that Bloch learned directly from Carcopino of his rescue.

At the same time he also received the ministry's permission to leave for the United States with his wife, mother, and six children, "to pursue his research in economic history."[42] But by then his plan

---

39 CGQJ to Ministre de l'Education Nationale, 14 Mar. 1942, CDJC: CIX-125; also report, 25 Sept. 1943, CDJC, LXXIX-102. On Carcopino, see Marrus and Paxton, *Vichy France*, pp. 151, 208.

40 Bloch to Maugain, 21 Feb. 1941, ADBR, AL 154 P8/15; also Bloch to Ullman, Clermont-Ferrand, 2 Apr. 1941, and Bloch to Febvre, 17 Aug. 1941, AN, MI 318 1.

41 Despite the opposition of the Militärbefehlshaber in France and Belgium, Mayer and Debré remained at their Paris posts, while Halphen, aided by Carcopino, went to the University of Grenoble in June 1941: Louis Halphen dossier, AN, AJ 16 6017; Carcopino, *Souvenirs*, p. 360. Militärbefehlshaber, Verwaltungsstab, documents of 24, 31 Jan., 19 Feb., 11, 14, 24, 28 Mar., 16 Apr., 30 May 1941, AN, AJ 40 555.

42 Bloch to Maugain, 21 Feb. 1941, and Arrêté, 24 Feb. 1941, ADBR, AL 154 P8/15.

to "strike camp" with nine people, a cumbersome proposition at best, had been complicated by his mother's sudden illness. Although Johnson (who had contacted the State Department) sent assurances that there should be no delays in obtaining the nonquota visas in Martinique, Bloch, fearing to leave his mother alone even for a short period, now abandoned the idea of departing at once for the West Indies without either visas in hand or firm guarantees. He made two trips to Marseille, there to be told that his "financial resources were too small" to support his whole family in New York. His fate rested in Lyon and in Washington.[43]

Again he appealed to New York to help expedite his case with the State Department, but apparently little could be done in Washington. Local visa offices had almost total control over their procedures.[44] In Lyon the consular staff had been slightly augmented, but the caseload had increased tenfold.[45] On learning of this situation, Bloch on 13 February told an American official in Lyon that he and his family would remain in France for three months, "until all of their cases could receive final consideration," and travel together to the United States. Johnson considered this a risky calculation. To assuage the consulate's financial concerns, he was able to persuade the Rockefeller Foundation to increase Bloch's travel subvention from $1,000 to $3,000. But the growing exodus promised to create difficulties in booking ship passage for nine people and in obtaining transit visas for Spain and Portugal. Johnson reluctantly accepted Bloch's decision to wait, but urged the

---

43 Bloch to Johnson, 15 Feb. 1941, RACEP. Background: Johnson to Eliot B. Coulter, Acting Chief, Visa Division, U.S. Dept. of State, 15, 20 Jan. 1941; A. M. Warren, Chief, Visa Division, to Johnson, 3 Feb. 1941; Johnson to Bloch, cables 7, 14 Feb. 1941; Bloch cable to Johnson, n.d.; Johnson to Warren, 14 Feb. 1941 ("...I want only to call your attention to the fact that there is not a single professor of history in our American universities who would not be enthusiastic to learn that Professor Bloch is coming over and the fact that events are moving so rapidly in France that our chances to save him for American science diminish almost hourly"), RACEP; also Bloch to Febvre, 5 Feb. 1941, AN, MI 318 1.

44 Warren to Johnson, 19 Feb. 1941, and Else Staudinger to Mrs. Michel, 20 Feb. 1941, RACEP.

45 Leahy to State Dept., 12 Feb. 1941, NARS, USDS 811.111 Refugees/959.

Martinique solution, which would enable them all to "leave the continent earlier."[46]

Poised between two worlds, ostensibly about to "desert" his native land to save his children, but still under the threat of further discrimination, Bloch at age fifty-four wrote his testament. In three short paragraphs he summarized the beliefs and creed that had governed his life, which he hoped would be read by a friend over his grave – either in France or abroad.[47]

Instead of the Hebrew prayers that had accompanied all his ancestors to their final rest, Bloch wanted but the simple epitaph *Dilexit veritatem* (I have loved the truth), a phrase he had applied earlier to his teacher Christian Pfister.[48] True to his principles and his horror of falsehood, at his "last farewell" he rejected invoking a religious orthodoxy that he had never recognized.

He nevertheless refused to deny that he was "born a Jew."

In a world assailed by the most atrocious barbarism, is not the generous tradition of the Hebrew prophets, which Christianity in its purest sense has adopted and expanded, one of the best reasons to live, to believe, and to fight?

But above all Bloch was a "good Frenchman":

A stranger to all credal dogmas as to all alleged racial solidarity, I have throughout my life thought of myself as above all and quite simply a Frenchman. Attached to my country by a long family tradition, nourished by its spiritual heritage and its history, and, indeed, incapable of conceiving another land whose air I could breathe with such ease, I have

46 Bloch to Johnson, undated cable, letter 9 Mar. 1941; Willits to Johnson, 11 Mar., Johnson to Willits, 14 Mar., Johnson to Bloch, cable 13 Mar., Bloch to Johnson, 25 Mar., Johnson to Bloch, 31 Mar., RACEP.

Alexander Makinsky, the Rockefeller Foundation's agent in Lisbon, who had been in touch with Bloch and the consulate, reported on 28 April 1941 that Bloch's insistence on the family's traveling together was foolhardy: "Unless he is willing to wait until the late fall, he will never be able to get eight [sic] places on the same boat." RFA.

47 "Dernières volontés," Clermont-Ferrand, 18 Mar. 1941, courtesy of Etienne Bloch, reprinted in *ED*, pp. 223–24.

48 Marc Bloch, "Christian Pfister, 1857–1933: Ses oeuvres," *RH* 172 (1933): 567.

loved it very much and served it with all my strength. I have never felt that my being a Jew has at all hindered these sentiments. In the course of two wars it has not been my lot to die for France. At least I can, in all sincerity, declare that I have died, as I have lived, a good Frenchman.[49]

This warm and serene patriotism and Bloch's hopes and composure were at once tested. On Easter Sunday 1941 his mother had a stroke. The day before, his wife had collapsed with an attack of pleurisy and a high temperature. Forced to remain in Fougères to nurse them, Bloch had to delay his return to Clermont and cancel his teaching. Sarah Bloch died on 27 April and was buried in the village cemetery of Le Bourg d'Hem. Simonne Bloch remained bedridden until the middle of May. In practical terms these calamities both simplified and complicated their future. Their émigré band was reduced by one. But should Bloch's emigration plans miscarry because his wife's weak health made it impossible to contemplate another long, dark, wet winter in Clermont-Ferrand, he had to seek another post. On a deeper level, at the moment when his bond with the *patrie* had become precarious Bloch's loss of his mother, the last of his immediate family and his sole link with a happier past, his long-standing confidante and guide, was an agonizing blow.[50] The extended illness and lingering fragility of his wife, who for twenty-two years had been his mainstay and beloved companion, weakened his own health and diminished his spirits and his confidence.[51]

Still, the war was not over, and Bloch retained a small measure of outward optimism. Although the Germans were in Salonika and were threatening Suez, "if they could be in London they would not need Salonika, and if they had access to Liverpool they would not

---

49 After which Bloch requested that, if the texts could be obtained, his five military citations be read.
50 "Je me sens déchiré et mutilé, et je n'ai même pas la douceur de penser que la vieillesse de ma mère aura été sereine." Bloch to Febvre, 16 May 1941, AN, MI 318 1; also 17 Aug. 1941, ibid.
51 Bloch to Etienne Bloch, 19 Apr. 1941, EBC; Bloch to Febvre, 16 Apr., 7, 16 May 1941, AN, MI 318 1; Bloch to Maugain, 19 Apr. 1941, ADBR, AL 154 P8/15; Bloch to Boutruche, 7 May 1941, RB; Bloch to Carcopino, 12 May 1941, AN, 3W 122/78; Bloch to Lot, 10 Aug. 1941, Lot papers, IF.

Clermont-Ferrand, le 18 mars 1941

Où que je doive mourir, en France ou sur la terre
étrangère, et à quelque moment que ce soit, je laisse
à ma chère femme ou, à son défaut, à mes enfants
le soin de régler mes obsèques, comme ils le jugeront
bien. Ce seront des obsèques purement civiles; les
miens savent bien que je n'en aurais pas voulu
d'autres. Mais je souhaiterais que ce jour-là, soit à
la maison mortuaire, soit au cimetière, un ami
accepte de donner lecture des quelques mots
que voici

« Je n'ai point demandé que, sur ma tombe,
fussent récitées les prières hébraïques, dont les
cadences, pourtant, accompagnèrent, vers leur dernier
repos, tant de mes ancêtres et mon père lui-même.
Je me suis, toute ma vie durant, efforcé de mon
mieux, vers une sincérité totale de l'expression et
de l'esprit. Je tiens la complaisance envers le
mensonge, de quelques prétextes qu'elle puisse
se parer, pour la pire lèpre de l'âme. Comme
un beaucoup plus grand que moi, je souhaiterais
volontiers que, pour toute devise, on gravât
sur ma pierre tombale, ces simples mots "Dilexit
veritatem". C'est pourquoi il m'était impossible
d'admettre qu'en cette heure des suprêmes
adieux, où tout homme a pour devoir de se

25. Marc Bloch's testament, March 1941

258

2. Se résumer soi-même, aucun appel fait fait, en mon nom, aux effusions d'une orthodoxie, dont je ne reconnais point le credo.

Mais il me serait plus odieux encore que dans cet acte de probité personne pût rien voir qui ressemblât à un lâche reniement. J'affirme donc, s'il le faut, face à la mort, que je suis né Juif; que je n'ai jamais songé à m'en défendre ni trouvé aucun motif d'être tenté de le faire. Dans un monde assailli par la plus atroce barbarie, la généreuse tradition des prophètes hébreux, que le christianisme, en ce qu'il eut de plus pur, reprit, pour l'élargir, ne demeure-t-elle pas une de nos meilleures raisons de vivre, de croire et de lutter ?

Étranger à tout formalisme confessionnel comme à toute solidarité prétendument raciale, je me suis senti, durant ma vie entière, avant tout et très simplement Français. Attaché à ma patrie par une tradition familiale déjà longue, nourri de son héritage spirituel et de son histoire, incapable, en vérité, d'en concevoir une autre où je pusse respirer à l'aise, je l'ai beaucoup aimée et servie de toutes mes forces, et je n'ai jamais éprouvé que ma qualité de Juif mit à ces sentiments le moindre obstacle. Au cours de deux guerres, il ne m'a pas été donné de mourir pour la France. Du moins, puis-je, en toute sincérité, ne rendre ce témoignage : je meurs, comme j'ai vécu, en bon Français. »

Il a seu ensuite — s'il a été possible de s'en procurer le texte — donné lecture de mes cinq citations.

have to attack the Canal."[52] As usual in such difficult moments, Bloch's antidote was work. He flung himself into his teaching, which that year had been chaotic at best. He fretted over the frequent disruptions in his contact with the handful of students preparing for the *agrégation*, but he persevered with his classes. To the extent possible and prudent, he participated voluntarily in the collegial life of the University of Strasbourg-in-exile.[53] In early May he asked to serve as *rapporteur* of the jury of his former student and present colleague Robert Boutruche, whose doctoral thesis he had guided for several years and now strongly recommended for publication.[54] Bloch read continually – Erasmus, Spinoza, and Montesquieu – and kept a diary which he called "Mea" that included historical and philosophical reflections on contemporary events. During this bleak spring of 1941 Bloch outlined projects he had scant hope of publishing, among them a small pamphlet on the formation of France,[55] a history of French currency, studies of the first German Empire and of the settlement of the United States, a murder mystery, and the work begun during the *drôle de guerre*, his reflections on history and historical method, his future *Apologie pour l'histoire*.[56]

52 Excerpt of letter to his former student Robert Folz, quoted in Robert Boutruche, "Marc Bloch vu par ses élèves," in *Mémorial des années 1939–1945*, Publications de la Faculté des Lettres de l'Université de Strasbourg (Paris: Belles Lettres, 1947), p. 206.

53 Ibid., p. 206: "Le groupe alsacien de Clermont est admirable de foi en l'avenir, de ténacité, de courage. Leur exemple nous est à tous une leçon. Et je crois qu'au fond ils ont raison, et que les prétendus 'réalistes' ont tort."

54 Bloch to Maugain, 7 May 1941, and Maugain to Terracher, 14 May 1941, ADBR, AL 154 P8/15. On the basis of his publications and mobilization and according to a recent decree, Boutruche was exempt from presenting a second thesis. Bloch, "Rapport," ibid. Bloch's faculty participation: ADBR, AL 154 P2/3.

55 Bloch was both flattered and apprehensive about the request by his former colleague and rival Albert Grenier, who was no doubt unaware of the delicacy of having Bloch's name attached to such a subject. Bloch to Febvre, 16 Apr., 16 May 1941, AN, MI 318 1. Draft letter to Grenier ("C'est un bel acte de courage à l'heure actuelle que d'inviter un homme de mon nom...d'y écrire sur la formation de la France"). AN, AB XIX 3824.

56 "Livres à écrire," notebook "Mea," EBC.

The fate of the *Annales* was now in question. Since October, when he had returned somewhat reluctantly and apprehensively to Paris, Febvre had again carried the main responsibility for the journal and had directed production of the two issues of 1940. Bloch's expected departure for the United States had kept the future in suspense.[57] By spring, however, there were important matters to be settled in the occupied capital in regard to the survival of their joint enterprise. With its non-Aryan co-proprietor, the *Annales* risked seizure or liquidation by German or French authorities.[58]

At the very moment when his wife and mother were stricken and his American plans stalled, Bloch was forced to engage in an intense month-long debate with Febvre over the future of the *Annales*, their third and harshest dispute in the history of their collaboration.[59] On Easter Sunday Febvre wrote Bloch, asking him to break the contract, relinquish his place, and give him full ownership of the *Annales*.[60]

Bloch initially refused. His pride and honor were injured by the two iniquities: maintaining their joint creation in the occupied zone and removing his name from its masthead. From his perspective there could be no compromise with the rule of the swastika. He refused to follow Meinecke in submitting to a dismissal from his post. Until France was liberated, the *Annales* must either move to the unoccupied zone or die, perhaps to be succeeded temporarily by two new independent creations by Bloch and by Febvre. He insisted:

---

57 Febvre to Bloch, 3 Oct. 1940, AN, MI 318 2.
58 Ibid. Bloch to Febvre, 5 Feb. 1941, AN, MI 318 1. As early as 20 May 1940 the Germans issued an ordinance envisaging the administration of enemy property in the conquered territories, which went into effect in northern France on 21 June. By autumn, the occupying authorities began to register Jewish properties, assign provisional administrators, and prevent Jews who had fled from returning to the occupied zone; an ordinance of 26 April 1941 gave administrators the power to sell Jewish properties or liquidate them. The Vichy government, intent on wresting aryanization from German hands, in early December created a Service du Contrôle des Administrateurs Provisoires, and on 23 March 1941 appointed a commissioner-general for Jewish affairs, Xavier Vallat, who proceeded to draft Vichy's own Aryanization law of 22 July. Paxton, *Vichy France*, pp. 176–80.
59 Febvre, "Marc Bloch: Témoignages," pp. 21–25.
60 Febvre to Bloch, Easter (13 Apr. 1941), AN, MI 318 3.

If our work has had any meaning at all, it has been its independence, its refusal to accept the pressure of what Péguy – the odd patron of a clientele that would have astonished him – called the "temporal" in the form of narrow academicism, adherence to a specific school of thought, or anything similar. The suppression of my name would be an abdication. . . .[61]

Febvre responded angrily to Bloch's "death sentence" for the *Annales*. He lamented his co-director's "desertion" and betrayal of his (not "our") country; it would give the enemy "another victory." From his side of the demarcation line, Febvre demolished Bloch's palliative proposals. Under current occupation regulations, no new journal could be founded. An *Annales* moved to the unoccupied zone would scarcely be free of censorship. Moreover, works published there could not be distributed to the greater part (two-thirds) of France, to its major cities and intellectual centers, or be sent abroad to readers in the Netherlands, Belgium, Switzerland, and Germany without special, and likely unattainable, authorization.

Febvre appealed to Bloch's sense of duty and self-abnegation, insisting that the only name that counted was the *Annales'*. He appealed to Bloch's patriotism. In that dismal time they must promote unity instead of schism. "Unity" meant Paris, and in Paris, suffering the heaviest yoke of occupation, the universal resolve was "to preserve" (*maintenir*). Febvre reported that their closest friends, while sympathizing with Bloch's sacrifice, were nevertheless unanimous that the *Annales* must continue to be published in the capital. Journals such as the *Revue Historique* were making accommodations. On the *Année Sociologique* their colleague Marcel Mauss had gallantly agreed to become an anonymous contributor. Febvre, vowing to "swim until he drowned," pledged his efforts, his labor, and his hope. With a flattering reference to Voltaire and Diderot's heroic publishing activity under another oppressive regime, he promised Bloch a continuing, if unofficial, role in their enterprise. Finally, no doubt in desperation, he taunted Bloch that a man who had appealed to his friends to help rescue his library ought not himself destroy an object whose spirit was even more precious than its material existence.[62]

61 Bloch to Febvre, 16 Apr. 1941, AN, MI 318 1; Meinecke reference: Bloch to Febvre, 7 May 1941, ibid.
62 Febvre to Bloch, 19 Apr. (2 drafts), 3 May, n.d. ("printemps"; 2 drafts) 1941, AN, MI 318 3 (887–907).

Bloch, initially unpersuaded, held out against his partner's torrent of criticism and vituperation, whereupon Febvre escalated his attack. Emphasizing the immediate threat of liquidation, he insisted that a life must not be extinguished for a principle.[63] On 16 May Bloch reluctantly surrendered to Febvre's practical "politics," but not without a warning that his violated principles would inevitably haunt them in the form of future repression and exclusion.[64]

It is not easy to determine why Bloch capitulated, for he was far from convinced by Febvre's arguments. A schism had opened between the two directors as between the two Frances. Out of a sense of duty, loyalty, and patriotism, or because of his grief, his helplessness to control events, and his uncertainty over the future, Bloch reluctantly succumbed.

Now his travel plans were less promising than ever. Just one day after he yielded to Febvre, Bloch informed the director of the Rockefeller Foundation of his mounting difficulties. First, he had encountered obstacles in booking a transatlantic passage for all the members of his family, either from Lisbon to the United States, which necessitated transit visas, or via Martinique, which required a special safe-conduct from the minister of colonies and booking on equally crowded ships. Second, since recent French legislation prohibited the emigration of males between the ages of eighteen and forty-nine, his two sons now needed exit visas, most likely for Martinique, which were considered easier to obtain than for foreign countries. Third, there was his wife's poor health and slow convalescence, which affected their prospects of immediate travel. Finally, there were the long-awaited U.S. visas, which had not yet been granted.[65]

In his own defense for having insisted on all the visas, Bloch complained mildly about the seemingly excessive delay in handling

---

63 Bloch to Febvre, 7 May 1941, AN, MI 318 1; Febvre to Bloch, n.d. (ca. 9 May 1941), AN, MI 318 3.

64 Bloch to Febvre, postcard and letter on 16 May 1941, AN, MI 318 1. Febvre to Bloch, 25 May, 2 June 1941, AN, MI 318 3.

65 Cable from Strode to Rockefeller Foundation, 10 Apr. 1941, quoted in Peter M. Rutkoff and William B. Scott, "Letters to America: The Correspondence of Marc Bloch, 1940–41," *French Historical Studies* 12 (Fall 1981): 296 (which includes a useful selection of the correspondence); Bloch to Willits, 17 May 1941, RACEP.

their case in Lyon and the impossibility of obtaining help in Marseille, which had prevented him from leaving earlier when there were fewer impediments on the French side. Though still hoping to be able to avail himself of the generous offer of the New School and pledging all his efforts to make it possible, Bloch was no longer sure he would succeed.[66]

He therefore had to arrange for his immediate future, which involved securing a teaching post for the following year in a more salubrious climate. His friend Carcopino obliged by recommending his appointment to the University of Montpellier. Bloch had known the city thirty years earlier. It was "infinitely more attractive than Clermont," with a better climate for his wife and the prospect of fruitful collaboration with new colleagues. On his preliminary visit in June 1941 he also went to nearby Toulouse, the refuge of many Parisian Jewish intellectuals, where he found a sympathetic environment. His exiled friends took his side on the struggle over the *Annales* and commiserated over his lost battle. He was also invited to participate in sessions of the newly founded Société d'Etudes Psychologiques, which touched one of Bloch's interests, the psychology of work and of technology. He saw a former *Annales* collaborator, Georges Friedmann, who, banned by the Statut from teaching, was now engaged in resistance activities.[67]

Bloch discovered that his relocation to Montpellier would not be simple. The university, despite its sprinkling of émigré Paris intellectuals, was the first institution to have formally invited Pétain and Darlan to visit in February 1941. The dean of the Faculty of Letters was a fellow *normalien*, Augustin Fliche, an ultra-conservative church historian who nursed a long-standing resentment against Bloch because of a bad review and who would do his utmost to obstruct the nomination. Fliche warned his superior that a public

66 Bloch to Willits, 17 May 1941, RACEP.
67 Bloch to Febvre, 26 June 1941, EBC. On Friedmann: H. R. Kedward, *Resistance in Vichy France* (Oxford: Oxford University Press, 1978), p. 158; *Une nouvelle civilisation? Hommage à Georges Friedmann* (Paris: Gallimard, 1973). Société d'Etudes: AN, AB XIX 3851.
  A lecture Bloch delivered to this group, "Les transformations des techniques comme problème de psychologie collective," was published posthumously in the *Journal de Psychologie Normale et Pathologique* 41 (Jan.–Mar. 1948): 104–15.

course by Marc Bloch might provoke hostile demonstrations and said he would take no responsibility for such incidents.[68] In the meantime Vichy on 2 June 1941 had revised the Statut des Juifs, closing loopholes and preparing for a "massive purge" of Jews from public life. There was to be a Jewish census, and Jewish property in the unoccupied zone was to be Aryanized.[69] The loyal Carcopino continued to aid his colleague. On 11 July 1941 he issued a decree formally maintaining Bloch in service on the basis of his earlier exemption, and on 15 July Bloch was assigned to Montpellier.[70]

At the end of July his extended offer from the New School was about to expire, and Bloch, in Fougères, was still without visas for his overage children. It was then that he wrote to inform Alvin Johnson that he could not leave for the United States and expected to go to Montpellier for the following academic year. Though their future was not without danger, to Johnson Bloch, buoyed as usual by the "hope and courage" of his rural Creusois neighbors, expressed optimism that conditions for French Jews would eventually improve. On the other hand, he would readily emigrate if his two sons could accompany him.[71] Across the Atlantic Bloch's delay had become untenable in view of the mounting uncertainty and expense of transatlantic travel and his "visa difficulties." It was undoubtedly imperative to offer rescue to more mobile applicants. Upon re-

---

68 Fliche to Bloch, 12, 18 June 1941, and Bloch to Fliche, 17 June 1941, EBC; Bloch to Carcopino, 18 June 1941, AN, 3w 340/68; Rector, University of Montpellier, to Ourliac, Chef-adjoint du Cabinet de M. le Secrétaire d'Etat à l'Education Nationale, 19 July 1941, ADH; Carcopino, *Souvenirs*, p. 361. On the faculty of the University of Montpellier, see Bremer and Rabuse report, NARS, Germany AA T-120 K1634/4744/K402928–30; also *Histoire de Montpellier* (Toulouse: Privat, 1984), pp. 349–50.

69 *Journal Officiel*, 14 June 1941; Marrus and Paxton, *Vichy France*, pp. 96–101.

70 According to Carcopino, the *décret* of 5 January 1941, though never published, was not invalidated by the new racial-exclusion law of 3 June 1941 and therefore remained in force: Carcopino to Bloch, 17, 18 June 1941, EBC; Carcopino to Rector, Université de Paris, 28 June, and Carcopino, Arrêtés, 11, 15 June 1941, EBC. Bloch to Lot, 10 Aug. 1941, Lot papers, IF.

71 Bloch telegram, n.d. (received 1 Aug. 1941) and letter to Johnson, 31 July 1941, RACEP. Cf. Bloch to Febvre, 16 Apr. 1941, on the comfort of his rural neighbors ("un peuple encore profondement sain"), and 7 May 1941, AN, MI 318 1.

ceiving Bloch's letter, the patient Johnson canceled the invitation to the New School, thereby eliminating Bloch's American option forever.[72]

Bloch's year-long abortive efforts to reach the United States to this day remain ambiguous. Rumors circulated for several months afterwards about his arrival and about his decision. Speculation about the latter survives to this day.[73] Was it a prudent and realistic strategy to await the delayed delivery of visas for his older children from harassed and overworked American officials who at the time were engaged in issuing documents for thousands of endangered foreigners?[74] On the other hand, could he have struck camp earlier for Martinique without risks to those he sought to save? Would a detour to the Antilles have sent the wrong signal to Vichy, on whose support he counted, dispelling the fiction that his trip to the New World was temporary and professionally oriented? Had he succeeded

---

72 Johnson to Bloch, 18 Aug. 1941, and Johnson to Appleget (Rockefeller Foundation), 18 Aug. 1941; Kittredge to Johnson, 23 Sept. 1941 (rescinding Bloch's grant), RACEP.

Bloch had not been excluded from the United States under the new State Department regulations of 5 June 1941 withholding nonquota visas from those having to leave immediate family members behind in Europe (as stated in Rutkoff and Scott, *New School*, p. 133), since this new restrictive policy did not apply to "native-born French citizens": Sumner Welles to Fullerton (U.S. Consul Marseille), 21 June 1941, and to Eleanor Roosevelt, 6 July 1941, NARS, USDS 811.111 Refugees/1623.

73 Several scholars, including Lynn White, Sylvia Thrupp, and Austin Evans, inquired of the foundation and of the New School about Bloch in the fall of 1941. Johnson replied to Evans that Bloch "could not make up his mind to leave France without one of his children who is of military age." Johnson to Evans, 8 Dec. 1941, RACEP.

William Mendel Newman's diary, in the custody of Professor Giles Constable, Institute for Advanced Study, Princeton, N.J., recorded the rumors that Bloch was being brought over by the Institute for Foreign Scholars (25 Nov. 1940), and that though not yet out of France he had obtained an appointment at the University of California (2 May 1941), a conjecture that still persists.

74 Leahy to Welles, Vichy, 12 Feb. 1941, NARS, USDS Refugees/959; also Fullerton (U.S. Consul General) to Welles, Marseille, 11 Apr. 1941, NARS, 811.111 France/26; Peck to Welles, 5 May 1941, NARS, 811.111 Refugees 1481.

in bringing his family to a secure foreign shore, would Bloch have remained so far away from France?[75] Indeed, was America perhaps only a vague chimera that Bloch, with his heavy family burdens, felt obligated to investigate, but which he pursued without sufficient resolve to attain, because it represented another retreat, another "desertion"? Despite all his present and foreseeable trials, Marc Bloch wanted to stay in France.[76]

That France, however, became increasingly inhospitable. During their cold "rutabaga summer" in Fougères, cheered somewhat by visits from his students, a discouraged and fatigued Bloch worked desultorily on his *Apologie pour l'histoire* while awaiting definite word on his appointment to Montpellier. Though regretting his departure from his excellent Strasbourg comrades, Bloch was intent on establishing his wife and family in a warmer climate. Predictably, complications arose as a result of Fliche's negative intervention. Carcopino, fearing hostile demonstrations, delayed signing the appointment and offered to search for an alternative location.[77] Bloch balked at this gesture. As a veteran of two world wars he refused to shrink before either threats of violence or Fliche's antipathy. He declined an offer to continue teaching in Clermont-Ferrand and commute on weekends to Montpellier, preferring to keep the family together even in a less friendly environment.[78] Following a harrowing trip to

---

75 The opinion of his oldest son: "I remain convinced that if it had succeeded my father would have returned to London after an indeterminate sojourn in the United States." Etienne Bloch, *Marc Bloch: Father, Patriot, and Teacher* (Poughkeepsie, N.Y.: Vassar College, 1987), p. 10.

76 "Du moins n'y a t'il pas l'océan entre vous et moi, – ni entre moi et mon pays." Bloch to Febvre, Fougères, 17 Aug. 1941, AN, MI 318 1. Ten months later: "En tout cas, et quoi qu'il arrive, je suis heureux d'être ici, non là où j'ai failli aller. Ces derniers mois que je prévois si durs, c'est dans mon pays que je les veux vivre; non à l'abri." Bloch to Febvre, Montpellier, 22 June 1942, EBC. Also Febvre, writing in 1945 ("Le vrai c'est qu'il ne voulait pas partir") in "Marc Bloch: Témoignages," p. 25; and Etienne Bloch, *Marc Bloch*, p. 10.

77 Carcopino to Bloch, Vichy, 16 Aug. 1941, EBC; Bloch to Febvre, Fougères, 17 Aug. 1941, AN, MI 318 1.

78 Bloch to Maugain, Fougères, 5 Aug. 1941, and Maugain to Rector, 9 Aug. 1941 ADBR, AL 154 P8/15; Bloch to Carcopino, 21 Aug. 1941, AN, 3W 340/68. See Bloch's farewell remarks to the Strasbourg Faculty Council, 11 July 1941, ADBR, AL 154 P1/2.

Vichy to press his case, Bloch won a small victory. Toward the end of August he was finally assured that he could teach in Montpellier, under the sole condition that he abstain from teaching a public course.[79]

Adding to Bloch's regret at uprooting his children from Clermont were the ill tidings in Montpellier. A new law of 21 June 1941, amplifying the Statut des Juifs, established a 3 percent quota of Jewish students in French higher education. Notwithstanding Bloch's special status, in order for his older son to study law at the University of Montpellier he had to apply for an exemption to the quota.[80] Bloch thus was compelled to assemble documentation proving five generations of French citizenship on both sides of the family as well as the family's exceptional services to the French state. This long, illustrious genealogy, verifying that Simonne Bloch's ancestor, a Nîmes merchant, in 1786 had received *lettres patentes* from Louis XVI and that Bloch's great-grandfather had fought in the year I at Mainz, represented the escalating price of survival in Vichy France.[81]

Then there was Bloch's library. During the past year, in the course of its plunder of Jewish artwork and libraries the Einsatzstab Reichsleiter Rosenberg (ERR) had also targeted intellectuals, including Bloch's predecessor, the economic historian Henri Hauser, who had been teaching at Rennes.[82] Bloch had asked for help from his Parisian

79 Bloch to Febvre, 25 Aug. 1941, AN, MI 318 1; Carcopino to Bloch, 26 Aug. 1941, EBC; Bloch to Carcopino, 28 Aug. 1941, AN, 3W 340/69. The restriction also applied to the Germanophobe Germanist Edmond Vermeil: See Bremer and Rabuse Report, NARS, Germany AA T-120 K1634/4744/K420928; Robert Minder, "Edmond Vermeil (1878–1964)," *Etudes Germaniques* 19, no. 2 (Apr.–June 1964): i–iv.

80 Copy of 21 June law (distributed by the Faculty of Letters, University of Strasbourg, 9 Sept. 1941), EBC. Background in Marrus and Paxton, *Vichy France*, pp. 123–25. Bloch to Febvre, 26 June, 8, 31 Oct. 1941, EBC; Bloch to Vallat, Fougères, 11 Aug. 1941, and Chef de Cabinet, Commissariat Général aux Questions Juives to Bloch, Vichy, 18 Aug. 1941, EBC.

81 "I doubt that he found it pleasant to help me prepare my request." Etienne Bloch, *Marc Bloch*, p. 9. Cf. Vallat to Bloch, Vichy, 26 Sept. 1941, and Arrêté (signed by Carcopino), 9 Oct. 1941, file "Numerus clausus," EBC.

82 Bremer, Aufzeichnung für den Herrn Botschafter (Abetz), "Geschlagnahme der Bibliothek des Geschichtsprofessors Henri Hauser durch den Einsatzstab

relatives and colleagues, and had also enlisted a legal advisor to try to transfer his library to the unoccupied zone, but with no success. Because there was insufficient space in their modest Montpellier dwelling for his library, he hoped to have it moved to his country home in Fougères.[83]

In the fall of 1941 Bloch returned to Montpellier after three decades, an isolated but resolute exile in still another temporary shelter. He wrote to Febvre that he was determined to exercise his duties as a "French professor" and teach "a history [that was] not without usefulness under current conditions." Assigned new courses on modern European and French economic and monetary history, he lacked adequate resources to prepare them. His trips to the library to check his references were "three-quarters of the time in vain."[84]

Rosenberg," 7 March 1941, complains of this ill-advised *Sonderaktion* ("... übrigens die Linie unserer Kulturpolitik durchaus widerspricht"), NARS, Germany AA T-120 4742/K1673/E208974; also E208973, 975–76. Hauser protested about the pillage to his government, which in turn protested, in vain, to the Armistice Commission in Wiesbaden. Febvre to Bloch (undated [July–Aug. 1941], AN, MI 318 3) refers to the disappearance of all the papers and books of Emile Durkheim.

   On the ERR: See U.S. Chief of Counsel for Prosecution, *Nazi Conspiracy and Aggression* (Washington, D.C., 1946–48), III pp. 184–203, and supp. B (Interrogation of Alfred Rosenberg), pp. 1333–37; also Donald E. Collins and Herbert P. Rothfeder, "The Einsatzstab Reichsleiter Rosenberg and the Looting of Jewish and Masonic Libraries during World War II," *Journal of Library History* 18, no. 1 (Winter 1983): 21–36.

83 Carcopino, *Souvenirs*, pp. 363–64; Bloch to Febvre, 27 Sept., 19 Nov. 1941, EBC.

84 "Je me suis trouvé dépourvu de la plus grande partie de mon travail habituel. Je n'ai disposé que d'une bibliothèque où il y a d'évidentes lacunes." Bloch, course introduction, AN, AB XIX 3839; research notes in 3824, 3838–39; Bloch to Febvre, Montpellier, 27 Sept. 1941, AN, MI 318 1; 31 Oct., 19 Nov. 1941, EBC; 11 Dec. 1941, AN, MI 318 1. Simonne Bloch to Alice Bloch, 20 Nov. 1941, EBC; Bloch to Boutruche, 20 Nov. 1941, RB.

   On Bloch's work in economic and monetary history, see excerpts from his letter to his former student René Baehrel, Montpellier, 1 Mar. 1942: "Prix-monnaies-courbes," *AESC* 1, no. 4 (Oct.–Dec. 1946): 355–57. On his teaching: interviews with Etienne Bloch; Francine Moussu to Etienne Bloch, 3 Sept. 1983.

Montpellier, also swollen with refugees, was slightly smaller but more physically attractive than Clermont. Bloch found his neighbors and some of his colleagues congenial. However, the climate, though an improvement on the bleak skies of Clermont, was chilly. That winter there was inadequate heating to protect them against the constant mistral, the cold north wind of southern France. Also there were regular food shortages in Montpellier, only partially alleviated by foraging trips to their country home in Fougères. At the opening of a new academic year Bloch complained of his rheumatism, of his "lassitude," and of missing Febvre, from whom he had been separated for almost two years.[85]

Bloch was also increasingly apprehensive about anti-Semitism, public and private, which by insidious stages sought to remove French Jews from national life. The recently decreed census set an ominous tone, suggesting further exclusion and spoliation. Bloch believed that even among the best people there lived a "spirit of discrimination" more lethal than the stupid and violent forms of racism. By assigning a variety of individuals to a racial category ("Jewish high finance" or, for that matter, "Jewish intellectuals") and imputing to them interests that separated them from the French nation, they gave subtle and powerful sanction to the official policy of prejudice. Bloch condemned all distinctions. Anti-Semitism would begin to disappear, he insisted to Febvre, when the so-called cultivated public was able to condemn cads and capitalists alike without reference to their religious origins. And it would finally expire when France's notables acknowledged their persistent error

85 Bloch to Febvre, Montpellier, 27 Sept., 31 Oct. 1941, AN, MI 318 1, and 19 Nov. 1941, EBC; also Simonne Bloch to Alice Bloch, 13, 20 Nov. 1941, EBC. On food shortages (the diminished rations of bread, sugar, and cheese provoked a women's food demonstration in February 1942): Kedward, *Resistance*, p. 221; Jean Baumel, *De la guerre au camps de concentration* (Montpellier: C.G.C., 1974), p. 44; Roger Austin, "Propaganda and Public Opinion in Vichy France: The Department of Hérault, 1940–44," *European Studies Review* 13 (Oct. 1983): 466–69; provisions: Marc Bloch to André Bloch, 19 Feb. 1942, EBC.

Febvre's last preserved letter to Bloch, undated (July–Aug. 1941) and written on the stationery of the Comité de l'Encyclopédie Française (AN, MI 318 3), was a long, contentious missive on such subjects as the continuation of the *Annales*, anti-Semitism, and contemporary politics and personalities.

that one group produced a monopoly of both.[86] Such bigotry, according to Bloch, was foreign to the real France of his rural neighbors and his former companions at arms.[87]

Bloch was also wary of the reaction of French Jews. He feared that the initial stages of intolerance and persecution, from the worst of which he had been mercifully spared, would trigger a tendency toward separatism. In Lyon, where he had vainly sought required visas from the U.S. consulate, Bloch had encountered a group of displaced intellectuals attempting to establish a research center for Jewish studies under the auspices of the Consistoire, the governing body of French Judaism.[88] Asked to collaborate, he counseled extreme limits on their investigations in order not to undermine, and indeed primarily to reinforce, their "legitimate place in the French community, which formally we have never left." They must avoid providing ammunition to those "who would consign us to any sort of ghetto."[89]

Bloch made concrete suggestions for the group's proposed research. He urged that they avoid secrecy in their deliberations and in their work, and above all reject the support and leadership of Jewish financiers, which might reignite the accusation of a "syndicate." They should include sympathetic Christians and take pains to represent the whole spectrum of French Jewish opinion. Finally, without renouncing the hospitality and aid granted by France and its Jews to foreign Jews, they must make clear that "their cause is not exactly our own."[90]

86 "Le jour où, dans les milieux les plus 'sympathiques,' comme vous dites, on ne pensera plus: 'ce Juif se conduit mal,' mais 'ce haut bourgeois se conduit comme il est presque inévitable que de hauts bourgeois se conduisent'; ce pleutre se conduit en pleutre,' et où l'on ajoutera, 'd'ailleurs nous ne voyons guère que les pleutres; les autres, il y a quelques bonnes raisons pour que nous ne les voyons pas,' ce jour là l'antisémitisme larvé, de beaucoup le plus redoutable chez nous, commencera de mourir." Bloch to Febvre, 17 Aug. 1941, AN, MI 318 I.
87 Ibid. Also Bloch to Febvre, Montpellier, 27 Sept. 1941, AN, MI 318 I. Like his father, Bloch persisted in believing that current French racism had its origins, and imitated practices from, across the Rhine.
88 Bloch to Febvre, Fougères, 17 Aug. 1941, AN, MI 318 I.
89 Bloch to J. Ullman, Clermont-Ferrand, 2 Apr. 1941, AN, MI 318 I.
90 Bloch, "La méthode pour traiter du problème juif," AN, MI 318 I, 469–70; Ullman to Bloch, 7 May 1941, ibid., 468.

Though unable to participate actively, Bloch suggested a three-part plan to counter the dangerous notion that "all Jews form a solid, homogeneous mass, endowed with identical traits, and subject to the same destiny." Initially, they must apply critical analysis to the primitive, widely disseminated abstraction of the "wretched Jew," one of the worst results of which was to force some of its targets to internalize their alleged separateness and accept a "territorial" solution (expulsion). After puncturing these "phantasmagoria," they must comprehend a complex historical reality. Finally, they were to recognize two distinct Jewish communities, the assimilated (French) and the nonassimilated (foreign). While the fate of the former depended on its complete integration and the preservation of its legal guarantees, the survival of the latter might well depend upon some form of emigration.[91]

Nevertheless, the Vichy government – to be sure, under considerable German prodding – was committed to establishing and controlling a segregated existence for all Jews. The law of 29 November 1941 created the Union Générale des Israélites de France (UGIF), a compulsory giant Jewish Council for the entire country, which absorbed all existing social and philanthropic agencies under a unified administrative structure, subordinated to the Commissariat Général aux Questions Juives (CGQJ) led by Xavier Vallat. Offically charged with "representing Jews to the public authorities" for welfare purposes, the UGIF was manifestly a tool for subjugating an entire community.[92]

Decades later it has been recognized that the handling of Jewish affairs represented one of the few areas of Nazi-Vichy rivalry as well as collaboration over the treatment of a marked people. This concerned the fate not only of the masses of German and East European refugees who had flooded both zones and were menaced by

91 Bloch, "Méthode," AN, MI 318 1, 469–70; also outline, "Trois divisions," AN, MI 318 1, 471–72.
92 *Journal Officiel*, 2 Dec. 1941; Lubetzski, *La condition des Juifs*, pp. 102–9; also Cynthia J. Haft, *The Bargain and the Bridle: The General Union of the Israelites of France, 1941–44* (Chicago: Dialog, 1983), pp. 6–9; Richard I. Cohen, *The Burden of Conscience: French Jewish Leadership during the Holocaust* (Bloomington: Indiana University Press, 1987). chap. 3; Marrus and Paxton, *Vichy France*, pp. 107–11.

round-ups and deportation, but also that of French Jews, who step by step were being stripped of their rights, their employment, and their property by their own government as well as by the Nazis. Ironically, Vichy originally created the UGIF to assert its authority in both zones. But after the independent nationalist Vallat was forced out by the Germans and replaced in May 1942 by the more fanatic anti-Semite Louis Darquier de Pellepoix, the Union essentially became a tool for Nazi manipulation and domination of all the Jews in France.[93]

French Jews were startled by the creation of this obligatory racial organization, now their new legal representative. With its title "Israélites de France" instead of "Israélites français," the UGIF menacingly lumped them together with foreign Jews, submerging their claims and rights into the greater numbers and peril of the latter and threatening further restrictions and expropriation. For example, the new law of 16 January 1942, associating the UGIF with the prohibition against transferring Jewish assets into the unoccupied zone, set an ominous precedent.[94] There was fervid opposition by the Consistoire, which was imbued with a strong national identity and feared exclusion from French society, laws, and institutions. However the UGIF controversy did not simply pit French citizens against foreigners. Numerous refugees refused to join, and it was a group of French Jewish leaders, like those in similar conditions throughout Nazi Europe, who agreed to become UGIF council members in the two zones and serve as intermediaries to "stave off the worst."[95]

93 Haft, *Bargain*, pp. 43–44; Marrus and Paxton, *Vichy France*, pp. 108–11, 283–86; Yerachmiel (Richard) Cohen, "The Jewish Community of France in the Face of Vichy–German Persecution, 1940–44," in *The Jews in Modern France*, ed. Frances Malino and Bernard Wasserstein (Hanover, N.H.: University Press of New England, 1985), pp. 181–206.

94 *Journal Officiel*, 18 Jan. 1942; Bloch, "Note au sujet de l'Union des Israélites de France," 1 May 1942, CDJC, CCXIV-75. Also René Mayer to Vallat, 2 Dec. 1941, cited in Marrus and Paxton, *Vichy France*, p. 109; Lubetzski, *La condition des Juifs*, p. 110.

95 Zosa Szajkowski, "The Organization of the 'UGIF' in Nazi-Occupied France," *Jewish Social Studies* 9 (1947): 239–56. Cohen, "Jewish Leader," pp. 296–99; Simon Schwarzfuchs, *Les Juifs de France* (Paris: Albin Michel, 1975), pp. 299–308.

Marc Bloch decided to voice opposition to the Union. After discussions with friends and colleagues in the southern zone, he drafted a protest to the head of the UGIF.[96] Speaking in the name of "Israélites français" bound by love, tradition, and service to their Catholic and Protestant compatriots, Bloch declared them to be "faithful sons" of their "common mother" France. Despite recent legislation, they recognized no other people than the French.[97] While acknowledging the nobility and necessity of its official welfare tasks, Bloch urged the UGIF to avoid any action that by "sanctioning or aggravating" the "moral isolation of the *Israélites français*," might provoke or alienate their loyal French compatriots. Notwithstanding the present dangers before them and their children, he insisted, "We have no concern which exceeds our attachment to France. We are French. . . . We cannot conceive another destiny than a French one."[98]

96 Draft (19 Feb. 1942) in AN, AB XIX 3838.
97 "La France, que nous avons servie de notre mieux et pour laquelle comme l'on fait un si grand nombre des nôtres, nous sacrifierons volontiers, demain encore, notre sang ou celui de nos enfants, est notre patrie au même titre que nos compatriotes, d'origine Catholique ou Protestante, parmi lesquels nous comptons tant d'amis très chers et d'anciens camarades de combat, nous nous sentons les fils loyaux et reconnaissants de cette commune mère.
    "Les espoirs comme les deuils de la France sont les nôtres. Les valeurs de civilisation, auxquelles nous demeurons passionnément attachés, sont celles qu'elle nous a enseignées. Quelles que puissent être dans leur diversité nos convictions philosophiques, politiques, ou religieuses, le peuple français est notre peuple. Nous ne nous en connaissons point d'autre." Copy of typewritten text from Marc Bloch to Georges Friedmann, dated 1 Feb. 1942, Commissariat Général aux Questions Juives (CGQJ), dossier 11013 M45, now in CDJC, XXVII a, 22.
98 "Nous nous fions donc à vous et à vos collègues du Conseil d'Administration pour vous efforcer de maintenir, entre nos frères français, et nous, une union aussi étroite que possible, pour ne rien proposer, ne rien faire, ne rien tenter qui, fut-ce dans le dessein de soulager les plus respectables infortunes, puisse avoir pour effet, direct ou non, de nous isoler moralement de la communauté nationale dont, même frappés par la Loi, nous voulons rester les membres fidèles; pour vous élever, selon les formes qui vous paraîtront convenables et dans les limites de vos droits, contre toute suggestion qui aboutirait à créer, aggraver ou consacrer une telle scission. Nous savons la nécessité et la beauté des oeuvres de secours. Nous sommes entièrement à leur service. Mais nous pensons qu'elles doivent avant tout éviter de se faire les instruments, même pleinement

The final draft, "Note au sujet de l'Union des Israélites de France," circulated on 1 May 1942, was signed by only three eminent people: the literary scholar Benjamin Crémieux (who in 1942 was deported to Bergen-Belsen and Buchenwald and died in Weimar),[99] the former president of the French bar and barrister of the Court of Appeals in Toulouse, René Milhaud, and Bloch. Repeating verbatim Bloch's original protest of loyalty to France, they declared their refusal to acknowledge the UGIF's leaders as their representatives, calling on their compatriots to "prepare and protect" the only possible future − "a French one."[100]

Bloch's forceful foray into Vichy politics requires explanation. He clearly had no intention of defying the government that he still served and whose officials regularly read his mail.[101] Nonetheless, Bloch was appalled by the UGIF leadership, some of whom he suspected of Zionist sympathies and others of naiveté in believing that the organization could be limited to welfare purposes. In February 1942, when the Final Solution had already begun, Bloch recognized the UGIF as part of a "hostile plot" to strip French Jews

---

involontaires, d'une séparation qui irait contre les sentiments les plus profonds des Israélites français. La générosité d'âme de tant de nos compatriotes d'autre origine nous est d'ailleurs trop bien connue, nous avons reçu d'eux trop de touchants témoignages de solidarité pour ne pas juger inutile, autant que redoutable, s'il risquait jamais d'être envisagé, un pareil repliement dans l'entr'aide.

"En un mot quelque cruel que soit, à l'heure actuelle, le sort de beaucoup d'entre nous, quelque menace qui pèse sur nos enfants, nous n'avons point de souci qui prime notre attachement à la France. Nous sommes Français. Nous n'imaginons pas que nous puissions cesser de l'être. Ni pour nous, ni pour nos enfants, nous ne saurions concevoir d'autre destinée qu'un avenir français. C'est cet avenir là que nous vous demandons de préparer ou de protéger." Ibid.

99 Louis Parrot, *L'intelligence en guerre: Panorame de la pensée française dans la clandestinité* (Paris: La Jeune Parque, 1945), pp. 54−58.

100 The CGQJ entitled this document "Déclaration de trois personnalités juives contre [sic] la politique de Vichy"; see CDJC, CCXIV-75.

101 See Bloch to Jacquet, 23 Nov. 1941, preface to A.-V. Jacquet, *Refus de parvenir: Roman-témoignage* (Blainville-sur-Mer: L'Amitié par le Livre, 1956), p. 13.

Bloch's letters to Henri Lévy-Bruhl and Georges Friedmann and his 1 Feb. 1942 draft found their way to the local CGQJ office: CDJC, XXVII a 22. Also Bloch to Febvre, 29 Sept. 1942, AN, MI 318 1.

of their "true nationality." By dissolving them, along with foreign refugees, into an arbitrary construct called "the Jewish people," it prepared the way for "the ghetto or expulsion."[102]

It was characteristic, not disloyal or inconsistent, for Bloch to deny a racial bond with German and East European Jews and, for that matter, with certain French Jews as well.[103] Bloch was aware of the mounting danger of Nazi exactions and Vichy's equivocations. He acknowledged, but did not shrink from, the eternal burden of Jewish ancestry, which had spurred his striving for exceptional achievement and the worry and pressure he directed toward his children.[104] Faced with a collapse of law and justice, and the belated revenge of the anti-Dreyfusards, Marc Bloch clung all the more tenaciously to his French identity, giving no sign to his countrymen that the Statut or anything else could break his loyalty to, and just claims on, France.[105]

That faith would be sorely tried again over the issue of his library. As the year moved on, Bloch had begun to despair of retrieving it. On 31 December 1941 Hitler approved Alfred Rosenberg's proposal to liquidate all vacated Jewish properties in Paris, and the Einsatzstab accelerated its raids on unoccupied apartments. Bloch prepared for the worst, recognizing that his impending loss was but a "modest drama in an immense tragedy."[106] Carcopino suggested a solution: Donate the library to the University of Montpellier as a means of removing it from the occupied zone, but Bloch, unwilling to alienate his property, stuck to the principle that his books belonged to his children.[107]

Early in February he learned from a faithful student that the

102 Draft letter, 19 Feb. 1942, AN, AB XIX 3826.
103 "Il y a beaucoup de maisons dans la demeure de mon père et même quelques mauvais lieux." Bloch to Febvre, 16 Apr. 1941, AN, MI 318 1.
104 "Ce n'est pas après tout un grand malheur. La facilité de vie n'est pas un bien si souhaitable." Bloch to Etienne Bloch, Fougères, 13 Sept. 1942, EBC.
105 Bloch sent a copy of his protest note to the UGIF council to Carcopino (1 Apr. 1942, AN, 3W 122/86).
106 Bloch to Febvre, 16 Jan. 1942; also 24 Dec. 1941, 5 Jan. 1942, EBC; Bloch to Boutruche, 6 Jan. 1942, RB. On the accelerated Rosenberg operation: Rademacher, Aufzeichnung, Berlin, 31 Jan. 1942, NARS, Germany AA T-120 2257/1205/478671.
107 Bloch to Carcopino, 5, 22 Jan. 1942, and Carcopino to Bloch, 13 Jan. 1942, AN, 3W 122, 340/70, 71, 84; cf. Carcopino, *Souvenirs*, pp. 363–64.

upper, seventh, floor of his apartment at 17, rue de Sèvres had been occupied by soldiers of the Third Reich. All his books and some extra furniture were removed to the sixth floor. Then, around the beginning of April, all his books along with four bookcases were removed. The news reached Bloch in Montpellier two months later.[108]

The origins of the theft, which was reported at once to the Militärbefehlshaber by one of its ss liaison officers,[109] remain mysterious. The least probable culprit was Rosenberg's office, with its generalized plunder of Jewish property. More likely it was perpetrated by the ss, either as part of its punitive strikes against exiles and enemies or to add to its own growing "scientific research" collection, or by the military itself, simply to clean out the lower floor to make space for additional inhabitants. From his informants Bloch learned only that his books had been "seized by the occupying authority, taken from the apartment, and dispatched to an unknown destination."[110]

It was another unequal struggle, another ostensibly mishandled effort, another defeat, and another cause for rancor between Bloch and Febvre, who ostensibly had tried to help.[111] After brooding for a short time, Bloch became resigned to the fait accompli. He nevertheless drafted a letter to the new minister of national education, the pro-fascist essayist Abel Bonnard, protesting the illegal confiscation of his indispensable teaching and research tools. "Absent from Paris on official orders" from Bonnard's predecessor (Bloch's friend Carcopino was one of the *pétainistes* who had left office

108 Simonne Bloch to Alice Bloch, 1 Feb. 1942; Bloch to Febvre, 14 Feb., 6 June 1942; C. Marcilhacy to Bloch, 18 June, 4 July 1942, EBC.
109 Der Beauftragte des Chefs der Sicherheitspolizei und des SD für den Bereich des Militärbefehlshabers in Frankreich Paris an die Dienststelle L 20 736 z. Hd. von Herrn Hauptmann Romey (Paris: Palais Luxembourg), Paris, 2 Apr. 1942: "Es wird hiermit bestätigt, dass aus der Wohnung des jüdischen Emigranten Marc Bloch, Paris VIe, 17, rue de Sèvres, die gesamte Bibliothek sowie 4 einfache Bücherregale beschlagnahmt wurden." EBC.
110 Draft letter, undated, to Minister of National Education protesting the seizure, EBC. Most, but not all of the library was returned to Bloch's children after the war: France, Ministère des Affaires Etrangères, Formules de décharge, 17 Feb. 1948, 4 May, 30 Sept. 1949, EBC.
111 Bloch to Febvre, 22 June, 26 July 1942, AN, MI 318 1.

in April 1942 when Laval returned to power), Bloch denied any dereliction on his part that could justify the act. He denounced the spoliation as both "contrary to human rights" and a subversion of the ministry's service. But Bloch's loss, which was only a minor incident among the escalating depredations against French Jews, could no longer be accorded special treatment. Under the Laval government, Vichy was now totally committed to collaboration with the Third Reich and would tolerate even harsher measures against Jewish citizens.[112]

Over the past year, incensed by Vichy's equivocations and betrayals and outraged by its leadership, Bloch had searched for sources of France's renewal. Though the powerful Grand Alliance was now battling Nazi Germany, he believed that France's freedom would also have to be regained from within, the corruption purged by sacrifice and blood.[113] In dark times Bloch found comfort outside his usual milieu, in his rural neighbors, in France's youth, and in some of their teachers. In his extended correspondence with the independent, headstrong schoolmaster A.-V. Jacquet he praised the combination of solid rural values and individual self-cultivation.[114]

Like Febvre, Bloch was preoccupied by "the problem of two zones" that divided France. Despite the dissimilar conditions under which they now lived, one element was omnipresent, "the impossibility for each of us to know what our closest neighbor thinks. We

---

112 Bloch to Minister (undated), signed "Professeur d'histoire économique à la Sorbonne, Chevalier de la Légion d'Honneur au titre militaire; Croix de guerre 1914–1918; Croix de guerre 1940." Copies in CDJC, CCXXXIX-153, EBC.

Before leaving office, Carcopino on 17 March 1942 had authorized Bloch's promotion to "2e classe"; cf. ADH, 485-w-49: Bloch, however, continued to have difficulties with payment of his salary, especially since it originated in Paris: Bloch to Treasurer of the Sorbonne, 31 Mar., 30 June 1942, AN, AJ 16 5876.

On Vichy's turning point in spring–summer 1942: Azéma, *Munich to the Liberation*, pp. 117–20; Paxton, *Vichy France*, pp. 131–35; Marrus and Paxton, *Vichy France*, chap. 6; Joseph Billig, "La condition des Juifs en France," *Histoire de la Deuxième Guerre Mondiale* 6, no. 21 (Jan. 1956): 45–53.

113 *ED*, pp. 218–19; cf. Marc Bloch to Sarah Bloch, 9 June 1940, EBC: "Après il y aura d'ailleurs bien des comptes à regler."

114 Bloch to Jacquet, 23 Nov. 1941, quoted in preface to Jacquet, *Refus de parvenir*, pp. 8–12; also Bloch to Febvre, 10 Dec. 1941, EBC.

live surrounded by monads." Vichy, though ruling with a softer rein than the Nazis, stepped up local spectacles and its propaganda barrage. Bloch nevertheless detected almost imperceptible "vibrations" in his seemingly peaceable corner of the south.[115] Beneath the surface was an omnipresent threat of violence. Bloch was routinely escorted to his class, and in March 1942 right-wing students rioted at the university. On the other hand, the tiny forces of resistance in Montpellier had already doubled.[116]

Bloch was, of course, well acquainted with the emerging Resistance in the unoccupied zone. He had known the leaders of the group "Combat" in Clermont-Ferrand. In Montpellier his younger colleagues René Courtin and Pierre-Henri Teitjen led Combat and were also the founders of the Comité Général d'Etudes (CGE), a political discussion group.[117] He also knew several young *résistants* personally: Georges Friedmann, Jean Cavaillès, the two sons-in-law of his medievalist *maître* Ferdinand Lot, and his two nephews, Jean and Henry Bloch-Michel.[118] Bloch's two older sons were

115 Bloch to Febvre, 8 May 1942, AN, MI 318 1; also 18 May 1942, EBC. On 11 May 1942 there was the obligatory parade in Montpellier marking the birthday of Jeanne d'Arc, one of Vichy's favorite symbols. Simonne Bloch to Alice Bloch, 8 May 1942, EBC; also Nick Atkin, "The Cult of Joan of Arc in French Schools, 1940–1944," in R. Kedward and R. Austin, eds., *Vichy France and the Resistance: Culture and Ideology* (Totowa, N.J.: Barnes and Noble, 1985), pp. 265–73.

   In June Pétain visited Hérault, in July Philippe Henriot delivered an address at the Peyrou, and in August Darlan came to inspect troops of the 16th Military Division (Austin, "Propaganda," p. 473).

116 *Histoire de Montpellier*, p. 350. Baumel, *De la guerre*, p. 54, estimates that there were approximately 200 *résistants* at the end of 1940 and between 300 and 400 by the end of 1942.

117 "Témoignages de M. René Courtin," 27 May 1946, "Notes de conversations recueillies auprès M. René Courtin par H. Michel," 13 Mar. 1950, AN, 72 AJ 45 CGE; also Kedward, *Resistance*, pp. 74, 245 and passim; Diane de Bellescize, *Les neuf sages de la résistance: Le Comité général d'études dans la clandestinité* (Paris: Plon, 1979), chap. 2; Baumel, *De la guerre*, pp. 43, 48–49 and passim.

118 Friedmann: Bloch to Febvre, 26 June 1941 and passim, EBC. Cavaillès: Bloch to Febvre, 17 Oct. 1942, AN, MI 318 1, and to Boutruche, Montpellier, 20 Oct. 1942, RB; also Georges Friedmann, "Au delà de 'l'engagement': Marc Bloch, Jean Cavaillès," *Europe* 10 (Oct. 1946): 32–43. *(note cont. p. 280)*

members of Combat, a small group whose activities included acts of sabotage, publication and distribution of anti-Laval and anti-Hitler tracts, inscribing the cross of Lorraine and the "V" on the walls of Montpellier, and painting the spectacular graffito "I Would Never Have Collaborated!" on the base of the Louis XIV statue in the Peyrou garden.[119]

Bloch's own activities during this period are, of course, obscure, but he was certainly not completely passive. He may have helped organize Combat. He attended several meetings of the CGE to discuss the political and economic reconstruction of postwar France and may have helped draft one of its papers.[120] In April 1942 Bloch was invited by a former Strasbourg colleague to deliver a series of lectures in Clermont-Ferrand. To Febvre he cryptically dis-

---

Lot's sons-in-law: Boris Vildé, a member of the Musée de l'Homme group in Paris, who was arrested and shot at Mt. Valerien on 25 Feb. 1942 (six weeks afterwards, Lot himself was arrested by the Gestapo and imprisoned for three days at Fresnes), and Jean-Berthold Mahn, who eventually left for Morocco to join the Free French: Bloch to Lot, 10 Aug. 1941, Lot papers, IF; Bloch to Febvre, 11 Apr., 8 May 1942, AN, MI 318 1; Martin Blumenson, *The Vildé Affair: Beginnings of the French Resistance* (Boston: Houghton Mifflin, 1977), pp. 62–64, 80, 92, 95, 222–23, 254, Charles-Edmond Perrin, *Un historien français: Ferdinand Lot* (Geneva: Droz, 1968), p. 114.

Interviews with Josette and Henry Bloch-Michel (1980) and Jean Bloch-Michel (1982); Henry Bloch-Michel, "Témoignage," 29 Oct. 1956, AN, 72 AJ 47; Simonne Bloch to Etienne Bloch, Fougères, 25 June 1942, EBC.

119 Bloch to Febvre, Montpellier, 18 Apr. 1942, AN, MI 318 1; Combat in Montpellier: Missa, "Témoignage," 5 Oct. 1948, and Sussel, "Témoignage," 21 Mar. 1946, AN, 72 AJ 132 (Hérault). Cf. interviews with Etienne Bloch; Etienne Bloch, *Marc Bloch*, p. 14; *Histoire de Montpellier*, p. 315.

120 Inserted in an old research file labeled "Affranchissements" (AN, AB XIX 3806) were the following CGE documents: "Thèses à discuter pour l'éventualité d'une victoire anglaise et d'une résurrection de la France" (author: Bloch?), "Observations du cercle d'études de Montpellier sur le projet de charge économique et professionnelle" (author: Courtin?), "Rapport sur les travaux du cercle de Montpellier" (author: Courtin or Teitjen). Suggestions of authorship courtesy of Etienne Bloch. Bloch's attendance at CGE meetings in Bellescize, *Les neuf sages de la résistance*, pp. 39, 66; also interview, 1983 with Vincent Badie, the former socialist deputy from Montpellier, who in the summer of 1940 was one of the few opponents of suspending the 1875 constitution.

closed his subject ("contemporary England") and his "nonacademic" audience.[121] One of his closest friends and colleagues in Montpellier later referred to Bloch's contribution to the clandestine Ecole Supérieure de Guerre, which had been set up to instruct the General Staff of the Armée Secrète.[122] In pleading with Febvre for a reunion, Bloch frequently hinted of, and wished to discuss, his interesting and important activities. "You understand," he wrote, "that I do not think only of the Middle Ages."[123]

Indeed, Bloch in his isolation gathered documentation on his and France's plight.[124] He corresponded with his English colleagues, avidly read German and foreign newspapers and, from the Paris and Vichy press, kept track of the perfidy of former eminences. He scrutinized the postmortem literature on the debacle. In the summer of 1942, drawing on his own conclusions and on recently published secret General Staff papers, he added annotations to the text of his still-hidden memoir *L'étrange défaite*.[125]

Bloch was continually preoccupied with the Jewish question and with French responses. In early fall his tranquil Creusois countryside

121 "Auditoire: à peu près celui qui nous haranguions, il y a plus longtemps encore, à l'ombre d'une cathédrale rhénane" (the French officers who attended the Centre des Etudes Germaniques in Mainz). Bloch to Febvre, 11 Apr. 1942, AN, MI 318 1; also 18 Apr., 8 May 1942, ibid.; Bloch to André Bloch, 25 Apr. 1942, EBC.
122 Paul Marres, "Un martyr de la résistance: Le professeur Marc Bloch," *Midi Libre*, 10 Mar. 1945.
123 Bloch to Febvre, 11, 18 Apr. 1942, AN, MI 318 1.
124 "Quelques documents sur l'avant-guerre, la guerre et l'après-guerre," EBC, including "Statistique des internés de Compiègne établie officiellement au milieu de janvier 1942." In another file Bloch collected "Extraits de diverse journaux de la N.S.D.A.P.," Sept. 1941.
125 Bloch to Febvre, Fougères, 26 July 1942, AN, MI 318 1. *ED*, pp. 50, 68–69, 106, 114; cf. *Les documents secrets de l'Etat-Major général français* (Berlin: Deutscher Verlag, 1941), pp. 240, 130, 98, 57, 132. Bloch also cited *L'annuaire militaire de la S.D. N.*; Paul Reynaud, *Le problème militaire français* (Paris: Flammarion, 1937); Jean de Pierrefeu, *Plutarque a menti* (Paris: Grasset, 1923); Bertrand de Jouvenel, *La décomposition de l'Europe libérale* (Paris: Plon, 1941); and Joffre's *Mémoires*, 2 vols. (Paris: Plon, 1932). He had recently read and (too late) profited from Jacques Benoist-Méchin's *Histoire de l'armée allemande (1919–1936)*, 2 vols. (Paris: Albin Michel, 1936–38): Bloch to Febvre, Montpellier, 27 Sept. 1941, EBC.

reverberated to a wave of arrests and deportations of foreign Jews. Bloch himself saw the truck transports. Even his least "political" neighbors had grumbled in outrage. There was grim news from Clermont-Ferrand, where students of the University of Strasbourg had been expelled for allegedly subversive activities.[126]

During these bleak months Bloch attempted to maintain his scholarship, despite long bouts of discouragement and distraction, fatigue and weak health, the result of age as well as practical difficulties. He explored the roots of fascism and Nazism, and also read J. M. Keynes and Walter Lippmann, Goethe and Valéry. Though he haunted archives and diligently read new works, he described his efforts as "storage" rather than major production.[127] His teaching revived his fascination with economic history and theory, his journeys stimulated his interest in the region. He visited and studied the nearby city of Narbonne, which had been the site of a flourishing medieval Jewish community and whose name would be identified with his one year later.[128]

Another dimension is revealed in Bloch's poetry. The subjects included love ballads to his wife, dreams, meditations on death, and a lament over a dead comrade in Flanders.[129] Bloch's wit had not failed him. On the occasion of a thesis defense in Montpellier, on which he sat as an outside (Paris) examiner, Bloch penned a witty verse:

---

126 Bloch to Febvre, Fougères, 17 Aug., 28, 29 Sept. 1942, AN, MI 318 1.
127 Bloch to Febvre, Montpellier, 5, 22 Jan., 14 Feb. 1942, EBC, and 11 Apr., 8 May 1942, AN, MI 318 1; Bloch to Boutruche, 6 Jan. 1942, RB; Bloch to René Baehrel, 14 Feb. 1942, in "Deux lettres de Marc Bloch," AESC 2 (July–Sept. 1947): 364–65; Simonne Bloch to Alice Bloch, 8 Jan., 11 Mar. 1942, EBC; Bloch to Philippe Wolff, 14 Mar. 1942, courtesy of Professor Wolff.
128 Bloch to Febvre, Montpellier, 6 June 1942, and Simonne Bloch to Alice Bloch, 10 June 1942, EBC. Courses: AN, AB XIX 3838.
   Bloch's Narbonne materials, including his extensive notes on the thesis of Jean Régné (a student of Ferdinand Lot), Etude sur la condition des Juifs de Narbonne du Ve au XIVe siècle (Narbonne: Caillard, 1912), in AN, AB XIX 3826.
129 "Ballade triste," "Fièvre," "Stances," "Ecrit la nuit," "A qui regrettant de mourir," "Epitaphe," "Rêves," "Ich hatte einen Kamarad," EBC.

Written for a Thesis

The candidate verbosely discourses on his thesis
With his elbows on the table, making the green glass [lampshade] vibrate,
He announces, "Gentlemen, according to my documents it is evident. . . ."
The judge interrupts, "Conjecture, nonsense. . . ."

Oh God! Dear Lord, how boring this is!
What if, to amuse myself I pulled out *Combat*,
Or used my finger to stuff my pipe with tobacco,
Or interrupted Fliche in the middle of a phrase!

But no, I shall remain hopelessly correct
And everything will turn out "very honorably"
For although we know that distinctions tend to be false
According to custom, we shall grant the utmost.[130]

In spite of his passive role in its direction, Bloch remained intensely committed to the *Annales*.[131] Though praising the first installment of the 1941 volume, which he received early in 1942, he could not conceal his emotion at the stark announcement "Directeur responsable: Lucien Febvre." In the two abbreviated issues of 1941

130   Ecrit à une thèse

Le candidat disertement parle sa thèse
Les coudes sur la table où vibre un verre vert,
Il dit: "De mes documents, Messieurs, il appert. . . ."
Le juge lui répond "Conjecture, fadaise. . . ."

Ce qu'on se rase, ô Dieux! Doux Seigneur, ce qu'on se rase!
Si, pour nous amuser, je deployais *Combat*,
Si je bourrais du doigt ma pipe de tabac,
Si j'interrompais Fliche au milieu d'une phrase!

Mais non je resterai désespérément sage
Et tout se dénouera très honorablement
Car, bien que nous sachions que la mention ment
Nous donnerons le fin du fin, selon l'usage.

Text in EBC. Thesis jury, 25–36 May 1942, ADH; cf. Bloch to Lot, 16 May 1942, Lot papers, IF.

131 Bloch to Febvre, 17 Aug. 1941, AN, MI 318 1, and 19, 20 Nov., 10, 24 Dec. 1941, EBC.

283

there were a total of only twenty-seven articles, *enquêtes*, and extended reviews. Of these, thirteen were by Febvre and four over Bloch's new pseudonym, "Fougères." One timely piece, by René Maunier, examined the queue as a "social group."[132]

The tone of this wartime *Annales* was far less combative than its predecessor. Febvre, who reported the deaths of two former collaborators, Jules Sion and Albert Demangeon, was noticeably more circumspect in his prose. "Fougères" concentrated primarily on rural history, while Febvre, who had contemplated also using a pseudonym for some of his profuse contributions, ranged over a host of subjects, including sensibility and history, politics and economics in the age of Louis XI, and an analysis of a property inventory in Amiens at the time of the Reformation and Counter-Reformation.

It was Febvre who in the *Annales* announced the publication of a new series, "Le paysan et la terre," published by Gallimard under the direction of Marc Bloch, whose name was now missing as editor of this collection. In his remarkably tactful review of the volume on France, which Bloch had not accepted, Febvre stressed his former co-director's "classic" contribution to French rural history, *Les caractères originaux de l'histoire rurale française*.[133] Febvre also reviewed the second volume of Bloch's *Société féodale* in a tone far less acerbic than his critique of the first. He nevertheless observed that the author's undoubted intelligence but inadequate "sensibility" had left significant gaps in his understanding of the mind and spirit of inhabitants of the past. Bloch rushed to defend himself, privately at least.[134]

132 Bloch to Febvre, Montpellier, 22 Jan. 1942, EBC; Febvre, "Marc Bloch: Témoignages," p. 24.

133 *AHS* (1941): 179, 180–81; cf. Bloch to Febvre, 7 Feb. 1942, EBC; 8 May 1942, AN, MI 318 1; 18 May 1942, EBC. Bloch's large, important file "Le paysan et la terre," EBC.

134 "Il me semble que ces féodaux, selon Marc Bloch, sont vraiment trop peu sensibles et que, sur le très ardu problème des rapports qu'entretiennent, à une époque lointaine, avec une sensibilité aux manifestations souvent plus bruyantes que les nôtres, la volonté tendue, la brutalité impérieuse et barbare des hommes, le livre passe un peu vite." Febvre, "La société féodale," *AHS* (1941): 241. Bloch's response, 8 May 1942, AN, MI 318 1.

Grateful for Febvre's solitary labors that had kept their journal alive, Bloch persisted in his hopes of maintaining a silent co-directorship and renewing their lapsed contact. However, he did not fail to chide Febvre for creating the *Annales'* new "diplomatic" tone.[135] When publication was temporarily stalled, Bloch continued to send in his articles and reviews. In mid-August 1942 the journal reappeared, renamed the *Mélanges d'Histoire Sociale*. The new title reflected Febvre's strategy of bypassing Vichy and Nazi regulations regarding periodicals. With its irregular appearance the *Mélanges* would escape these controls.[136]

Volume 1 of the *Mélanges*, though still of modest size, featured two young authors (Charles Morazé and Philippe Wolff) and two veterans (Georges Espinas and Charles-Edmond Perrin) as well as five extended pieces by Febvre and one by "Fougères." Bloch also wrote a considerable number of short reviews of works on France, England, Germany, and Italy as well as on southeastern Europe in his former vigorous style, demanding precision in terminology, attacking artificial time barriers, and stressing comparison of similarities as well as differences.[137] Febvre headlined a review of a book on the physical destruction of the ancient buildings of Paris: "Maintenir [preserve]."[138] He also announced the deaths of three more collaborators,[139] the incarceration in German prisoner-of-war camps of three more,[140] and several appointments, including that of

135 Bloch to Febvre, 11 Apr. (3 postcards), 18 Apr., 3, 8 May 1942, AN, MI 318 1, and 18 May 1942, EBC: "Vous êtes plus à l'aise dans le c.r. vigoureusement critique que dans le c.r. diplomatique."

136 Bloch to Febvre, 8 May, 17 July 1942, AN, MI 318 1; Febvre, "Marc Bloch: Témoignages," p. 24; Bloch to Febvre, Fougères, 17 Aug. 1942, AN, MI 318 1: "...un beau succès. Je pense que tout le monde comprendra. Si d'aventure quelques imbéciles se bouchent les yeux, je renonce à les eclairer."

137 "Un mot dangereux," *MHS* 1 (1942): 111; "De Rome au Moyen Age: Seigneurie et tenure en Italie," pp. 112–13; "Villages et terroirs de Bulgarie," pp. 118–19; "Sur les terres d'une grande abbaye anglaise," p. 108.

138 "Paris qu'on tue," *MHS* 1 (1942): 89.

139 Henri Laurent, killed in battle, and the unexpected deaths of Lucie Varga and André-E. Sayous.

140 Henri Brunschwig, P. Vilar, and Fernand Braudel, "qui, avec une admirable énergie, rédige en captivité une thèse, qui fera époque, sur la *Méditerranée au temps de Philippe II*."

C.-E. Labrousse to the Sorbonne, "substituting for M. Bloch, who is teaching at Montpellier."[141]

Although Febvre contributed the bulk of articles and reviews to the *Mélanges*, "Fougères" wrote several significant pieces. In volume 2 he composed a lengthy, balanced analysis of the giant two-volume thesis *La vie rurale en Bourgogne, jusqu'au début du XIe siècle* by his former student André Deléage as well as a detailed, enthusiastic critique of the work of his Montpellier colleague René Courtin.[142] In volume 3 "Fougères" revived the *enquêtes*. On the basis of his recent research in the archives of the Auvergne and Hérault, he revised and corrected Marc Bloch's 1929 article on French *plans parcellaires*.[143] He also penned twenty-three reviews.

Febvre was undoubtedly the dominant partner, and Bloch, excluded from the day-to-day work of the *Mélanges*, complained repeatedly about not receiving proofs from the printer in Limoges. He found it embarrassing to have to reply to Morazé's query that he saw articles "only when his *Annales* [sic] issue arrived." Febvre countered with a torrent of his own accusations, reopening the wounds of their battle eighteen months earlier. When volume 2 arrived, although its lead article was by his old rival, Emile Coornaert, Bloch relented. He rejoiced in the journal's survival and that "they" – that is, Febvre – had continued. On the eve of his last *rentrée* in the fall of 1942 he pleaded that they bury the past and work together toward the future.[144]

Bloch carried back to Montpellier the draft of his last book, *Apologie pour l'histoire*, on which he had worked intermittently

---

141 *MHS* 1 (1942): 87–88. Febvre also announced the election of their former colleague and collaborator André Piganiol from the Sorbonne to the chair in Roman civilization at the Collège de France.

142 "Origines de notre société rurale," *MHS* 2 (1942): 45–55 (Bloch to Febvre, 14 Feb., 11, 18 Apr. 1942, AN, MI 318 1); "Diagnostic et thérapeutique d'économiste," pp. 96–97 (Bloch to Febvre, 11 Apr. 1942, AN, MI 318 1).

143 "Les plans cadastraux de l'ancien régime," *MHS* 3 (1943): 53–70 (Bloch to Febvre, 11 Apr., 26 July, 17 Aug. 1942, AN, MI 318 1; also AN, AB XIX 3852).

144 Bloch to Febvre, Montpellier, 18 May, 22 June 1942, EBC; Fougères, 29 Sept. 1942, Montpellier, 9, 17, 22 Oct. 1942, AN, MI 318 1; 20 Oct., 9 Nov. 1942, EBC.

for three years and with greater concentration during the past summer.[145] Like *L'étrange défaite*, Bloch's *Apologie* was in many respects a memoir, arising from the deprivations and unquenched hopes of his dark times. The dedication, written in May 1941, was to his mother, who had just died: "In memoriam matris amicae." But also, just at the climax of the quarrel over the *Annales'* future and the denouement of the American escape plan, Bloch composed a second dedication, to Lucien Febvre:

Long ago we fought together for a larger and more human history. At this moment our common task is threatened.... The time will come, I am sure, when our collaboration can again as in the past be public and be free. In the meantime, on these pages filled with your presence, on my part it continues.[146]

The book opens with his son's question: "Tell me, Daddy, what is the use of history?" (Papa, explique-moi donc à quoi sert l'histoire?). In response to this innocent but exigent query Bloch, like Socrates, had decided to "render his accounts." The answer would justify not only his own lifelong commitment, but also the underlying creed of Western civilization, which was based on a continuous and vital relationship with the past. Only a few months earlier, on the day the Germans had entered Paris, a young General Staff officer had

145 See n. 56 and Bloch to Febvre, 17 Aug. 1941, AN, MI 318 1 ("J'ai écrit un peu sur l'Histoire"); 12 Jan. 1942, EBC ("Je suis encore loin du but"); 17 Aug. 1942, AN, MI 318 1 ("Exercise difficile, exercise instructif"); 29 Sept. 1942, ibid. ("Drôle de livre, décidément...poussé—ce que me rassure un peu – par un besoin intérieur"); 9 Oct. 1942, ibid. ("...dans ma situation on travaille pour la muse"). Bloch to Etienne Bloch, 13 Sept. 1942, EBC ("Il avance bien lentement. Mais enfin, il avance; et – malgré les moments habituels de doute – il ne me semble pas sans intérêt").

146 "A Lucien Febvre; en manière de dédicace," Fougères, 10 May 1941, sent to Febvre in Bloch's letter of 17 Oct. 1942, AN, MI 318 1; cf. *AH*, p. 17. The autobiographical quality has also been noted in A. J. P. Taylor, "Historical Wisdom: *The Historian's Craft*," *New Statesman and Nation*, 5 June 1954; W. M. Brewer, "The Historian's Craft," *Journal of Negro History* 39 (1954): 71; John Larner, "Marc Bloch and the Historian's Craft," *Philosophical Journal* 2 (1965): 123–32; and esp. A. J. Gurevich, "Marc Bloch i 'Apologija istorii,'" postface to the Russian edition, *Apologija istorii ili remeslo istorika*, 2d ed. (Moscow: Nauka, 1986), pp. 182–231.

actually cried: "Are we to believe that history has betrayed us?"[147]

The first reason for studying history, according to Bloch, was its enduring appeal to the imagination and intelligence. As an old, devoted practitioner, he would not deny history's poetic qualities, the "subtle enchantment of the unfamiliar." The second and more important purpose, in a world numbed by war and on the threshold of atomic and interstellar exploration, was that history was essential to providing intelligibility to, and achieving understanding of, the human story. History's detractors accused it of superficiality and perniciousness. In his *Apologie* Bloch, like the ancient Greek teacher, shunned an abstruse philosophical debate. Instead he proceeded to present his own tools and his method. Hence the second, better-known title: *Métier d'historien* (The Historian's Craft). Let the reader decide on history's usefulness. At the outset he acknowledged that history was still a "young" science which, like contemporary physics, lacked immutable laws. His conclusions placed him at odds both with his "timid" master Seignobos ("It is useful to ask oneself questions, *but very dangerous to answer them*")[148] and with any kind of artificial determinism, including Durkheimian sociology. For Bloch, the opportunity to take up the challenge and hazards of the Einsteinian world of uncertainty, armed with his intelligence, daring, and extraordinary sense of responsibility, was without doubt the essence of his dedication to his craft.[149]

The *Apologie* contains four completed chapters and one fragment. Defining history as "the science of men in time," Bloch attacked his old demons, the "idol of origins" and the artificial barriers between past and present, and preached "historical sensitivity." As in the prefaces to many of his courses, Bloch ranged broadly over space and time and liberally inserted examples and anecdotes from the recent

147 *AH*, pp. 19–21. For a different interpretation of this agonized query, see *ED*, pp. 155–56. Bloch could not commence without a preliminary excuse. Through a "malign destiny" over which he had no control, he was bereft of his library and dependent solely on his memory and notes (*AH*, p. 21).

148 *AH*, p. 29, based on Seignobos's statement during the debate of May 1907. Cf. *Bulletin de la Société Française de Philosophie* 7, no. 7 (July 1907), p. 304. Bloch also noted that in their text Langlois and Seignobos judged his son's question "idle" (*AH*, p. 165 n. 1).

149 *AH*, pp. 21–30.

past. He outlined his personal version of the historian's procedures, the search for evidence as a pursuit of "tracks" through a variety of documents; the rigorous critique of sources; and, in the analysis of data, the striving for an appropriate vocabulary and impartiality. The last chapter, on historical causation, ended abruptly: "In history, as elsewhere, the causes cannot be assumed. They are to be looked for..." By destiny or some internal logic Bloch left the search to those who came after him.[150]

Bloch's painstaking attempt to honor and update his masters, to evenhandedly declare the defects both of pedantic historians obsessed with chronology and ahistorical theoreticians who ignored change, and to relate the fruits of his three decades of work, combined with his engaging wit, optimism, and self-confidence, have placed the *Apologie* in a special category of works, admired by scholars of widely differing ideological casts and backgrounds. Bloch was enough of a historian, and sufficiently knowledgeable of the social sciences, to launch an enduring challenge to both camps. While conscientiously seeking explanation in history, neither discipline must neglect the fluidity inherent in all individual and social phenomena as well as in the observer's perspective.

Despite his gallant second dedication, it is probably incorrect to define this work as a joint production with Febvre.[151] And it is indeed anachronistic to characterize Bloch's *Apologie* as a harbinger of what later became known as "*Annales* history," with its emphasis on the social and behavioral sciences, material factors, and structural

150 Bloch to Febvre, 2 Mar. 1943 (EBC), gave the outline for *AH*. Cf. Febvre, "Comment se présentaient les manuscrits de 'Métier d'historien,'" *AH*, pp. 161–64: There were to be two more chapters – "Historical Explanation" and "The Problem of Prevision" (which Febvre believed would have contained Bloch's most original contribution), and in his conclusion there was to be a study of the role of history in citizenship and education and an appendix on the teaching of history.

The original manuscript is in three locations: AN, the Maison des Sciences de l'Homme, and EBC. Cf. Massimo Mastrogregori, "Le manuscrit interrompu: *Metier d'historien* de Marc Bloch," *AESC* 44, no. 1 (Jan.–Feb. 1989): 147–59; also Mastrogregori, "Nota sul testo dell' 'Apologie pour l'histoire' di Marc Bloch," *Rivista di Storia della Storiografia Moderna* 7, no. 3 (1986): 5–32.

151 See esp. Bloch to Febvre, 18 May 1942, EBC; 9, 17 Oct. 1942, AN, MI 318 1.

analysis.[152] Bloch's treatise was not particularly noteworthy for its scientific, methodological, or philosophical originality. Nor did it contain a specific blueprint or strategy for "total" history. Faced with the forces of barbarism and destruction and still retaining his hope for survival and freedom, facing the impediments and difficulties of aging and trying to comprehend meaningful links between generations, between civilizations, and between time past and time present, Bloch's *Apologie / Métier* – in however indirect and mutilated form it has reached us – is the meditation of a shrewd, diligent, and masterful worker who, like Montaigne, stimulates and inspires the reader with the honest inventory of his convictions. It was also a testimony of his hope for the future.[153]

Buoyed by a less arduous and more productive summer than he had expected and also by the news of the Soviet counterattack at Stalingrad, Bloch returned hopefully to Montpellier in early October for the *rentrée*. Like everyone else, Bloch fervently followed the news of the Allied buildup prior to the invasion of North Africa.[154]

At once the old troubles resurfaced. Rations had been reduced in July, and food was scarce and expensive. Montpellier, one of the eight worst cities from the point of view of basic nourishment (milk, meat, fats, eggs, and bread), also had severe shortages of clothing, shoes, petrol, and tires, as well as a flourishing black market. Bloch

152 Mastrogregori, "Nota sul testo," p. 31; also Friedrich J. Lucas, "Einleitung für den deutschen Leser," in Marc Bloch, *Apologie der Geschichte, oder der Beruf des Historikers* (Stuttgart: Klett, 1974), pp. 7–18; A. Gurevich, "Medieval Culture and Mentality According to the New French Historiography," *Archives Européennes de Sociologie* 1 (1983): 168.

153 "Que de tâches attendent les hommes de bonne volonté! Ne serait-ce, pour aller au plus proche de notre métier, que la refonte totale de l'enseignement, de A jusqu'à Z. L'action commune sera nécessaire. Elle sera rude. Elle ne sera possible que si nous savons avoir foi les uns dans les autres, nous comprendre avant de nous juger et accepter nos diversités." Bloch to Febvre, 9 Oct. 1942, AN, MI 318 1. See review by Georges Lefebvre, *RH* 210 (July–Sept. 1953): 94, and the remarks by Natalie Zemon Davis in "History's Two Bodies," *AHR* 93, no. 1 (Feb. 1988): 23–25.

154 Bloch to Febvre, Montpellier, 6, 22 (2 cards) June 1942, 28 Sept. 1942, EBC; Fougères, 17, 26 July, 17 Aug., 29 Sept., 9 Oct. 1942, AN, MI 318 1; Bloch to Etienne Bloch, Fougères, 13 Sept. 1942, EBC.

fretted over his wife's fragile health, which was further weakened by the food queues she was forced to join at 5 a.m. each day.[155] He was anxious about his older children's careers and their safety, particularly in view of the compulsory labor laws that were passed by Vichy in September. While the lovely fall weather stimulated hope, outwardly people were circumspect, isolated, and silent. The heavily censored press was forbidden to report any meaningful news. There was evidence of the Gestapo's presence in the increased number of mail interceptions and arrests. At the university's opening ceremony on 5 November 1942, Dean Fliche exhorted his listeners to "work hard" and be "quiet." In his annual report on the accomplishments of the faculty he omitted the work of Marc Bloch.[156]

Bloch was scheduled to teach two courses, on the economic evolution of the United States and on the peasantry and seigneury in France in the Middle Ages.[157] He had scarcely begun when news arrived of the Allied landings in North Africa on the night of 7−8 November followed by "Operation Attila," the German invasion of the unoccupied zone, which took place, with ironic timing, on 11 November 1942.[158] Faced directly by the enemy and warned by the authorities to leave at once, Bloch and his family, with the exception of his daughter Alice, who was working as a guardian of seventy-nine orphaned children near the Spanish border, fled hastily in two

155 On deteriorating material conditions in Montpellier, see Jean Sagnes, *L'Hérault dans la guerre, 1939−1945: La vie quotidienne sous l'occupation* (Les Etines: Horvath, 1986), pp. 32−42; Baumel, *De la guerre*, pp. 50−65.
156 Rentrée, 5 Nov. 1942, Université de Montpellier, ADH; see also Bloch to Febvre, 9, 17, 20, 23 Oct. 1942, EBC; Bloch to Boutruche, 20 Oct. 1942, RB.
  On Fliche, see Bloch's witty poem, "Epitaphe":
     Le mort qui sous cette dalle répose
     Fut conseiller municipal, doyen
        Voire académicien
     En un mot, il fut donc beaucoup de choses
     Et se crut historien.
157 "Histoire et peuplement des Etats-Unis," EBC; "La société paysanne et la seigneurie rurale," AN, AB XIX 3841; cf. Bloch to Febvre, 17 Oct. 1942, AN, MI 318 I.
158 Sagnes, *L'Hérault*, pp. 77−84, on the occupation and deportation of French citizens as well as foreigners.

convoys to Fougères, where they were joined by his wife's sister and her children.[159]

Bloch was again bereft of his few books and all his notes, which were abandoned along with many other things on their precipitate flight. He was summarily relieved of his functions for desertion in the face of the enemy. Assisted by his two older sons, he immediately set up a veritable collège in their country home to instruct the younger children for the remainder of the trimester. He inquired about correspondence courses and courses over the radio. He also sought a plan for the future.[160]

Once the veil of Vichy's independence had been brutally removed by Operation Attila and by Pétain and Laval's compliance, Bloch could have few illusions about work or protection for himself or for his children. In December came the orders to stamp "Juif" or "Juive" on the identification and ration cards which were essential for life but which also spelled danger for Jews, both foreign and French. With the Allies now building their resources nearby for a strike against metropolitan France, Hitler ordered the arrest and deportation of the Reich's enemies, Jews, communists, and Gaullists.[161] At this moment of peril, to have faith in the future Marc Bloch had to make it himself.[162]

159 Bloch to Febvre, 16 Nov. 1942, EBC.
160 The schedule, Monday through Saturday, 8:30–12:30 and 5:00–7:00, had Bloch teaching Greek, Latin, Spanish, and history. Bloch to Alice Bloch, 23 Nov. 1942, EBC. That letter also mentions his inquiry to the minister about the possibility of enrolling his older son at Clermont-Ferrand and of teaching there again.
161 Lubetzski, La condition des Juifs, pp. 110–11; Marrus and Paxton, Vichy France, pp. 302–5. At least 23,000 French Jews were deported.
162 In his notebook "Mea," EBC, sometime between December 1940 and February 1941 Bloch had written this quotation from Michelet's introduction to Le peuple: "Je croyais à l'avenir, parce que je le faisais moi-même."

11. Narbonne

We wait and hope and prepaie to our utmost.[1]

France, awaiting deliverance from the Allies, now fell almost completely under the German yoke. The "unoccupied" zone, with its small margin of safety, had disappeared. Except for the eight départements east of the Rhône which were occupied by Italy until its surrender in the summer of 1943,[2] France was no longer physically divided. Division, however, existed within the population itself, between the diehard or simply passive collaborators still wedded to the Pétain–Laval regime, and the growing number of active or tacit resisters who opposed the weakened conqueror. Without doubt the Third Reich would be defeated, but the question remained how, when, and at what price.[3]

France now endured a time of extreme danger. While the Allies issued proclamations and slowly built up their invasion forces to liberate Western Europe, Nazi Germany, like a mortally wounded animal, committed its most lethal acts: the attacks on the Resistance and the massive arrests and deportations of the Jews. In November 1942 SS First Lieutenant (*Obersturmführer*) Klaus Barbie arrived in Lyon to head the Gestapo. Vichy, on its part, was collaborating with the Third Reich by vigorously implementing its labor-conscription law, the Service du Travail Obligatoire (STO). In January 1943 it

1 Bloch to Etienne and Louis Bloch, Lyon, 28 Feb. 1944, EBC.
2 Drôme, Isère, Hautes-Alpes, Basses-Alpes, Alpes-Maritimes, Savoie, Haute Savoie, and Var.
3 Charles Rist, *Une saison gâtée: Journal de la guerre et de l'occupation, 1939–1945* (Paris: Fayard, 1983), pp. 289–90 (entry 11 Nov. 1942).

created the Milice to war against Jews, communists, Freemasons, and other enemies of the militant counterrevolution.[4]

The events of late 1942 had also stimulated the unification of the French underground. Earlier the northern and southern movements, operating against two different enemies, had maintained separate tactics and leadership. Moreover in the south, before the Germans crossed the demarcation line there had been a welter of disparate, autonomous groups led by independent chieftains. Unification was a gradual process, built by establishing links at home and abroad. The original architect was Jean Moulin, who even before the Allied landings had laid the essential basis for internal consolidation under the leadership of Charles de Gaulle. Public opinion in late 1942 began to turn against an exacting but now vulnerable conqueror and an increasingly feeble Vichy. The Allies, cautiously balancing rival political factions in North Africa, began to intensify their interest in and support for the resistance organizations in metropolitan France. And de Gaulle, emerging as the major recognized and unyielding symbol of a free France, directed his full efforts at consolidation. There was an almost irrepressible movement inside France toward the creation of a national resistance, welding north and south, balancing central and local control, coordinating the military, political, social-service, and labor arms, and integrating the leadership and organizations of the interior with Algiers and London. In early 1943, as a result of Moulin's prodding, the three major noncommunist southern groups agreed to merge into the MUR, the Mouvements Unis de la Résistance, which became the model for the future nationwide Conseil National de la Résistance (CNR).[5]

4 Details on the new Gestapo leader in Alan A. Ryan, *Klaus Barbie and the United States Government: A Report to the Attorney General of the United States* (Washington, D.C.: U.S. Department of Justice, Criminal Division, 1983), pp. 3–22. Intensified measures against foreign and French Jews in Michael R. Marrus and Robert O. Paxton, *Vichy France and the Jews* (New York: Basic, 1981), pp. 302–10.

5 Documentation on the creation of the MUR and the CNR: AN, 72 AJ 65 (AIII). Also Henry Frenay, *The Night Will End: Memoirs of a Revolutionary*, trans. D. Hofstadter (New York: McGraw-Hill, 1976), pp. 223–43; Henri Michel, *Jean Moulin l'unificateur* (Paris: Hachette, 1964); John F. Sweets, *The Politics of Resistance in France: A History of the Mouvements Unis de la Résistance* (De Kalb: Northern Illinois University Press, 1976), pp. 18–60. *(note cont. p. 295)*

Marc Bloch, who as an "old medievalist" recognized that "the Antichrist had to precede the coming of the Messiah," was conscious of the imminent peril as well as the hope.[6] At age fifty-six, he was out of work and without good prospects of another teaching post but not prepared to retire. His financial resources were greatly diminished, and he was responsible for a large, still young family and several dependent relatives. His wife was ailing and his own health was fragile. He could have remained sheltered in the country, minding his flock, working, and waiting for deliverance. But this passive course posed obvious dangers as well as personal obstacles, not the least of which was Bloch's overriding sense of his "uselessness." The alternative was action.[7]

Sometime in late 1942 or early 1943 Marc Bloch decided to join the Resistance. During the previous half-year a "second generation" of young volunteers, fleeing the STO or the Germans, had swelled the ranks of the underground. Many of the original southern chiefs had departed for Paris, Algiers, or London. A new local and regional leadership was emerging. Its main task was to establish the political structure as well as the fighting forces for France's liberation. It was here that Bloch decided to contribute his main efforts.

Bloch's motivations must include his patriotism and sense of honor. Membership in the Resistance gave Bloch the opportunity to serve France at a crucial time and manifest his loyalty to the *patrie*. He also felt a personal commitment to maintaining the bond, five generations long, linking his Jewish identity with France. In the Resistance, Marc Bloch, like a number of patriotic assimilated Jews, found the means to reclaim his maimed citizenship and assert "civis gallicus sum."[8] Bloch's love of action and his ambition also in-

---

Estimates of the numbers of French resisters vary from 2 to 5 percent of the adult population. Margaret Rossiter (*Women in the Resistance* [New York: Praeger, 1986], pp. 220–22), who includes intelligence networks, escape lines, publishing, and paramilitary activities, estimates that 50,000 males and females were occupied in intelligence networks alone.

6 Bloch to Febvre, Montpellier, 9 Oct. 1942, AN, MI 318 1.

7 Bloch to Alice Bloch, 23 Nov. 1942, EBC; to Boutruche, 6 Jan. 1943, RB; to Febvre, 22 Jan. 1943, EBC.

8 Cf. Georges Friedmann, *Fin du peuple juif?* (Paris: Gallimard, 1965), pp. 8–10; see also Claude Lévy, "La résistance intérieure et les Juifs," and Dominique Veillon, "Franc-Tireur et les Juifs," in *La France et la question juive, 1940–1944*

fluenced his decision. Given the obvious risks of capture and death, he made a great gamble. Should he survive, there would be the opportunity for leadership in a resurrected republic. Should he perish, his family would at least take consolation from the legacy of a fallen martyr.

Bloch now fully entered the public realm which he had avoided in the past, but without a specific political ideology. Like many in the Resistance he retained his distaste for parties, partisanship, and the defunct parliamentary regime of the Third Republic. As an individual and a historian he was driven by a deep antifascism and by a certain conception of France as the champion of human liberty. In the countryside he had reread Montaigne, who during the dark times four centuries earlier had been a firm, solitary spokesman for humanism and freedom.[9] Given Marc Bloch's background, intelligence and energy, ambition, and strong sense of responsibility, the decision to join developed out of both rational calculation and deeper necessity. And although the nadir of his fortunes coincided with a moment of opportunity to participate in the national resurrection, this in no way diminishes the genuineness, depth, and even, perhaps, the inevitability of his choice. Such major decisions, rarely articulated or completely explained, indeed have the power of illuminating an entire life.[10]

(Paris: S. Messinger, 1981), pp. 297–314, 315–29; Claude Singer, "Des universitaires juifs dans la Résistance," in Association pour la Recherche sur l'Histoire Contemporaine des Juifs, *Les Juifs dans la Résistance et la Libération* (Paris: Editions du Scribe, 1985), pp. 71–81.

Other Jews in leadership positions in the mainstream of the French Resistance included: Jacques Bordier-Brunschwig, Raymond Aubrac, Maurice Kriegel-Varlimont (Libération-Sud); Max Heilbronn (Résistance-Fer); Jean-Pierre Lévy, Georges Altman (Franc-Tireur); André Kaan, Georgette Lévy (Ceux de la Résistance), Léo Hamon (Action Ouvrière de Combat, Comité Parisien de Libération), Daniel Mayer, Jean-Maurice Hermann (Socialists); René Cassin, Georges Boris, André Weill-Curiel, René Mayer, Pierre Mendès-France (France Combattante, London); and also Admiral Louis Kahn who, representing the Free French, aided the Allies' antisubmarine warfare in the Atlantic. *Les Juifs*, pp. 47–89 and passim; Marcel Baudot, "Les mouvements de Résistance devant la persécution des Juifs," in *France et la question juive*, p. 294.

9 Bloch to Febvre, Fougères, 2 Mar. 1943, EBC; notes on Montaigne in AN, AB XIX 3852, and in "Mea," EBC.

10 Good discussions of the motivation of *résistants* in Roderick Kedward, *Resistance*

Before joining, there were practical details to attend to. To save them from the STO or worse dangers, and enable them possibly to join the Free French in North Africa or in London, Bloch in late December accompanied his two older sons and a nephew to Montpellier, where they were escorted by a Resistance contact to the Spanish border.[11] His older daughter was now working in a children's home near Limoges. His wife and their three younger children, along with her youngest sister and her three young children, remained at the country home in Fougères. His brother-in-law Arnold Hanff, a chief engineer in the postal service and an active *résistant*, would serve as the crucial liaison between Bloch and his wife.

It was not easy to join the leadership ranks of the underground in early 1943. Made up of tiny, tight networks based upon personal contact and confidence, and under constant threat of surveillance and betrayal, the southern Resistance was not readily opened to an outsider, especially to an elderly bourgeois intellectual. Bloch's main contacts were in Clermont-Ferrand, recently the scene of accelerated resistance activity and arrests. Under the vigorous direction of the regional chief, Dr. Henry Ingrand, the newly established Auvergne (R.6) branch of the MUR was in the process of consolidating the three groups Combat, Franc-Tireur, and Libération, organizing maquis operations in the countryside and student–worker campaigns in the cities, and rooting out spies.[12] An outside applicant needed significant support and a specific affiliation to enter at this feverish and dangerous stage.

It was through his old friend on the Strasbourg faculty in Clermont, Dr. Robert Waitz, who was one of the local leaders of Franc-Tireur, that Bloch entered through the smallest member of

in *Vichy France* (Oxford: Oxford University Press, 1978), pp. 75–81; Sweets, *Politics of Resistance*, pp. 9–17; and esp. Alban Vistel, *L'héritage spirituel de la Résistance* (Lyon: Lugdunum, 1955), pp. 56–90. Cf. Bloch to Febvre, 2 Mar. 1943, EBC.

11 Francis Missa, "Témoignage," 5 Oct. 1948, AN, 72 AJ 132 (Hérault); Etienne Bloch, *Marc Bloch: Father, Patriot, and Teacher* (Poughkeepsie, N. Y.: Vassar College, 1987), p. 8.

12 Henri Ingrand, "Témoignage," 17 May 1956, AN, 72 AJ 55; John F. Sweets, *Choices in Vichy France* (New York: Oxford University Press, 1986), pp. 210–14; interview with Jean-Pierre Lévy, 1983.

the MUR.[13] Franc-Tireur was the successor to France-Liberté, a group spontaneously established in Lyon in late 1940 to publish rebuttals to Vichy propaganda. The organization Franc-Tireur was founded at the beginning of 1941 by this association of former radicals, left-wing Catholics, and communists. It was led by a young demobilized reserve artillery lieutenant, Jean-Pierre Lévy, a refugee Alsatian businessman reestablished in Lyon who traveled extensively in the southern zone and was thus able to expand the group's contacts with and support from the middle-class exile community. Throughout its existence the heart of Franc-Tireur was its clandestine newspaper, "a monthly insofar as possible and by the grace of the Marshal's police" (with the addition, after November 1942, of "and the Gestapo"). Using a chain of loyal printers and distributors and produced by professional journalists, *Le Franc-Tireur* was notable for its terse, biting prose. On its masthead was *Liberté – égalité – fraternité.*[14]

Like Combat and Libération, Franc-Tireur represented a fairly broad spectrum of political opinion, though it was generally regarded as a moderate, independent republican group: democratic, antiracist, antibolshevik, and pro-European.[15] In 1942 it rallied to

---

13 Simonne Bloch to Alice Bloch, Fougères, 4, 16 Apr. 1943, EBC; interviews with Maurice Pessis, 1981, 1983. Sweets, *Politics of Resistance*, p. 48, estimates that in January 1943 there were 75,000 members of Combat, 30,000 members of Franc-Tireur, and a figure in between for Libération. Waitz (whose code name was "Prudent") four months later, in July 1943, was arrested and deported, but he returned after the war. Georges Altman ("Chabot"), "Témoignage," 14 June 1946, AN, 72 AJ 55.

14 According to Antoine Avenin's figures, AN, 72 AJ 55, the first edition, appearing on 8 December 1941, was printed in 6,000 copies. Subsequent printings as follows: Apr. 1942, 35,000; Jan. 1943, 50,000; Sept. 1943, 100,000; Jan. 1944 (with a special edition for Paris and the northern zone, published in Paris), 150,000.

15 In its first number the paper's policy was described: "Nous ne voulons ni de dictature prolétarienne, ni de dictature capitaliste, ni de dictature militaire, ni de dictature religieuse.... Nous voulons un gouvernement fort au sein du quel toutes les classes et toutes les tendances seront représentées, où les intérêts de chacun pourront s'exprimer sans que l'intérêt d'un seul ou d'une groupe prime sur l'intérêt des autres. Nous voulons un système représentatif libéré des erreurs passées. Nous rejetons comme une duperie un syndicalisme obligatoire où

de Gaulle, first cautiously, then with enthusiasm, and also to the Mouvements Unis de la Résistance, where it served as mediator between its larger partners. As the MUR began to function in 1943, it predictably tended to blur its members' distinctiveness. Nevertheless, Franc-Tireur, its name deliberately recalling the hearty volunteers of 1870–71, always maintained its intense anti-Vichy viewpoint, which well matched the sentiments of Marc Bloch.[16]

Waitz introduced Bloch to a twenty-year-old philosophy student, Maurice Pessis, one of the stalwarts of the movement, who was attached to the leadership in Lyon. After struggling for ten days to persuade his superiors to admit the eager and distinguished candidate, Pessis proudly presented his "new recruit," perhaps in March but more likely in early April 1943. The chief editor of *Le Franc-Tireur*, Georges Altman, two years later recalled:

A gentleman of fifty, with a rosette in his buttonhole, a refined face under silver-gray hair, keen eyes behind a pair of spectacles, a briefcase in one hand, a walking stick in the other; at first my visitor was a little stiff, but

---

le travailleur n'est plus qu'un figurant. . . . Nous répudions formellement le bolchevisme totalitaire et meurtrier. Nous désirons voir se fonder la communauté des peuples unis et fédérés librement hors de la domination du capitalisme international et des oligarchies quelles qu'elles soient."

Opposed to anti-Semitism and a vengeful peace that would repeat the "erreurs de Versailles," it nevertheless insisted: "Nous pensons qu'une paix véritable ne sera possible tant que l'hitlérisme ne sera pas écrasé et que l'Allemagne n'aura pas fait son 'mea culpa.'"

Repudiating any party allegiance, it declared its aim to be the liberation of France: "Nous voulons grouper tous les Français, sans distinction de croyances ou d'opinions, pour la croisade libératrice. Pour l'instant, une seule tâche: résister, organiser, préparer le sursaut national qui nous fera à nouveau maîtres de notre destin."

16 "Renseignements fournis par Avinin, 5 Mar. 1945 ('Franc-Tireur')," AN, 72 AJ 55; Noel Clavier, "Franc-Tireur: Tel que je l'ai vu naître," *Bulletin des AMUR* no. 6 (June 1947): 4; Dominique Veillon, *Le Franc-Tireur: Un journal clandestin, un mouvement de Résistance 1940–1944* (Paris: Flammarion, 1977) (indispensable); interviews with Marc Gerschel (1983); Jean-Pierre Lévy (1981, 1983); Eugène Claudius Petit (1981). Marcel Ruby, *La résistance à Lyon*, 2 vols. (Lyon: L'Hermès, 1979), I, p. 215, identified Franc-Tireur as the "most specifically *Lyonnais* of the three major southern groups." The group was occasionally confused with the communist Francs-Tireurs et Partisans Français (FTPF).

26. Last photograph of Bloch, 1944

before long he smiled, held out his hand, and said politely: "Yes, I'm Maurice's 'colt.' "[17]

Lyon, Bloch's birthplace and the scene of his futile interviews two years earlier in the U.S. consulate, now became his last place of residence. Despite the exodus of many of the original leaders, the ancient Gallic capital and France's third-largest city retained its identity as the "capital of the Resistance." Almost halfway between Paris and Marseille, at the confluence of the Rhône and the Saône, and also the hub of the nation's principal rail lines and national highways, Lyon was a well-located and relatively safe place for underground activity. In its old homes and warehouses along the banks of the two rivers, in its buildings on the hills of Fourvière and the Croix Rousse with their seemingly endless staircases, entries on different levels, and passageways (*traboules*), in its labyrinthine alleyways and along the avenues of its working-class quarters, there were ample opportunities to distribute and gather information, take shelter, and carry out evasive maneuvers. The main Resistance press was still located in Lyon, as were the main headquarters of the Armée Secrète. On Bastille Day in 1942 a hundred thousand Lyonnais had assembled between 6:30 and 8 p.m. in the city's center for a great republican manifestation.[18]

After the Germans returned in November 1942, Lyon became an extremely tense city. Desperately short of lodging, food, and essential supplies, it maintained a vigorous black market occasionally punished by the police. The population chafed under the intermittent punitive curfews. It was sullen over clumsy displays of Vichy or Nazi power, and resented the periodic sweeps by French and German police to round up Jews or conscripts for the labor

17 Georges Altman ("Chabot"), "Notre 'Narbonne' de la Résistance," *CP* 8 (Mar. 1945): 2. Altman's recollections reprinted in *AHS* (1945), – "Hommages à Marc Bloch" – I: 11–14 and enlarged in *ED*, pp. 7–18. Cf. interviews with Maurice Pessis.
18 Aufzeichnung, 14 July 1942 (NARS, Germany AA T-120 5800/2723/ E422538–39), gives further details of "Lyon: Resistance capital"; also Dupont, *Combats dans l'ombre* (Lyon: P. Derain, 1945); Paul Garcin, *Interdit par la censure, 1942–44* (Lyon: Lugdunum, 1944); Henri Amoretti, *Lyon capitale 1940–1944* (Paris: Editions France-Empire, 1964); Bernard Aulas, *Vie et mort des Lyonnais en guerre, 1939–1945* (Roanne: Horvath, 1974).

27. Lyon: the Rhône, ca. February 1944

force, as well as over the periodic mass arrests of members of the Resistance. Few any longer believed in collaboration, but most feared their masters' capacity for violence and retribution.[19]

Marc Bloch's resistance career began inauspiciously. Originally assigned to work under Altman, until he found his own niche he had little to do but menial tasks, mainly delivering messages and newspapers. He had to overcome the neglect and suspicion of his new comrades along with his own doubts and dismay. During his first weeks in Lyon as "Monsieur Rolin" he led a wandering existence in a series of furnished flats. It was a new life of waiting and isolation in a relatively unfamiliar environment. His first separation from his wife and family was made more difficult by the irregular, risky paths of communication and the infrequent trips to

19 See Prefect's reports, 8 Dec. 1942, 12 Feb., 7 Mar., 8 Apr., 9 May, 10 June 1943, AN, FI CIII 1200; OSS documents: "Apperçu sur la situation intérieure en France métropolitaine," Algiers, 26 May 1943, NARS, RG 226 38267, and "Conditions in Southern France," 1 June 1943, NARS, RG 226 37711; also Jacques Natali, *L'occupant et l'occupation allemande à Lyon de 1940 à 1944*, Mémoire de Maîtrise: Université de Lyon II (1975).

Fougères. There was the fleeting hope of a leadership position in Limoges, which did not materialize.[20]

But Bloch was scarcely inactive. As "Fougères," he completed his reviewing assignments for volumes 4 and 5 of the *Mélanges*. At Easter he was for the first time able to pay a visit to Lucien Febvre in his country home in Le Souget.[21] Through secret channels he also remained in contact with his English friends.[22]

Furthermore, Bloch was now greatly preoccupied with the political and economic changes that would be essential in a resurrected France.[23] Above all, he dreamed of a "revolution" in French education. As the aspiring successor to Abel Bonnard at the head of the Ministry of National Education he would abolish all special schools, end the servitude to examinations and the tyranny of Latin and Greek, introduce global studies, encourage innovation in teaching methods, and reorganize research.[24]

Bloch's proposals on educational reform appeared in the third issue of a new Resistance journal, *Les Cahiers Politiques*.[25] Founded and originally published in Lyon by the Comité Général d'Etudes, it had been inspired by Moulin, who sought a clandestine counterpart to the *New Statesman* and a rival to the *Revue des Deux Mondes*. The *Cahiers* was aimed at a limited readership of French intellectuals, for

20 Interviews with Henri Falque (1982), Maurice Pessis, Irène Altman Allier (1981), Eugène Claudius Petit, Jean-Pierre Lévy; Bloch to Febvre, 12 May 1943, EBC; Veillon, *Franc-Tireur*, pp. 175, 382.

21 Bloch to Febvre, 12, 28 May 1943, and Febvre to Etienne Bloch, 28 Aug. 1946, EBC. See esp. "Entr'aide et piété: Les associations urbaines au Moyen Age," *MHS* 5 (1944): 100–6, Bloch's last extended critical review.

22 Draft letter to Postan and Tawney, from "somewhere in France," 14 June 1943, papers of Lucien Febvre, Maison des Sciences de l'Homme; M. M. Postan, "Marc Bloch: An Obituary Note," *Economic History Review* 14, no. 2 (1944): 161–62.

23 See Bloch's notes on political parties and political life "after the victory," Lucien Febvre files, Maison des Sciences de l'Homme. Cf. Bloch to Lot, 29 June 1943, Lot papers, IF.

24 "Rêves, anticipations. Mais que faire en ce moment, sinon rêver?" Bloch to Febvre, 28 May 1943, EBC; also Bloch to Febvre, 2 Mar. 1943, EBC.

25 "Notes pour une révolution de l'enseignement," *CP 3* (Aug. 1943): 17–24. Etienne Bloch (to Alice Bloch, 17 Nov. 1944, EBC) recalled reading his father's unsigned but unmistakable writing after he arrived in London.

whom it hoped to articulate the "political, economic, and social" direction for the liberation and the postwar regime. Bloch, through his CGE contacts, was named editor-in-chief of the *Cahiers*, a role to which he contributed not only his extensive publishing experience but also his strong "historian's" interest in dealing with the practical problems of reconstruction.[26]

Late spring brought a pleasant "southern wind" to Lyon, the news of the Anglo-American victories in Tunisia that moved the Allies' forces ever closer to the Continent.[27] But the occupier quickly retaliated. Lyon was shocked by a series of arrests of major Resistance leaders, culminating on 21 June in the capture of Jean Moulin in the suburb of Caluire and his subsequent death. This tragic and in many ways still mysterious incident greatly hindered the movement toward the unification of the Resistance on the national and local levels.[28]

In accordance with their merger negotiations, national services were to be centrally administered by the MUR, but the three founding groups retained control over their own press and propaganda. In the division of responsibilities, Henri Frenay, the leader of Combat, oversaw military affairs; Emmanuel d'Astier de la Vigerie, head of Libération, saw to political affairs; and Lévy managed intelligence, security, and material resources. Moving down the pyramid to the key regional level, it would take time, effort, and diplomacy before

26 See Bloch, "Suite à notre conversation du 9 juin" (undated), Lucien Febvre files, Maison des Sciences de l'Homme; François de Menthon, "A la mémoire de Marc Bloch," *CP* 8 (Mar. 1945): 1; also Diane de Bellescize, *Les neuf sages de la Résistance* (Paris: Plon, 1979), pp. 80–85. Michel Debré (letter to author, 16 Sept. 1981) recalls sharing editorial chores with Bloch on the review.

According to the "Table analytique des matières publiées dans *Les Cahiers Politiques* depuis leur création," *CP* 16 (Dec. 1945): 92, Bloch is credited with authoring the article "Pourquoi je suis Républicain: Réponse d'un historien," *CP* 2 (July 1943): 9–11 (*MH* II, p. 1101); but the style is not his, and Bellescize also rejects the notion.

27 Bloch to Febvre, 12 May 1943, EBC; Prefect's reports, 9 May, 10 June 1943, AN, FI CIII 1200.

28 Ruby, *La résistance* I, pp. 499–505; Henri Noguères, *Histoire de la Résistance en France de 1940 à 1945* III (Paris: Laffont, 1972).

the newborn MUR began to overcome the "feudal" propensities and rivalries of its founding groups.[29]

In Lyon, the MUR's leaders had either departed or would soon move out, and newer members were rapidly being promoted to national posts. Bloch's testing period ended abruptly in July 1943 when he replaced Pierre Gacon as Franc-Tireur's chief of R. 1 (the region Rhône–Alpes) and its representative on the three-man regional directory of the MUR.[30] The new R. 1 directory consisted of Bloch (whose code name now was "Narbonne") for Franc-Tireur, Marcel Peck ("Battesti") for Combat, and A. Malleret ("Baudoin," later "Bourdelle") for Libération. In the leadership of southern France, Combat – with the largest and best-organized network – had provided five of the MUR's six regional chiefs. However, in R. 1 it was the Libération representative who in March 1943 had been named by the national committee to head the regional directory. This reflected the well-entrenched and active nature of all three organizations in Lyon and also the fact that Combat's candidate had presented political and security problems. Franc-Tireur appears to have given its support to the Libération candidate, "Baudoin." Though technically a coalition partner, Franc-Tireur's regional delegate was more often an observer and mediator between the chief and his stronger rival, with their ongoing personal rivalry and two distinct conceptions of the leadership and organization of the Resistance's southeastern heartland.[31]

In July Marc Bloch inherited the responsibilities of his predecessor as organizer of the region's social services and inspector of

29 Ruby, *La résistance* I, pp. 492–96; Veillon, *Franc-Tireur*, pp. 331–48; Alban Vistel, *La nuit sans ombre: Histoire des mouvements unis de résistance, leur rôle dans la libération du sud-est* (Paris: Fayard, 1970), pp. 375–78.
30 Gacon ("Hughes"), a slightly earlier professorial recruit, was appointed by the national committee as the MUR's delegate to the Lyon youth organization, Forces Unies de la Jeunesse. Veillon, *Franc-Tireur*, p. 176; Ruby, *La résistance* I, pp. 519–23.
31 Ruby, *La résistance* I, pp. 289–96; II, pp. 990–91; Veillon, *Franc-Tireur*, pp. 345–48; Vistel, *Nuit*, pp. 377–79; also Marie Granet and Henri Michel, *Combat: Histoire d'un mouvement de résistance, de juillet 1940 à juillet 1943* (Paris: Presses Universitaires de France, 1957).

the region's ten départements. He also maintained a liaison between the MUR and its local constituent organizations: intelligence and false papers and the Armée Secrète and the maquis, as well as with the railway and postal services. In his office on the border between Lyon and the suburb of Villeurbanne he and his handful of agents decoded and recoded messages which they then delivered to other agents on the streets of Lyon. In the book he always carried there were slips of paper recording his appointments, carefully disguised to protect his contacts.[32]

Now his main resistance career began, and Marc Bloch had tasks that well suited his ability and inclinations. At once he distinguished himself by bringing order and discipline to a hitherto chaotic organization.[33] His responsibilities suddenly multiplied and his contacts grew, as did his freedom and his authority. Bloch was assigned the special task of preparing the region for "Jour-J" – the Allies' debarkation – which was to be accompanied by uprisings in all ten départements. He worked on setting up the "Liberation Committee" that would govern Lyon and the region, as well as on all the technical details concerning personnel, transport, and liaisons, possibly anticipating his own appointment as president of the committee.[34]

Bloch lived the double life of a clandestine leader. Thanks to a Resistance contact, as the traveling businessman "M. Blanchard" he found a safe permanent lodging in Caluire. He lived on the quiet, almost rural rue de l'Orangerie, far from the bustling city with its periodic *rafles* and vexatious curfews. Here his wife could visit, and here he could take some of his meals and establish a more "normal" existence. From the country Simonne Bloch frequently sent him

32 Veillon, *Franc-Tireur*, pp. 175–77; letters to the author from Denise Vernay ("Miarka"), 19 Aug. 1981, and Dr. Maurice Laforgue ("Cadum"), 15 June 1982; interviews with Jacques Godechot (1980), Raymond Péju (1982), Cecile Hermann (1983).

33 Altman, "Notre 'Narbonne,'" p. 2; letters to the author by Henri Falque ("Gaucher"), in charge of propaganda diffusion, 1 Jan., 6 May 1982, and interview; also interview, Irène Altman Allier.

34 Bloch to Simonne Bloch, 20 Aug. 1943, EBC; Dr. Laforgue to author, 15 June 1982; Alice Bloch to author, 22 Dec. 1982; interviews with Raymond Péju, J.-P. Lévy. Also "Notice sur la vie de Marc Bloch dans la Résistance," courtesy of Alice Bloch.

food, clothing, books, and supplies that were indispensable for his survival and comfort. "Blanchard" used his stove to incinerate his mounting piles of documents. His neighbors were entirely unaware of his activities.[35]

There were, of course, long periods of unaccustomed solitude. Bloch spent his fifty-seventh birthday alone. Through contacts he anxiously followed the fate of his two exiled sons, from their long internment in a Spanish prison to their release and escape to the Free French in North Africa.[36] He was constantly worried about the safety of his older daughter, Alice, who was guardian of some eighty four- to twelve-year-olds at the children's home Le Masgelier, where they were "visited" twice, once by French police searching for arms and once by German soldiers looking for Jews.[37] Because his son Daniel, approaching age eighteen, was endangered by the conscript-labor laws, Bloch fretted over his study problems and put pressure on him to enroll in a good agricultural school, Neuvic in Ardèche.[38] His next son, Jean-Paul, who in the fall of 1943 became a day boarder in the lycée in Guéret, had health problems that also worried Bloch.[39] Bloch missed his children and his wife. During

---

35 Bloch to Simonne Bloch, 9 July, 4, 8, 22 Aug. 1943, EBC; Altman, "Notre 'Narbonne,'" pp. 3–4; also Jean-Claude Weill (who lived near Bloch in Caluire in 1944) to Michel Barridon, 13 Mar. 1988, with thanks to Professor Barridon for this communication.

36 "Drôle" birthday: Marc Bloch to Simonne Bloch, 7 July 1943, EBC. Sons: Bloch to Simonne Bloch, 22 June 1943 (their situation unchanged), EBC; to Lucien Febvre, 15 Aug. 1943, AN, MI 318 1 (announces Louis Bloch's departure for North Africa); to Alice Bloch, 5 Dec. 1943, EBC (announces that Etienne Bloch had "reached his destination"); also Simonne Bloch and Marc Bloch to Louis and Etienne Bloch, 7 Oct. 1943, EBC.

Louis Bloch became an intelligence officer on de Gaulle's staff. Etienne Bloch reached Morocco, where he enlisted in the 2d French Armored Division, which later took part in the Allied campaign in France and Germany. Simonne Bloch's cousin René Mayer, a cabinet member in the provisional government in North Africa, appears to have been Bloch's contact person concerning his sons.

37 Bloch to Ferdinand Lot, 29 Dec. 1943, Lot papers, IF; Alice Bloch to author, 22 Dec. 1982.

38 Bloch to Daniel Bloch, 5 July, 5 Sept., 4 Nov. 1943, EBC; Bloch to Simonne Bloch, 3, 27 July, 1 Aug., 11, 23 Sept., 11 Oct. 1943, EBC.

39 See, e.g., Bloch to Simonne Bloch, 1, 4, 22 Aug., 11, 19, 23 Sept. 1943, EBC.

307

their long periods of separation he found his life "heavy," and he was chagrined at having "abandoned them."[40]

In Lyon there were two kinds of *résistants*: those who led normal lives as well as participating in underground activities and those in a full-time clandestine existence. The former were primarily native Lyonnais, and the latter were French and foreign refugees with few ties to the local population. Bloch established himself in the second milieu. He had a "clan" of in-laws, the Weill family, who provided hospitality and profited from his concern and advice. He was also in contact with his two nephews and niece who were active in Combat. He established a close circle of friends among his Resistance colleagues, Altman and Elie Péju and especially the young Pessis, with whom he ate regularly.

Singularly adept at fitting in, Bloch now had a new family of young, dedicated combatants with whom he shared his daily tasks. For security reasons, all *résistants* withheld their identity, but Marc Bloch was easily identifiable. He was described by one former young courier as a "small elderly gentleman, smiling and affable" with whom she met as if by accident to transfer messages on one of the many bridges of Lyon.[41] In his office Bloch maintained an egalitarian relationship in all their tasks, but he was immediately recognized as one of the more practical, penetrating, and articulate elders of the movement. Most of Bloch's young comrades established a loyal, trusting, filial relationship with the elegant Parisian gentleman who nevertheless avoided the almost universal *tutoiement*. Bloch was a model leader for times that required daring and planning, individualism and group rapport, silence and skill in communication, and, above all, a sense of commitment to a cause. He had loved soldiering and being a responsible officer. Despite the many privations, he generally had a jaunty air, and seemed to relish the personal freedom and physical and material austerity of an underground activist.[42]

40 Bloch to Simonne Bloch, 8 Aug., 16, 24 Oct. 1943, EBC.
41 Denise Vernay ("Miarka") to author, 19 Aug. 1981.
42 Important descriptions of underground life in Lyon in 1943–44 in papers of Hans Hubert von Ranke (a German exile, active in Combat and close to Altman and Georges Bidault), Institut für Zeitgeschichte, Munich, ED 161; interviews with "Lillie" Szary (1983), Maurice Pessis, Jean Bloch-Michel, Henri Falque. Also Altman, "Notre 'Narbonne.'"

This new life also made Bloch mobile again. As a regional chief he made inspection trips throughout the area, which also facilitated brief family visits.[43] Before long he also began a series of monthly journeys to Paris for meetings with the national leaders of the Comité Général d'Etudes to discuss administrative matters for the post-liberation period and also to work on the transplanted *Cahiers Politiques*.[44] Back in the capital after a three-year absence, Bloch was captivated by its late-summer beauty, the air that was fresher than the air one breathed in Lyon, and the lovely light over the Seine. Despite the *boches*, the swastika flying over the Senate, the streets stripped of auto and bus traffic, the packed metros, and the disruption of periodic *alertes*, Bloch would have stayed if he could.[45] During the next five months he made six more trips to Paris, the last one with his wife. He ate at good restaurants, went to the cinema, and gazed at his former home, now housing German officers and with an antiaircraft spotlight on the balcony. He visited his relatives and each time called on Lucien Febvre, who found him ever the same: "lucid, optimistic, active."[46] Often last-minute, dangerous, and

---

43 Bloch to Febvre, 15 Aug. 1943, AN, MI 318 1. Bloch's code expression was "travel to libraries and archives."

44 Letters from Bloch to Simonne Bloch (8, 11, 16, 20 Aug. 1943, EBC) anticipate his first Paris journey; letter from Alice Bloch to author, 22 Dec. 1982, on some of Bloch's activities.

45 Bloch to Simonne Bloch, 16 Sept. 1943, EBC, also recalled an expensive, delicious meal in a (black-market) restaurant.

46 Bloch to Simonne Bloch, 9, 26 Sept., 11, 28 Oct., 28, 30 Nov. 1943, 24 Jan., 21 Feb. 1944; Bloch to Louis and Etienne Bloch, 28 Feb. 1944, EBC. Lucien Febvre, "Marc Bloch et Strasbourg," *Combats pour l'histoire* (Paris: Armand Colin, 1953), pp. 405–6: "Je le vis plusieurs fois, pendant les mois d'angoisse, toutes les fois qu'il se rendait de Lyon à Paris, pour assister à quelque réunion centrale de son organisation. Brusquement, un soir, je recevais un coup de téléphone: 'Oui, c'est moi!...Je viendrai dîner chez vous demain, voulez-vous?' Il descendait très loin du Quartier, du côté du Père Lachaise, par prudence. Il se méfiait beaucoup des abords de la Sorbonne et de l'Ecole Normale, et j'étais le seul des hôtes de ces lieux qu'il prévint et visitât. Parfois, il me demandait de convoquer un ou deux amis, Paul Etard, Georges Lefebvre. Je le retrouvais toujours le même, lucide, optimiste, agissant. Très préoccupé des lendemains de la Libération et, en particulier, de la réforme nécessaire – non, de la *révolution* nécessaire de l'enseignement." Also Mme. Richard (Febvre's daughter) to author, May 1982. On at least two occasions Bloch slept on the divan in Febvre's study.

uncomfortable, these voyages nonetheless provided the Lyon Resistance leader with valuable human contacts, influence, information, and resolve.

Bloch was involved in a considerable amount of publication. He certainly contributed to the newspaper *Le Franc-Tireur*. With Altman he also founded and edited a new periodical, *La Revue Libre*, and produced two remarkable issues. With its scholarly structure of articles, documents, testimonies, reviews, and announcements of other Resistance publications, with its terse, biting prose and its dedication to a "revolutionary transformation of French society," the *Revue* bore Bloch's unmistakable stamp.[47] In addition, he wrote several anonymous articles for *Les Cahiers Politiques*, on the causes of the debacle of 1940,[48] on the propaganda base of Nazism,[49] on racism and elitism in the French academy,[50] on the prospects of economic and trade cooperation in the postwar world,[51] and on the need for a thorough, sweeping purge (*épuration*) after the liberation, where he insisted that the "real season of judges...will come tomorrow."[52] Even more caustic than in his scholarly prose, Bloch's outpouring reflected a more radical political orientation than had been revealed formerly. It is possible he was author, compiler, or editor of the anonymous MUR circulars that repeatedly urged

47 "Quand la liberté sera reconquise, nous nous ferons un plaisir de faire connaître au public les noms de nos collaborateurs." *La Revue Libre* 1 (Dec. 1943). The second issue appeared in February 1944. See "Recent Clandestine French Publications," 14 Jan. 1944, NARS, OSS RG 226 53747; also Veillon, *Franc-Tireur*, pp. 91–92.
48 "A propos d'un livre trop peu connu: Général Chauvineau, *Une invasion est-elle encore possible?*" *CP* 6 (Apr. 1944): 22–25.
49 "Le Dr. Goebbels analyse la psychologie du peuple allemand," *CP* 4 (Nov. 1943): 26–27.
50 "Un philosophe de bonne compagnie," *CP* 5 (Dec. 1943): 27–29.
51 "L'alimentation humaine et les échanges internationaux d'après les débats de Hot Springs," *CP* 4 (Nov. 1943): 20–25.
52 "La vraie saison des juges," *CP* 4 (Nov. 1943): 28–30, a biting review of former minister Anatole de Monzie's *La saison des juges* (Paris: Flammarion, 1943): "La France du renouveau sera une France énergique et dure, une France qui saura répudier toute solidarité avec ceux qui l'ont vendue, bernée, assassinée, qui, implacable envers les crimes du passé, ne craindra pas de continuer dans le présent, d'appliquer la rigueur de lois équitables." (p. 30). Cf. Bloch to Simonne Bloch, 22 Aug. 1943, EBC.

the mobilization of the people behind the Liberation Committees, stressing that the insurrection must occur as a "popular local uprising."[53]

In September 1943 Bloch savored two moments of elation and hope, first with the news of the Allies' amphibious landings in southern Italy, later with the Russians' recapture of Smolensk.[54] But as autumn dragged on and the days grew shorter, grayer, damper, and windier, and the cold and his solitude weighed on his spirits, Bloch succumbed to the generalized sense of lassitude spreading through occupied France, mixed with bitterness and impatience. When would liberation come?[55]

Winter brought more waiting and despair as well as mounting danger. In December 1943, in anticipation of the Allied landings and the internal insurrection, the fanatical Joseph Darnand was appointed head of the Milice. At once, in full collaboration with the Germans, Darnand unleashed a widespread brutal campaign against the Resistance.[56] As the wave of terror moved closer to Lyon, Bloch made cautious plans for an escape. He awaited his own fate with stoicism and courage, having made the necessary financial arrangements and also having alerted his wife to the scholarly work he still hoped to publish. After almost a full year in the Resistance, Marc Bloch was approaching the maximum period of danger. He knew too many people, had taken too many risks, and was too

53 Sweets, *Politics of Resistance*, p. 93.
54 Bloch to Simonne Bloch, 9, 26 Sept. 1943, EBC.
55 See esp. Bloch to Simonne Bloch, 12, 20 Nov. 1943; Bloch to Alice Bloch, 5 Dec. 1943, EBC.
56 "Darnand and the Vichy Police," 15 Jan. 1944; "The Internal Situation in France," Lisbon, 3 Mar. 1944; "Darnand Campaign against the French Resistance," 16 Mar. 1944; "The Vichy Militia," 30 Mar. 1944, NARS, OSS RG 226 62163, 73925, 62365, 66600. Himmler, "Bekämpfung der reichs-feindlichen Bestrebungen durch die deutsche Sicherheitspolizei und Folgerungen für die allgemeinen Sicherheitslage in Frankreich" (for Hitler), NARS, Germany AA T-120 712/350/262402−27; Militärbefehlshaber in Frankreich, Sicherheitspolizei (SD), 1942−44, reported the increased German arrest figures for March 1944, AN AJ 40/1632. Also Robert Paxton, *Vichy France: Old Guard and New Order, 1940−1944* (New York: Norton, 1971), pp. 297−98; Henri Noguères, *Histoire de la Résistance en France* IV (Paris: Laffont, 1976), pp. 454−55.

incautious about his own safety. Sensing the signals, he knew his arrest was imminent.[57]

On the eve of his capture Bloch thought of others, of his brave, stoic *maître*, Ferdinand Lot,[58] his former students,[59] and especially his family. He tried to console his daughter, whose work had ended when the children's home was closed, with his hopes for the future.[60] To his distant sons he expressed satisfaction with his unaccustomed, fatiguing, but necessary way of life.[61] With great reluctance he acquiesced in his son Daniel's decision to join the maquis, and set to work at once to help him. And on the morning of his arrest he asked his wife's forgiveness for "being so far away."[62]

Marc Bloch was terribly exposed. For almost two months he had been the acting head of the regional directory for Rhône–Alpes, after Malleret ("Bourdelle") had departed precipitately for Paris in early January and his replacement, Alban Vistel ("François"), was stricken with pneumonia. Now he was the veteran chief vis-à-vis the two new local leaders, Vistel and R. Blanc ("Drac") from Combat (who had replaced Peck, arrested in November). Blanc's adjunct was Jean Bloch-Michel ("Lombard"), Marc Bloch's brother's older son, whom he had earlier helped to raise. In February 1944 Bloch established a new bureau in the central part of Lyon, at 1, rue de Quatre Chapeaux (the Cordeliers Building) on the sixth floor of a needlework factory. Through a local university connection, as "M.

---

57 Bloch to Simonne Bloch, 22 Dec. 1943, 4, 10 Jan., 27, 28 Feb. 1944, EBC. One plan was to take shelter in Lucien Febvre's country home. On Bloch's premonition of "une mort horrible": Febvre, "Marc Bloch et Strasbourg," p. 406.

58 Bloch to Lot, Fougères, 29 Dec. 1943, Lot papers, IF.

59 Bloch to "Mlle.," Fougères, 30 Dec. 1943, courtesy of the recipient, Mme Monfren. After providing a two-page list of references, Bloch declined her request for a meeting, explaining, "Je mène moi-même une vie passablement nomade et vous ne me trouverez ici que par intermittences."

60 Bloch to Alice Bloch, 7, 27 Feb. 1944, EBC.

61 "Je m'efforce de servir. C'est le moins qu'on puisse faire en ce moment." Bloch to Etienne and Louis Bloch, 28 Feb. 1944, EBC.

62 "Malgré ton courage et ta raison, je t'imagine un peu troublée par toutes les décisions à prendre. Pardon d'être si loin." Bloch to Simonne Bloch (his last letter), 8 Mar. 1944, EBC. Cf. Bloch to Daniel Bloch (who turned 18 on 11 Mar. 1944), 31 Jan., 7 Feb. 1944, EBC.

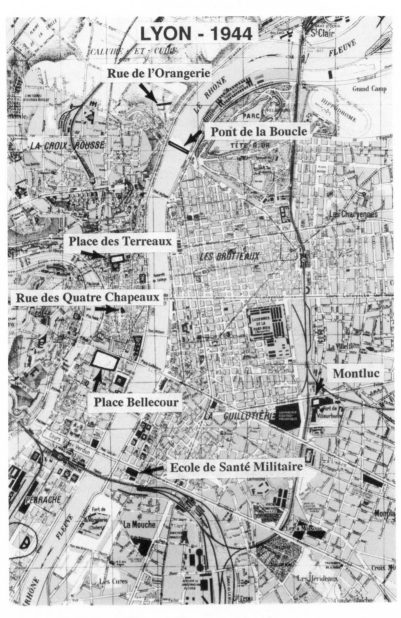

Rue de l'Orangerie

Pont de la Boucle

Place des Terreaux

Rue des Quatre Chapeaux

Montluc

Place Bellecour

Ecole de Santé Militaire

28. Center of Lyon, with principal locations

313

Blanchard" he sublet the office for his scientific work, scattering German books and scholarly papers on the premises. As "Narbonne," with his secretary and two assistants he worked diligently to keep the MUR organization sound and secure. A plenary meeting of the regional directory was set for 8 March 1944 at 3 p.m. to discuss various matters, including settling the problem of succession.[63]

The major arrests began on 7 March. That day at 12:15 p.m. "François" had arranged a meeting with "Drac" to prepare for the plenary on the eighth. When after three-quarters of an hour his Combat colleague failed to appear, Vistel sensed that something grave had occurred. Indeed, by the time he arrived at the rendezvous five key persons had been arrested by the Gestapo: "Jacqueline" (the head of the local Action Ouvrière), "Velin" (Service Propagande-Diffusion), "Bertrand" (the directory's liaison agent), "Lombard," and "Drac."[64]

An hour earlier Bloch had met "Chardon," a recent arrival from Haute-Savoie attached to Combat, who informed him of the Gestapo raid on "Drac's" office.[65] After searching for his nephew, "Lombard," who failed to appear for lunch, and for "Drac," who missed their appointment at the Place des Terraux, Bloch learned of their arrest from "Chardon," who offered to deliver "Drac's" archive to him between 5 and 5:30 p.m. Afterward Bloch dined with "Chardon" and the faithful "Maurice," and later attended a small gathering at his neighbors' in Caluire.[66]

The next morning at about eight-thirty a Gestapo car arrived in Bloch's neighborhood. Its occupants interrogated the shopkeepers

63 Vistel, *La nuit*, pp. 393–404. Bloch ("Narbonne") to Vistel, 26 Jan. 1944, Vistel papers, AN, 72 AJ 626.
64 Vistel, *La nuit*, p. 404. Vistel's file "Dossier concernant les arrestations de mars 1944 à Lyon, dont celle de Marc Bloch (Narbonne)" (AN, 72 AJ 626; hereafter Vistel, "Dossier") is the main source for these events.
65 Previously "Chardon" had worked with and was a close friend of "Poulain" (Dr. Henry Bloch-Michel), Bloch's younger nephew. "Chazaud" to "Magny" (Vistel's new pseudonym), 17 Apr. 1944, Vistel, "Dossier."
66 "Baccarat" (i.e., "Chardon") to "François," 26 Mar. 1944, "Chazaud" report, 17 Apr. 1944, in Vistel, "Dossier." Also Jean-Claude Weill to Michel Barridon, 21 Mar. 1988. (Weill, who attended the gathering, remembers greeting Bloch the next morning, minutes before his arrest.)

about an elderly resident named Blanchard. The owner of the *boulangerie* pointed them in the direction that Bloch, carrying a valise, had just followed. He was seized and arrested on the Pont de la Boucle at around nine o'clock.[67]

When "Narbonne" failed to appear for a noon appointment, his deputy, René Seyroux ("Chazaud"), spread the alarm. Full of presentiment, "François" hastily departed when neither "Narbonne" nor "Drac" materialized that afternoon for the meeting of the regional directory. "Chardon" was worried about the important papers in Bloch's possession. When Bloch's secretary "Nathalie" (Nina Morgueleff) arrived at 5 p.m. at the Cordeliers and ascended the private elevator to the sixth floor, "Chardon" and the head dressmaker, Mme. Jacotot, met her with the news of her chief's arrest. "Chardon" advised her to hide the most crucial dossiers concerning politics, finances, and Jour-J. Jacotot agreed to carry some of the archives in a valise for safekeeping with the friend who had introduced her to Bloch, Professor Florence.[68]

The next morning, 9 March, the Gestapo raided Bloch's office and announced the discovery of a receiving device and a number of incriminating documents "proving that the occupant was a member of the Resistance." The Germans also searched his lodgings. Before they arrived at his secretary's residence "Nathalie," forewarned, was able to escape. That day the Cordeliers proprietor, Mme. Brun, was arrested; in the afternoon Jacotot and Florence were seized in a café. The office and house raids continued for one week. In all there were about sixty-three arrests of key MUR personnel and its affiliated administrative, engineering, rail, postal, labor, intelligence, and military services.[69]

From Vichy on 15 March, Minister of Information Philippe Henriot announced the huge seizure of men, funds, documents, and

67 "Rapport," n.d.; "Chazaud" report, 17 Apr. 1944, Vistel, "Dossier." Marcel Fonfrede to Etienne Bloch, 11 Aug. 1987.
68 "Rapport," n.d.; "Baccarat" ("Chardon") to "François," 26 Mar. 1944; "Chazaud" report, 17 Apr. 1944, Vistel "Dossier"; Vistel, *La nuit*, p. 407. On Florence, see n. 81.
69 "Arrestations mars à Lyon," n.d.; "Extraits d'un rapport de la G."; "Copin" to "Magny," 13 Apr. 1944; "Rapport," n.d., Vistel, "Dossier." Also Noguères, *Histoire* IV, pp. 454–56.

arms and boasted that "Lyon, the capital of the Resistance, is destroyed."[70] The collaborationist press trumpeted the annihilation "by the police and the Milice" of Lyon's "nest of vipers," a group of terrorists waging a brutal civil war, disposing of 173 million francs per month, committing over three thousand attacks on Frenchmen (and scarcely eighty against the occupier), camouflaged as followers of de Gaulle but in reality slavish adherents of Moscow.[71]

Much journalistic emphasis was placed on the identity of the captured leader of the "terrorist general staff" as a "Jew who had taken the pseudonym of a French southern city."[72] In praising Laval's energetic attack on French terrorism, the *Völkischer Beobachter* stressed the point that Bloch as "chief of the assassination band," handsomely financed by London and Moscow, had provided incontrovertible evidence of National Socialist claims that the Jewish element was dedicated to destroying the other nations of Europe.[73]

Extensive and costly as they were, the March roundups did not, as Vichy's propagandists boasted, "decapitate" the Resistance. Taking the reins, Vistel at once reassured his comrades: "The Resistance continues..." On 11 March he issued a defiant public retort to Henriot's boast and to his "lies" about the underground. A hundred thousand copies of Vistel's text were distributed between 17 and 22 March, and the new regional chief moved rapidly to revive and regroup his forces.[74]

For the Germans the arrests represented a mixed accomplishment.

---

70 *L'Oeuvre*, 16 Mar. 1944; *New York Times*, 16 Mar. 1944; also Vistel, *La nuit*, pp. 405–7.

71 E.g., *Le Petit Parisien*, 16 Mar. 1944.

72 *Aujourd'hui*, 16 Mar. 1944; also *Le Matin*, 16 Mar. 1944; *Pariser Zeitung*, 16 Mar. 1944; *Paris Soir*, 17 Mar. 1944; *Journal des Débats*, 17 Mar. 1944. Another Jew, Captain Fould (who apparently had taken as a pseudonym the name of a national French leader), was also captured.

73 "Jude leitete die Mordbanden in Frankreich," *Völkischer Beobachter*, Munich ed., 18 Mar. 1944. Ambassador Abetz (to the Auswartiges Amt, Berlin) reported on 21 March that the "chief of the general staff of the French resistance movement in Lyon was a French Jew named Block [sic], whose pseudonym was Narbonne." NARS, Germany AA T-120 K1509/4668/K435470.

74 Vistel, *La nuit*, pp. 408–11; Prefect reports, 15 Mar., 14 Apr. 1944, AN, FI CIII 1200. The *chant des partisans* declared: "Friend, if you fall, a friend will step in to take your place."

Henriot's announcement underscored the Vichy regime's solidarity with the occupier in the onslaught against the Resistance, though his bombastic statement, which had not been authorized by higher officials of the ss, greatly exaggerated the roles of Darnand and Laval.[75] The raids had indeed been successful, producing extensive discoveries of local political, administrative, economic, press, labor, and counterespionage materials. On the other hand the ss and army intelligence had already obtained the basic outline of the nationwide plans for Jour-J, which they now amplified with local details. Therefore the authorities tended to regard the Lyon operation as one of a group of striking regional incidents. In fact, it exacerbated relations with the population and with local French officials without significantly reducing the level of "terrorism" on the eve of Jour-J in and around Lyon.[76]

Almost at once Vistel launched an inquiry into Bloch's capture and the decimation of the regional directory. The investigation was hindered by heavy losses, disappearances, and *fausses nouvelles*, but was also facilitated by unexpected releases and the sudden reappearance and testimony of key actors.[77] The initial suspect was the outsider "Chardon," whose organization, Combat, had been hardest hit. He had been in close contact with "Narbonne" and had dis-

75 See *Kriegstagebuch des Oberkommandos der Wehrmacht* IV (1 Jan. 1944–22 May 1945) (Frankfurt am Main: Bernard and Graefe, 1961), p. 294 ("Die französische Polizei"), for an entry referring to the radio announcement of Bloch's arrest. Also Oberkommandos der Wehrmacht, excerpts from ss report "Aushebung einer Zentralstelle der Vereinigten Widerstandsbewegungen (MUR)" (Secret), 18 Mar. 1944, Zentrales Staatsarchiv, Potsdam.

76 Hilger to Embassy Paris, Berlin, 16, 20 Mar. 1944; Abetz to AA, Paris, 18 Mar., and Pfeiffer to AA, Paris, 29 Mar. 1944, NARS, Germany AA T-120 255/234/165856, 876, 882, 915–16; Militärbefehlshaber in Frankreich (geheim): "Organisation und Pläne der Widerstandsbewegung für den Tag 'J,'" Paris, 9 Mar. 1944, Bundesarchiv/Militärarchiv, Freiburg/Breisgau, RW 35/84 (abbreviated translated copy in Vistel, "Dossier"). Aftermath in Prefect's report, 16 May 1944, AN, FI CIII 1200; Donovan memorandum to President, 16 June 1944, OSS Situation report on France, 7 June 1944, FDR Presidential Library, Hyde Park, N.Y.

77 "Vialley," released on 9 March, gave the first information that the five major leaders – "Drac," "Narbonne," "Lombard," "Jacqueline," and an unnamed fifth person ("Velin"?) – were all in Montluc prison. "Rapport," n.d., and "Arrestations mars à Lyon" in Vistel, "Dossier."

appeared immediately after his arrest. But "Chardon's" explanation appeared to be credible. The story was indeed more complicated.[78]

Bloch's arrest was apparently the result of a series of apprehensions, divulgences, and, perhaps, betrayals of the MUR, starting in the beginning of March in Paris and moving at once to Lyon.[79] Vistel's investigation led to "Chatoux," who had been responsible for the distribution of the newspaper *Combat*, knew all the leaders, and appeared to have talked after his arrest on 6 March. On the next day he was reportedly seen in a Gestapo vehicle indicating rendezvous sites. "Drac," caught on 7 March, was accused by "Lombard" of giving further information under torture. "Lombard" subsequently admitted that he had revealed his uncle's address under torture.[80] Another suspected person was Mme. Jacotot; released on 11 March, she was seen afterwards in a Gestapo car and was reportedly aware of and boastful about the activities of the distinguished elderly occupant of the sixth floor.[81] Once the Gestapo had been able to puncture a few vulnerable points, Bloch, with his distinctive combination of prudence and indifference to his personal safety, was easily caught.

After his arrest Bloch had been taken to the headquarters of the Gestapo on the avenue Berthelot, the Ecole de Santé Militaire. Directed by Klaus Barbie, this establishment had become notorious for its grim array of torture – the scorching and icy baths, beatings

78 "Chazaud" report, 17 Apr. 1944, made the accusation; "Baccarat" ("Chardon") to "François," 26 Mar. 1944, denied it, as did the testimony of "Poulain"; see "Arrestations mars à Lyon: Feuille Joint A. – 'Chardon,'" Vistel, "Dossier"; cf. Vistel, *La nuit*, p. 413.
79 "Rapport sur l'arrestations des chefs régionaux" and "Arrestations mars à Lyon: Résumé chronologique des faits," Vistel "Dossier"; also Vistel, *La nuit*, p. 403.
80 "Velin" testimony; "Rapport de Lombard après sa libération; affaire mars-début juin 1944"; Cf. "Drac" to "ex-François," 18 July 1944, Vistel, "Dossier."
81 "Arrestations mars à Lyon"; "Copin" to "Magny," 13 Apr. 1944; "Chazaud" to "Magny," 17 Apr. 1944, Vistel, "Dossier."
    Mme. Brun, the proprietor, and her other workers were eventually released. Gabriel Florence, professor in the Faculty of Medicine and Pharmacy of the University of Lyon, who had been responsible for regional medical services for the Resistance, was reportedly tortured by the Gestapo and died during his deportation. Robert Debré, *L'honneur de vivre: Témoignage* (Paris: Hermann, 1974), p. 244.

and bludgeonings – as well as the executions in the basement.[82] On the next day, after prolonged interrogation and torture Bloch was brought to Montluc prison, where he was seen by his nephew "Lombard" in a "very bad state of health." Following his second interrogation and torture, he spent four weeks in the infirmary suffering from double bronchial pneumonia and serious contusions.[83]

Bloch told the Germans nothing except his real name, perhaps in the hope of outside intervention, perhaps out of pride or a desire for better treatment. After his release from the infirmary he was interrogated twice again, on 22 and 25 May, and again refused to give information. While the Gestapo appeared to have lost interest in most of their captives, some of whom were released, a person of Bloch's stature, with his suspected ties to the CGE and other national officials, commanded special attention. Examined several times by the deputy governor of Montluc, he apparently failed to satisfy his captors.[84]

During his long agony Bloch remained calm and stoic. Less than two kilometers from the heart of Lyon, he was incarcerated in a crowded, impenetrable early-nineteenth-century military fortress which was infamous for its poor food and hygiene. To "pass the time" he resumed the role of the Sorbonne professor, teaching French history and explaining field patterns to a young *résistant*. He

82 "Lombard's" report asserted that "Narbonne" was identified at Gestapo headquarters by "Drac"; "Drac" to "ex-François," 18 July 1944, denied this (Vistel, "Dossier"). On torture at the Ecole de Santé, see NARS Suitland, translation of French Ministry of the Interior, Criminal Investigation Dept., "War Crimes": Charles Perrin report, 13 June 1950; I thank David Marwell for this document. On the French accomplices to the baths and the beatings, see "Au procès de la Gestapo lyonnaise," *Voix du Peuple* (Lyon), 18 July 1946. Also Amoretti, *Lyon capitale*, p. 306.

83 "Lombard" report, Vistel, "Dossier"; interviews, Jean Bloch-Michel; Jean Gay to Etienne Bloch, 30 Mar. 1983; deposition of Marcel Fonfrede, 6 Mar. 1984, Permanent Military Tribunal, Lyon (records concerning the case of Klaus Barbie) (hereafter PMT), EBC.

84 When the Gestapo headquarters were under bombardment on 24 May, most of the prisoners were sheltered in a cave and then returned to Montluc, but Bloch was not among them. "Lombard" (who was released at the end of May) report, Vistel, "Dossier"; interviews, Jean Bloch-Michel.

was reportedly alert to informants inside the cell.[85] With little hope of release or of escape, Bloch awaited his fate.

As the Allied invasion drew nearer, the Germans, preparing their retreat, began disposing of their mounting number of captives. Some were deported to camps in the Third Reich. But starting in April and accelerating in early June there were a series of nightly transports to isolated locations around Lyon, to avoid detection and retaliation by Resistance forces, where groups of prisoners were shot.[86]

From the new arrivals the inhabitants of Montluc learned almost at once of the 6 June Allied landings in Normandy. The long-awaited joyous tidings were transmitted from cell to cell by coded knocks on the wall. Within a few days, by the middle of June, Marc Bloch was transferred to a new cell.[87]

On the night of 16 June, at approximately eight o'clock, twenty-eight prisoners of Montluc were assembled from various cells and, handcuffed two by two, were placed in an open truck (a camionette). Escorted in the front and at the rear by cars carrying German officers and subofficers with aimed tommy guns, they were driven to the Place Bellecour, which after the May bombings had become the new main headquarters of the Gestapo. They waited in the van for about twenty minutes, during which time a drunken German officer insulted them and bragged that London was about to be destroyed by the v-1 rocket.[88]

85 "Lombard" report, Vistel, "Dossier"; interviews, Jean Bloch-Michel. Also Fonfrede deposition, and Fonfrede to Etienne Bloch, 11 Aug. 1987. Description of Montluc in Christian Pineau, *La simple vérité, 1940–1945* (Paris: R. Julliard, 1960).

86 Between the first shootings on 21 April and 6 May and the final shooting on 1 September approximately 713 prisoners were killed, only slightly fewer than the total of victims in the eight other départements of the region Rhône-Alpes: République Française, Commissariat Regional Rhône-Alpes, Memorial Lyon, 25 Sept. 1944, NARS Suitland, oss RG 266129 558. The Prefect's report, 13 July 1944 (AN, FI CIII 1200), notes that these "massive executions" had stirred "considerable emotion" among the Lyonnais.

87 Fonfrede to Etienne Bloch, 11 Aug. 1987.

88 Saint-Didier-de-Formans: testimony of Charles Perrin ("Vauban"), one of the two survivors of the 16 June shootings, "Mémorial de l'oppression," EBC (hereafter Perrin, testimony).

29. Saint-Didier-de-Formans: the field of the shootings. The memorial to the victims is in the background.

Having found its direction, the cortege made its way northward along the Saône, past Caluire, Neuville-sur-Saône, and Trévoux. A few kilometers north of Trévoux and just before the village of Saint-Didier-de-Formans, in a place called La Roussille, the truck stopped next to a meadow which was surrounded by high bushes. The two vehicles were stationed perpendicular to the truck, fifty meters in front and behind. It was approximately nine o'clock. The Germans ordered four prisoners to descend from the van. Their hands were untied and they were led through the narrow entry into the meadow from where, seconds later, came the sound of machine-gun fire. Four more were called, one of whom made a futile try to escape. Four by four they were led into the meadow and shot by four uniformed soldiers at close range until all twenty-eight had fallen. There were no cries of supplication; some of the victims called out "Vive la France!" "Adieu ma femme!" etc.[89]

The executions took between ten and twenty minutes. Then the Germans circulated among the bodies, delivering final shots to

89 "Tous montrent aux boches comment les Français savent mourir." Perrin, testimony. According to Georges Altman, Bloch, who was in the first group of four, at the last minute comforted a frightened youth with the assurance that the bullets would not hurt. Reportedly the first victim to fall, he cried out, "Vive la France!" *CP* 8 (1945): 2.

heads and the napes of necks. After destroying all pieces of identification, they hurriedly departed in the truck and two cars. The scene of the carnage was brutally chaotic – bodies resting on their backs, stomachs, or sides, and some curled up. Among them was a blind man holding his cane, another had an artificial right arm, and there was a corpse wearing the insignia of the Legion of Honor. Miraculously there were two survivors, Jean Crespo and Charles Perrin, who were able to recount the incident.[90]

The next morning the bodies were found by Marcel Pouvaret, the local schoolmaster and assistant to the mayor of Saint-Didier. The mayor called in the *gendarmerie* of Trévoux. Because none of the victims could be identified, the police summoned forensic authorities from Lyon, who proceeded to photograph, fingerprint, and gather scraps of evidence from the twenty-six corpses. Then the bodies were placed in coffins and buried in Saint-Didier.[91]

Bloch's disappearance in March 1944 had naturally produced alarm. His closest colleague, "Maurice," trusting Bloch's strength and composure, did not flee and, learning of his agony, tried unsuccessfully to free him.[92] After finding shelter for the two youngest children, Marc Bloch's wife and daughter came to Lyon to search for him. Already ill with an undiagnosed stomach cancer, Simonne Bloch survived her husband by less than a month without recognizing his photograph. Bloch's brother-in-law Arnold Hanff, who had been arrested at almost the same time in Limoges, was killed by the Germans in the mass shootings at Brantôme on 26 March 1944 after digging his own grave. His wife Jeanne was

---

90 Crespo and Perrin depositions, 31 Jan., 2 Feb. 1946, PMT, VI-1/30/6, 9.
91 "Cahier No. 7: 28 [sic] cadavers découverts à St. Didier-de-Formans (Ain) le 17 juin 1944"; "Copie du rapport no. 29/2, 31 Oct. 1944, de la brigade de gendarmerie de Trévoux"; Pouvaret testimony, 27 Jan. 1946, PMT VI/30/3, 8.
92 Interviews with Maurice Pessis. Altman, "Notre 'Narbonne,'" pp. 1–2, relates the reaction of Bloch's friends and Resistance comrades when they learned the news of his torture: "[He was] bleeding from the mouth (this blood-stained gash in place of that mischievous smile he had last bestowed me on a street corner just before the horror had occurred). . . . 'he was bleeding.' The tears of rage leapt to our eyes."

deported and died at Auschwitz.[93] Sometime after it was deserted in May 1944, the Bloch home in Fougères was occupied and pillaged, presumably by communist partisans. The furniture remained, but many precious private belongings disappeared.[94]

Lucien Febvre, who had learned of Bloch's arrest from one of their colleagues, spread the word prudently in Paris.[95] At first he hoped Bloch might have been deported to Germany. But Febvre was also one of the first to learn, through another reliable contact, about the shootings at Saint-Didier. Lyon was finally liberated on 3 September 1944 by American, Free French, and Resistance forces. Soon afterwards Febvre made a melancholy solo journey there to seek information about his missing friend.[96]

Two months later, in early November 1944, Bloch's death was officially established when his daughter Alice and his sister-in-law Hélène Weill finally identified his personal effects: his spectacles,

93 Simonne Bloch died on 2 July 1944 at age fifty after surgery in a Lyon hospital (certificate no. 1998, 3d arrondissement, signed by the mayor), and she was buried in a common grave. Interviews, Alice Bloch (1982), Jean Bloch-Michel. Also Gabriel Fournier, "Nécrologie: Marc Bloch (1886–1944)," *Mémoires de la Société des Sciences Naturelles et Archéologiques de la Creuse* (1945): 289. Hanff: Alice Bloch to author, 22 Dec. 1982; "Nos martyrs," *La Marseillaise du Centre* (regional organ of the MLN, formerly MUR), 30 Sept. 1944.

94 Hélène Weill to Febvre, 18 Oct. 1944, AN, MI 318 1.

95 Rist, *Saison gâtée*, p. 398 (entry 3 Apr. 1944).

96 Febvre had learned of Bloch's arrest from Albert Bayet. Member of the editorial committee of *Le Franc-Tireur* and Bloch's colleague and occasional rival, Bayet was a former *normalien* and Sorbonne professor as well as a radical activist and journalist in the 1930s. Suspended from his position after the armistice, he had taken refuge in the unoccupied zone where he met Altman and collaborated on several Resistance newspapers. Veillon, *Franc-Tireur*, passim; interview with Henri Falque.

   It was from Pierre Abraham, their former collaborator on the *Annales*, that Febvre learned of the 16 June shootings. One of Abraham's friends knew a survivor (either Crespo or, more likely, Perrin), who testified that among the group of victims was "an elderly, gray-haired, short man, with gold-rimmed glasses, called 'Marcel Blanchard' and who was a professor at the Sorbonne." Febvre (not knowing of her death) to Simonne Bloch, 23 July 1944, EBC; Febvre to "Monsieur le Secrétaire General," n.d. (ca. Oct. 1944), AN, MI 318 1.

pieces of his jacket and tie, the three decorations he always wore, and the incontrovertible evidence of his fingerprints.[97] From a France now almost entirely freed from German occupation came the tragic news of the slaying of a noble historian, teacher, soldier, and patriot. For his children, three of whom were still in arms, it was an even more terrible loss.[98]

97 Weill to Febvre, 30 Sept. 1944, AN, MI 318 1; "Marc Bloch (Narbonne)," *Lyon Libre*, 1 Nov. 1944; interview, Alice Bloch.
98 Etienne Bloch to Alice Bloch, 17 Nov. 1944. EBC.

12. The Legacy

The good historian resembles the ogre in the fairy tale. Whenever he scents human flesh he recognizes his prey.[1]

Behind the euphoria over France's liberation and the Allied victory in May 1945 lay a somber picture of considerable human loss, a shattered economy and paralyzed transportation system, and, in violent reaction against the four years of Vichy rule, a widespread purge (*épuration*) of collaborators. Under the provisional government led by de Gaulle and by former Resistance leaders that ruled France until October 1946 there was some significant social and economic legislation. But there was also bitter conflict between Resistance forces and the traditional parties as well as between the left and the right over France's political future.[2]

As France took count of the victims, Marc Bloch's heroic death was mourned and honored at home and abroad.[3] There were eulogies

---

1 *AH*, p. 35.
2 Jean-Pierre Rioux, *The Fourth Republic, 1944–1958*, trans. G. Rogers (Cambridge: Cambridge University Press, 1987), pp. 3–94; Jean-Jacques Becker, *Histoire politique de la France depuis 1945* (Paris: Armand Colin, 1988), pp. 5–40; also Herbert R. Lottman, *The Purge: The Purification of French Collaborators after World War II* (New York: Morrow, 1986).
3 See, e.g., M. M. Postan, "Marc Bloch: An Obituary Note," *Economic History Review* 14, no. 2 (1944): 161–62; "Hommage à Marc Bloch," read on 5 May 1945 to the Société d'Histoire et d'Archéologie, Nîmes; Charles Parain, "Marc Bloch," *La Pensée* 6 (Jan.–Mar. 1946): 65–72; Georges Friedmann, "Au delà de 'l'engagement': Marc Bloch, Jean Cavaillès," *Europe* 10 (Oct. 1946): 24–46; G. I. Brătianu, "Un savant et un soldat: Marc Bloch (1886–1944)" (Communication à l'Institut d'Histoire Universelle 'N. Iorga,' Bucharest), *Revue Historique de Sud-Est Européen* 23 (1946): 5–20; Faculté des Lettres de l'Université de Strasbourg, *De l'université aux camps de concentration: Témoignages strasbourgeois* (Paris, 1947).

in the press, an official memorial ceremony in the great amphitheater of the Sorbonne, and special commemorative articles in *Les Cahiers Politiques* and in the resurrected *Annales d'Histoire Sociale*.[4] In recognition of his lost collaborator Febvre published the text of Bloch's course on the Germanic invasions and also his contribution to the historical debate on the origins of modern France – subjects of considerable pertinence – in the *Annales* and in the *Revue de Synthèse*.[5]

In 1946 Franc-Tireur published Marc Bloch's long-hidden testimony of the fall of France under the title *L'étrange défaite*. It contained a moving preface by Georges Altman, with details of "Narbonne's" life and death in the Resistance. At that moment it was an act of homage to release a text that was painful and difficult for most Frenchmen who had newly recovered their freedom to absorb, but in time *L'étrange défaite* became one of Bloch's most durable and accessible works. Appreciation of his historical insight has been demonstrated by the subsequent editions and translations, and particularly by the numerous citations of *L'étrange défaite*. Scholars have adopted this title, which Bloch himself had not given it, to depict one of modern France's greatest catastrophes.[6] Bloch's posthumous presence was thus established early in the postwar period as

4 *Hommage solennel de l'Université et de la Résistance à la mémoire de Marc Bloch*, 26 June 1944; *Le Monde*, 26 June 1944; *CP* 8 (Mar. 1945): 1–11. The two volumes of *AHS* (1945) were subtitled "Hommages à Marc Bloch."

5 "Marc Bloch: Reliquiae. Les invasions: Deux structures économiques" and "Les invasions: Occupation du sol et peuplement," *AHS* (1945), "Hommages" – I: 33–46; "Hommages" – II: 13–28; "Sur les grandes invasions: Quelques positions de problèmes," *Revue de Synthèse* 60 (1945): 55–81.

6 See, e.g., John C. Cairns, "Some Recent Historians and the 'Strange Defeat' of 1940," Journal of Modern History 46 (1974): 60–85.

There have been an English edition in 1949, a second French edition (which included the 1941 testament and several clandestine articles) in 1957, an American edition in 1968, an Italian edition in 1970, and a Japanese edition, but up to now no German edition.

Significant reviews and scholarly discussion: David Thomson in *International Affairs* 23 (1947): 413; Aldo Garosci in *Rivista Storica Italiana* 71 (1959): 163–69; Gordon Wright in *AHR* 63 (1958–59): 487; Elvira Gencarelli, "Bloch e la testimonianza storica," *Quaderni del Movimento di Liberazione in Italia* (Apr.-June 1971): 99–114. Also Anthony Cheal Pugh, "Defeat May 1940: Claude Simon, Marc Bloch, and the Writing of Disaster," *Forum of Modern Language Studies* 21, no. 1 (Jan. 1985): 59–70.

both a savant and a martyr: a pioneering scholar, brave soldier, and acerbic critic of the Third Republic, but also one of a handful of French professors who had sacrificed their lives for *la patrie*.

The Fourth Republic, which began functioning in 1947 – a largely unpopular compromise regime tinged with party rivalries and bureaucratic ossification reminiscent of the Third – lasted only eleven years. In the shadow of the Cold War, France receded from its former role of major power. Its economic accomplishments and remarkable population growth were counterbalanced by foreign-policy and colonial defeats and by the deficiencies of its fragmented leadership. On the other hand, during this politically frustrating decade France retained and even increased its distinction in the arts, humanities, and social sciences, and slowly laid the groundwork for a modern, democratic "polyculture."[7]

In another "world in ruins," bereft of his younger friend and collaborator and burdened by a host of suspended projects, Febvre was nevertheless determined to continue the *Annales*. To meet the challenges of the atomic and global age, he gave the journal a new format and a new, more expansive title: *Annales: Economies, Sociétés, Civilisations*.[8] Febvre gathered his younger colleagues Fernand Braudel, Georges Friedmann, and Charles Morazé onto the journal's *comité de direction* and added a group of new collaborators with diverse horizons. At age sixty-eight Febvre plunged into a decade of renewed struggle to serve humanity accented by a rekindled combative tone that declared "our history the real history."[9] If the first postwar meeting of the International Congress of Historical Sciences in Paris in 1950 signaled a victory for Febvre and his followers, it was also a tribute to the absent and honored Marc Bloch.[10]

7 Gordon Wright, *France in Modern Times*, 3d ed. (New York: Norton, 1981), pp. 420–33; Rioux, *Fourth Republic*, passim, esp. chaps. 18, 19.

8 Depending on one's perspective, the removal of history from the title meant either its triumph in incorporating the other social sciences or that it itself had dissolved. François Dosse, *L'histoire en miettes: Des "Annales" à la "nouvelle histoire"* (Paris: Editions la Découverte, 1987), pp. 96, 118.

9 Lucien Febvre, "Face au vent: Manifeste des *Annales* nouvelles," *AESC* 1, no. 1 (Jan.–Mar. 1946): 1–8.

10 Karl Dietrich Erdmann, *Die Ökumene der Historiker: Geschichte der Internationalen Historikerkongresse und des Comité International des Sciences Historiques* (Göttingen: Vandenhoeck and Ruprecht, 1987), pp. 265–98.

30. Lucien Febvre (1878–1956)

Among the most striking developments in postwar France was the proliferation of private, governmental, and international support for research. In contrast to the 1930s, when Bloch and Febvre commanded relatively meager resources for their projects, history after World War II joined the spectacularly expanding social, biological, and physical sciences as the object of generous subventions. To be sure, these created intense rivalries among individuals and disciplines as well as a proliferation of institutions, and were no doubt also a political and ideological component in the struggle for academic power.[11]

A new direction in French historiography was set in 1947 by the founding of a new institution, the Sixth Section (of Economic and Social Sciences) of the Ecole Pratique des Hautes Etudes. The Sixth Section was linked firmly to history, and to the *Annales*, through the efforts of Febvre's energetic trio Braudel, Friedmann, and (especially) Morazé, who obtained funds from the Rockefeller Foundation as well as government approval of their project over stiff competition from the social scientists. Here was a new generation, trained in the 1920s and early 30s, blocked by the Depression and tempered by the Second World War, now eager to take the helm. Febvre, who had little to do with the preliminary negotiations, agreed to become the Section's first president. Morazé established the Marc Bloch Association to collect and channel private funding into its teaching, research, and publications. Led by scholars affiliated with the *Annales*, the Sixième Section became an important institutional base for the postwar journal. As a non-degree-granting graduate school in economic and social history and the social sciences, it was to some extent the fulfillment of Bloch and Febvre's earlier hopes for interdisciplinary collaboration between historians and social scientists.[12]

Bloch's personal legacy expanded when two of his former students, Robert Boutruche and Philippe Dollinger, published articles re-

---

11 Cf. Brigitte Mazon, "Fondations américaines et sciences sociales en France: 1920–1960" (thèse de 3e cycle, Ecole des Hautes Etudes en Sciences Sociales, 1985); also Frédéric Blancpain, "La création du CNRS: Histoire d'une décision," *Bulletin de l'Institut International d'Administration Publique* 34 (1974): 99–143; Robert F. Arnove, *Philanthropy and Cultural Imperialism: The Foundations at Home and Abroad* (Boston: G. K. Hall, 1980); Alain Drouard, "Réflexions sur une chronologie: Le développement des sciences sociales en France de 1945 à la fin des années soixante," *Revue Française de Sociologie* 23 (1982): 55–85.

12 Febvre, "Vingt ans après," *AESC* 4 (Jan.–Mar. 1949): 1–3; Mazon, "Fondations américaines," pp. 110–31, 232–56; Giuliana Gemelli, "La VI Sezione dell' 'Ecole Pratique des Hautes Etudes' e l'unificazione delle scienze economico-sociali in Francia," *Inchiesta* (Jan.-June 1984): 129–44.

counting his immense contributions as a teacher.[13] The esteemed scholar and Resistance hero was now also celebrated as a brilliant, devoted *maître*. Behind the meticulously organized courses, rigorous standards, and occasionally caustic criticism was a man who had lavished time, respect, and encouragement on novice historians almost until the end of his life. Bloch's protégés, who, dispersed in many different research fields and teaching positions, made their own notable contributions, have provided a prodigious tribute to his efforts and inspiration. Among them were André Deléage,[14] François Chevalier, Michel Mollat, Robert Folz, Robert Boutruche, Henri Brunschwig, Philippe Dollinger, Pierre Goubert, and the American doctoral student William Mendel Newman,[15] as well as the two devoted young colleagues he never taught, Philippe Wolff and Charles Morazé.

Bloch's achievements as a scholar were also recognized, especially his important contributions to historical geography and rural history.[16] In the first concise intellectual biography, published in 1948, Charles-Edmond Perrin, Bloch's former colleague at Strasbourg and Paris, detailed Bloch's innovative methods and praised his extensive oeuvre.[17] And from younger scholars then taking their places in the profession came words of appreciation for Bloch's

---

13 Philippe Dollinger, "Notre maître Marc Bloch: L'historien et sa méthode," *Revue d'Histoire Economique et Sociale* 27 (1948–49): 109–26; Robert Boutruche, "Marc Bloch vu par ses élèves," in *Mémorial des années 1939–1945*, Publications de la Faculté des Lettres de l'Université de Strasbourg (Paris: Belles Lettres, 1947), pp. 195–207.

14 Who died in December 1944 during the last German offensive in the Ardennes.

15 Who, despite his difficulties with Bloch as a teacher, respected him as a scholar of medieval and economic history and was saddened by his death. Newman diary, 26 Mar. 1947, 14 Feb., 4 Apr. 1948, courtesy of Professor Giles Constable, Institute for Advanced Study, Princeton, N. J.

16 Henri Baulig, "Marc Bloch: Géographe," *AHS* (1945), "Hommages" – II: 5–12; G. Debien, "Marc Bloch and Rural History," *Agricultural History* (July 1947): 187–89.

17 "L'oeuvre historique de Marc Bloch," *RH* 199, no. 2 (1948): 161–88. Perrin (to Carl Stephenson, 31 Jan. 1948, Stephenson papers, Cornell University, Ithaca, N. Y.) mentions the long delay in its publication, caused by Perrin's heavy responsibilities at the Sorbonne.

human and scholarly accomplishments and his enduring influence.[18]

Bloch's oldest son, Etienne, who gave up an early interest in history to become a judge and writer on human rights issues and penal reform, devoted himself to his father's legacy. He gave Febvre the bulk of Bloch's uncompleted manuscripts as well as his teaching and research notes. Through his and Febvre's efforts, the unfinished *Apologie pour l'histoire* finally appeared in 1949, arousing as strong admiration for the man as for his historical creed.[19] Despite its truncated presentation, it has become Bloch's most famous work, now in its seventh French edition and with translations into Italian, Portuguese, English, German, Russian, Czech, Polish, Hungarian, and Japanese.[20] Etienne Bloch was also instrumental in the publication of a new edition of *Les caractères originaux de l'histoire rurale française* in 1952, supplemented in 1956 by a second volume derived from his father's notes and edited by a former student.[21]

18 See, e.g., Philippe Ariès, "L'histoire existentielle" (1949), *Le temps de l'histoire* (Monaco: Editions de Rocher, 1954), pp. 291–311; also Giuliano Procacci, "Marc Bloch," *Belfagor* (1952): 662–75; I. S. Kon and A. D. Ljublinskaja, "Raboty francuzskogo istorika M. Blocha," *Voprosy Istorii* 8 (1955): 147–59.
19 "Marc Bloch fut un héros et je tiens à honneur qu'il m'ait jugé digne de son estime et son amitié." Georges Lefebvre in *RH* 210 (July–Sept. 1953): 94.
20 Lucien Febvre, "Vers une autre histoire," *Combats pour l'histoire* (Paris: Armand Colin, 1953), pp. 419–38. Other significant reviews include: Dennis Hay in *English Historical Review* 65 (1950): 384–87; Beatrice F. Hyslop in *AHR* 55 (1950): 866–68; R. Franchini in *Lo Spettatore Italiano* 5 (1951): 128–31; G. Giannantoni in *Rassegna di Filosofia* 2 (1952): 182–83; Jean Stenghers in *AESC* 8 (1953): 329–37; Michael Kraus in *Journal of American History* 40 (1954): 721–22; A. J. P. Taylor in *New Statesman and Nation*, 5 June 1954.

Important introductions: František Graus, "Doslov," *Obrana historie aneb historik a jeho řemeslo* (Prague: Nakladatelstvi Svoboda, 1967); Friedrich J. Lucas, "Einleitung für den deutschen Leser," *Apologie der Geschichte oder der Beruf des Historikers* (Stuttgart: Klett, 1974); and A. Gurevich, "Marc Bloch i 'Apologija istorii,'" postface to *Apologija istorii ili remeslo istorika*, 2d ed. (Moscow: Nauka, 1986).

Massimo Mastrogregori, "Nota sul testo dell' 'Apologie pour l'histoire' di Marc Bloch," *Rivista di Storia della Storiografia Moderna* 7, no. 3 (1986): 5–32 gives details on the editorial difficulties and shortcomings.
21 There were also English, Spanish, Italian, and Russian translations. See Lucien Febvre, "Une nouvelle contribution de Marc Bloch à l'histoire rurale de la France," *AESC* 11 (Oct.–Dec. 1956): 499–501, and A. D. Ljublinskaja,

Less fortunate was Febvre's decision to publish Bloch's course material on European monetary history from the end of the Roman empire, *Esquisse d'une histoire monétaire de l'Europe* (1954), not aimed at an audience of specialists but meant to provide beginning students with Bloch's introduction to the basics. Less than one hundred pages of incomplete, disjointed lecture notes, the *Histoire monétaire* contained flashes of Bloch's insight and his skillful and provocative framing of such problems as the character and consequences of monetary mutations. But as an act of fealty it was marred by haphazard organization, insufficient annotation, and a few errors.[22]

On the tenth anniversary of Bloch's death, in 1954, Febvre kept the flame of remembrance alive with memorial articles in the *Annales* and in the press. But, as he admitted, the craft of history as manifested in the new *Annales* had changed significantly.[23] World conditions had also moved well beyond Marc Bloch's experience. In 1954 the French army in Indochina was surrounded at Dien Bien Phu, and the insurrection began in Algeria. In the wake of Stalin's death new reformist forces had emerged in Russia and Eastern Europe that would lead two years later both to Khrushchev's denunciation of the long, brutal dictatorship and to the Soviet repression in Poland and Hungary. The French left was baffled and demoralized, while French moderates would be shaken by the debacle at Suez and the deepening conflict in Algeria that eroded the fragile authority of the Fourth Republic.[24]

In the tense autumn of 1956, on 26 September, Lucien Febvre

"Préface à l'édition russe des *Caractères originaux de l'histoire rurale française*," *AESC* 14 (Jan.–Mar. 1959): 92–105. Also reviews in *Journal of Economic History* 17 (1957): 85–86 (French edition); and *Economic History Review* N.S. 20 (1967): 411–12; *Journal of Economic History* 27 (1967): 400–1; *Agricultural History* 42 (1968): 279–80; *The Historian* 30 (1968): 254–55 (U.S. edition).

22 Lucien Febvre, "Deux mots d'explication," in Bloch, *Esquisse d'une histoire monétaire de l'Europe* (Paris: Armand Colin, 1954). Criticism in *Economic History Review* 9 (1956): 158; *Journal of Economic History* 16 (1956): 243–44; *English Historical Review* 72 (1957): 727. There was an Italian translation in 1975.

23 Lucien Febvre, "Marc Bloch: Dix ans après," *AESC* 8 (1954): 145–47. See *Combat*, 16 June 1954 (articles by Lucien Febvre, Fernand Braudel, Ernest Labrousse, Claude Delmas, and Minister of National Education André Marie); also, *Le Figaro Littéraire*, 12 June 1954; *Le Franc-Tireur*, 16 June 1954.

24 Rioux, *Fourth Republic*, chap. 14; Becker, *Histoire politique*, pp. 55–72.

died at age seventy-eight of a heart attack at his beloved country home in Le Souget. In his last days he was still fully active with his research and writing, direction of the Sixth Section and the *Annales*, and a long list of influential editorial and administrative posts.[25] Febvre had devoted over a half-century to history. While not neglecting economic and social history, he had made his chief contributions to the history of culture, ideas, and psychology. During the twelve years following Marc Bloch's death, Febvre, with his energy and leadership, had overcome their old demons, German historicism and French positivism, had forged a measure of cooperation with the burgeoning social sciences, and had secured for the *Annales* an influential place in French historical scholarship.[26]

Febvre's place at the head of the *Annales* and of the Sixth Section of the Ecole Pratique des Hautes Etudes was assumed by his protégé and friend Fernand Braudel (1902–1985), author of the acclaimed doctoral thesis *La Méditerranée et le monde méditerranéen à l'époque de Philippe II*.[27] Conceived under Febvre's influence before World War II, written largely without notes or documents during Braudel's five-year captivity in a German prisoner-of-war camp, and first published in 1949 (the year of *Apologie pour l'histoire*), *La Méditerranée* signaled a new direction. It was a departure not only from chronological and

25 Elected member of the Académie des Sciences Morales et Politiques, Febvre at the time of his death was also president of the committee of the revived *Encyclopédie*, of the historical section of the Centre National de la Recherche Scientifique (CNRS), vice-president of the Fondation Nationale des Sciences Politiques, president of the Comité d'Histoire de la Seconde Guerre Mondiale, director of the "Cahiers d'histoire mondiale" published by UNESCO, and director of the collection "Destins du monde." Robert Mandrou, "Lucien Febvre, 1878–1956," *Revue Universitaire* 66 (1957): 3–7.

26 Fernand Braudel, "Lucien Febvre, 1878–1956," *AESC* 11, no. 3 (July-Sept. 1956): 289–91; Charles Morazé, "Lucien Febvre et l'histoire vivante," *RH* 217 (1957): 1–19. Also *Eventail de l'histoire vivante: Hommage à Lucien Febvre* (Paris: Armand Colin, 1953); Hans-Dieter Mann, *Lucien Febvre: La pensée vivante d'un historien* (Paris: Armand Colin, 1971); Guy Massicotte, *L'histoire problème: La méthode de Lucien Febvre* (Saint-Hyacinthe: Edisem; Paris: Maloine, 1981).

27 Braudel, "Les *Annales* continuent..." *AESC* 12, no. 1 (Jan.-Mar. 1957): 1–2. See in the special issue of the *Journal of Modern History* devoted to Braudel (44 [Dec. 1972]): Braudel, "Personal Testimony," pp. 448–67; H. R. Trevor-Roper, "Fernand Braudel, the *Annales*, and the Mediterranean," pp. 468–79; J. H. Hexter, "Fernand Braudel and the *Monde Braudellien*..." pp. 480–539.

fact-based history but also from problem-oriented history, to a history directed primarily toward understanding the "long duration": a total, or global, history with vast scope and comprehensive approach. Braudel's world, unlike Marc Bloch's, divided historical time into "short," "medium," and "long" durations and also tended to denigrate the act and the individual.[28]

Braudel had been a major collaborator in the post-1945 resurgence of the *Annales*. Named director of the Sixième Section's Centre de Recherches Historiques, in 1949 he was elected to the chair of modern civilization at the Collège de France and also appointed to the influential post of *président du jury d'agrégation d'histoire* (the chair of the history section of the national program of teacher certification). At fifty-four Braudel was not only heir apparent to Febvre but a distinguished personage himself, with disciples who applied his principles to specific countries and to the regions of France.[29]

Two years after Febvre's death, in 1958, Charles de Gaulle returned to power and founded the Fifth Republic. Within four years he was able to extricate France from the costly and divisive Algerian conflict. Until 1968 Gaullist France produced an expanding economy bolstered by membership in the Common Market, regained its prestige in international affairs, and maintained its stature in intellectual and cultural domains. French structuralism became a dominant force in a variety of disciplines, and the debate over its impact and usefulness made Paris once again one of the world's foremost and "heated incubators of ideas."[30]

Braudel's tenure as head of the *Annales* paralleled this brilliant decade. Continuing in many of Febvre's offices and missions and maintaining the old struggle with the social sciences, Braudel in 1963 obtained a Ford Foundation grant and funding from the Min-

28 "Down with occurrences, especially vexing ones! I had to believe that history, destiny, was written at a much more profound level." Braudel, "Personal Testimony," p. 454. Cf. review by Febvre of *La Méditerranée, RH* 203 (1950): 217; also Bernard Bailyn, "Braudel's Geohistory – A Reconsideration," *Journal of Economic History* 11 (1951): 277–82; Braudel in *AESC* 13 (1958): 725–53.

29 Dosse, "Braudel le bâtisseur," *L'histoire*, pp. 105–38; F. Roy Willis, "The Contribution of the *Annales* School to Agrarian History: A Review Essay," *Agricultural History* 52, no. 1 (Oct. 1978): 543–46.

30 Wright, *France*, p. 473.

istry of National Education for the establishment of a Maison des Sciences de l'Homme, to group research units of the "human sciences" under one roof. In 1966 *La Méditerranée* was reissued in a revised and expanded format, soon to be translated into several languages. The *Annales'* themes and methods influenced scholarship in Western and Eastern Europe as well as in North America.[31]

Now at the helm of a prestigious establishment, Braudel always saw himself as a humble successor. He insisted that the "decisive stage" in the *Annales*, the creative development that had laid the groundwork for its postwar victory, had taken place in his young adulthood, between 1929 and 1940. Crediting his elders with the triumph of a "new history," Braudel wrapped Bloch and Febvre in an aura of classic rebellion against the French academic establishment, and also saw them as model partners whose long collaboration had produced the journal's variety and elegance. Without enemies or a companion, Braudel proceeded serenely to carve out his own niche and produced his multivolume history of capitalism in the preindustrial world between the fifteenth and the eighteenth century.[32].

Like Febvre, Braudel was committed to keeping Marc Bloch's name alive, though he admittedly had only limited first-hand acquaintance with the man.[33] A new edition of *Les rois thaumaturges*

---

31 Traian Stoianovich, *French Historical Method: The 'Annales' Paradigm* (Ithaca, N. Y.: Cornell University Press, 1976), pp. 43–46.

32 *Civilisation matérielle et capitalisme, XVe-XVIIIe siècle* (Paris: Armand Colin, 1967); *Civilisation matérielle, économie et capitalisme, XVe-XVIIIe siècle*, 3 vols. (Paris: Armand Colin, 1979).

Braudel, "Personal Testimony," pp. 461–67, and foreword to Stoianovich, *French Historical Method*, pp. 10–13.

Also John Day, "Fernand Braudel and the Rise of Capitalism," *Social Research* 47 (Autumn 1980): 507–18; M. Aymard, "Fernand Braudel," in *Dictionnaire des sciences historiques* (Paris: Presses Universitaires de France, 1986), pp. 98–101.

33 "Unfortunately, I scarcely knew Marc Bloch personally, having seen him only three times in Paris in 1938 and 1939." Braudel, "Personal Testimony," p. 464; interview with Braudel, 1983. Also Braudel, "1944–1964: Marc Bloch," *AESC* 19 (Sept.–Oct. 1964): 833–34, and "Marc Bloch," *International Encyclopedia of the Social Sciences* II (New York: Macmillan and Free Press, 1968), pp. 93–95; related correspondence in AN, MI 318 1, 476–86.

was issued in 1961; foreign translations followed. But Braudel perhaps unwisely decided to publish two fragments based on Bloch's former courses at Strasbourg and at the Sorbonne: *La France sous les derniers Capétiens (1223–1338)* (1958) and *Seigneurie française et manoir anglais* (1960). Critics appreciated these reminders of Marc Bloch's acute vision and probing questions but doubted the scientific value of such uneven, partially outdated elementary surveys.[34]

More successful was the 1963 publication of the *Mélanges historiques*, a two-volume collection of Bloch's major articles with an illuminating preface by Perrin and a seventy-two-page bibliography.[35] Forty-two pieces were grouped under nine headings that Bloch himself had established for his bibliography in 1934 when he had been a candidate at the Collège de France: history and historians; societies of the High Middle Ages; feudal institutions; serfdom in European society; Germany and the Holy Roman Empire; rural life; historical geography; history of economy and technology; and aspects of the medieval mentality. The *Mélanges* gathered in one place scattered works, key ideas, and a clear demonstration of Marc Bloch's "lucid and complex intelligence, his vast and profound knowledge, and his extraordinary working capacity."[36] Out of the *Mélanges* came a number of translations, making Bloch's important essays accessible to a larger audience.[37]

In the mid-sixties, the springtime of social history and the social sciences, Marc Bloch's reputation expanded. If his contributions as a medievalist underwent specific correction and revision, he was still considered the forerunner of modern scholarship in economic and

---

34 "To read a work by Marc Bloch and gain little from it!" Review by David Herlihy of *La France sous les derniers Capétiens, 1223–1328* in *Journal of Economic History* 19 (1959): 622; similar reviews of *Seigneurie française* in *Speculum* 36 (1961): 459–60; *English Historical Review* 77 (1962): 135.

35 (Paris: S.E.V.P.E.N., 1963). There is considerable correspondence between Etienne Bloch and Perrin on this publication in EBC.

36 Review by Virginia Rau in *Journal of Economic History* 24 (1964): 390–91; see also R. H. Hilton in *English Historical Review* 80 (1965): 345–48.

37 English: *Land and Work in Medieval Europe: Selected Papers by Marc Bloch*, trans. J. E. Anderson (Berkeley and Los Angeles: University of California Press, 1967), and *Slavery and Serfdom in the Middle Ages: Selected Essays by Marc Bloch*, trans. William R. Beer (Berkeley and Los Angeles: University of California Press, 1975); Hungarian: *A Történelem Védelmében* (Budapest: Gondolat, 1974).

rural history, in comparative history, and in the history of *mentalités*. On the twentieth anniversary of his death, his former colleagues and students honored him by following his example and critically evaluating the present status of his scholarly conclusions.[38] Historians outside France recognized Marc Bloch's remarkable spirit, methods, and contributions.[39] Journals modeled on the *Annales*, such as *Past and Present* (founded in 1952) and the *Journal of Social History* (founded in 1966), testified to its international prestige. Its history entered European intellectual history, with emphasis on Bloch's erudition and the extraordinary scholarly and temperamental symbiosis he had forged with Febvre, which between the two world wars had given "new unity to the study of man."[40]

The events of May – June 1968, when French workers and students demonstrated together against the Gaullist republic, shook the general's strength and authority and led eventually to his resignation. Under his successors Georges Pompidou and Valéry Giscard d'Estaing, France moved away from Gaullist grandeur and independence to a more flexible multiparty state and a more European orientation. There was a wave of reforms, especially in education, where, for example, the once monolithic Sorbonne was divided into smaller, more decentralized units.[41]

38 B. Guenée, "Marc Bloch vingt ans après," *Bulletin de la Faculté des Lettres de l'Université de Strasbourg* 43 (1964–65): 419–20. Also see Henri Brunschwig, "Vingt ans après (1964): Souvenirs sur Marc Bloch," later published in *Etudes Africaines: Offertes à Henri Brunschwig* (Paris: Editions de l'Ecole des Hautes Etudes en Sciences Sociales, 1982), pp. xiii–xvii.

39 See, e.g., Bryce Lyon, "The Feudalism of Marc Bloch," *Tijdschrift voor Geschiedenis* 76 (1963): 275–83; Carlo Ginzburg, "A proposito della raccolta dei saggi storici di M. Bloch," *Studi Medioevali* (1965): 335–53; Felix Gilbert, "Three Twentieth Century Historians: Meinecke, Bloch, Chabod," in John Higham, Leonard Krieger, and Felix Gilbert, *History* (Englewood Cliffs, N. J.: Prentice-Hall, 1965), pp. 359–81; R. R. Davies, "Marc Bloch," *History* 52 (Oct. 1967): 267–82; William H. Sewell, Jr., "Marc Bloch and the Logic of Comparative History," *History and Theory* 6, no. 2 (1967): 208–18; Oscar Mourat, *Marc Bloch* (Montevideo: Faculted de Humanidades y Ciencias, 1969).

40 An influential work on Bloch, Febvre, and the *Annales* was H. Stuart Hughes, *The Obstructed Path: French Social Thought in the Years of Desperation* (New York: Harper and Row, 1966), chap. 2. A German parallel to the *Annales*, *Geschichte und Gesellschaft*, was founded in 1975.

41 Becker, *Histoire politique*, pp. 122–29.

In 1968 the sixty-six-year-old Braudel stepped down from his directorship of the *Annales*, turning the journal over to a trio of younger specialists in medieval, modern, and contemporary history. From 1969 onward, the *Annales* had a larger format, more emphasis on contemporary history and societies, more discussion of related methodologies (linguistics, semiotics, comparative mythology, anthropology, and climatology), and special numbers devoted to major historical and interdisciplinary themes. This "third-generation" *Annales* was led by a small, relatively homogeneous group of historians, gifted, ambitious, and self-confident, whose entry into the profession had been facilitated by Febvre and Braudel's triumphs. The most notable example was Emmanuel Le Roy Ladurie, Braudel's successor in the chair of modern civilization at the Collège de France, who in his two-volume thesis, *Les paysans de Languedoc* (1966), had examined all aspects of a regional peasant society from the Middle Ages to the Enlightenment as a protoype of the economic transformation of France and Europe.[42]

Success was represented in physical terms as well. In 1970 the new multistory steel and glass headquarters of the Maison des Sciences de l'Homme opened its doors at 54, boulevard Raspail on the premises of the former prison of Cherche Midi (where Dreyfus was once tried), which had been demolished in 1961. Under Braudel's presidency the Maison brought together a large number of scholarly activities. The building housed the offices of the *Annales* as well as the Sixième Section, which as a result of the post–de Gaulle reforms in 1975 became an independent doctoral-granting institution: the Ecole des Hautes Etudes en Sciences Sociales.[43]

In the 1970s, an "*Annales* school" of history, centered on the journal and the Ecole, was firmly entrenched in Paris and was also being exported.[44] Now only loosely associated with Bloch and Febvre

---

42 John Day, foreword to the English edition, *The Peasants of Languedoc*, trans. John Day (Urbana: University of Illinois Press, 1974), pp. ix–xii; also Emmanuel Le Roy Ladurie, *Le territoire de l'historien* (Paris: Gallimard, 1973), and *Paris-Montpellier: P.C.-P.S.U., 1945–1963* (Paris: Gallimard, 1982); François Furet, "Beyond the *Annales,*" *Journal of Modern History* 55, no. 3 (Sept. 1983): 389–94; Stoianovich, *French Historical Method*, pp. 40–61.

43 Mazon, "Fondations américaines," pp. 199–231. The Marc Bloch Association was dissolved in 1984 (pp. 255–56).

44 Fernand Braudel, "Les 'nouvelles' *Annales,*" AESC 24 (May–June 1969): 1.

(whose scholarship had become increasingly outdated), "*Annales* history" tended to desert its old mainstays of agricultural history, technology, geography, and economics and moved in two directions: toward minute analysis of material and social life, using linguistics, demography, and quantification; and toward explorations of popular consciousness, utilizing anthropology, popular culture, and the study of *mentalités*. Comparative history had largely disappeared along with Febvre's special treatment of the history of ideas.

Braudel, who stepped down from his directorship of the Ecole in 1972, continued to preside over the Maison. Until his death in 1985 he remained France's most illustrious historian, although he was not without critics.[45] The younger *Annalistes* renounced his "total" canvas and his emphasis on material life for French regional and village studies and for such themes as sexuality and death. The highly visible, well-financed *Annales* school attracted admirers and imitators, but also critics, who deplored the disintegration (*émiettement*) of Bloch and Febvre's unified vision of history, complained about its jargon and obscure microstudies, and noted the discrepancy between its scholarly and institutional activism and its political conservatism.[46]

45 See Geoffrey Parker, "Braudel's 'Mediterranean': The Making and Marketing of a Masterpiece," *History* 59 (1974): 238–43; "Fernand Braudel (1902–1985)," *AESC* (Jan.–Feb. 1986): 3–6; Olwen Huften, "Fernand Braudel," *Past and Present* no. 112 (Aug. 1986): 208–13; cf. H. Kellner, "Disorderly Conduct: Braudel's Mediterranean Satire," *History and Theory* 2 (1979): 197–222; S. Kinser, "Capitalism Enshrined: Braudel's Triptych of Modern Economic History," *Journal of French Studies* 16 (1979): 419–23, and "*Annales* Paradigm: The Geo-Historical Structuralism of Fernand Braudel," *AHR* 86 (1981): 63–105. In 1977 a Fernand Braudel Center for the Study of Economies, Historical Systems, and Civilizations was inaugurated at the State University of New York at Binghamton under the direction of Braudel's disciple Immanuel Wallerstein, with a journal, *Review*, inspired in part by Braudel's work.

46 The vast literature on the *Annales* school includes: Manfred Wüstemeyer, "Die 'Annales': Grundsätze und Methoden ihren 'neuen Geschichtswissenschaft,'" *Vierteljahrsschrift für Sozial- und Wirtschaftsgeschichte* 58 (1971): 1–45; Dieter Groh, "Structurgeschichte als 'totale' Geschichte?" ibid., pp. 289–322; Maurice Aymard, "The 'Annales' and French Historiography," *Journal of European Economic History* 1 (1972): 491–511; Volker Rittner, "Ein Versuch systematischer Aneignung von Geschichte: Die 'Schule der Annales,'" in Immanuel Geiss and Rainer Tamchina, eds., *Ansichten einer künftigen Geschichtswissenschaft* 1 (Munich: Hansen, 1974), pp. 153–72; Georg Iggers, "Die 'Annales' und ihre Kritiker: Probleme moderner französischer Sozialgeschichte," *Historische Zeit-*

The period of consolidation of the *Annales*, which brought international renown to boulevard Raspail, also created a cottage industry of its own history, culminating in the journal's half-century celebration in 1979: Exhibitions, conferences, and publications revived the memory of the two founders.[47]

In the *Annales'* triumphant age Marc Bloch was transformed from a living presence into a distant, honored elder, routinely praised for

schrift (1974): 578–608; Claudia Honegger, "Geschichte im Entstehen: Notizen zum Werdegang der *Annales*," in Claudia Honegger, ed., *Marc Bloch, Fernand Braudel, u.a.* (Frankfurt: Suhrkamp, 1977); M. Cedronio, F. Diaz, and C. Russo, *Storiografia francese di ieri e di oggi* (Naples: Guida, 1977); Robert Forster, "Achievements of the *Annales* School," *Journal of Economic History* 38 (Mar. 1978): 58–76; Richard Elmore, "View from the Rive Gauche: A Comment on *Annales* Historiography," *Psychohistory Review* 7 (Fall 1978): 30–35; J. Stephen Hazlett, "The New History and French Schooling," *History of Education Quarterly* 18 (Fall 1978): 323–47; M. Harsgor, "Total History: The 'Annales' School," *Journal of Contemporary History* 13 (1978): 1–13; M. Erbe, *Zur neueren französischen Sozialgeschichtsforschung: Die Gruppe um die 'Annales'* (Darmstadt: Wissenschaftliche Buchgesellschaft, 1979); Immanuel Wallerstein, "The *Annales* School: The War on Two Fronts," *Annals of Scholarship* 1, no. 3 (Summer 1980): 85–91; I. N. Afanas'ev, "Evoliutsiia theoreticheskikh osnov shkoly 'Annalov,'" *Voprosy Istorii* 9 (1981): 77–92; and esp. papers at the Inaugural Conference of the Fernand Braudel Center for the Study of Economies, Historical Systems, and Civilizations: "Impact of the *Annales* School on the Social Sciences," SUNY Binghamton, 12–15 May 1977, published in *Review* 1, nos. 3–4 (1978).

47 Paul Leuilliot, "Aux origines des 'Annales d'histoire économique et sociale' (1928), Contribution à l'historiographie française," in *Mélanges en l'honneur de Fernand Braudel* II (Toulouse: Privat, 1979): 317–24; Jacques Revel, "Histoire et sciences sociales: Les paradigmes des *Annales*," *AESC* (Nov.–Dec. 1979): 1360–76; André Burguière, "Histoire d'une histoire: La naissance des *Annales*," ibid., pp. 1347–59; F. Ruiz Martin, "El cincuentenario de '*Annales* E. S. C.,'" *Rivista Española de Investigaciones Sociologicas* 12 (1980): 9–14; Georges Huppert, "Lucien Febvre and Marc Bloch: The Creation of the *Annales*," *French Review* 4 (1982): 510–13. See also: the collection entitled *La nouvelle histoire* (Les Encyclopédies du savoir moderne) (Paris: Retz, 1978); "Lucien Febvre (1878–1956)," exhibition, BN, Nov. 1978, "Marc Bloch, 1886–1944," exhibition catalogue, Ecole des Hautes Etudes en Sciences Sociales (May 1979); and the proceedings of a colloquium in honor of the *Annales'* half-century, held in Strasbourg, 11–13 Oct. 1979, which were published in *Au berceau des Annales*, eds. Charles-Olivier Carbonell and Georges Livet (Toulouse: Presses de l'Institut d'Etudes Politiques de Toulouse, 1983).

his personal courage and tough-minded erudition, and still occasionally revised and corrected by scholars.[48] It was natural that a man formed before World War I had become increasingly remote to historians of the last third of the twentieth century, with their new training and techniques, their new subjects such as women's history, and their politically charged debates over the treatment of the Holocaust and the history of the Third Reich. Bloch had nonetheless never lost his special place as a national hero. To a modernizing France, now also coming to terms with the realities of its own Vichy past, he remained the unswerving patriot and tragic sacrifice. Thirty-three years after his death, in 1977, there was a reburial ceremony in the Creuse, which was attended by representatives of the University system, the Resistance, and the government. Bloch's testament was read for the first time by his oldest surviving student, Henri Brunschwig.[49]

The victory of socialist presidential candidate François Mitterrand in 1981 paradoxically sent France in a more conservative direction. The immediate euphoria accompanying the establishment of France's first leftist regime in a half-century was followed by a revival of traditionalism – economic, diplomatic, political, and also cultural. With new attention throughout Western societies devoted to celebrating national heritages and mainstream values and, in history, to the resurrection of traditional subjects and narrative, the *Annales* school has paid the price of its earlier success. The widespread triumph of its social history and its history of mentalities led

48 See preface by Georges Duby to 7th ed. of *Apologie pour l'histoire* (Paris: Armand Colin, 1974); R. C. Rhodes, "E. Durkheim and the Historical Thought of Marc Bloch," *Theory and Society* 5, no. 1 (1978): 45–73; Lawrence Walker, "A Note on Historical Linguistics and Marc Bloch's Comparative Method," *History and Theory* 2 (1980); 154–64; Elizabeth A. R. Brown, "The Tyranny of a Construct: Feudalism and Historians of Medieval Europe," *AHR* 79 (Oct. 1974): 1063–88; James A. Henretta, "Social History as Lived and Written," *AHR* 84 (Dec. 1979): 1293–1322; "Marc Bloch and Comparative History" (article and reply by Arlette Hill and Boyd Hill; comments by William H. Sewell and Sylvia L. Thrupp), *AHR* 85 (Oct. 1980): 828–57.
49 That year the first full-length study of Franc-Tireur detailed Bloch's contributions: Dominique Veillon, *Le Franc-Tireur: Un journal clandestin, un mouvement de Résistance 1940–1944* (Paris: Flammarion, 1977).

almost inevitably to fragmentation, competition, and challenges.[50]

With the natural erosion of its unity and leadership has come a relative decline of the school's singularity and influence. Its championship of the poor, powerless, and inarticulate, its interdisciplinary bent, and heavy emphasis on structure and method have diminished. Indeed, some of the main spokesmen have abandoned the semblance of a unified mission and moved on to more conventional subjects and methodology.[51] There is discussion of the "return to the event," to descriptive and narrative history, and even to biography.[52] This group that for so long withstood criticism from both the left and the right for its avoidance of the great subjects of modern and contemporary history, for its failure to treat short-term crises or confront the centrality of politics in human affairs, has increasingly lost its hold on the center because of its prolonged indifference to questions of power, conflict, and change.[53]

Marc Bloch's reputation has not been diminished by the eclipse of his spiritual grandchildren. His life, work, and relationship with

50 Guy Bourdé and Hervé Martin, *Les écoles historiques* (Paris: Editions du Seuil, 1983); Hervé Coutau-Bégarie, *Le phénomène 'Nouvelle Histoire': Stratégie et idéologie des nouveaux historiens* (Paris: Economica, 1983); A. J. Gurevich, "Medieval Culture and Mentality According to the New French Historiography," *Archives Européennes de Sociologie* 24 (1983): 167–95; Lynn Hunt, "French History in the Last Twenty Years: The Rise and Fall of the *Annales* Paradigm," *Journal of Contemporary History* 21 (Apr. 1986): 209–24; Hartmut Kaelble, "Sozialgeschichte in Frankreich und der Bundesrepublik: Annales gegen historische Sozialwissenschaften?" *Geschichte und Gesellschaft* 13, no. 1 (1987): 77–93.

51 Jacques Revel, "The *Annales*: Continuities and Discontinuities," *Review* 1 (1978): 9–18; Furet, "Beyond the *Annales*," pp. 389–410.

52 Lawrence Stone, "The Revival of Narrative: Reflections on a New Old History," *Past and Present* no. 85 (1979): 3–24; reply by Eric Hobsbawm, "The Revival of Narrative: Some Comments," ibid. 86 (1980): 3–8; Barrie M. Ratcliffe, "The Decline of Biography in French Historiography: The Ambivalent Legacy of the 'Annales' Tradition," *Western Society for French History: Proceedings* 8 (1980): 556–67; M. Moretti, "Parlando di 'eventi': Un aspetto del dibattito storiografico attorno alle 'Annales' dal secondo dopoguerra ad oggi," *Società e Storia* 6 (1985): 373–442.

53 For two contrasting but parallel criticisms, see Elizabeth Fox-Genovese and Eugene D. Genovese, "The Political Crisis of Social History: A Marxist Perspective," *Journal of Social History* 10 (Winter 1976): 205–19; and Gertrude Himmelfarb, *The New History and the Old* (Cambridge: Harvard University Press, 1987), chaps. 1, 2, 5.

342

Febvre have remained subjects of considerable scholarly interest.[54] Since 1978 the Ecole des Hautes Etudes en Sciences Sociales has, with its annual Marc Bloch lecture, invited some of the world's most distinguished savants to speak in Paris in his honor. In 1983 *Les rois thaumaturges* was again reissued, with a long preface by the medievalist Jacques Le Goff emphasizing Bloch's important contribution to political history.[55] In June 1986 the centenary of his birth was commemorated with a three-day international colloquium at the Ecole Normale Supérieure, which was co-sponsored by the Ecole des Hautes Etudes en Sciences Sociales and the German Historical Institute of Paris, whose director was the prolific medievalist Karl Ferdinand Werner (a student of Bloch's former student Robert Boutruche). There were also centenary celebrations for Marc Bloch in Venezuela and in the United States.[56]

Now there is a fuller, more balanced picture of Marc Bloch. Based on newly available private letters and other documents as well as fresh analysis of his environment, Bloch has to a great extent been liberated from the *Annales* mystique and has spoken in his own

54 See, e.g., John Cannon, "Marc Bloch," *The Historian at Work* (London: Allen and Unwin, 1980), pp. 121–35; Peter Rutkoff and William Scott, "Letters to America: The Correspondence of Marc Bloch, 1940–41," *French Historical Studies* (1981): 277–303; Eugen Weber, "About Marc Bloch," *American Scholar* 51 (1981–82): 73–82; Ivana Holzbachovai, "Marc Bloch – Historie jako skutečnost a jako věda," *Československy Časopis Historicky* 30 (1982): 426–47; A. S. Hodonov, "Marc Bloch v sovetskoy istoriografii," *Voprosy vseobschei istorii i istoriografii* (Tomsk: Izolatel'stvo Tomskogo Universiteta, 1982) pp. 122–29; Pier Luigi Orsi, "La storia delle mentalità in Bloch e Febvre," *Rivista di Storia Contemporanea* (1983): 370–85; André Burguière, "La notion de 'mentalités' chez Marc Bloch et Lucien Febvre: Deux conceptions, deux filiations," *Revue de Synthèse*, no. 111 (July 1983): 333–48; John Day, "The History of Money in the Writings of Marc Bloch," in *Problems of Medieval Coinage in the Iberian Area* II, ed. Mário Gomes Marques and M. Crusafont I Sabater (Aviles, 1986), pp. 15–27.

55 "Histoire: Le grand air de Marc Bloch. Un entretien avec Jacques Le Goff," *Le Nouvel Observateur*, 26 Aug. 1983. Also, new ed. of *Les caractères originaux de l'histoire rurale française* (Paris: Armand Colin, 1988) with preface by Pierre Toubert.

56 Commemorative sessions in the United States were presented at the Southern Historical Association in November 1986 and the American Historical Association in December 1986.

voice.[57] Scholars have examined his Jewish identity and its relationship to his role in the Resistance. Bloch's fervent patriotism, imbued with a traditional attachment to reason and a modern appeal to democracy, distinguished him from Frenchmen and Jews who sought, and still seek, to separate peoples along lines of blood.[58]

Not simply the co-founder of the wave of "new history," Marc Bloch has emerged as a shrewd, courageous respondent to broad, universal questions that were raised in the first half of this century, questions he answered with the unity of his work and his life, in messages that remain ever pertinent and eloquent. It is not surprising that one of Bloch's foremost disciples is the brilliant, courageous Polish medievalist Bronislaw Geremek, author of several important works on the poor and marginal in the Middle Ages, who is also the principal intellectual advisor to Solidarity leader Lech Walesa. Prevented by the Warsaw police from attending the centenary ceremony for Marc Bloch, Geremek delivered a message that linked their convictions: "One can die for Danzig."[59]

57 See Carole Fink, "Marc Bloch: The Life and Ideas of a French Patriot," *Canadian Review of Studies in Nationalism* 10 (Fall 1983): 235–52; Daniel Chirot, "The Social and Historical Landscape of Marc Bloch," in Theda Skocpol, ed., *Vision and Method in Historical Sociology* (Cambridge: Cambridge University Press, 1984), pp. 22–46; Marleen Wessel, "De persoonlijke factor: Nieuw licht op Marc Bloch en Lucien Febvre," *Skript: Historisch Tijdschrift* 7, no. 4 (Dec. 1985): 251–63; Bryce Lyon, "Marc Bloch: Did He Repudiate *Annales* History?" *Journal of Medieval History* 11 (1985): 181–91; and Natalie Zemon Davis, "History's Two Bodies," *AHR* 93 (Feb. 1988): 18–30.

58 See David Diamont, *Combattants, héros et martyrs de la Résistance* (Paris: Editions Renouveau, 1984); *Les Juifs dans la Résistance et la Libération* (Paris: Editions du Scribe, 1985); *The Jews in Modern France*, ed. F. Malino and B. Wasserstein (Hanover, N. H.: University Press of New England, 1985); Jean-Pierre Rioux, "Marc Bloch, historien, combattant," in *Visages de la Résistance* (La liberté de l'esprit, no. 16) (Lyon: La Manufacture, 1987).

In the literature critical of Bloch's adherence to a nonaccepting France, see Leo Trepp, "Marc Bloch Seen in Jewish Perspective," *Conservative Judaism* 25, no. 3 (Spring 1971): 64–74, which judged Bloch's renunciation of the Kaddish at his own funeral and his sacrifice for the *patrie* "futile and without meaning."

59 Roger Chartier, "Geremek: 'On peut mourir pour Dantzig,'" *Libération*, 20 June 1986. Geremek's speech, the eighth Marc Bloch lecture sponsored by the Ecole des Hautes Etudes en Sciences Sociales, entitled "Marc Bloch, historien et résistant," was read in his enforced absence in Warsaw by Jacques Le Goff on 17 June 1986. Text published in *AESC* (Sept.–Oct. 1986): 1091–1105.

Marc Bloch was a gifted, diligent, rigorous, and innovative historian, able to range over a vast terrain of human experience in its social and physical context. He formulated basic, often timely historical questions, and while acknowledging the limits of his sources (and his own resources), he achieved an extraordinary level of historical understanding on subjects ranging from agricultural production, money and finance, and technological change, to rural society, feudal relationships, and royal power.

History was no doubt a political subject for Marc Bloch. He entered the profession at a specific time and with an implicit conviction which grew and evolved throughout his life. From the start he was committed to supplanting French positivism and German historicism not with the flat theoretical formulations of the social sciences that sacrificed the unique aspects of historical inquiry for technical elegance, but with a vibrant human history. Bloch's fascination with and support of the auxiliary sciences stopped short of surrendering to the pan-scientific ideal, just as his indebtedness to and emulation of a host of erudite historian *maîtres* could not prevent him from shattering venerable boundaries of time, space, and methodology. To be a comparative historian – his own label under which he presented himself unsuccessfully to the Collège de France – enabled Marc Bloch to become a new kind of historian: to see the back as well as the front of things, to see reality in its unruly fullness, to grapple with permanence as well as with change.

Bloch was an assimilated Jew of the Third Republic, of capitalist and imperialist Western Europe, who experienced at first hand two

---

Rescued as a child from the Warsaw ghetto, Geremek after the war became a Marxist, but resigned from the Polish Communist party in 1968 in protest against the invasion of Czechoslovakia. In 1980 he offered his services to the striking Gdansk (Danzig) miners, after the crackdown in 1981 spent long periods in detention and prison, and continues to function as an activist intellectual.

A student of medieval social history, his publications include: *Le salariat dans l'artisanat parisien aux XIII–XV siècles* (Paris: Mouton, 1968); *Les marginaux parisiens aux XIV et XV siècles* (Paris: Flammarion, 1976); *Truands et misérables dans l'Europe moderne* (Paris: Gallimard, 1980) as well as "Men without Masters: Marginal Society during the Pre-Industrial Era," *Diogenes* 98 (Summer 1977): 28–54.

world wars, bolshevism, fascism, and militant anti-Semitism. His mental world ranged over hundreds of years and several continents, landscapes, and tongues. He was a patriot who loved France and a relentless cosmopolitan who measured its history and achievements against the wider world. He was a rationalist keenly aware of the power and ubiquitousness of irrational forces. Despite the omnipresence and utility of myths, Bloch fought mythmaking all his life, not only because it distorted reality but also because it served arbitrarily, and often vainly, to preserve the status quo in ways that primarily benefited the powerful.

As a historian Bloch applied reason to the understanding of the process of change in human affairs: all kinds of change both from within and without, not following any prescribed pattern, accompanied by an insistent and amazing human capacity for adaptation, and discernible through critical and comparative investigation. This was a liberal's creed, infused with an exuberant tension that valued the process as much as the end product.[60] Bloch had the gift of presenting reality both as movement and stillness.[61] He had shunned a life of pure erudition. Like the fairy-tale ogre, he had pursued human life throughout the ages, in its various roles, activities, groups, and environments. Faithful to "the science of change," the historian had gained understanding and mastery of the present and had helped shape the future.

Bloch's personal reality was infused with the historian's insights, experience, and accomplishments. There were many parts to his identity: son, husband, and father; teacher, editor, and researcher; Jew, Frenchman, and European. If his private world was fairly traditional, his scholarly life was bold and inventive. In the persona of "Narbonne," Marc Bloch entered history itself, wrestling the angel who stands guard over the age-long quest for knowledge and self-knowledge. Perhaps he won.

60 "To paraphrase Péguy, the good husbandman takes as much pleasure in plowing and sowing as in the harvest." *AH*, p. 30.
61 "Bloch's work constituted a privileged moment in historical practice [which mastered] the conflicting claims of spatial and temporal, substantive and theoretical, structural and dynamic." Fox-Genovese and Genovese, "Political Crisis," p. 208.

Appendix: Selected Bibliography of
Marc Bloch's Publications

Included here are all of Bloch's books and the majority of his articles, but only a small sampling of his reviews, which number in the hundreds. Within each section, each category of publication – books, articles, reviews – is arranged in chronological order. An almost complete list is in Vol. II of Bloch's *Mélanges historiques* (Paris: S.E.V.P.E.N., 1963).

The first twelve sections are those Bloch himself established for his bibliography in his application to the Collège de France in 1934.

Entries with an asterisk were published posthumously; only *L'étrange défaite* was complete and intended for publication.

I. ROYALTY

Les rois thaumaturges: Etude sur le caractère surnaturel attribué à la puissance royale, particulièrement en France et en Angleterre (Strasbourg, 1924; Paris, 1961, 1983). English trans. *The Royal Touch* (London and Montreal, 1973).

Review of Fritz Kern, *Gottesgnadentum und Widerstandsrecht im früheren Mittelalter: Zur Entwicklungsgeschichte der Monarchie*, in *RH* 138 (1921): 247–53.

Review of H. Mitteis, *Die deutsche Königswahl*, and P. Schramm, *Geschichte des englischen Königtums im Lichte der Krönung*, in *AHS* 2 (1940): 143–45.

2. SOCIETIES OF THE HIGH MIDDLE AGES

*La France sous les derniers Capétiens (1223–1328) (Paris, 1958).

"L'organización de los dominios reales Carolingios y las teorias de Dopsch," *Anuario de Historia del Derecho Español* 3 (1926): 89–119.

"La société du haut moyen âge et ses origines," *Journal des Savants* (1926): 403–20.

*"Les invasions: Deux structures économiques," *AHS* (1945), "Hommages à Marc Bloch" – I: 33–46.

347

*"Occupation du sol et peuplement," *AHS* (1945), "Hommages à Marc Bloch" – II: 13−28.
*"Sur les grandes invasions: Quelques positions de problèmes," *Revue de Synthèse* 60 (1945): 55−81.
Review of G. des Marez, *Le problème de la colonisation franque et du régime agraire dans la Basse-Belgique*, in *RSH* 42 (1926): 93−99.
Review of Erna Patzelt, *Die fränkische Kultur und der Islam*, in *AHES* 5 (1933): 399−400.
Review of J. R. Strayer, *The Administration of Normandy under Saint Louis*, in *AHES* 6 (1934): 196−97.
Review of Henri Pirenne, *Mahomet et Charlemagne*, in *AHES* 10 (1938): 25−30.
Review of G. Espinas, *Les origines de l'association*, in *MHS* 5 (1944): 100−6.

3. "FEUDAL" INSTITUTIONS

La société féodale, vol. 1: *La formation des liens de dépendance* (Paris, 1939); vol. 2: *Les classes et le gouvernement des hommes* (Paris, 1940). English trans. *Feudal Society*, 2 vols. (London, 1961).
Seigneurie française et manoir anglais (Paris, 1960).
"Les formes de la rupture de l'hommage dans l'ancien droit féodal," *Nouvelle Revue Historique de Droit Français et Etranger* 36 (1912): 141−77.
"M. Flach et les origines de l'ancienne France," *RSH* 31 (1920): 150−52.
"Feudalism: European," *Encyclopedia of the Social Sciences* VI (1931), pp. 203−10.
"The Rise of Dependent Cultivation and Seignorial Institutions," *The Cambridge Economic History of Europe* (Cambridge, 1941), I, chap. VI, pp. 224−77.

4. CLASSES AND GROUPS IN MEDIEVAL SOCIETY

Rois et serfs: Un chapitre d'histoire capétienne (Paris, 1920).
"Blanche de Castille et les serfs du chapitre de Paris," *Mémoires de la Société de l'Histoire de Paris et de l'Ile-de-France* 38 (1911): 224−72.
"Serf de la glèbe: Histoire d'une expression toute faite," *RH* 136 (1921): 220−42.
"Les 'colliberti': Etude sur la formation de la classe servile," *RH* 157 (1928): 1−48, 225−63.
"Un problème d'histoire comparée: La ministérialité en France et en

Allemagne," *Revue Historique de Droit Français et d'Etranger* ser. 4, 7 (Jan.–Mar. 1928): 46–91.

"Liberté et servitude personnelles au Moyen Age, particulièrement en France," *Anuario de Historia del Derecho Español* 10 (1933): 19–115.

"De la cour royale à la cour de Rome: Le procès des serfs de Rosny-sous-Bois," *Studi di storia e diritto in onore di E. Besta* (Milan, 1939), II, pp. 149–64.

Review of Henri Pirenne, *Les villes du Moyen Age*, in *Revue Critique d'Histoire et de Littérature* (1928): 203–6.

Review of G. I. Brătianu, *Recherches sur "Vicina" et "Cetatea Alba,"* in *AHES* 8 (1936): 107–8.

Review of Peter von Váczy, *Die erste Epoche des Ungarischen Königtums*, in *RH* 177 (1936): 187–88.

5. GERMANY AND THE HOLY ROMAN EMPIRE

"L'empire et l'idée d'empire sous les Hohenstaufen," *Revue des Cours et Conférences* 60 (1929): 481–94, 577–89, 759–68.

Review of Georg von Below, *Der deutsche Staat des Mittelalters*, vol. 1, in *RH* 128 (1918): 343–47.

"Bulletin historique: Histoire d'Allemagne. Moyen Age" (review essays), *RH* 158 (1928): 108–58; 163 (1930): 331–73; 164 (1930): 134–60; 169 (1932): 615–55; 170 (1932): 61–101; (with C.-E. Perrin) 181 (1937): 405–58; 184 (1938): 79–112, 146–90.

Review of P. Ernst Schramm, *Kaiser, Rom, und Renovation*, in *Revue Critique d'Histoire et de Littérature* (1931): 9–11.

Review of G. Dumézil, *Mythes et Dieux des Germains*, in *RH* 188 (1940): 274–76.

Review of F. Markmann, *Zur Geschichte des Magdeburger Rechtes*, in *MHS* 6 (1944): 123–24.

6. GREAT BRITAIN

"La vie de saint Edouard le Confesseur, par Osbert de Clare, avec Introduction sur Osbert et les premières vies de saint Edouard," *Analecta Bollandiana* 41 (1923): 1–131.

*"La structure politique et sociale de la Grande-Bretagne: Leçons professées au Centre d'Etudes Européennes de l'Université de Strasbourg en 1940–41 [1942]," *Bulletin de la Faculté des Lettres de l'Université de Strasbourg* 32, no. 5 (Feb. 1954): 191–206; no. 6 (Mar. 1954): 233–58; no. 7 (Apr. 1954): 281–90.

Review of W. Stubbs, *Histoire constitutionnelle de l'Angleterre*, vol. III, in *Le Moyen Age* 29 (1928): 72–76.

Review of W. A. Morris, *The Medieval English Sheriff to 1300* and *The Early English County Court*, in *Le Moyen Age* 29 (1928): 76–78, 343–44.

Review of F. M. Powicke, *Medieval England, 1066–1485*, in *AHES* 5 (1933): 418–19.

Review of Elie Halévy, *Histoire du peuple anglais au XIX siècle. Epilogue (1895–1914)*, vol. II: *Vers la democratie sociale et vers la guerre (1905–1914)*, in *AHES* 5 (1933): 430–31.

Review of Eileen Power and Michael Postan, *Studies in English Trade in the Fifteenth Century*, in *AHES* 6 (1934): 316–18.

Review of H. R. Trevor-Roper, *Archbishop Laud: 1573–1645*, in *MHS* 1 (1942): 110.

7. ITALY

"Une expérience historique: La Sardaigne médiévale," *AHES* 10 (1938): 50–52.

Review of Gino Luzzato, *La commenda nella vita economica dei secoli XIII e XIV con particolare riguardo a Venezia*, in *AHES* 8 (1936): 110–11.

Review of Roberto Lopez, *Storia delle colonie genovesi nel Mediterraneo*, in *MHS* 1 (1942): 114–15.

8. RURAL LIFE

Les caractères originaux de l'histoire rurale française (Oslo, 1931; Paris, 1952, 1988). English trans. *French Rural History: An Essay on Its Basic Characteristics* (Berkeley and Los Angeles, 1970).

*Vol. II: *Supplément établi d'après les travaux de l'auteur*, by Robert Dauvergne (Paris, 1956).

"La lutte pour l'individualisme agraire dans la France du XVIIIe siècle," *AHES* 2 (1930): 329–83; 511–43; 543–56.

"Le problème des régimes agraires," *Bulletin de l'Institut Français de Sociologie* (1932): 45–92.

"Les plans cadastraux de l'ancien régime," *MHS* 3 (1943): 55–70.

Review of G. G. Coulton, *The Medieval Village*, in *Revue Critique d'Histoire et de Littérature* (1926): 281–83.

9. REGIONAL STUDIES AND PROBLEMS OF HISTORICAL GEOGRAPHY

L'Ile-de-France: Les pays autour de Paris (Paris, 1913). English trans. *The Ile-de-France: The Country around Paris* (Ithaca, N.Y., 1971).

"Cerny ou Serin?" *Annales de la Société Historique et Archéologique du Gâtinais* 30 (1912): 157−60.

Review of Lucien Febvre, *Histoire de Franche-Comté*, in *RSH* 28 (1914): 354−56.

Review of Lucien Febvre, *La terre et l'évolution humaine*, in *RH* 145 (1924): 235−40.

Review of Albert Demangeon and Lucien Febvre, *Le Rhin*, 2 vols., in *AHES* 5 (1933): 85−87; 7 (1935): 505−6.

Review of André Deléage, *La vie rurale en Bourgogne jusqu'au début du XIe siècle*, in *MHS* 2 (1942): 45−55.

10. DIVERSE PROBLEMS OF ECONOMIC HISTORY
[includes inventions]

Aspects économiques du règne de Louis XIV (Paris: Les Cours de Sorbonne, 1939).

*Esquisse d'une histoire monétaire de l'Europe (Paris, 1954).

"Technique et évolution sociale. A propos de l'histoire de l'attelage et celle de l'esclavage," *RSH* 41 (1926): 91−99.

"La force motrice animale et le rôle des inventions techniques," *RSH* 43 (1927): 83−91.

"Le problème de l'or au Moyen Age," *AHES* 5 (1933): 1−34.

"Le salaire et les fluctuations économiques à longue période," *RH* 173 (Jan.−June 1934): 1−31.

"Avènement et conquêtes du moulin à eau," *AHES* 7 (1935): 538−63.

"Economie-nature ou économie-argent: Un pseudo-dilemme," *AHS* 1 (1939): 7−16.

Review of J. H. Clapham, *An Economic History of Modern Britain: The Early Railway Age, 1820−1850* in *RSH* 44 (1927): 157−59.

Review of J. Rutkowski, *Histoire économique de la Pologne avant les partages*, in *AHES* 1 (1929): 147−50.

Review of Henri Hauser, *Les débuts du capitalisme*, in *RSH* 47 (1929): 112−13.

Review of A. Payton Usher, *A History of Mechanical Inventions*, in *AHES* 3 (1931): 278−79.

Review of E. F. Heckscher, *Der Merkantilismus*, in *AHES* 6 (1934): 160–63.
Review of Fritz Rörig, *Mittelalterliche Weltwirtschaft*, in *AHES* 6 (1934): 511–12.

11. SEVERAL ASPECTS OF THE MEDIEVAL MENTALITY

"Saint Martin de Tours: A propos d'une polémique," *Revue d'Histoire et de Littérature Religieuse* 7 (1921): 44–57.

"La vie d'outre-tombe du roi Salomon," *Revue Belge de Philologie et d'Histoire* 4 (1925): 349–77.

Review of Ernest Tonnelat, *La chanson des Niebelungen*, in *RH* 151 (1926): 256–59.

Review of Johann Huizinga, *Herbst des Mittelalters*, in *Bulletin de la Faculté des Lettres de l'Université de Strasbourg* 7 (1928–29): 33–35.

Review of E. Faral, *La légende arthurienne*, in *RSH* 51 (1931): 95–111.

Review of Guy de Tervarent, *La légende de sainte Ursule*, in *RH* 171 (1933): 626–28.

Review of Lucie Varga, *Das Schlagwort vom "finsteren Mittelalter,"* in *RH* 170 (1932): 345.

12. PROBLEMS OF METHOD AND ORGANIZATION OF WORK: HISTORY AND HISTORIANS

Critique historique et critique du témoignage (Amiens, 1914), reprinted in *AESC* 5 (Jan.–Mar. 1950): 1–8.

Projet d'un enseignement d'histoire comparée des sociétés européennes (Strasbourg, 1933).

*Apologie pour l'histoire, ou Métier d'historien (Paris, 1949). English trans. *The Historian's Craft* (New York, 1953).

"Réflexions d'un historien sur les fausses nouvelles de la guerre," *RSH* 33 (1921): 41–57.

"Pour une histoire comparée des sociétés européennes," *RSH* 46 (1928): 15–50.

"Comparaison," *Bulletin du Centre International de Synthèse – Section de Synthèse Historique* 9 (June 1930): 31–39.

"Henri Pirenne, historien de la Belgique," *AHES* 4 (1932): 478–81.

"Christian Pfister, 1857–1933: Les oeuvres," *RH* 172 (1933): 563–70.

"Henri Pirenne (23 déc. 1862–24 oct. 1935)," *RH* 176 (1935): 671–79.

"Que demander à l'histoire?" *Centre Polytechnicien d'Etudes Economiques* 34 (1937): 15–22.

"Technique et évolution sociale: Réflexions d'un historien," *Europe* 47 (1938): 23–32.
*"Les transformations des techniques comme problème de psychologie collective," *Journal de Psychologie Normale et Pathologique* 41 (Jan.–Mar. 1948): 104–15.
Review of Maurice Halbwachs, *Les cadres sociaux de la mémoire*, in *RSH* 40 (1925): 73–83.
Review of Charles Blondel, *Introduction à la psychologie collective*, in *RH* 160 (1929): 398–99.
Bibliographical note: "*L'Année Sociologique*, Nouvelle série, t. II (1924–1925)," in *RH* 165 (1930): 380–81.
Review of Maurice Halbwachs, *Les causes du suicide*, in *AHES* 3 (1931): 590–92.
Review of M. Schelle, *Wesen und Glaube in der Geschichtswissenschaft*, in *RH* 170 (1932): 553.
Review of Georges Lefebvre, *La grande peur de 1789*, in *AHES* 5 (1933): 301–4.
Review of Paul Harsin, *Comment on écrit l'histoire*, in *AHES* 8 (1936): 51–52.
Bibliographical note: "Allemagne: *Bericht über der 18. Versammlung deutschen Historiker in Göttingen, 2–5 August 1932*," in *RH* 180 (1937): 362.
Review of Maurice Halbwachs, *Morphologie sociale*, in *AHS* 1 (1939): 315–16.
Review of Friedrich Meinecke, *Die Entstehung des Historismus*, in *AHS* 1 (1939): 429–30.

13. CONTEMPORARY HISTORY, SOCIETY, AND POLITICS

**L'étrange défaite: Témoignage écrit en 1940* (Paris, 1946, 1957). English trans. *Strange Defeat* (New York, 1953).
**Souvenirs de guerre, 1914–1915* (Paris, 1969). English trans. *Memoirs of War, 1914–15* (Ithaca, N.Y., 1980; Cambridge, 1988).
(With Lucien Febvre) "Pour le renouveau de l'enseignement historique: Le problème de l'agrégation," *AHES* 9 (1937): 113–29.
"Notes pour une révolution de l'enseignement," *CP* 3 (Aug. 1943): 17–24.
"Le Dr. Goebbels analyse la psychologie du peuple allemand," *CP* 4 (Nov. 1943): 26–27.
"La vraie saison des juges," *CP* 4 (Nov. 1943): 28–30.
"L'alimentation humaine et les échanges internationaux d'après des débats de Hot Springs," *CP* 4 (Nov. 1943): 20–25.

"A propos d'un livre trop peu connu: Général Chauvineau, *Une invasion est-elle encore possible?*" *CP* 8 (Apr. 1944): 22–25.
Review of H. Labouret, *A la recherche d'une politique indigène dans l'Ouest Africain*, in *AHES* 5 (1933): 397–98.

14. COLLECTED ARTICLES

*Mélanges historiques, 2 vols. (Paris, 1963). Selections in *Land and Work in Medieval Europe* (London, 1967) and in *Slavery and Serfdom in the Middle Ages* (Berkeley and Los Angeles, 1975).

Note on Sources

Specific references for the statements in this book are indicated in the footnotes. Listed below, for the convenience of the reader, are the principal materials that have contributed to the biography of Marc Bloch. I should like to express my deepest appreciation to the individuals and the institutions that have aided my research.

I. PRIVATE COLLECTIONS

Etienne Bloch collection (EBC), La Haye, France. Marc Bloch's oldest son and literary heir has generously shared his large, meticulously organized collection of family and professional correspondence, personal and official documents, scholarly materials, and photographs, illuminating all phases of his father's life and career, which have been indispensable for this study. At the time of my research he also retained a portion of Bloch's correspondence with Lucien Febvre, which has since been integrated with the collection at the Archives Nationales (see below).

Letters from Bloch and Febvre to Henri Pirenne (HP). Professor Bryce Lyon, Brown University, Providence, Rhode Island, has made available, with the permission of Count Jacques-Henri Pirenne, copies of the correspondence between Bloch and Febvre and Henri Pirenne between 1920 and 1935, which contributes significantly to the history of the *Annales*.

Robert Boutruche collection (RB). During a period of ten years Bloch wrote fifty-two letters pertaining to personal as well as professional matters to his student and eventual colleague at Clermont-Ferrand. The Boutruche file, seen by courtesy of Mme. Boutruche, Montpellier, also contains several photographs and Boutruche's memorial to his former teacher.

Lucien Febvre collection, Maison des Sciences de l'Homme. Seen by courtesy of the late Fernand Braudel, this includes drafts of *Apologie pour l'histoire*, various research notes by Marc Bloch given by Etienne Bloch, miscellaneous papers and correspondence, and drafts by Febvre in preparation for his publications on Marc Bloch.

Other. Marc Bloch was a prolific writer, and several of his correspondents, including Henri Brunschwig, Mme. Claude Anne (for Roberto) Lopez, Michel Mollat, Mme. Monfren, Erna Patzelt, Jean Stenghers, and Philippe Wolff, have kindly shared copies of letters they received from him.

2. ARCHIVES: PAPERS AND CORRESPONDENCE

Archives Nationales (AN), Paris. Among its holdings are fifty-six boxes of Marc Bloch's professional papers, AB XIX 3796–852 (whose consultation requires the permission of Etienne Bloch), a massive collection of Bloch's research notes spanning three and a half decades, which also includes course materials, lectures, reviews and drafts of his letters and publications. Despite some missing files, this is an invaluable resource for an investigation of Marc Bloch's intellectual development.

The AN also houses the Bloch-Febvre correspondence in the original and on microfilm (MI 318 1–3), donated by Fernand Braudel and Etienne Bloch. This consists of over two hundred letters written during a fifteen-year period, containing detailed and often frank comments about personal, professional, and political matters. Complementary documentation on Bloch and Febvre was also added with the assistance of Professor Hilah Thomas, including records of Bloch's education, his fellowship at the Fondation Thiers, his military citations, miscellaneous correspondence, and views on the Jewish question, documents pertaining to his death, and materials for Braudel's article in the *International Encyclopedia of the Social Sciences.*

The Gustave Cohen collection contains letters from Bloch as well as from several other of Cohen's former colleagues at Strasbourg.

Institut de France (IF), Paris. The IF has important letters from Gustave and Marc Bloch to Jérôme Carcopino, and from Marc Bloch to Ferdinand Lot. Also there is Marc Bloch's correspondence with Henri Dehérain and René Cagnat concerning the *Revue des Savants.*

Bibliothèque Nationale (BN), Paris. The papers of Henry Omont contain documents in connection with Bloch's request in 1928 for a research subvention to study French agrarian systems.

Pontifical Institute of Medieval Studies, Toronto. Through the courtesy of J. Ambrose Raftis, I have been able to obtain copies of the letters deposited in this institute from Bloch and Febvre to Etienne Gilson concerning Bloch's candidature for the Collège de France.

Other. The letters from Bloch and Febvre to André Siegfried are in the Siegfried collection, Fondation Nationale des Sciences Politiques, Paris. Copies of Bloch's and Perrin's letters to Carl Stephenson were graciously sent by the Cornell University Library, Ithaca, New York; Bloch's correspondence with Luigi Einaudi, by the Fondazione Luigi Einaudi, Turin; and his correspondence with R. H. Tawney, by the archives of the London School of Economics.

2. ARCHIVES: DOCUMENTARY SOURCES

Archives Nationales (AN). There are records pertaining to Marc Bloch in the files of the Ecole Normale Supérieure (61 AJ 110–15, 119, 157, 197, 205–6, 233, 236, etc.) and the Université de Paris (student: AJ 16 4764X, 4766; professor: AJ 16 5876).

Other important collections include the official ministerial records of Gustave Bloch, Louis Bloch-Michel, and Paul Vidal as well as Bloch's colleagues Halphen, Halbwachs, and Lefebvre. The Albert Thomas papers include documentation on the reestablishment of the University of Strasbourg.

The captured documents of the German Military Government (Militärbefehlshaber in Frankreich) include materials on the suppression of the French Resistance as well as the activities of the Rosenberg staff. The reports of the prefect of Lyon in 1943–44 (FI CIII 1200) give excellent detail on conditions in that city. The Carcopino dossier (La Haute Cour de Justice contre Jérôme Carcopino, 3W 122, 230, 78–86, seen by special permission) provides information on Carcopino's efforts on Bloch's behalf in 1940–41.

There is also a large collection on the French Resistance, formerly housed and consulted in the Institut d'Histoire du Temps Présent, which includes documents on Franc-Tireur, the MUR, and the CGE, as well as the papers of Albin Vistel.

Archives Départementales du Bas-Rhin (ADBR), Strasbourg. There are extensive records of the University of Strasbourg during Bloch's tenure, including correspondence with the dean, minutes of the faculty council and assembly, official papers, budgets, and reports.

National Archives and Records Service (NARS), Washington, D.C. The most important holdings are the captured records on microfilm of the German Foreign Ministry (AA T-120), the Wehrmacht, and the SS during the occupation of France. There are also records of the office of the State Department dealing with refugees, and the Office of Strategic Services on the French Resistance.

Rockefeller Foundation Archives (RFA), Tarrytown, N.Y., and the Records of the American Council for Emigrés in the Professions (RACEP), Library of the State University of New York at Albany. Both collections contain extensive correspondence (with a considerable amount of, but not total, duplication) pertaining to Bloch's application to the New School in 1940–41.

A selection has been published in Peter M. Rutkoff and William B. Scott, "Letters to America: The Correspondence of Marc Bloch, 1940–41," *French Historical Studies* (Fall 1981): 277–303.

Service Historique de l'Armée de Terre (SHV), Château de Vincennes. This archive has Bloch's military records and also indispensable maps, narratives, and publications on both world wars.

Collège de France (CdF), Paris. In addition to the files on Marc Bloch's and Lucien Febvre's candidacies, there are records of the Assembly's deliberations.

Centre de Documentation Juive Contemporaine (CDJC), Paris. This small but significant collection includes documents on Marc Bloch's protest against the UGIF and his arrest in 1944.

Archives Départementales de l'Hérault (ADH). There are only a handful of papers here pertaining to Bloch's appointments as lycée professor (1912–13) and university professor (1941–42).

Institut für Zeitgeschichte, Munich. The institute has copies of all the documents from the Eichmann trial, including the implementation of the Final Solution in France. Also there are the papers of Hans Hubert von Ranke (seen with the permission of Frau von Ranke), who as "Camille" was an activist in the Lyon underground.

3. ORAL HISTORY: INTERVIEWS

I have been privileged to obtain interviews from many people who knew Marc Bloch. These have included members of his family, Alice, Etienne,

Louis, Daniel, and Jean-Paul Bloch; Jean, Henry, and Josette Bloch-Michel; and Catherine Hanff; his former students Marie-Thérèse Alverny, Mme. Boutruche, Jean Braun, Henri Brunschwig, François Chevalier, Philippe Dollinger, Pierre Goubert, François-Jacques Himly, André Hoepffner, Fernand L'Huillier, Paul Leuilliot, Georges Livet, Mme. Monfren, Jean Schneider, and Pierre Sudreau; and his younger colleagues Raymond Aron, Victor Badie, Fernand Braudel, René Brouillet, Jacques Godechot, Ernest Labrousse, Charles Morazé, and Philippe Wolff.

In connection with the Resistance, I have interviewed Irène Altman Allier, Eugène Claudius-Petit, Henri Falque, Jean-Pierre Lévy, Cecille Hermann, Raymond Péju, and Bloch's devoted "Maurice" (Pessis).

I have received helpful written information from Denise Vernay, Mme. René Courtin, Mme. (Febvre) Richard, Maurice Laforgue, Jean Gay, Wilhelm Kohlhaas, and Michel Debré.

I am very grateful to Lillie Szary, of Hampstead, North Carolina, who did not know Marc Bloch but who in two lengthy interviews provided an extraordinary amount of detail of her life and work as a *résistante* in Lyon.

Index

Abraham, Pierre, 323n
Alfaric, Prosper, 90
Algeria
  reaction to Dreyfus Affair, 20
  French draft protests, 1916, 69
  war of independence, 332, 334
Allies
  World War I, 74, 75
  World War II: initial inactivity, 207–8,
    214, 215; poor cooperation, 211–
    12,221–22; North Africa campaign,
    291; support for Resistance, 294;
    landings in Normandy, 320
Alsace
  ceded to Germany, 1871, 5
  reunification with France, 80
  autonomy movements, 98, 99n, 168
  German annexation, 1940, 241n, 247
L'Alsace Française, 100
Altman, Georges, 299–300, 302, 308,
  310, 320, 322n
American Historical Review, 128
Amiens, 49, 53, 55, 76
Andler, Charles, 19, 174
Annales de Géographie, 31, 133
Annales d'Histoire Economique et Sociale, 38,
  105, 130
  title, choice of, 133–34
  editorial committee, 134
  staff, 135
  statement of purpose, 141–42
  scope and characteristics, 143–44,
    146–48, 150–58, 163, 164
  structure, 145; articles section, 146–51,
    162; book review section, 151–53;
    professional news section, 153–55,
    163; directed investigations, 155–57,
    163; general problems section,
    157–60, 162–63
Annales d'Histoire Sociale, 160, 162–63,
  200; wartime issues, 261, 283–85;
  Bloch's dissociation, 261–63;
  commemorative articles on Bloch, 326

Mélanges d'Histoire Sociale, 285–86
Annales: Economies, Sociétés, Civilisations,
  327, 334, 338
"*Annales* history," 164, 289–90, 335,
  338–40, 341–42
Année Sociologique, 33, 108, 129, 134, 262
anti-Semitism (*see also* Jews, French; France:
  Vichy Jewish policy), 202, 270
  in Third Republic, 17–18, 175, 188
  in Strasbourg, 168
  at Collège de France, 175, 184, 187
Apologie pour l'histoire (Bloch), 210n, 260,
  267, 286–90, 331
Appell, Paul, 83
Arbos, Philippe, 26
Armand Colin, 133, 143, 160
Armée Secrète, 281, 301, 306
army, British, 211–12, 221–22
army, French (*see also* Dreyfus Affair), 22, 54
  World War I (*see also* World War I: trench
    warfare): military strategy, 1914, 54;
    Battle of the Frontiers, 55; retreat after
    Ardennes, 56; victory at Marne,
    57–58; western front stabilizes, 1914,
    59; preparation and supplies, 62;
    typhoid epidemic, 64–65; 72d
    Infantry Regiment, 67, 68–69, 71,
    76–77, 78; Champagne offensive, 68;
    German offensive repelled in Argonne,
    68; attack on Hindenburg line, 70
  World War II, 213–14, 217–22,
    225–27, 231–33; mobilization,
    206–7; evacuation at Dunkirk,
    227–30
army, German
  World War I (*see also* World War I: trench
    warfare), 56, 57, 59–61, 67–68,
    74–75, 76–77; Battle of the Frontiers,
    54–55
  World War II, 220, 221; attack on
    Denmark and Norway, 215; invasion of
    Belgium, 217; Manstein plan,
    219–20; at Dunkirk, 227, 229–30;

108–9, 114, 192–93; views on
discipline of history, 35–38, 50–52,
286–90; and political economy
theories, 37; comparative method, 42,
44, 52, 94, 117–19, 139, 156, 160,
171–72; on racial theories of
nationalism, 44, 125; documentary
criticism, 45, 94, 96; critique of
Febvre's history, 49–50; and historical
doctrines, 95, 108; on German
historians, 97, 156; influence of
Pirenne, 106; critics of, 114–15;
questionnaires, use of, 118; work
compared with Febvre's, 139–40, 149;
critique of Meinecke, 162–63, 193;
evaluation of Simiand, 176
works: *Rois et serfs*, 44, 92–94;
"Blanche de Castille et les serfs du
chapitre de Paris," 44–45; "Cerny ou
Serin?" 45; *L'Ile de France*, 45–46; "Les
formes de la rupture de l'hommage dans
l'ancien droit féodal," 45, 92; *Les rois
thaumaturges*, 48, 88, 109–11, 240,
335–36, 343; "Réflexions d'un
historien sur les fausses nouvelles de la
guerre," 112–13; *Les caractères
originaux de l'histoire rurale française*,
124–27, 284, 331; *La société féodale*,
143, 157, 195–96, 200, 284;
Cambridge Economic History chapter,
183, 194; *Apologie pour l'histoire*, 210n,
260, 267, 286–90, 331; *L'étrange
défaite*, 237–40, 281, 326; *Esquisse
d'une histoire monétaire de l'Europe*, 332;
Mélanges historiques, 336; *La France sous
les derniers Capétiens (1223– 1338)*,
336; *Seigneurie française et manoir
anglais*, 336
career: Montpellier lycée post, 46–47;
Amiens lycée post, 49, 83; at
University of Strasbourg, 83–84,
88–91, 167; head, Institute of the
History of the Middle Ages, 88, 176;
Collège de France candidacy, 135,
170–72, 174–76, 177–78, 182,
183–84, 185, 186; Sorbonne
candidacy, 182, 185–86; at Sorbonne,
190–92; Institute of Economic and
Social History co-founder, 190; Ecole
Normale directorship candidacy,
200–2; at University of Strasbourg,
Clermont-Ferrand, 243–44, 245, 247,
260; application to New School,
248–49, 264, 265–66; appointment

to University of Montpellier, 264–65,
268, 269, 291, 292; posthumous
recognition and publications, 325–27,
330–32, 335–37, 342–43
military service, World War I, 53,
55–78; *Souvenirs de guerre* begun, 66;
criticism of French army, 66, 68, 73;
decorations, 67, 68, 73, 77
as teacher, views and style, 95–98;
criticism of French education system,
94, 150; collaboration with Febvre,
97–98; educational reform proposals,
303
political views, 100–3, 166; and Dreyfus
Affair, 19–24; skepticism of press,
22–23; reparations issue, 101; view of
individual in society, 102–3; distress
over right-wing strength, 179–82; on
France's decline, 197–98; and Munich
agreement, 199; patriotism, 203,
256–57, 276, 295, 344
Annales d'Histoire Economique et Sociale,
105, 130–33; publisher, 133; editorial
committee and staff, 134–35; demands
of *Annales* work, 143; articles and
reviews; 147, 151, 152–53, 162–63,
183; directed investigations, 155–57;
promotion of views in, 159–60;
published with Febvre, 160; goals for,
162, 164–65; dissociation from,
261–63; wartime issues, 283–86, 303
personal and family life, 141, 169, 176,
183, 190; birth and youth, 13–17;
marriage, 84; love of travel, 107–8;
relationship with Febvre, 136, 139,
150, 161–62, 176–77, 180, 185,
200, 261–63, 270, 286, 303, 309,
343; move to Paris, 166–69, 189–90;
Fougères home, 169; health problems,
169, 176, 183; application for U.S.
visas, 249–50, 255–56, 263–64; last
testament, 256–57; loss of library,
268, 276–78; poetry, 282–83; flight
to Fougères, 291–92
reserve unit training, 1933, 1938, 1939,
176, 199, 204
military service, World War II, 204,
206–34; liaison with British, 211–12;
in charge of petrol supplies, 212, 217,
218, 223, 226; evacuation at Dunkirk,
227–29; not captured, 233–35
Resistance work, 280, 295–303,
305–10, 311–14; *Les Cahiers
Politiques*, editor, 303–4; writings for,

Langlois, Charles-Victor, 29, 30, 38, 39, 41
Lanson, Gustave, 19
Laval, Pierre, 184n, 241, 278, 292, 317
Lavisse, Ernest, 16, 25, 28, 29, 41, 109, 173
Lazare, Bernard, 19
    Une erreur judiciaire: La vérité sur l'Affaire Dreyfus, 20
Le Bras, Gabriel, 91, 111, 210n
Le Goff, Jacques, 343
Le Roy Ladurie, Emmanuel: *Les paysans de Languedoc*, 338
League of Nations, 131, 142, 214
Leclerc, Max, 133, 134
Lefebvre, Georges, 111, 123, 135, 148–49, 309n
    Annales articles, 147, 150, 153, 158
    on *Annales* editorial committee, 161n
Lefebvre des Noëttes, Richard, 160
Leopold III: capitulation to Germany, 225
Leroux, Emmanuel, 26
Leuilliot, Paul, 135, 151
Lévi-Strauss, Claude, 248
Lévy, Jean-Pierre, 298, 304
Lévy, Paul, 26
Lévy-Bruhl, Lucien, 137
Liard, Louis, 28
Libération (Resistance group), 297, 298, 304, 305
La Libre Parole, 20
Ligue des Droits de l'Homme, 201
Little Entente, 197
Locarno agreements, 1925, 100, 131
"Lombard," *see* Bloch-Michel, Jean
London School of Economics: Bloch lectures, 178
Lopez, Roberto, 147
Lorraine
    ceded to Germany, 5
    reunification with France, 80–81
    German occupation, 1940, 241n
Lot, Ferdinand, 30, 279, 280n, 312
Loubet, Emile, 20
Louis X: emancipation ordinances, 1315,· 92–93
Lycée Louis-le-Grand, 24, 137
Lyon (*see also* Resistance: Lyon), 293, 301

Maginot Line, 102, 204, 206, 210–11
Maison des Sciences de l'Homme, 335, 338
Maitland, Frederick William, 123
Malleret, A., 305, 312
Marc Bloch Association, 329
Massigli, Jacques, 26

Mathiez, Albert, 137
Matignon, Camille, 182
Maurras, Charles, 39
Mauss, Marcel, 262
Mayer, André, 252, 254
Mayer, René, 307n
La Méditerranée et le monde méditerranéen à l'époque de Philippe II (Braudel), 333–34,335
Meillet, Antoine, 137, 184n
    and comparative method, 32
Meinecke, Friedrich: *Die Entstehung des Historismus*, 162–63, 193–94
Meitzen, August, 123, 125, 156
Mélanges d'Histoire Sociale, see *Annales d'Histoire Economique et Sociale*
Mélanges historiques (Bloch), 336
mentalités, history of, 111, 114, 115, 140, 194, 339
Métier d'historien, see *Apologie pour l'histoire*
Michelet, Jules, 31, 38, 50n, 109, 173
Milhaud, René, 275
Militärbefehlshaber, 236, 241, 277
Millerand, Alexandre, 83, 84
Mitterand, François, 341
Mollat, Michel, 192, 330
Mommsen, Theodor, 7
Monod, Gabriel, 19, 29, 34, 41, 137, 173
Montluc prison, 319
Montpellier (*see also* Resistance: Montpellier; University of Montpellier), 46, 270
    wartime living conditions, 270, 290
Monzie, Anatole de, 173, 310n
Morazé, Charles, 285, 286, 327, 329, 330
Moret, Alexandre, 184n
Morgueleff, Nina, 315
Mougin, Henri, 158
Moulin, Jean, 294, 303, 304
Mouvements Unis de la Résistance (MUR), 294, 297, 298, 304–5, 306, 310
    arrests of leaders, 315–17
Munich conference, 199
Musée de l'Homme, 188, 242

"Narbonne," *see* Bloch, Marc Léopold Benjamin: Resistance work
"Nathalie," *see* Morgueleff, Nina
National Socialism, Germany, 166, 194
New School for Social Research, 248–49, 264, 265
Newman, William Mendel, 167n, 266n, 330
Niebuhr, Barthold Georg, 7
Nivelle, Robert, 70

368

Russia, Soviet: nonaggression pact with Germany, 1939, 204, 205
Russo-Finnish war, 214, 215

Saar: reunification with Germany, 184
Sayous, André-Emile, 147, 285n
Scheurer-Kestner, Charles Auguste, 19
Schreuer, Hans, 47, 48
scrofula, 110
Séchan, Louis, 26
Sedan, 16, 55
Sée, Henri, 123
Seebohm, Frederick, 123
Seigneurie française et manoir anglais (Bloch), 336
Seignobos, Charles, 29–30, 34, 35, 38, 39, 92, 137, 163, 288
   Histoire politique de l'Europe contemporaine, 30
   criticism of sociology, 33
serfdom in France, 41–45, 92–93, 119–21
Sering, Max, 37
Service du Travail Obligatoire (STO), 293, 297
Seyroux, René, 315
Siegfried, André, 134, 161n, 184n
Simiand, François, 185
   defense of social sciences, 33–34
   evaluated by Bloch, 115, 176
Sion, Jules, 123, 137, 151, 284
Société des Professeurs d'Histoire et de Géographie, 192
Société d'Etudes Psychologiques, 264
Société d'Histoire Moderne, 33, 180
La société féodale (Bloch), 143, 157, 195–96, 200, 284
Société Française de Philosophie, 34
sociology: and history, 33–34
Sorbonne, *see* University of Paris
Sorel, Albert, 137
Souvenirs de guerre (Bloch), 66
Spain: Civil War, 141, 188, 203
Spengler, Oswald, 108
Stavisky, Serge, 178, 179
Stinnes, Hugo, 101
Strasbourg
   German siege, 5
   French rule, 79, 80, 100
   German rule, 79–80
   growing Nazi influences, 168
   World War II, 206
Sudreau, Pierre, 192
Sybel, Heinrich von, 128n

Tableau de la géographie de la France (Vidal de la Blache), 31
Tannery, Jules, 19
Tawney, Richard Henry, 123, 178
Teitjen, Pierre-Henri, 279
Thomas, Albert, 135
Tonnelat, Ernest, 137, 174n
Treaty of Frankfurt, 5
typhoid fever during World War I, 64–65

Union Générale des Israélites de France (UGIF), 272–76
United States of America
   refugee policy, 248
   Lyon consulate, 249–50, 255
University of Montpellier, 264, 268
University of Paris, 25, 39, 337
   modernization and expansion, 28
University of Strasbourg (*see also* Kaiser-Wilhelms-Universität Strassburg), 79, 81–83, 84, 87–91
   réunions du samedi, 12, 90–91, 168
   Institute of the History of the Middle Ages, 88, 176
   pedagogic reform, 94–95
   isolation of faculty, 98–100, 102–3
   Institute of Modern History, 138
   steady loss of faculty, 167–68
   exile in Clermont-Ferrand, 168, 243–44, 245–47, 282

Vaillant, Casimir Julien, 26–27
Vallat, Xavier, 188, 261n, 272, 273
Varagnac, André, 163
Varga, Lucie, 162, 285n
Vermeil, Edmond, 90, 268n
Vidal, Paul, 84–85, 169n
Vidal de la Blache, Paul, 31–32, 129, 137
   Tableau de la géographie de la France, 31
La vie rurale en Bourgogne, jusqu'au début du XIe siècle (Deléage), 286
Vierteljahrsschrift für Sozial- und Wirtschaftsgeschichte, 129, 130, 134
Vinogradoff, Paul, 123
Vistel, Alban, 312, 314, 315, 316, 317
Voltaire, François Marie Arouet de, 38, 109, 262
Vrain-Lucas, Denis, 23

Waitz, Georg, 29
Waitz, Robert, 297, 299
Wallon, Henri, 137, 183
Weber, Max, 105

Weill, Hélène, 308, 323
Wells, H. G., 108
Werner, Karl Ferdinand, 343
Weygand, Maxime, 221, 227, 231–32
Wilhelmian Reich, *see* Germany: Second
  Reich
Wolff, Philippe, 285, 330
World War I (*see also* Allies: World War I;
  army, French: World War I; army,
  German: World War I; France: World
  War I; Germany: World War I)
  outbreak, 52–53
  Battle of the Frontiers, 55
  Battle of Ardennes, 56

Battle of the Marne, 57–58
trench warfare, 59–61, 63–64
World War II (*see also* Allies: World War II;
  army, French: World War II; army,
  German: World War II; France: World
  War II; Germany: World War II; Great
  Britain: World War II)
  events leading up to, 203–4
Wurmser, René, 252

Zay, Jean, 186, 190n, 202n, 254
Zentgraff, Jean Joachim, 88
Zola, Emile, 19
  "J'accuse," 20